Computational Science and Engineering

Computational Science and Engineering

Edited by
Rushel Davis

WILLFORD PRESS

www.willfordpress.com

Published by Willford Press,
118-35 Queens Blvd., Suite 400,
Forest Hills, NY 11375, USA

ISBN: 978-1-68285-643-7

Cataloging-in-Publication Data

Computational science and engineering / edited by Rushel Davis.
    p. cm.
Includes bibliographical references and index.
ISBN 978-1-68285-643-7
1. Computer science. 2. Computer engineering. 3. Computational complexity.
4. Mathematics--Data processing. 5. Engineering mathematics. I. Davis, Rushel.
QA76 .C66 2019
004--dc23

For information on all Willford Press publications
visit our website at www.willfordpress.com

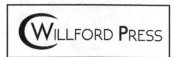

Contents

Preface..VII

Chapter 1   **Implicit Large Eddy Simulation of Flow in a Micro-Orifice with the Cumulant Lattice Boltzmann Method** 1
Ehsan Kian Far, Martin Geier, Konstantin Kutscher and Manfred Krafczyk

Chapter 2   **Levy-Lieb-Based Monte Carlo Study of the Dimensionality Behaviour of the Electronic Kinetic Functional** 21
Seshaditya A., Luca M. Ghiringhelli and Luigi Delle Site

Chapter 3   **Artificial Immune Classifier Based on ELLipsoidal Regions (AICELL)** 31
Aris Lanaridis, Giorgos Siolas and Andreas Stafylopatis

Chapter 4   **Analyzing the Effect and Performance of Lossy Compression on Aeroacoustic Simulation of Gas Injector** 55
Seyyed Mahdi Najmabadi, Philipp Offenhäuser, Moritz Hamann,
Guhathakurta Jajnabalkya, Fabian Hempert, Colin W. Glass and Sven Simon

Chapter 5   **Using an Interactive Lattice Boltzmann Solver in Fluid Mechanics Instruction** 78
Mirjam S. Glessmer and Christian F. Janßen

Chapter 6   **CFD-PBM Approach with Different Inlet Locations for the Gas-Liquid Flow in a Laboratory-Scale Bubble Column with Activated Sludge/Water** 100
Le Wang, Qiang Pan, Jie Chen and Shunsheng Yang

Chapter 7   **Performance Comparison of Feed-Forward Neural Networks Trained with Different Learning Algorithms for Recommender Systems** 118
Mohammed Hassan and Mohamed Hamada

Chapter 8   **Multiresolution Modeling of Semidilute Polymer Solutions: Coarse-Graining using Wavelet-Accelerated Monte Carlo** 136
Animesh Agarwal, Brooks D. Rabideau and Ahmed E. Ismail

Chapter 9   **Deformable Cell Model of Tissue Growth** 156
Nikolai Bessonov and Vitaly Volpert

Chapter 10   **Energetic Study of Clusters and Reaction Barrier Heights from Efficient Semilocal Density Functionals** 174
Guocai Tian, Yuxiang Mo and Jianmin Tao

Chapter 11   **A Discrete Approach to Meshless Lagrangian Solid Modeling** 184
Matthew Marko

Chapter 12   **Numerical Simulation of the Laminar Forced Convective Heat Transfer between Two Concentric Cylinders** **197**
Ioan Sarbu and Anton Iosif

Permissions

List of Contributors

Index

Preface

Computational science is the field that is concerned with the development of computational models and simulations to understand natural systems and solve complex problems. The methods and frameworks used in this field include high-performance computing, modeling and simulation, algorithms, mathematical foundations, analysis and visualization of data. Computer programming, parallel computing and algorithms are crucial to computational science and engineering. FORTRAN, C and C++, MATLAB, PYTHON, etc. are widely used programming languages in this field. The applications of computational science and engineering are found in the varied domains of engineering, astrophysical systems, medicine, numerical weather prediction, finance, etc. There has been rapid progress in this field and its applications are finding their way across multiple industries. Most of the topics introduced in this book cover new techniques and applications of computational science and engineering. Students, researchers, experts and all associated with this field will benefit alike from this book.

The information contained in this book is the result of intensive hard work done by researchers in this field. All due efforts have been made to make this book serve as a complete guiding source for students and researchers. The topics in this book have been comprehensively explained to help readers understand the growing trends in the field.

I would like to thank the entire group of writers who made sincere efforts in this book and my family who supported me in my efforts of working on this book. I take this opportunity to thank all those who have been a guiding force throughout my life.

Editor

Implicit Large Eddy Simulation of Flow in a Micro-Orifice with the Cumulant Lattice Boltzmann Method

Ehsan Kian Far, Martin Geier *, Konstantin Kutscher and Manfred Krafczyk

Institute for Computational Modeling in Civil Engineering, TU Braunschweig, 38106 Braunschweig, Germany; ehsan@irmb.tu-bs.de (E.K.F.); kutscher@irmb.tu-bs.de (K.K.); kraft@irmb.tu-bs.de (M.K.)

* Correspondence: geier@irmb.tu-bs.de

Academic Editor: Christian F. Janßen

Abstract: A detailed numerical study of turbulent flow through a micro-orifice is presented in this work. The flow becomes turbulent due to the orifice at the considered Reynolds numbers ($\sim 10^4$). The obtained flow rates are in good agreement with the experimental measurements. The discharge coefficient and the pressure loss are presented for two input pressures. The laminar stress and the generated turbulent stresses are investigated in detail, and the location of the vena contracta is quantitatively reproduced.

Keywords: lattice Boltzmann method; orifice; discharge coefficient; implicit large eddy simulation

---

1. Introduction

Flow through orifices is observed in many industrial applications. One example is the orifice meter used for measuring flow rates via the pressure drop induced by the constriction of the flow [1–4]. The main characteristic of flow through an orifice is that the flow velocity increases by substantially decreasing the cross-sectional flow area. Turbulent shear stresses are created downstream of the orifice. A "vena contracta" is formed inside the orifice. Turbulent eddies and recirculation of flow occur both upstream and downstream of the orifice. Theory and applications of orifice meters for measurement purposes can be found in [5–9].

Orifices can be used for increasing the shear stress in the flow (e.g., in order to break up suspended particles). The geometry studied in this paper was designed for this purpose, but the methodology used here applies in the same way for any kind of turbulent flow through an orifice at subsonic speeds [10,11].

Few studies have been conducted to simulate an orifice with the help of computational fluid dynamics (CFD) [12–17], and are usually focused on experimental investigations. However, measurements are not possible under all conditions (e.g., due to high pressure), and some quantities like local shear stress distributions are difficult to obtain experimentally. Most of the above-cited CFD studies considered laminar flow in the orifice or they used explicit turbulence modeling in order to capture turbulent eddies. These simplifications may reduce the overall accuracy of the CFD approach [13,18,19]. The advancement in CFD theory and in high performance computing motivates us to study orifice flow with a high-fidelity CFD method that resolves the relevant flow features in space and time. Here we use the cumulant lattice Boltzmann method (LBM) that allows the simulation of time-resolved turbulent flows at acceptable cost [20–23].

2. Aim of This Work

The aim of this work is to simulate turbulent flow in a micro-orifice [24] while resolving all essential flow features. The micro-orifice has a width of 80 μm, a height of 50 μm, and a length of 300 μm (Figure 1). It is located in the center of a channel of two centimeters in length. Only half of the geometry is displayed, since the shape is symmetric in the x-direction (however, the simulation included the full geometry). There is an asymmetry in the z-direction. Pressure, velocity, and stress distributions are studied for this special orifice. The laminar and turbulent stresses in the orifice are calculated and presented in detail.

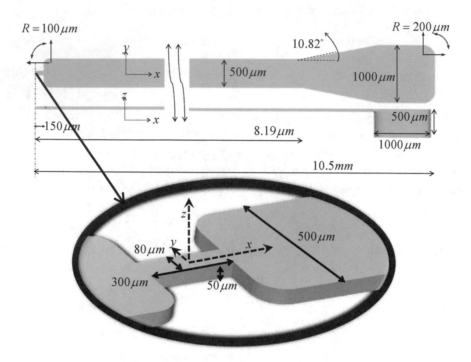

Figure 1. A schematic of the micro-orifice meter.

Three input pressures corresponding to pressure drops of 100 bar, 200 bar, and 500 bar, respectively, between the entrance and the exit of the device are considered in this study. All pressures and stresses in this paper are given in bar, with 1 bar = 10^5 Pa. All pressures are measured with reference to the pressure at the outlet, where we assume the pressure to be zero. In the real device, a sufficiently high pressure was applied at the outlet to suppress cavitation inside the device. This absolute pressure at the outlet can be determined a posteriori from the simulation results, and is hence no input parameter to the simulation itself. The flow setup was chosen to accurately simulate the pressure drop of 200 bar by adjusting the resolution to the boundary layer thickness.

In CFD simulations, more resolution is required when higher pressure drops are imposed, leading to larger mass fluxes and thinner boundary layers. The simulation for a pressure drop of 500 bar is already slightly under-resolved. Therefore, the results for this case have to be used with some caution, as they are expected to be less accurate than the results for the pressure drop of 200 bar.

3. The Cumulant Lattice Boltzmann Method

This study applies the cumulant lattice Boltzmann method [20]. Turbulent flow can be simulated accurately with the use of this method, as long as the computational domain is resolved adequately. The classical lattice Boltzmann equation without an external force can be written as follows:

$$f_i(x + e_{xi}c\Delta t, y + e_{yi}c\Delta t, z + e_{zi}c\Delta t, t + \Delta t) - f_i(x, y, z, t) = \Omega_i \tag{1}$$

where f_i and Ω_i are the discrete momentum distribution function and the collision operator, respectively. Here x, y, and z are positions of the lattice nodes. The lattice speed $c = \frac{\Delta x}{\Delta t}$ is defined as the ratio of the lattice spacing to the time step such that the distributions are shifted by $e_{xi} c \Delta t$ from one lattice node to another on a Cartesian grid during one time step.

In order to obtain the lattice Boltzmann equation in the cumulant space, we have to transform the distribution functions into cumulants [20,25]. The lattice Boltzmann equation in cumulant space is:

$$c^*_{\xi^m v^n \zeta^l} = c_{\xi^m v^n \zeta^l} + \omega_{\xi^m v^n \zeta^l} \left(c^{eq}_{\xi^m v^n \zeta^l} - c_{\xi^m v^n \zeta^l} \right) \tag{2}$$

where c_{eq} is the cumulant for the equilibrium state and ξ, v, and ζ are three discrete random variables corresponding to the normalized microscopic velocities in x, y, and z directions.

4. Simulation Results

The simulation domain was discretized with nested Cartesian grids [26,27] using a block-structured code based on Esoteric Twist [28] with resolution varying from 4.96 μm to 0.62 μm for the 100 bar case and down to 0.31 μm in the 200 bar and 500 bar cases. The grid for the 100 bar case contained approximately 57 million grid nodes, the one for the 200 bar case had 65 million grid nodes, and the grid for the 500 bar case had 79 million grid nodes. The setup is shown in Figure 2, and further details are given in [21]. Turbulence emerges naturally in the cumulant lattice Boltzmann method. No fluctuations were added to the flow field. In general, high velocity gradients are observed close to the wall, which is why the highest grid resolution has to be spent there. A commonly-used grid independence criterion for CFD simulations is that the $y+$ value is on the order of one or smaller [29]. For that reason, one additional grid level was spent for the pressure drops of 200 bar and 500 bar in comparison to the 100 bar case in order to keep the $y+$ value close to one. The simulation required about 15 days on 120 Intel Nehalem compute nodes (2.6 GHz) with eight cores each to simulate 655 μs real time for the 200 bar case. Due to the different numbers of lattice nodes, the 100 bar case required about half the compute time of the 200 bar case, and the 500 bar case required about 1.5 times the time of the 200 bar case to reach the same real time.

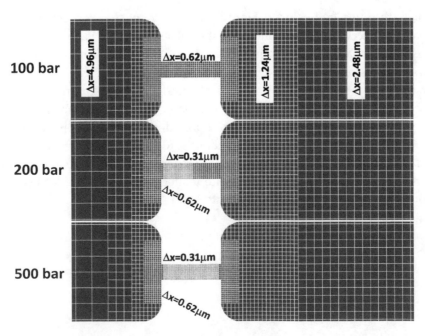

Figure 2. Zoom into the grids at the orifice. Each block in the picture contains $16 \times 16 \times 16$ lattice nodes.

The flow rates acquired by our simulations are compared with the experimental measurement to validate our results [11]. The deviations between the LBM simulation and the experiment for the 100 bar, 200 bar, and 500 bar pressure drops are 1.57%, 1.51%, and 2.84%, respectively. It is observed that our results are in close agreement with the experimental results (see Figure 3).

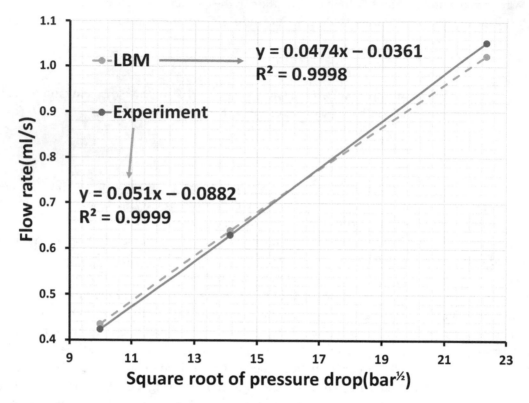

Figure 3. Variation in flow rate with square root of pressure drop across orifice. Comparison between flow rates obtained by the LBM simulation and by experiment for the three pressure drops of 100 bar, 200 bar, and 500 bar. LBM: lattice Boltzmann method.

In addition to the averaged velocity, Figure 4 demonstrates the vena contracta effect. The vena contracta reduces the effective area and increases the velocity. Thus, it is observed that the velocity in position 2, V_2, is greater than the velocity in position 3, V_3. This phenomenon is a classical problem in fluid mechanics, and researchers try to eliminate it in some ways, such as by rounding the entrance region [30]. An orifice usually has two loss coefficients: the loss coefficient due to a sudden contraction, and the loss coefficient due to a sudden expansion. Streeter [31] calculated the loss coefficient for both a sudden contraction and a sudden expansion, and provided approximations for these coefficients in relation to the ratios of the cross-sections. For example, for a cylindrical orifice, the loss coefficients extracted from his plot are 0.42 and 0.68 for the sudden expansion and the sudden contraction, respectively. In general, these loss coefficients are related to the pressure loss calculated from the energy equation between points 1 and 2 and points 3 and 4 [30].

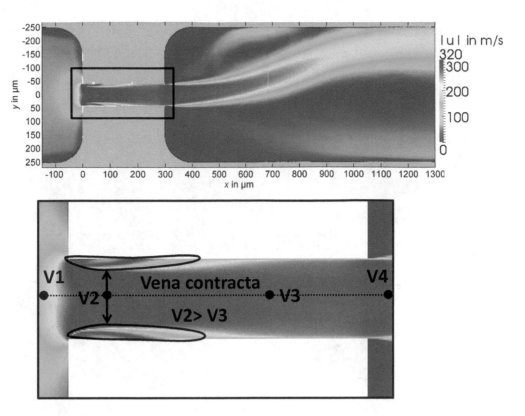

Figure 4. The upper figure shows an average of 40,000 time steps of the simulation of the device, corresponding to a real time interval of 24.5 microseconds at a pressure difference of 500 bar. The lower picture shows a zoom into the velocity field. The effect of the vena contracta is demonstrated.

The center line magnitude velocities for three different pressure drops of 100 bar, 200 bar, and 500 bar are shown in Figure 5. The plot area covers a distance from 50 μm before the orifice entrance to 50 μm after the orifice exit. The position $x = 0$ coincides with the entrance of the orifice. The velocity in each case reaches the maximum value at point V_2 (Figure 4).

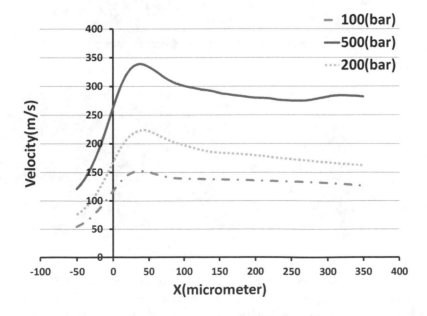

Figure 5. The center line magnitude velocity for three different pressure drops. The positions $x = 0$ and $x = 300$ μm coincide with the entrance and the exit of the orifice, respectively.

The time-averaged pressure in and behind the orifice is depicted for the 100 bar and 500 bar cases in Figure 6. It is shown for two different planes: $z = -17$ μm and $z = -34$ μm, according to Figure 1.

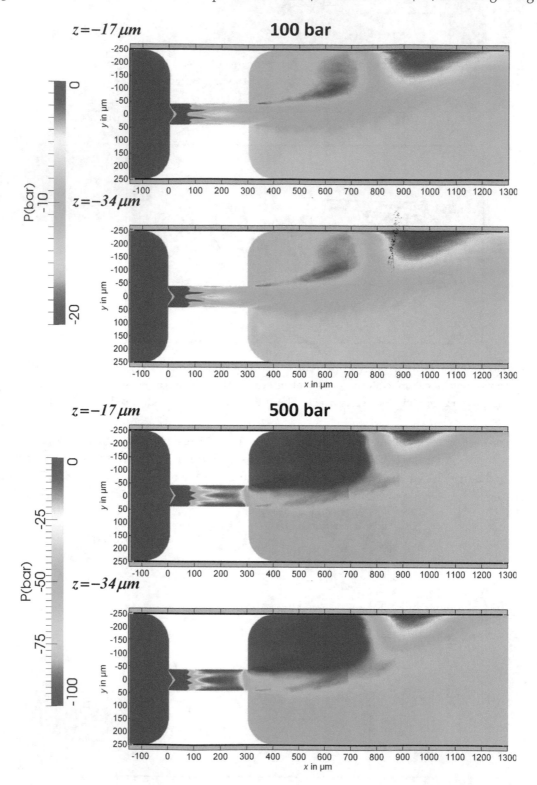

Figure 6. The time-averaged pressure for the 100 bar and 500 bar cases at two different planes. The upper picture for each set shows the pressure for plane $z = -17$ μm, and the lower shows the pressure for $z = -34$ μm. All pressure is measured relative to the pressure at the outlet.

The pressure is seen to have negative values in comparison to the pressure at the outlet of the device (assumed to be zero). The device is susceptible to cavitation, which is undesired since it leads to the erosion and eventually to the destruction of the device. Cavitation is suppressed in the operation of the device by applying a sufficiently high absolute pressure at the outlet such that the minimal absolute pressure inside the device does not drop below the vapor pressure of water. Part of the purpose of the simulation was to determine the minimum pressure required at the outlet to suppress the cavitation. Since this can be done a posteriori, it was not required to consider the cavitation in the simulation itself. We note here that cavitation can be simulated with the lattice Boltzmann method, if required [32].

Figure 6 shows the reason why the jet is attached to the wall after leaving the orifice. In the volume confined by the jet and the wall in negative y direction, the pressure decreases due to the suction effect of the moving jet. This lowers the pressure in the confined volume relative to the pressure in the open volume on the other side of the jet. The pressure difference between the confined and the open volume drives the jet towards the confined volume. While the jet oscillates downstream of the orifice, it was never observed in the simulation or the experiment that the jet would switch to the other wall once it was attached.

The time-averaged pressure is averaged again over the $y - z$ planes and plotted along the main flow direction (x direction) for the 100 bar and 500 bar cases in Figure 7. The orifice entrance is located at $x = 0$. The pressure drops suddenly at the entrance, and reaches its minimum value where the velocity has its maximum. The pressure drops further at the exit of the orifice. This effect is much more pronounced in the 500 bar case than in the 100 bar case. The plot displayed in Figure 7 is used to calculate the pressure loss between two points along the x direction [30]. With the flow rate known, the only required parameter for the energy equation is the pressure drop between the two points, and the discharge coefficient can be calculated (defined as the ratio of the actual flow to the theoretical flow—mean velocity × cross-section × density). The following equation has been used to calculate C_D [33]:

$$C_D = \frac{V\sqrt{(1-\beta^4)}}{\sqrt{\Delta p/\rho}} \qquad (3)$$

where V is the averaged velocity in the orifice and Δp is the pressure difference between upstream of the orifice and the vena contracta—at which the wall pressure is at its minimum. The ratio of the orifice diameter to the channel diameter is termed β. In our case, it is determined as $\beta = 80\,\mu m/500\,\mu m = 0.16$. The discharge coefficients for pressure drops 100 bar and 500 bar are $C_D = 0.8855$ and $C_D = 0.9432$, respectively. The actual location of the vena contracta changes with the flow rate, and this location can be obtained from Figure 5 or Figure 7.

Tables in hydraulic handbooks list the loss coefficient only for a limited number of specific geometries. In other cases, CFD simulations as presented in this work can be used to obtain this coefficient. The averaged pressure and velocity can be extracted from Figures 3 and 7, respectively. The pressure loss can be easily calculated by inserting the obtained pressures and velocities into the energy equation.

The pressure loss per length l can be calculated by the use of the following equation [34]:

$$\frac{\Delta p}{l} = \lambda\left(\frac{V^2}{2D_h}\right) \qquad (4)$$

where the mean velocity V is calculated from the numerically-determined mass flow, ρ is the density of water, and λ is the friction factor. Since the studied orifice has a rectangular shape, the hydraulic diameter must be considered, D_h. The Reynolds number Re at the smallest cross-sectional areas of the orifice is defined as:

$$Re = \frac{VD_h\rho}{\mu} \qquad (5)$$

here μ is the dynamic viscosity. When the device simulated here was designed, no simulations were available and the geometry was chosen based on simple considerations using the Blasius equation for round channels [10], even though the orifice is neither round nor a channel in the sense used by Blasis [35]. The roughness of the orifice is below 20 nm [10,11]; thus, the friction factor of hydraulically smooth channels at the respective Reynolds numbers ($2320 < Re < 10^5$) was chosen [35]:

$$\lambda = 0.3164(Re)^{-1/4} \tag{6}$$

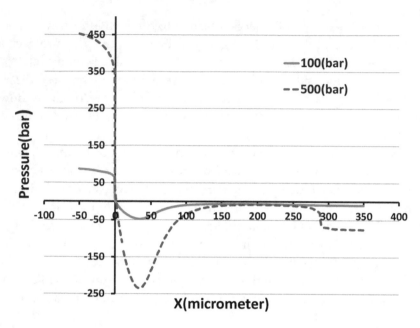

Figure 7. The time averaged pressure over z direction through the orifice for the 100 bar case and the 500 bar case. The positions $x = 0$ and $x = 300$ μm coincide with the entrance and the exit of the orifice, respectively. All pressure is measured relative to the pressure at the outlet.

The calculated pressure losses per millimeter in the orifice segments with the smallest cross-sectional area are 33.00 bar/mm and 150.12 bar/mm for the two pressure drops 100 bar and 500 bar, respectively.

4.1. Fluid Flow Intensity

The stresses are calculated by the velocity-gradient components. The strain rate tensor is composed of the nine velocity-gradient components, of which three are normal strain components and six are tangential strains components. The magnitude of the strain rate tensor can be written in terms of velocity gradients, as:

$$S^2 = \left[\frac{\partial u}{\partial x}\left(\frac{\partial u}{\partial x} + \frac{\partial u}{\partial x}\right) + \frac{\partial u}{\partial y}\left(\frac{\partial u}{\partial y} + \frac{\partial v}{\partial x}\right) + \frac{\partial u}{\partial z}\left(\frac{\partial u}{\partial z} + \frac{\partial w}{\partial x}\right) \right] +$$
$$\left[\frac{\partial v}{\partial x}\left(\frac{\partial v}{\partial x} + \frac{\partial u}{\partial y}\right) + \frac{\partial v}{\partial y}\left(\frac{\partial v}{\partial y} + \frac{\partial v}{\partial y}\right) + \frac{\partial v}{\partial z}\left(\frac{\partial v}{\partial z} + \frac{\partial w}{\partial y}\right) \right] + \tag{7}$$
$$\left[\frac{\partial w}{\partial x}\left(\frac{\partial w}{\partial x} + \frac{\partial u}{\partial z}\right) + \frac{\partial w}{\partial y}\left(\frac{\partial w}{\partial y} + \frac{\partial v}{\partial z}\right) + \frac{\partial w}{\partial z}\left(\frac{\partial w}{\partial z} + \frac{\partial w}{\partial z}\right) \right]$$

In order to obtain the velocity-gradients in this equation, a finite difference scheme is implemented in common CFD methods. Thus, each grid node needs information from its neighbors. In the LBM, the strain rate can be computed locally from the non-equilibrium part of the distribution function. The above equation is rewritten according to the strain rate instead of the velocity gradients as:

$$S^2 = 2(s_{xx}^2 + s_{yy}^2 + s_{zz}^2 + 2s_{xy}^2 + 2s_{xz}^2 + 2s_{yz}^2) \tag{8}$$

By convention, the magnitude of the strain rate tensor is defined as [36,37]:

$$S^2 = 2s : s = 2s_{ij}s_{ji} \tag{9}$$

where the strain rate component s_{ij} is:

$$s_{ij} = \frac{1}{2}\left(\frac{\partial u_i}{\partial x_j} + \frac{\partial u_j}{\partial x_i}\right) \tag{10}$$

The dissipation rate is a useful parameter for the characterization of the local hydrodynamic conditions and flow field intensities.

$$\epsilon = \nu S^2 \tag{11}$$

The total dissipation can be split up into the averaged energy dissipation rate and the turbulent dissipation rate according to the following equation [38]:

$$\epsilon_{total} = \epsilon_{fluctuation} + \epsilon_{mean} = 2\nu\overline{s'_{ij}s'_{ij}} + 2\nu\bar{s}_{ij}\bar{s}_{ij} \tag{12}$$

This is often done in the CFD literature due to the prevalence of Reynolds-averaged Navier–Stokes (RANS) methods. In such methods, only the average energy dissipation rate is directly accessible, and the turbulent dissipation rate must be estimated with some turbulence model. Our method provides the full information on the dissipation rate.

The corresponding stress can be acquired from:

$$\tau = \mu\sqrt{\epsilon/\nu} \tag{13}$$

Figure 8 shows the logarithm of the dissipation rates for the 100 bar and 500 bar cases from 50 μm before to 50 μm after the orifice. There is a substantial increase in the dissipation rate at the entrance of the orifice in comparison to 50 μm in front of the entrance. Two peaks are observed in the dissipation; one is exactly at the entrance, and another one is at position $x = 46$ μm. It is the same position where the maximal velocity and the minimal pressure are observed.

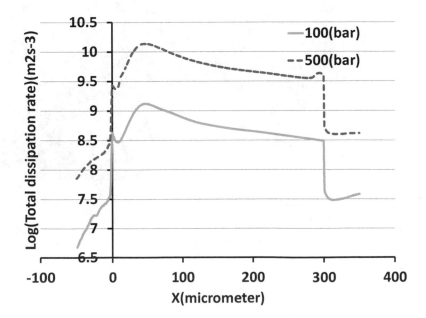

Figure 8. The logarithmic plot of the total dissipation rates versus x-direction for two pressure drops. The dissipation rates are averaged over the z direction. The position $x = 0$ coincides with the orifice entrance.

4.1.1. *Q*-Criterion

Both Eulerian and Lagrangian methods are available to detect coherent structures (eddies) in a flow [39,40]. Many of the Eulerian methods are based on the velocity gradient tensor [40–42]. One prominent example of such indicators is the *Q*-criterion [43], which is determined from the second invariant of the velocity gradient tensor, and is given by:

$$Q = \frac{1}{2}[|\Omega|^2 - |s|^2] \tag{14}$$

where the antisymmetric part or the vorticity tensor is:

$$\Omega_{ij} = \frac{1}{2}\left(\frac{\partial u_i}{\partial x_j} - \frac{\partial u_j}{\partial x_i}\right) \tag{15}$$

The *Q*-criterion is applied to detect the dominance of the vorticity over the strain. Vorticity is dominant when $Q > 0$, while strain is dominant for $Q < 0$. A zero contour of Q can be used to visualize vortices.

Figures 9–11 show contours for $Q = 0$ for the three cases. Q is calculated for the averaged velocity fields in these figures. Stretched vortex tubes are observed at the entrance of the orifice. With increasing pressure drop and Reynolds number, finer vortex structures develop in the orifice.

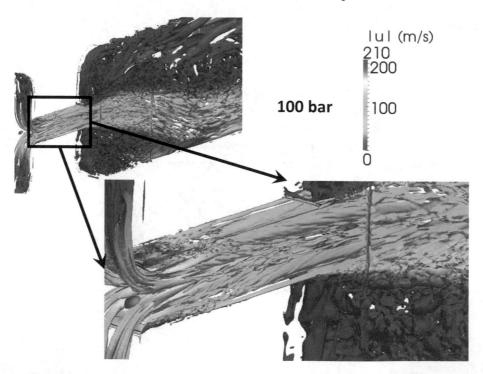

Figure 9. The *Q*-criterion for the time averaged flow through the device for the 100 bar case. The color shows the magnitude of the velocity.

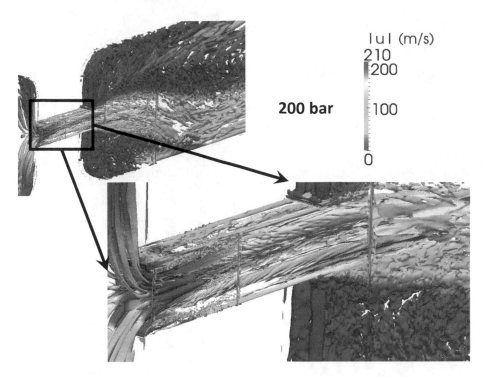

Figure 10. The Q-criterion for the time-averaged flow through the device for the 200 bar case. The color shows the magnitude of the velocity.

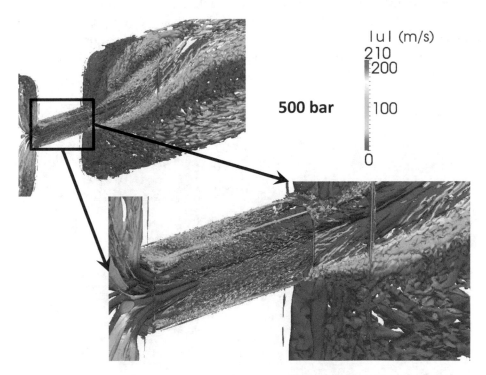

Figure 11. The Q-criterion for the time averaged flow through the device for the 500 bar case. The color shows the magnitude of the velocity.

4.1.2. Laminar and Turbulent Stresses

As with dissipation, the stresses generated by the fluid flow can be divided into laminar stresses and turbulent stresses [44–47].

$$\tau = \tau_l + \tau_t \tag{16}$$

where τ_l and τ_t are the laminar stress tensor and turbulent stress tensor, respectively. The stress tensor is given by:

$$\tau = \begin{bmatrix} \tau_{xx} & \tau_{xy} & \tau_{xz} \\ \tau_{yx} & \tau_{yy} & \tau_{yz} \\ \tau_{zx} & \tau_{zy} & \tau_{zz} \end{bmatrix} \tag{17}$$

The laminar stress tensor consists of the average velocity derivatives [44]:

$$\tau_l = \mu \begin{bmatrix} \tau_{xx} & \tau_{xy} & \tau_{xz} \\ \tau_{yx} & \tau_{yy} & \tau_{yz} \\ \tau_{zx} & \tau_{zy} & \tau_{zz} \end{bmatrix} = \mu \begin{bmatrix} \frac{\partial \bar{u}}{\partial x} + \frac{\partial \bar{u}}{\partial x} & \frac{\partial \bar{u}}{\partial y} + \frac{\partial \bar{v}}{\partial x} & \frac{\partial \bar{u}}{\partial w} + \frac{\partial \bar{w}}{\partial x} \\ \frac{\partial \bar{v}}{\partial x} + \frac{\partial \bar{u}}{\partial y} & \frac{\partial \bar{v}}{\partial y} + \frac{\partial \bar{v}}{\partial y} & \frac{\partial \bar{v}}{\partial z} + \frac{\partial \bar{w}}{\partial y} \\ \frac{\partial \bar{w}}{\partial x} + \frac{\partial \bar{u}}{\partial z} & \frac{\partial \bar{w}}{\partial y} + \frac{\partial \bar{v}}{\partial z} & \frac{\partial \bar{w}}{\partial z} + \frac{\partial \bar{w}}{\partial z} \end{bmatrix} \tag{18}$$

The turbulent stress tensor is identical to the Reynolds stress tensor ($\tau_{ij}^R = -\rho \overline{u_i' u_j'}$) [38,48]:

$$\tau_t = \begin{bmatrix} \tau_{xx} & \tau_{xy} & \tau_{xz} \\ \tau_{yx} & \tau_{yy} & \tau_{yz} \\ \tau_{zx} & \tau_{zy} & \tau_{zz} \end{bmatrix} = -\rho \begin{bmatrix} \overline{u'u'} & \overline{u'v'} & \overline{u'w'} \\ \overline{u'v'} & \overline{v'v'} & \overline{v'w'} \\ \overline{u'w'} & \overline{v'w'} & \overline{w'w'} \end{bmatrix} \tag{19}$$

The laminar stresses produced in the orifice for the 100 bar and 500 bar cases in the mid-plane are shown in Figures 12 and 13. The six independent stress components are depicted in each figure. In general, if the coordinate system is aligned with the flow direction, the diagonal components of the stress tensor cause a fluid element to be elongated. The diagonal components of the stress tensor in Figures 12 and 13 are dominant. From the non-diagonal components, only τ_{xy} has a significant contribution to the stress in the mid plane. However, the non-diagonal parts of the stress tensor become dominant closer to the wall, as depicted in Figure 14.

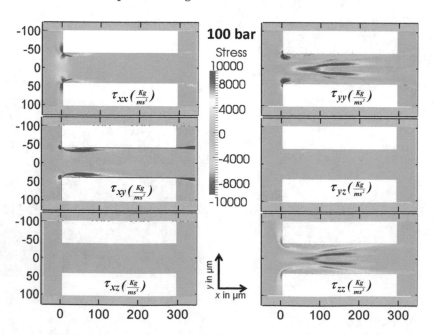

Figure 12. The laminar stress components generated in the orifice in the mid plane for a pressure drop of 100 bar.

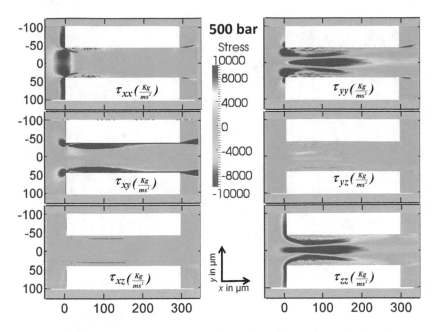

Figure 13. The laminar stress components generated in the orifice in the mid plane for a pressure drop of 500 bar.

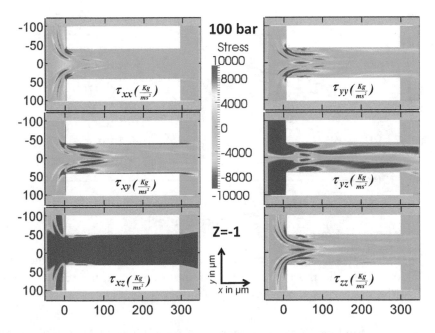

Figure 14. The laminar stress components generated in the orifice in the plane $z = -1$ for a pressure drop of 100 bar.

In order to quantitatively compare the effects of each stress component, the magnitude of the stress is averaged over $y - z$ planes and plotted along the length of the orifice (Figure 15). The upper figure shows the stress components from 50 µm before to 50 µm after the orifice. The lower figure shows a close-up of the upper figure. At the entrance, the diagonal components of the stress tensor τ_{xx} and τ_{yy} are dominant. The stress component τ_{xx} decreases along the orifice. The stress component τ_{xy} shows a complicated behavior. It starts from a low value and reaches its maximum a short distance in front of the entrance. After a short distance from the entrance, it reaches a local minimum.

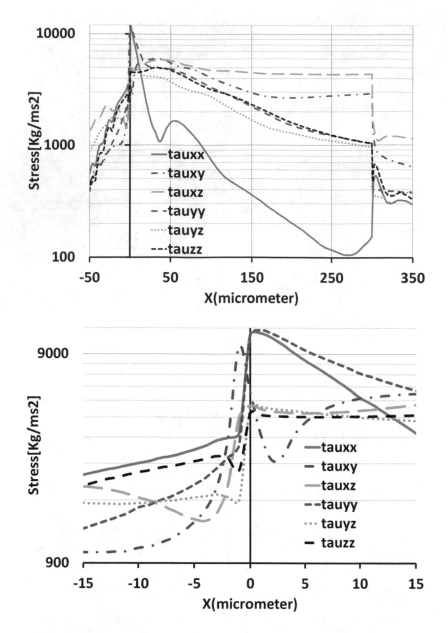

Figure 15. The laminar stress components averaged over the $y-z$ planes plotted in the x direction for a pressure drop of 100 bar. The upper figure shows the stress components from 50 μm before to 50 μm after the orifice. The lower figure shows a close-up of the upper figure.

The components of the turbulent stress tensor for the 100 bar and 500 bar cases are shown in Figures 16 and 17. These figures are taken in the mid-plane of the orifice. The trace of the turbulent stress tensor constitutes the turbulent kinetic energy of the fluid flow. The magnitude of the diagonal components is considerably larger than the non-diagonal components in the mid-plane. As for the laminar stresses, only τ_{xy} has a significant contribution among the non-diagonal stresses.

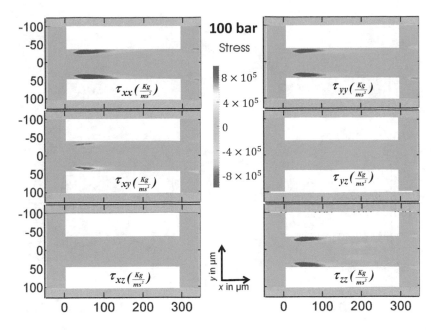

Figure 16. The turbulent stress components generated in the orifice in the mid-plane for a pressure drop of 100 bar.

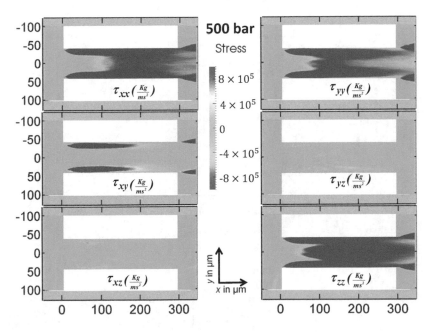

Figure 17. The turbulent stress components generated in the orifice in the mid-plane for a pressure drop of 500 bar.

Unlike the laminar stresses, turbulent stresses play no role at the entrance of the orifice. The turbulence is produced where the laminar stresses are high, and moves downstream with the flow. The turbulent flow near the wall in the plane $z = -1$ is shown in Figure 18. The values for the turbulent stresses are seen to be smaller close to the wall than in the mid-plane. The diagonal components of the turbulent stress tensor are dominant before, after, and inside of the orifice. This behavior can be seen in Figure 19. The upper figure shows the average magnitude of the turbulence stress for each component. The lower figure is a close-up of the upper figure.

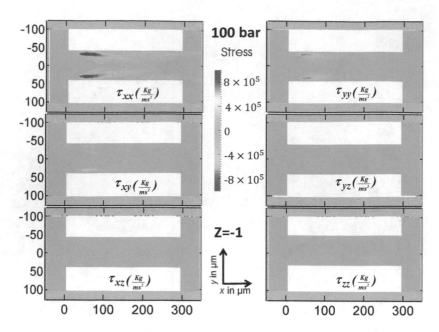

Figure 18. The averaged stress components generated in the orifice in the plane $z = -1$ for the pressure drop of 100 bar.

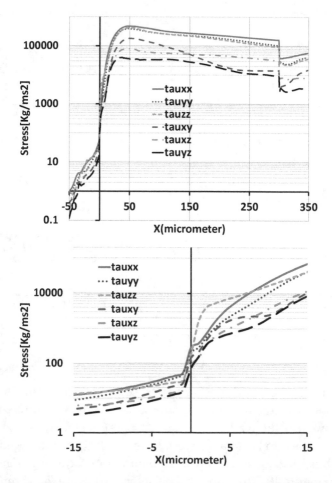

Figure 19. The turbulent stress components averaged over $y - z$ planes plotted in the x direction for a pressure drop of 100 bar. The upper figure shows the average magnitude of the turbulence stress for each component. The lower figure is a close-up of the upper figure.

The maximum of the turbulent stress is observed where the velocity obtains its peak value at about 50 μm behind the entrance of the orifice.

From comparing the turbulent stress in Figure 19 to the laminar stress in Figure 15, we see that the turbulent stress is generally one order of magnitude larger than the maximum of the laminar stress. Our result is therefore in disagreement with the result by Beinert et al. [49], who simulated the same device at the same pressure drop values and obtained turbulent stresses one order of magnitude larger than we did while simultaneously reporting laminar stresses one order of magnitude lower than ours. This difference merits some further discussion. Beinert et al. obtained their result by applying the commercial software ANSYS Fluent 14.0 using a Reynolds-stress model. The turbulent stresses in this software are obtained from empirical closure relations, which are not primarily designed to obtain microscopic stresses. Their approach is therefore based on the *assumption* that the modeled Reynolds-stresses are valid substitutes of the turbulent stresses. On the other hand, our approach does not rely on explicit turbulence models. The turbulent stresses in our model are essentially obtained by direct simulation of the Navier–Stokes equation. Yet, this does not prove that our result is correct. In order to check for the plausibility of their result, Beinert et al. estimated the size of the eddies necessary to comply with the stresses obtained from their turbulence model. For this, they had to estimate the velocity at which the eddy rotates; they chose the maximum velocity measured in the flow, which they give as 250 m/s for the case of 200 bar (we obtained a similar maximum velocity). With this, they obtained eddy sizes of 154 nm. This was compared to an estimate of the Kolmogorov scale obtained from the dissipation, which was estimated as v_{max}^3/l, with $v_{max} = 250$ m/s being the maximal velocity observed in the flow and l being the size of the largest eddies, corresponding to the diameter of the orifice. Under those assumptions, the Kolmogorov scale was estimated to be 33 nm, which was judged to be sufficiently smaller than the smallest estimated eddy size computed from the Reynolds-stress model to support the validity of their result. As our result for the same test case was different, we have re-examined this procedure. First of all, the hypothesis that the smallest eddies would rotate with a velocity equal to the global maximum in the flow does not appear to be very plausible. It should be noted that the argument depends crucially on this point, as the size of the smallest eddies required for their dissipation is inversely proportional to the assumed velocity. Under the assumption that the velocity of the smallest eddies would be five times smaller than the global maximum, the obtained eddies would already be smaller than the Kolmogorov length scale, which would render the results unphysical according to the criterion of Beinert et al. Another crucial point is that the estimates of Beinert et al. require that the smallest eddies are responsible for the largest stress, which is also only plausible under the assumption that the velocity of the smallest eddies was very high. Now we return to our own results and try to estimate Kolmogorov length. The Kolmogorov length η is computed from the turbulent dissipation ϵ and the kinematic viscosity of water v as:

$$\eta = \left(\frac{v^3}{\epsilon}\right)^{1/4} \tag{20}$$

The dissipation in the orifice according to our results is depicted in Figure 8. If we pick, e.g., a value of $\epsilon = 5.6 \times 10^8$ m²s⁻³ for the 100 bar case, we obtain a Kolmogorov scale of $\eta = 206$ nm, which is three times smaller than the smallest grid spacing in our simulation. In order to check the plausibility of this value, we also estimate the dissipation in another way. The global energy dissipation of the flow in the device is easily obtained from the measurement in Figure 3. It is calculated as the volume flux times the pressure drop; i.e., $Q \times \Delta p = 4.3$ W for the 100 bar case. In order to compute the dissipation rate, we have to specify a volume in which the dissipation takes place. Here we assume that all dissipation is confined to the orifice, which gives us:

$$\epsilon = \frac{4.3\,\text{W}}{80\,\mu\text{m} \times 50\,\mu\text{m} \times 300\,\mu\text{m} \times 1000\,\text{kgm}^{-3}} = 3.58 \times 10^9\,\text{m}^2\text{s}^{-3} \tag{21}$$

We see that this value is six times larger than the dissipation obtained directly from the simulation. This rough estimate neglects the fact that the jet behind the orifice participates in the dissipation, and that the remainder of the device is 30 times larger than the orifice itself. This estimate must therefore over-predict the real dissipation, which is compatible with the observation that the previous estimate is smaller. The corresponding Kolmogorov length obtained from this estimate is expected to under-predict the the real Kolmogorov scale. We obtain $\eta = 129$ nm. Note in particular that the last estimate of the Kolmogorov length was obtained entirely from the experimentally-measured flow rate, and did not use any data obtained from the simulation. The so-obtained Kolmogorov length—which underpredicts the real Kolmogorov length—is larger than the one estimated by Beinert et al. Thus, we conclude that the turbulent stresses and the associated dissipation rate is physically more plausible than the results obtained by Beinert et al.

5. Conclusions

We used a high-fidelity implicit large eddy simulation code based on the cumulant lattice Boltzmann method to simulate the turbulent flow through a mirco-orifice. In this paper, we especially focused on turbulent quantities like turbulent stresses and dissipation. In particular, we compare our results to the state-of-the-art approach to obtain turbulent stresses from the empirical Reynolds-stresses of standard turbulence models. It is found that our results for turbulent stresses disagree with published results obtained from RANS equations. The plausibility of our results is checked with the Kolmogorov theory, and it is found that the RANS model predictions for the smallest eddy sizes appear inconsistent. We conclude that our approach of a direct simulation without an explicit turbulence model is a priori more sound in terms of the underlying physics of the problem considered. The resolution in our simulation could support eddies up to about three times the Kolmogorov size, such that it can be considered as a very highly resolved LES. It is not possible to obtain turbulent shear stresses from experiments directly such that time- and space-resolved simulations such as the ones presented here are the only practical means to check the plausibility of RANS results in this regard. Since such resolved simulations are very expensive in terms of compute time, the results from RANS models are rarely challenged. Here we observed a clear indication that standard RANS turbulence models might have deficiencies in obtaining quantitative turbulent stresses for the problem class under consideration.

Acknowledgments: We thank the Deutsche Forschungsgemeinschaft for financial support of the research training group FOR 856 under fund number GE 1990/3-1.

Author Contributions: E.K.F. conducted the simulations and analyzed the results. M.G. developed the computational model and assisted in writing the paper. K.K. implemented larges parts of the simulation software. M.K. contributed in the computational setup and analysis of the results.

References

1. Husain, Z.D. Theoretical Uncertainty of Orifice Flow Measurement. In Proceedings of the International School of Hydrocarbon Measurement, Oklahoma City, OK, USA, 16–18 May 1995; pp. 70–75.
2. McCabe, W.L.; Smith, J.C.; Harriott, P. *Unit Operations of Chemical Engineering*; McGraw-Hill: New Delhi, India, 2005; p. 1140.
3. Doblhoff-Dier, K.; Kudlaty, K.; Wiesinger, M.; Gröschl, M. Time resolved measurement of pulsating flow using orifices. *Flow Meas. Instrum.* **2011**, *22*, 97–103.
4. Peters, F.; Groß, T. Flow rate measurement by an orifice in a slowly reciprocating gas flow. *Flow Meas. Instrum.* **2011**, *22*, 81–85.
5. Baker, R.C. *Flow Measurement Handbook: Industrial Designs, Operating Principles, Performance, and Applications*; Cambridge University Press: Cambridge, UK, 2000; p. 95.
6. Gallagher, J.E. *Natural Gas Measurement Handbook*; Gulf Publishing Company: Houston, TX, USA, 2006; p. 468.

7.   Cristancho, D.E.; Coy, L.A.; Hall, K.R.; Iglesias-Silva, G.A. An alternative formulation of the standard orifice equation for natural gas. *Flow Meas. Instrum.* **2010**, *21*, 299–301.

8.   Åman, R.; Handroos, H.; Eskola, T. Computationally efficient two-regime flow orifice model for real-time simulation. *Simul. Model. Pract. Theor.* **2008**, *16*, 945–961.

9.   Graves, D. Effects of Abnormal Conditions on Accuracy of Orifice Measurement. *Pipeline Gas J.* **2010**, *237*, 35–37.

10. Gothsch, T.; Finke, J.H.; Beinert, S.; Lesche, C.; Schur, J.; Büttgenbach, S.; Müller-Goymann, C.; Kwade, A. Effect of microchannel geometry on high-pressure dispersion and emulsification. *Chem. Engin. Technol.* **2011**, *34*, 335–343.

11. Gothsch, T.; Schilcher, C.; Richter, C.; Beinert, S.; Dietzel, A.; Büttgenbach, S.; Kwade, A. High-pressure microfluidic systems (HPMS): Flow and cavitation measurements in supported silicon microsystems. *Microfluid. Nanofluid.* **2015**, *18*, 121–130.

12. Chen, D.; Cui, B.; Zhu, Z. Numerical simulations for swirlmeter on flow fields and metrological performance. *Trans. Inst. Meas. Control* **2016**, in press.

13. Eiamsa-Ard, S.; Ridluan, A.; Somravysin, P.; Promvonge, P. Numerical investigation of turbulent flow through a circular orific. *KMITL Sci. J.* **2008**, *8*, 43–50.

14. Shah, M.S.; Joshi, J.B.; Kalsi, A.S.; Prasad, C.; Shukla, D.S. Analysis of flow through an orifice meter: CFD simulation. *Chem. Eng. Sci.* **2012**, *71*, 300–309.

15. Reader-Harris, M.; Barton, N.; Hodges, D. The effect of contaminated orifice plates on the discharge coefficient. *Flow Meas. Instrum.* **2012**, *25*, 2–7.

16. Nakao, M.; Kawashima, K.; Kagawa, T. Measurement-integrated simulation of wall pressure measurements using a turbulent model for analyzing oscillating orifice flow in a circular pipe. *Comput. Fluids* **2011**, *49*, 188–196.

17. Gronych, T.; Jeřáb, M.; Peksa, L.; Wild, J.; Staněk, F.; Vičar, M. Experimental study of gas flow through a multi-opening orifice. *Vacuum* **2012**, *86*, 1759–1763.

18. Durst, F.; Wang, A.B. Experimental and numerical investigations of the axisymmetric, turbulent pipe flow over a wall-mounted thin obstacle. In Proceedings of the 7th Symposium on Turbulent Shear Flows, Stanford, CA, USA, 21–23 August 1989.

19. Oliveira, N.M.; Vieira, L.G.; Damasceno, J.J.R. Numerical Methodology for Orifice Meter Calibration. *Mater. Sci. Forum* **2010**, *660–661*, 531–536.

20. Geier, M.; Schönherr, M.; Pasquali, A.; Krafczyk, M. The cumulant lattice Boltzmann equation in three dimensions: Theory and validation. *Comput. Math. Appl.* **2015**, *70*, 507–547.

21. Goraki Fard, E. A Cumulant LBM Approach for Large Eddy Simulation of Dispersion Microsystems. Ph.D. Thesis, TU Braunschweig, Braunschweig, Germany, 2015.

22. Kian Far, E.; Geier, M.; Kutscher, K.; Krafczyk, M. Distributed cumulant lattice Boltzmann simulation of the dispersion process of ceramic agglomerates. *J. Comput. Methods Sci. Eng.* **2016**, *16*, 231–252.

23. Far, E.K.; Geier, M.; Kutscher, K.; Krafczyk, M. Simulation of micro aggregate breakage in turbulent flows by the cumulant lattice Boltzmann method. *Comput. Fluids* **2016**, *140*, 222–231.

24. Richter, C.; Krah, T.; Büttgenbach, S. Novel 3D manufacturing method combining microelectrial discharge machining and electrochemical polishing. *Microsyst. Technol.* **2012**, *18*, 1109–1118.

25. Geier, M.; Greiner, A.; Korvink, J.G. A factorized central moment lattice Boltzmann method. *Eur. Phys. J. Spec. Top.* **2009**, *171*, 55–61.

26. Geier, M.; Greiner, A.; Korvink, J.G. Bubble functions for the lattice Boltzmann method and their application to grid refinement. *Eur. Phys. J. Spec. Top.* **2009**, *171*, 173–179.

27. Schönherr, M.; Kucher, K.; Geier, M.; Stiebler, M.; Freudiger, S.; Krafczyk, M. Multi-thread implementations of the lattice Boltzmann method on non-uniform grids for CPUs and GPUs. *Comput. Math. Appl.* **2011**, *61*, 3730–3743.

28. Geier, M.; Schönherr, M. Esoteric Twist: An Efficient in-Place Streaming Algorithmus for the Lattice Boltzmann Method on Massively Parallel Hardware. *Computation* **2017**, *5*, 19.

29. Gong, Y.; Tanner, F.X. Comparison of RANS and LES Models in the Laminar Limit for a Flow over a Backward-Facing Step Using OpenFOAM. In Proceedings of the Nineteenth International Multidimensional Engine Modeling Meeting at the SAE Congress, Detroit, MI, USA, 19 April 2009.

30. Munson, B.R.; Young, D.F.; Okiishi, T. *Fundamentals of Fluid Mechanics*, 4th ed.; John Wiley and Sons: Hoboken, NJ, USA, 2006; p. 481.

31. Streeter, V.L. *Handbook of Fluid Dynamics*; McGraw-Hill: New York, NY, USA, 1961; p. 413.

32. Kähler, G.; Bonelli, F.; Gonnella, G.; Lamura, A. Cavitation inception of a van der Waals fluid at a sack-wall obstacle. *Phys. Fluids* **2015**, *27*, 123307.

33. Shaaban, S. Optimization of orifice meter's energy consumption. *Chem. Eng. Res. Des.* **2014**, *92*, 1005–1015.

34. Munson, B.R.; Young, D.F. *Fundamentals of Fluid Mechanics*, 5th ed.; John Wiley and Sons: Hoboken, NJ, USA, 2009; p. 481.

35. Blasius, H. Das ähnlichkeitsgesetz bei reibungsvorgängen in flüssigkeiten. In *Mitteilungen Über Forschungsarbeiten Auf Dem Gebiete Des Ingenieurwesens*; Springer: Berlin/Heidelberg, Germany, 1913; pp. 1–41. (In German)

36. Fluent, A. *ANSYS Fluent 12.0 User's Guide*; ANSYS Inc.: Canonsburg, PA, USA, 2009; p. 48.

37. Shur, M.L.; Strelets, M.K.; Travin, A.K.; Spalart, P.R. Turbulence modeling in rotating and curved channels: Assessing the Spalart-Shur correction. *AIAA J.* **2000**, *38*, 784–792.

38. Schumann, U. Realizability of Reynolds-Stress Turbulence Models. *Phys. Fluids* **1977**, *20*, 721.

39. Haller, G. An objective definition of a vortex. *J. Fluid Mech.* **2005**, *525*, 1–26.

40. Green, M.A.; Rowley, C.W.; Haller, G. Detection of Lagrangian Coherent Structures in Three-Dimensional Turbulence. *J. Fluid Mech.* **2007**, *572*, 111.

41. Dubief , Y.; Delcayre, F. On coherent-vortex identification in turbulence. *J. Turbul.* **2000**, *1*, 11.

42. Chakraborty, P.; Balachandar, S.; Adrian, R.J. On the relationships between local vortex identification schemes. *J. Fluid Mech.* **2005**, *535*, 189–214.

43. Hunt, J.C.R.; Wray, A.A.; Moin, P. Eddies, streams, and convergence zones in turbulent flows. In Proceedings of the Summer Program on Studying Turbulence Using Numerical Simulation Databases, Stanford, CA, USA, 27 June–22 July 1988; pp. 193–208.

44. Kuo, K.K.; Acharya, R. *Fundamentals of Turbulent and Multiphase Combustion*; John Wiley & Sons, Inc.: Hoboken, NJ, USA, 2012; p. 220.

45. Landahl, M.T.; Mollo-Christensen, E. *Turbulence and Random Processes in Fluid Mechanics*; Cambridge University Press: Cambridge, UK, 1992; p. 45.

46. Tennekes, H.; Lumley, J.L. *A First Course in Turbulence*; MIT Press: Cambridge, MA, USA, 1972; p. 300.

47. Fröhlich, J.; von Terzi, D. Hybrid LES/RANS methods for the simulation of turbulent flows. *Prog. Aerosp. Sci.* **2008**, *44*, 349–377.

48. Blazek, J. *Computational Fluid Dynamics: Principles and Applications*; Elsevier: Amsterdam, The Netherlands, 2005; pp. 227–270.

49. Beinert, S.; Gothsch, T.; Kwade, A. Numerical evaluation of stresses acting on particles in high-pressure microsystems using a Reynolds stress model. *Chem. Eng. Sci.* **2015**, *123*, 197–206.

Levy-Lieb-Based Monte Carlo Study of the Dimensionality Behaviour of the Electronic Kinetic Functional

Seshaditya A. [1,†], Luca M. Ghiringhelli [2,†] and Luigi Delle Site [1,*]

[1]   Institute for Mathematics, Freie Universität Berlin, D-14195 Berlin, Germany; aditya@zedat.fu-berlin.de
[2]   Fritz-Haber Institute, Faradayweg 4-6, D-14195 Berlin, Germany; luca@fhi-berlin.mpg.de
[*]   Correspondence: luigi.dellesite@fu-berlin.de
[†]   These authors contributed equally to this work.

Academic Editor: Jianmin Tao

Abstract: We consider a gas of interacting electrons in the limit of nearly uniform density and treat the one dimensional (1D), two dimensional (2D) and three dimensional (3D) cases. We focus on the determination of the correlation part of the kinetic functional by employing a Monte Carlo sampling technique of electrons in space based on an analytic derivation via the Levy-Lieb constrained search principle. Of particular interest is the question of the behaviour of the functional as one passes from 1D to 3D; according to the basic principles of Density Functional Theory (DFT) the form of the universal functional should be independent of the dimensionality. However, in practice the straightforward use of current approximate functionals in different dimensions is problematic. Here, we show that going from the 3D to the 2D case the functional form is consistent (concave function) but in 1D becomes convex; such a drastic difference is peculiar of 1D electron systems as it is for other quantities. Given the interesting behaviour of the functional, this study represents a basic first-principle approach to the problem and suggests further investigations using highly accurate (though expensive) many-electron computational techniques, such as Quantum Monte Carlo.

Keywords: Levy-Lieb principle; Monte Carlo sampling of electrons; kinetic-energy functionals; dimensionality

---

1. Introduction

In the popular KS-DFT methodology [1], the kinetic energy of the electrons consists only of the non interacting part while the part concerning the correlation is included in the general term of the exchange-correlation functional which includes all the correlation contributions. In alternative approaches, such as that of Orbital-Free-DFT (OFDFT), it may be more useful to not include the correlation part of kinetic functional in a general correlation term, but to treat it explicitly, since one of the key quantities of OFDFT is the kinetic term [2–8]. Some of us have previously proposed a method based on the Levy-Lieb constrained formalism [9,10] to derive a form of the kinetic functional whose non-analytic part can be determined via a Monte Carlo sampling of the electron correlation in space [11–13]. For the test case of almost uniform gas in 3D resulted in a kinetic-correlation energy functional which follows the form $\int \rho(\mathbf{r}) \log \rho(\mathbf{r}) d\mathbf{r}$. Interestingly, the same qualitative behaviour was found also in state-of-the-art Quantum Monte Carlo calculations and opened interesting scenarios where electron correlations may be expressed within the framework of Information Theory [13–15]. An interesting question that can be addressed by this method is the following: in general the universal functional of DFT should have a form which is independent of the dimensionality, i.e., the functional behaviour should not depend on the spatial dimensions [16,17]. This is termed the dimensional crossover (DC) of density functionals and is a very important property of the universal functional, that guides the construction of approximate functionals. As a consequence, given the physical consistency of our approach for 3D and its relatively affordable computational costs, one can extend the study to 2D and 1D systems and see whether or not the functional form changes drastically. Results of this study can be taken as a basis for more accurate and far more expensive calculations of the kinetic correlation functional, e.g., by state-of-the-art Quantum Monte Carlo techniques. Our results show an interesting feature: in 2D and 3D the functional form is consistent (in both cases logarithmic or with a power law of 1/2, concave behaviour), however in 1D the change is drastic and consistent with results present in literature on other quantities (convex behaviour). This drastic difference is certainly intriguing and worth further investigations, and, if confirmed by other calculations, gives an interesting insight in the construction of energy functionals.

The paper is organized as follows: first we summarize the conceptual approach employed in this study, that is Levy-Lieb constrained search formalism for the design of kinetic energy functionals combined with Monte Carlo evaluation technique, next we introduce the problem of the dimensional-crossover of the kinetic-correlation energy functional and finally we report the technical aspects and the simulation results of the study.

2. Levy-Lieb Constrained Search Formalism and Monte Carlo Evaluation

In the Levy-Lieb constrained search formalism, the minimisation problem for the ground state of electrons is:

$$E_{GS} = \min_{\rho} \left[\min_{\Psi \to \rho} \langle \Psi | \hat{T} + \hat{V}_{ee} | \Psi \rangle + \int v(\mathbf{r})\rho(\mathbf{r})d\mathbf{r} \right], \tag{1}$$

where Ψ is the N-electron wavefunction, $\hat{T}$ and $\hat{V}_{ee}$ are the kinetic energy and electron-electron potential energy operators, respectively, $v(\mathbf{r})$ is the external potential, and $\rho(\mathbf{r})$ is the electron density. The inner minimisation of the universal functional is carried out with respect to the wavefunctions integrating to density $\rho(\mathbf{r})$ and the outer minimisation is done on all densities, preserving the N-representability (i.e., integrating to N). In an alternative representation, N-electron wavefunction can be substituted by its corresponding $3N-$dimensional probability density and expressed in terms of the one particle density $\rho(\mathbf{r}_1)$ and the $N-1$, conditional electron density [11,18]:

$$|\Psi|^2 = \rho(\mathbf{r}_1)f(\mathbf{r}_2, \mathbf{r}_3, ...\mathbf{r}_N|\mathbf{r}_1). \tag{2}$$

In order to assure the fermionic character $f(\mathbf{r}_2, \mathbf{r}_3, ...\mathbf{r}_N|\mathbf{r}_1)$ must satisfy the following necessary mathematical conditions:

$$\int f(\mathbf{r}_2, \mathbf{r}_3, ...\mathbf{r}_N|\mathbf{r}_1)d\mathbf{r}_2 d\mathbf{r}_3 ...d\mathbf{r}_N = 1. \tag{3}$$

$$f(\mathbf{r}_1, \mathbf{r}_2, ..\mathbf{r}_i..\mathbf{r}_N|\mathbf{r}_j) = 0, \forall i = j; j = 1, N. \tag{4}$$

Upon reformulating the expression of Equation (1), one obtains:

$$E_{GS} = \min_{\rho} \left(\min_{f} \Gamma[\rho(\mathbf{r}_1), f] + \int \frac{1}{8} \frac{|\nabla \rho(\mathbf{r}_1)|^2}{\rho(\mathbf{r}_1)} d\mathbf{r}_1 + \int v(\mathbf{r}_1)\rho(\mathbf{r}_1)d\mathbf{r}_1 \right). \tag{5}$$

where

$$\Gamma[\rho(\mathbf{r}_1), f] = \int \rho(\mathbf{r}_1)\left[\frac{1}{8} \int \frac{|\nabla_1 f|^2}{f} d\mathbf{r}_2 ...d\mathbf{r}_N + \frac{(N-1)}{2} \int \frac{f}{|\mathbf{r}_i - \mathbf{r}_j|} d\mathbf{r}_2 ...d\mathbf{r}_i ...d\mathbf{r}_j ...d\mathbf{r}_N\right]d\mathbf{r}_1. \tag{6}$$

which for convenience we express as:

$$\Gamma[\rho(\mathbf{r}_1), f] = I[\rho(\mathbf{r}_1), f] + C[\rho(\mathbf{r}_1), f]. \tag{7}$$

3. Monte Carlo Sampling for Nearly Uniform Electron Gas

3.1. Spinless Case

For the evaluation of the non-local part of the kinetic energy and Coulomb interaction, $\Gamma[\rho(\mathbf{r}), f]$ in Equation (6), first an ansatz about the form of f is done. Such an ansatz satisfies the mathematical requirements and basic physical principles (for details see [11,14]) and is derived for the spinless case, that is, spins are not explicitly considered:

$$f(\mathbf{r}_2...\mathbf{r}_N|\mathbf{r}_1) = e^{D_f(\mathbf{r}_1)} \prod_{n=2}^{N} e^{-\gamma E_H(\mathbf{r}_1, \mathbf{r}_n)} \prod_{i>j\neq 1} e^{-\beta E_H(\mathbf{r}_i, \mathbf{r}_j)}. \tag{8}$$

where the quantity $e^{D_f(r_1)}$ is the normalisation factor and

$$E_H(\mathbf{r}_1, \mathbf{r}_n) = \frac{1}{|\mathbf{r}_1 - \mathbf{r}_n|}, E_H(\mathbf{r}_i, \mathbf{r}_j) = \frac{1}{|\mathbf{r}_i - \mathbf{r}_j|}. \tag{9}$$

For the numerical evaluation, the expressions are transformed as:

$$\Gamma[\rho(r_1), f] = \frac{1}{M} \sum_{m=1}^{M} [\frac{1}{8}|\frac{\nabla_1 f}{f}|^2 + \frac{1}{N} \sum_{i=1}^{N} \sum_{j>i} \frac{1}{|\mathbf{r}_i - \mathbf{r}_j|}]_{\rho(\mathbf{r}_1), \gamma}. \tag{10}$$

and in this form, Metropolis Monte Carlo can be employed to evaluate the quantities, of interest, in fact the minimisation w.r.t. f in Equation (5) is now reduced to a minimisation (for a given density) w.r.t. γ and β; for simplicity, in previous studies we used $\gamma = \beta$. As a consequence, treating different densities and calculating I for each density we can numerically obtain the correlation part of the kinetic functional $I[\rho(\mathbf{r}_1), f]$; the numerical result can then be fit into an analytic expression. For the Monte Carlo moves, the acceptance ratio is given as

$$\frac{f_{new}}{f_{old}} = e^{-\gamma[E_H(\mathbf{r}_1, \mathbf{r}_k^{new}) - E_H(\mathbf{r}_1, \mathbf{r}_k^{old})]} \prod_{i\neq 1,k} e^{-\gamma[E_H(\mathbf{r}_i, \mathbf{r}_k^{new}) - E_H(\mathbf{r}_i, \mathbf{r}_k^{old})]}. \tag{11}$$

The analytic form obtained for the correlation part of the kinetic energy functional is:

$$I[\rho] = \int \rho(\mathbf{r})(A + B \ln \rho(\mathbf{r}))d\mathbf{r}, \tag{12}$$

and thus, from Equation (5), the total kinetic energy functional reads:

$$K[\rho(\mathbf{r})] = T_W[\rho(\mathbf{r})] + \int \rho(\mathbf{r})(A + B \ln \rho(\mathbf{r}))d\mathbf{r}, \tag{13}$$

where $T_W[\rho(\mathbf{r})] = \frac{1}{8} \int \frac{|\nabla\rho(\mathbf{r})|^2}{\rho(\mathbf{r})}d\mathbf{r}$, is the von Weizäcker kinetic energy [19], and A, B are the fitting parameters. In the above expressions, the indistinguishability of electrons allows to remove the labeling for the electron position.

3.2. Adding the Effects of Spin

An extension of the method was done in order to include the effects of the spin [13]. The Pauli exclusion principle even in the absence of Coulomb interactions tells us that two same-spin electrons cannot have the same position. This observation is introduced to extend the form of f via the introduction of an additional interaction between the so-called Pauli pairs; in simple terms, for every electron, the nearest electron (not already paired to any other electron and whose distance is denoted by $r_{pp(i)}$) is the corresponding Pauli companion and they are related via the Pauli weighting function

$$p = \prod_{\text{Paulipairs}} e^{-\alpha|\mathbf{r}_i - \mathbf{r}_{pp(i)}|}. \tag{14}$$

The modified conditional electron density:

$$g(\mathbf{r}_2...\mathbf{r}_N|\mathbf{r}_1) = p \cdot e^{D_g(\mathbf{r})} \prod_{n=2}^{N} e^{-\gamma E_H(\mathbf{r}_1,\mathbf{r}_N)} \prod_{i>j\neq 1} e^{-\beta E_H(\mathbf{r}_i,\mathbf{r}_j)}, \tag{15}$$

with

$$e^{-D_g(\mathbf{r}_1)} = \int d\mathbf{r}_2 d\mathbf{r}_3...d\mathbf{r}_N \prod_{\text{PauliPairs}} e^{-\alpha|\mathbf{r}_i - \mathbf{r}_{pp(i)}|} \prod_{n=2}^{N} e^{-\gamma E_H(\mathbf{r}_1,\mathbf{r}_N)} \prod_{i>j\neq 1} e^{-\beta E_H(\mathbf{r}_i,\mathbf{r}_j)}. \tag{16}$$

For the Monte Carlo evaluation of:

$$I[\rho(\mathbf{r}_1), f] = \langle \frac{1}{8} |\frac{\nabla_1 g}{g}|^2 \rangle \tag{17}$$

the new acceptance rule becomes:

$$\frac{g_{new}}{g_{old}} = \frac{p^{new}}{p^{old}} e^{-\gamma[E_H(\mathbf{r}_1,\mathbf{r}_k^{new}) - E_H(\mathbf{r}_1,\mathbf{r}_k^{old})]} \prod_{i\neq 1,k} e^{-\gamma[E_H(\mathbf{r}_i,\mathbf{r}_k^{new}) - E_H(\mathbf{r}_i,\mathbf{r}_k^{old})]}. \tag{18}$$

Upon moving an electron, all the Pauli pairs are re-evaluated and new pair-distances are considered. Upon inclusion of Pauli weighting function, the Kinetic-correlation energy $I[\rho(\mathbf{r}_1), f]$ consists of three main contributions (see Equation (31) in Reference [13]): a term which would be equivalent to the Thomas-Fermi kinetic functional if α is chosen to be $\sqrt{C_F}\rho^{1/3}$ with an analytic form: $T_{TF} = C_F \rho_0^{\frac{5}{3}}$ [20,21], and the two terms which needs to be evaluated, that is the kinetic-Coulomb correlation and kinetic-spin-cross correlation term,

$$I_C \cong \tilde{\gamma}^2 \sum_{i=2}^{N} \sum_{j=2}^{N} [\nabla_1 E_H(\mathbf{r}_1,\mathbf{r}_i) \cdot \nabla_1 E_H(\mathbf{r}_1,\mathbf{r}_j)], \tag{19}$$

and

$$I_{sC} \cong 2\alpha\tilde{\gamma}\mathbf{u}_p \cdot \sum_{i=2}^{N} \nabla_1 E_H(\mathbf{r}_1,\mathbf{r}_i). \tag{20}$$

In the above expressions, $\tilde{\gamma}$ is the value which minimises the energy functional at a given density. A scaling factor k is used for the parameter α for softening the spin interactions. Therefore, the modified parameter, $\alpha' = k\alpha$ and $0 \leq k \leq 2$ (going from spinless to full spin case). Numerical results show that despite the addition of effective spin, the functional form of the correlation term of the kinetic functional remains logarithmic and reads:

$$K_{spin}[\rho] = T_{TF} + T_W + \int \rho(\mathbf{r}_1)(A_C + B_C \ln\rho(\mathbf{r}_1))d\mathbf{r}_1 + \int \rho(\mathbf{r}_1)(A_{sC} + B_{sC} \ln\rho(\mathbf{r}_1))d\mathbf{r}_1. \tag{21}$$

The quantities A_C, B_C, A_{sC} and B_{sC} are the fitting parameters for I_C and I_{sC} respectively. In this study, since we are interested in the functional form of the correlation term of the kinetic functional, we will employ the spinless approach, however, for the 1D case, given the drastic change in the functional behaviour we will check whether the effect of the spin changes the conclusions reached.

4. Dimensional Behaviour of Electronic Kinetic Correlation Functional

Universality of density functionals means that the functional form should be conserved in any dimension. Studies on the behaviour of non-interacting kinetic energy (T_s) and Weizäcker (T_W) functionals clearly explain the dimensional crossover behaviour for kinetic energy functionals [17,22]. Based on these ideas, similar kinds of studies are performed for understanding the dimensional behaviour of kinetic correlation functional using (nearly) uniform electron gas in different dimensions. Interacting electrons of a gas at uniform density in 1D, 2D and 3D have also been studied extensively using various QMC approaches [23–25]; however, a direct comparison between our calculation and QMC calculations in 1D and 2D is not possible at this stage. In fact the quantity we are interested in, i.e., the correlation term of kinetic functional, has not been treated in the QMC studies in 1D and 2D, but only in 3D, where, as mentioned before, there is qualitative agreement with the results of our approach [15]. In this perspective, as underlined before and as will be discussed later on, QMC calculations of the correlation term of the kinetic functional are highly desired, given the results reported here. In general, electrons confined to two-dimensions (2D) have correlations that are predicted to be stronger than the correlations in a corresponding three-dimensional system at the same density. Usually in 2D, the system exhibits a Fermi-liquid behaviour at high densities whereas at low densities they form Wigner crystals [24,26]. Electrons in 1D-chains are very well described by the Tomonaga-Luttinger liquid theory and show drastically different behaviour from that of two and three-dimensional case [23,27]. This is due to the strong correlations in 1D as the electrons cannot avoid each other (only scattering possible in back and forth directions). Inspired by the discussions in literature an interesting question is to consider this issue within the Levy-Lieb derivation reported in the previous sections and eventually calculate the correlation term of the kinetic functional using the Monte Carlo procedure to see whether or not its functional form changes with the change of dimensionality. From Equation (5) it is clear that the analytic part of the kinetic functional: $T_W[\rho(\mathbf{r})] = \frac{1}{8} \int \frac{|\nabla \rho(\mathbf{r})|^2}{\rho(\mathbf{r})} d\mathbf{r}$, is indeed formally independent of the dimensionality, however the correlation term $I_C[\rho(\mathbf{r})]$ must be determined numerically. Our Monte Carlo approach reported above, allows us to calculate the correlation part of the kinetic functional in 1D, 2D and 3D; its dimensional behaviour may be very interesting for building general kinetic functionals, at least within the range of densities considered in this work. It must be noticed that the Levy-Lieb implicit functional: $\min_{\Psi \to \rho} \langle \Psi | \widehat{T} + \widehat{V}_{ee} | \Psi \rangle$, in term of the conditional probability: $\min_f \Gamma[\rho(\mathbf{r}_1), f] + \int \frac{1}{8} \frac{|\nabla \rho(\mathbf{r})|^2}{\rho(\mathbf{r})}$, is formally exact and that our approximations in building f lead to a final explicit Levy-Lieb functional (i.e., functional of ρ only) whose accuracy directly relates to the accuracy (and sufficiency) of the basic (first) principles of electron correlations in f. Thus our numerical functional is approximated only regarding the assumption of f, if one had f calculated with standard QMC then the functional would be (numerically) exact (within the accuracy of QMC). For this reason, although the universality of the functional can be assured only for the truly exact functional, accurate numerical approaches would lead to functionals whose dimensional behaviour should not deviate much from the behaviour of the ideal (exact) case. Finally, in 1D case, the form of electron-electron interaction is the $\frac{1}{r_{ij}}$ and there is no need for regularisation of the bare potential as the conditional probability function would be zero for $r_i = r_j$ by definition, thereby avoiding the singularity [28,29]. Moreover, it must be noticed that in our approach there are two distinct, though complementary, ways in which the physics of correlation can be investigated: (a) use the assumptions done for the 3D case for f and consider the 1D and 2D cases as straightforward limiting cases of 3D, as dimension x and y became small compared to dimension z; (b) modify f in 2D and 1D in order to get a desired consistency with the results of 3D and understand which assumptions are required and thus what is the relevant physics of correlation in 1D and 2D if we assume the 3D case as a reference for the form of the functional. We have so far explored only case (a), future work will investigate also option (b). In the next section we discuss the results obtained.

5. Results

For computational convenience we treat the spinless case since the functional form of the correlation term of the kinetic functional has been shown to be independent of the explicit inclusion of the spin. We calculate $I_C[\rho(\mathbf{r})]$ for different densities in 1D, 2D and 3D; for each density a minimisation study was done to derive the corresponding optimal $\tilde{\gamma}$. The numerical values of $I_C[\rho(\mathbf{r})]$ are fitted to an analytic form. In the 1D case, I_C is optimally fitted by a power law (see Figure 1): $I_C[\rho(\mathbf{r})] = 2.41\rho^2 + 0.11\rho + 0.025$. For 2D and 3D cases (see Figures 2 and 3): I_C follows the analytical fits of the form, $I_C[\rho(\mathbf{r})] = A + B\ln\rho(\mathbf{r})$ for 3D or a polynomial fitting with non integer power law: $I_C = -0.594\rho^{(2/3)}(\mathbf{r}) + 1.838\rho^{(1/3)}(\mathbf{r}) - 0.394$; for 2D instead the fitting formula is: $I_C = 0.167\rho(\mathbf{r}) + 1.851\rho^{(1/2)}(\mathbf{r}) - 0.360$. The physical meaning of the fitting functions may turn to be very interesting from a conceptual point of view, however it does not represents the main focus of this study and will be subject of further investigations in future work; instead the change in concavity of kinetic correlation energy upon reducing the dimensions is the evident and drastic difference between the 1D case and the higher dimensions cases. The striking difference in the functional dependence of I_C from $\rho(\mathbf{r})$, when comparing 1D to 2D and 3D, is the concavity: convex for 1D whereas concave for 2D and 3D. Given such a change, a question to ask is whether the role of spins, treated explicitly, may change the behaviour in 1D. Calculations with the explicit inclusion of the spin display the same power law behaviour found for the spinless case, for both the kinetic correlation $I_C[\rho(\mathbf{r})]$ and and the spin-cross correlation $I_{sC}[\rho(\mathbf{r})]$ terms. In detail, for different k-values and within the density range, the polynomial fits for I_C and I_{sC} are tabulated in Table 1 (energies and densities are in atomic units). Technical details are reported in the Appendix A.

Table 1. Polynomial Fits for I_C and I_{sC} values (with RMS errors in parenthesis) for 1D including the spin.

k Value	I_C	I_{sC}
$k = 0.5$	$I_C[\rho(\mathbf{r})] = 2.214\rho^2 - 0.101\rho + 0.031(0.0287)$	$I_{sC}[\rho(\mathbf{r})] = 0.631\rho^2 - 0.055\rho + 0.0126(0.0263)$
$k = 0.75$	$I_C[\rho(\mathbf{r})] = 2.231\rho^2 - 0.198\rho + 0.0465(0.0364)$	$I_{sC}[\rho(\mathbf{r})] = 1.016\rho^2 - 0.146\rho + 0.0291(0.0687)$
$k = 1.2$	$I_C[\rho(\mathbf{r})] = 2.204\rho^2 - 0.099\rho + 0.0327(0.0114)$	$I_{sC}[\rho(\mathbf{r})] = 1.609\rho^2 - 0.165\rho + 0.0363(0.0345)$

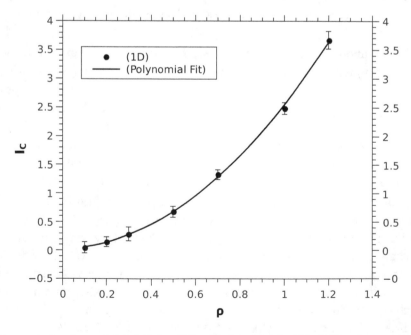

Figure 1. Computed values of $I_C[\rho(\mathbf{r})]$ for different densities in 1D obtained at optimal γ values. The analytical fit in this case is $I_C[\rho(\mathbf{r})] = 2.41\rho(\mathbf{r})^2 + 0.11\rho(\mathbf{r}) + 0.025$ with RMS error value 0.0165. All values are in atomic units.

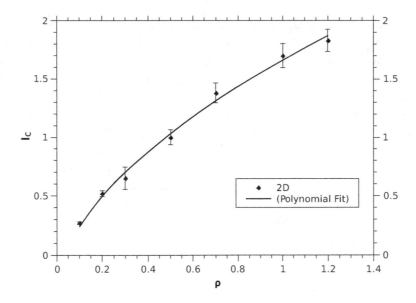

Figure 2. Computed values of $I_C[\rho(\mathbf{r})]$ for different densities in 2D obtained at optimal γ values. The Polynomial fit in this case is: $I_C = 0.167\rho(\mathbf{r}) + 1.851\rho^{(1/2)}(\mathbf{r}) - 0.360$ with error 0.0277. All values are in atomic units.

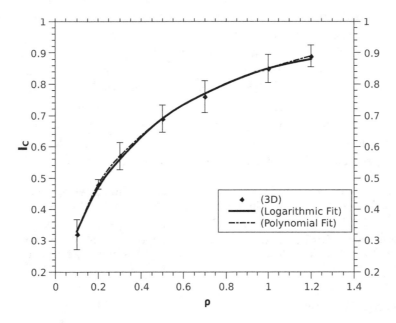

Figure 3. Computed values of $I_C[\rho(\mathbf{r})]$ for different densities in 3D obtained at optimal γ values. The analytic fit obtained in this case, $I_C[\rho(\mathbf{r})] = 0.847 + 0.241 \ln\rho(\mathbf{r})$ and the polynomial fit is given by $I_C = -0.594\rho^{(2/3)}(\mathbf{r}) + 1.838\rho^{(1/3)}(\mathbf{r}) - 0.394$ with RMS values 0.0273 and 0.0324 respectively. All values are in atomic units.

6. Discussion

It must be stated once more that except for the assumption of the form of coupling of electrons in f, which is essentially a Jastrow factor extensively used in literature for treating correlations [30,31], the approach is then free of other assumptions. This implies that if the Jastrow factor form of f is reasonable to describe the basic physics of interacting electrons, then the behaviour of the 1D case has a real physical meaning and it is not the artifact of the assumptions of the model. In fact in 1D for both spins and spinless systems, due to the break-down of Fermi-liquid behaviour a quadratic power law has been already observed; a similar power-law scaling behaviour in 1D electron gas is also observed experimentally for properties such as conductance, tunneling current $I(R)$, and density of states (DOS) while in 3D the behaviour is logarithmic [25,32,33]. An additional argument in favor of a real physical meaning of our results in 1D is the fact that for the 3D case the logarithmic behaviour of $I_C[\rho(\mathbf{r})]$ found with our approach was then qualitatively verified with state of art Quantum Monte Carlo calculations [15]; in addition, in Reference [14], it has been shown that the form of f chosen leads indeed to a first-principle form of electronic correlations, meaning that I_C is the average response in energy of the $N-1$ electrons to the displacement of the reference electron. It must be also reported that the conclusions of our previous work [12,13] have been strongly criticized by experts of OFDFT [34]. However the dispute was created due to a misunderstanding rather than by a conceptual or technical bug of our approach; in fact the analytic fit obtained with our approach must be considered valid only within the range of densities considered in the numerical calculations. In such a range then, the analytic fit is the closest functional form of the kinetic correlation functional (based on our sampling approach of the electron configuration in space). In this perspective the behaviour found for the 1D system in the range of densities considered and in comparison to the 3D and 2D case is worth of future attention and developments in the perspective of building valid analytic kinetic functionals.

7. Conclusions

Our results clearly suggest that the functional behaviour in 1D is different from the other two cases. The $\rho^2 + \rho$ power-law behaviour with respect to the density is observed in both spin and spinless 1D cases. These results could well be related to the power law behaviour of other quantities such as conductance, current and other electronic charge properties in 1D; in fact they are nothing else than a response to a perturbation; similarly the Monte Carlo procedure of our approach at each move perturbs the system by displaying an electron in space and observes its response. The main emphasis of this study is the drastic change in the behaviour of the kinetic correlation energy (from concave to convex) going from 3D to 1D rather than the specific fitting function. It must also be clarified that the intention of this paper is not to draw final conclusion about the power law behaviour of the non analytic term (correlation term) of the kinetic functional, but to provide a basis from which to start an investigation using methods with higher accuracy. Our study at a relatively affordable computational effort serves as an indicator of a possible path of interest in the development of kinetic-energy functionals.

Acknowledgments: This work was supported by the Deutsche Forschungsgemeinschaft (DFG) with the grant CRC 1114 (project C01). We are thankful to the high-performance computing service (Zedat-HPC) at Free University Berlin for providing the computational resources.

Author Contributions: Seshaditya A. performed the computations and all the authors developed the idea. Luigi Delle Site and Luca M. Ghiringhelli designed the research plan and wrote the paper.

Appendix A. Technical Details

All Monte Carlo (MC) computations are carried out according to the protocol laid out in Reference [13]. Using Metropolis algorithm studies on the spinless system in 1D, 2D and 3D are carried out. Calculations including the effective spin-interactions (with Pauli weighing function) in 1D are also performed. To rectify the sampling problems, the spin interactions are also softened using a scaling parameter K, with values 0.5, 0.75, and 1.2. For a 3D system, cubic lattice with almost uniform electron distribution is taken as the starting configuration. A randomly selected electron is given a trial move and the move is accepted with a probability, $\frac{f_{new}}{f_{old}}$. Periodic boundary conditions and minimum image convention are used. For different densities ($\rho = 0.1, 0.2, 0.3, 0.5, 0.7, 1.0, 1.2$), the optimal γ parameter minimising the $\Gamma[\rho(\mathbf{r}_1), f]$ are obtained. In all computations, different number of electrons ($N = 10, 20, 30, 25, 27, 35, 64$ and 100) for different densities and also same number of electrons for different densities are used (to check that the results to not depend on the number of electrons) [13]. In 3D for high densities, the evaluations are obtained using the biased MC acceptance rule due to the low γ value for accurate evaluations. In case of 2D and 1D, uniformly distributed electrons on a square and line are taken as the starting configurations respectively. Therefore the notion of density changes to $\frac{N}{L^2}$ and $\frac{N}{L}$ respectively for each case. Also in these cases, the acceptance probabilities are very low (close to 30 percent), so large number of MC samplings are used for obtaining the values.

The error bars for the kinetic-correlation energy values are computed by considering the errors in quadratic fitting of energies used for the estimation of γ minimum for a particular density followed by the difference in the kinetic-correlation energy values.

References

1. Hohenberg, P.; Kohn, W. Inhomogeneous electron gas. *Phys. Rev. B* **1964**, *136*, B864–B871.
2. Wang, Y.A.; Carter, E.A. Orbital-free kinetic-energy density functional theory. In *Theoretical Methods in Condensed Phase Chemistry*; Schwartz, S.D., Ed.; Kluwer: Dordrecht, The Netherlands, 2002; pp. 117–184.
3. Watson, S.; Carter, E.A. Linear-scaling parallel algorithms for the first principles treatment of metals. *Comp. Phys. Commun.* **2000**, *128*, 67–92.
4. Choly, N.; Kaxiras, E. Kinetic energy density functionals for non-periodic systems. *Solid State Commun.* **2002**, *121*, 281–286.
5. Chai, J.D.; Weeks, J.A. Modified statistical treatment of kinetic energy in the thomas-fermi model. *J. Phys. Chem. B* **2004**, *108*, 6870–6876.
6. Gavini, V.; Bhattacharya, K.; Ortiz, M. Quasi-continuum orbital-free density-functional theory: A route to multi-million atom non-periodic DFT calculation. *J. Mech. Phys. Solids* **2007**, *55*, 697–718.
7. Karasiev, V.V.; Trickey, S.B. Issues and challenges in orbital-free density functional calculations. *Comp. Phys. Commun.* **2012**, *183*, 2519–2527.
8. Wesolowski, T.A.; Wang, Y.A. Recent progress in orbital-free density functional theory. In *Recent Advances in Computational Chemistry*; World Scientific: Singapore, 2013.
9. Levy, M. Universal variational functionals of electron densities, first-order density matrices, and natural spin-orbitals and solution of the v-representability problem. *Proc. Natl. Acad. Sci. USA* **1979**, *76*, 6062–6065.
10. Lieb, E.H. Density functionals for Coulomb systems. *Int. J. Quantum Chem.* **1983**, *24*, 243–277.
11. Delle Site, L. Levy-Lieb constrained-search formulation as a minimization of the correlation functional. *J. Phys. A Math. Theor.* **2007**, *40*, 2787–2792.
12. Ghiringhelli, L.M.; Delle Site, L. Design of kinetic functionals for many-body electron systems: Combining analytical theory with Monte Carlo sampling of electronic configurations. *Phys. Rev. B* **2008**, *77*, 073104.
13. Ghiringhelli, L.M.; Hamilton, I.P.; Delle Site, L. Interacting electrons, spin statistics, and information theory. *J. Chem. Phys.* **2010**, *132*, 014106.
14. Delle Site, L. Kinetic functional of interacting electrons: A numerical procedure and its statistical interpretation. *J. Stat. Phys.* **2011**, *144*, 663–678.
15. Delle Site, L. Shannon entropy and many-electron correlations: Theoretical concepts, numerical results, and Collins conjecture. *Int. J. Quantum Chem.* **2015**, *115*, 1396–1404.
16. Garcia-Gonzalez, P. Dimensional crossover of the exchange-correlation density functional. *Phys. Rev. B* **2000**, *62*, 2321–2329.
17. Garcia-Gonzalez, P.; Alvarellos, J.E.; Chacon, E. Dimensional crossover of the kinetic-energy electronic density functional. *Phys. Rev. A* **2000**, *62*, 014501.
18. Sears, S.B.; Parr, R.G.; Dinur, U. On the quantum-mechanical kinetic energy as a measure of the information in a distribution. *Isr. J. Chem.* **1980**, *19*, 165–173.
19. Weizäcker, C.F. Zur theorie der kernmassen. *Z. Phys.* **1935**, *96*, 431–458.
20. Thomas, L.H. The calculation of atomic fields. *Proc. Camb. Philos. Soc.* **1927**, *23*, 542–548.
21. Fermi, E. Statistical method to determine some properties of atoms. *Rend. Lincei* **1927**, *6*, 602–607.
22. Pittalis, S.; Räsänen, E. Orbital-free energy functional for electrons in two dimensions. *Phys. Rev. B* **2009**, *80*, 165112.
23. Lee R.M.; Drummond, N.D. Ground-state properties of the one-dimensional electron liquid. *Phys. Rev. B* **2011**, *83*, 245114.
24. Drummond, N.D.; Needs, R.J. Phase diagram of the low-density two-dimensional homogeneous electron gas. *Phys. Rev. Lett.* **2009**, *102*, 126402.
25. Wagner, L.K.; Ceperley, D.M. Discovering correlated fermions using quantum Monte Carlo. *Rep. Prog. Phys.* **2016**, *79*, 1–9.

26. Drummond, N.D.; Needs, R.J. Quantum Monte Carlo study of the ground state of the two-dimensional Fermi fluid. *Phys. Rev. B* **2009**, *79*, 085414.

27. Haldane, F.D.M. 'Luttinger liquid theory' of one-dimensional quantum fluids. I. Properties of the Luttinger model and their extension to the general 1D interacting spinless Fermi gas. *J. Phys. C Solid State Phys.* **1981**, *14*, 2585–2609.

28. Astrakharchik, G.E.; Girardeau, M.D. Exact ground-state properties of a one-dimensional Coulomb gas. *Phys. Rev. B* **2011**, *83*, 153303.

29. Loos, P.-F.; Gill, P.M.W. Correlation energy of the one-dimensional Coulomb gas. *arXiv* **2012**, arXiv:1207.0908.

30. Jastrow, R. Many-body problem with strong forces. *Phys. Rev.* **1955**, *98*, 1479.

31. Drummond, N.D.; Towler, M.D.; Needs, R.J. Jastrow correlation factor for atoms, molecules, and solids. *Phys. Rev. B* **2004**, *70*, 235119.

32. Deshpande, V.V.; Vikram, V.; Bockrath, M.; Glazman, L.I.; Yacoby, A. Electron liquids and solids in one dimension. *Nature* **2010**, *464*, 209–216.

33. Kukkonen, C.A.; Overhauser, A.W. Electron-electron interaction in simple metals. *Phys. Rev. B* **1979**, *20*, 550–557.

34. Trickey, S.B.; Karasiev, V.V.; Vela, A. Positivity constraints and information-theoretical kinetic energy functional. *Phys. Rev. B* **2011**, *84*, 075146.

3

Artificial Immune Classifier Based on ELLipsoidal Regions (AICELL)[†]

Aris Lanaridis *, Giorgos Siolas and Andreas Stafylopatis

Intelligent Systems Laboratory, National Technical University of Athens, Athens 15780, Greece; giosiolas@gmail.com (G.S.); andreas@cslab.ntua.gr (A.S.)

* Correspondence: aristeides@gmail.com

† This paper is an extended of our paper published in Lanaridis, A.; Stafylopatis, A. An Artificial Immune Classifier Using Pseudo-Ellipsoid Rules. In Proceedings of the 26th International Symposium on Computer and Information Sciences, London, UK, 26–28 September 2011.

Abstract: Pattern classification is a central problem in machine learning, with a wide array of applications, and rule-based classifiers are one of the most prominent approaches. Among these classifiers, Incremental Rule Learning algorithms combine the advantages of classic Pittsburg and Michigan approaches, while, on the other hand, classifiers using fuzzy membership functions often result in systems with fewer rules and better generalization ability. To discover an optimal set of rules, learning classifier systems have always relied on bio-inspired models, mainly genetic algorithms. In this paper we propose a classification algorithm based on an efficient bio-inspired approach, Artificial Immune Networks. The proposed algorithm encodes the patterns as antigens, and evolves a set of antibodies, representing fuzzy classification rules of ellipsoidal surface, to cover the problem space. The innate immune mechanisms of affinity maturation and diversity preservation are modified and adapted to the classification context, resulting in a classifier that combines the advantages of both incremental rule learning and fuzzy classifier systems. The algorithm is compared to a number of state-of-the-art rule-based classifiers, as well as Support Vector Machines (SVM), producing very satisfying results, particularly in problems with large number of attributes and classes.

Keywords: artificial immune systems; artificial immune networks; pattern classification; learning classifier systems; evolutionary algorithms

---

1. Introduction

The immune system is a complex of cells, molecules and organs that aim at protecting the host organism from invading pathogens. The system's ability to recognize these pathogens is not innate, but can be acquired through a complex learning process, which adapts antibodies to recognizing specific types of antigens. However, the invading agents also evolve rapidly, and to combat them effectively the system must be able to generalize its recognition ability to similar, incomplete or corrupt forms of the antigen. In addition to this antigen-specific response, the system must regulate the diversity of its antibody population so that they are able, as a whole, to recognize a wide array of pathogens while, at the same time, not recognize each other, in order to be able to discriminate the pathogens from the organism's own healthy tissues. These abilities of learning, generalization, noise-tolerance and diversity regulation have made the immune system a suitable source of inspiration for a corresponding bio-inspired model, artificial immune networks.

The response of the immune system is primarily explained by two mechanisms. According to the Clonal Selection [1] principle, when an antigen is encountered antibodies are born to confront it. These antibodies have receptors that adapt their shape through a process similar to natural selection, except on a much faster time scale, in order to better match the corresponding antigen. This evolution is based of a repeated cycle of cloning, mutation and survival of the fittest antibodies, gradually resulting in a population of antibodies of increased ability to match the pathogens, a process known as affinity maturation. The best of these antibodies are stored as memory cells, to be recalled if the antigen is encountered again in the future. Additionally, according to the Immune Network Theory [2], the distinction between antibodies and antigens in not innate to the system. Instead the receptors of antibodies bind to any molecule of matching shape, forming a network of molecules that can recognize, as well as be recognized by, other molecules. To avoid mistaking its own antibodies for pathogens, which results in auto-immune disease, the immune system must ensure that antibodies not only match antigens, but do not match other antibodies. In combination, these two principles mean that the network must evolve in a manner that guarantees both the quality and the diversity of its population. These principles have been successfully applied to the development of engineering approaches, dealing with a variety of classification problems [3], multimodal function optimization [4,5], gene expression tree optimization [6], cascade airfoil optimization [7], breast cancer detection [8] and sensor drift mitigation [9].

We propose in this paper an algorithm applied to one of the central problems of machine learning, that of pattern classification. The proposed classifier encodes the patterns to be recognized as antigens, and evolves a set of antibodies encoding pattern recognition rules of ellipsoidal shape, which are efficient in covering oblique areas of the problem space, in contrast to most rule-based classifiers which are based on rectangular rules. We adapt the innate characteristics of the immune network diversity to ensure the cooperation between those rules, and employ fuzzy membership functions to avoid the exhaustive coverage of the space, which usually results in a large number of rules covering very few patterns, having negative impact on the generalization ability of the classifier. Finally, we modify the computational paradigm, so that the aim of the system is not the recognition, but the elimination of the antigens. This not only brings it closer to the biological model, but also enables us to adapt the fuzzy rules to the approach of Incremental Rule Learning, which combines some of the benefits of traditional Pittsburg and Michigan rule-based classifiers.

A preliminary version of the classifier has been presented in [10]. The current version constitutes a major extension of the former work, including several improvements with respect to both the technical content and the presentation. Among others, a new rule initialization method has been introduced, which, in synergy with the evaluation metric, leads the search to uncovered areas of the problem space, thus improving the performance and convergence of the algorithm. Additionally, the criteria of unfit antibody removal have been extended to include both recognition ability and space coverage. Also, the mutation probability has been adapted to the dimensionality of the problem. Finally, the algorithm has been extensively tested on a number of established benchmark problems, and compared to other state-of-the-art algorithms, using multiple statistical metrics.

The paper continues by giving an overview of learning classifier systems in Section 2. Section 3 provides a description of the modifications made to the immune paradigm and an outline of the proposed method. Individual aspects of the algorithm are discussed in the following sections. In particular, Section 4 describes the form of the classification rule encoded by the antibodies of the network, Section 5 discusses the mutation operator used to evolve it, and Section 6 proposes a fuzzy evaluation metric for selecting the best rules. A suitable rule initialization process is described in Sections 7 and 8 discusses the preservation of the network quality and diversity by removing unfit antibodies. Section 9 sums up the previous sections in a formal description of the algorithm, and the paper concludes with Section 10, which tests the proposed algorithm on a set of benchmark problems, compares it against state-of-the-art algorithms, and applies a number of significance tests to assess the results.

2. Overview of Learning Classifier Systems

Pattern classification aims at finding a function that maps a vector describing the features of a pattern to a category among a given set. The problem is approached in various ways, with some algorithms assigning the pattern to the class having the most similar patterns (a typical example being k-nearest neighbors algorithm), while others classify it based on some statistical attributes of the patterns in each class (the most well-known example being Naive Bayes Classifier). However, most algorithms approach the problem in a geometric manner, searching the vector space for hyper-surfaces that separate patterns of different classes. Typical examples of this approach are Support Vector Machines (SVM) and Neural Networks.

Another popular type of geometric classifiers are decision trees, which partition recursively each attribute's range of values into subranges, until a stopping criterion is met. In this manner, decision trees separate the problem space into subspaces, each described by a rule of the form **if** $x_i \in [l_i, u_i]$ **and** $x_j \in [l_j, u_j]$ **then** *class*. Although all geometric classifiers form a set of rules mapping a pattern to a subset of the problem space, rules of this particular form are easily interpretable, and for this reason, decision trees are often called rule-based classifiers.

However, finding the optimal set of such rules is an NP-complete problem [11], regardless of the optimality criterion used. As as result, most rule-based classifiers rely on greedy algorithms that partition the space iteratively, with the aim of maximizing some separation criterion, with information gain being the most common. The use of evolutionary algorithms was proposed by Holland [12] as an alternative, leading to learning classifier systems. To implement a such system, two important decisions have to be made, namely, how the chromosomes represent classification rules, and how the evolutionary algorithm is used to evolve them. Traditionally, there have been two main approaches (see [13] for details).

According to the Pittsburg approach [14], a chromosome encodes a set of rules forming a complete classifier. The genetic algorithm applies crossover and mutation to the best of these rules. Since each chromosome represents a complete classifier, evaluation is straight-forward. However, chromosomes tend to be long, making the search space too large. Morever, either the number of rules has to be decided in advance, or some variable-length mechanisms have to be employed, making optimization even harder. According to the alternative Michigan approach [15], each chromosome represents an invididual rule, resulting in much smaller search space, and easier optimization. However, evalution of the rules becomes much more complicated, since they have to be evaluted both individually, as well as in terms of their ability to co-operate, to form a complete classifier.

As a compromise between the two approaches, Incremental Rule Learning [16] algorithms were proposed. According to this approach, each chromosome encodes a single rule, as in Michigan classifiers. However, instead of evolving the complete set of chromosomes simultaneously, the algorithm begins with an empty set and adds a new rule at each iteration. Each rule evolves individually, while patterns that are covered by existing rules are removed from the dataset, to avoid overlap and ensure that newly-created rules search uncovered areas of the problem space. To a large extent, this approach combines the smaller search space of Michigan and cooperation of Pittsburg classifiers.

Regardless of which of the above approaches is followed, there is a number of additional implementation choices which have an important effect on the resulting algorithm.

- If the classifier rules are ordered, they form an *if-elseif-else* chain, and the pattern can be assigned to the first rule whose condition is satisfied. However, with unordered rules of *if-else* form, further actions are needed to ensure their co-operation, minimize the overlap, and assign the pattern to a class.

- The most common form of condition combines clauses of the form $x_i \in [l_i, u_i]$ for each dimension of the problem. These rules form a hyper-rectangle, whose faces are parallel to the axes. However, by using a linear combination of the pattern attributes, oblique areas of the problem space can be covered. These linear rules can be combined to form surfaces of arbitrary shape. Alternatively, inherently non-linear rules can be used, such as spheres, quadratic or ellipsoidal surfaces.

- If the patterns are presented to the classifier one at a time, the fitness of the rules that recognize the pattern increases, while for the others it decreases. If no rule matches the pattern, a new one is created. When the patterns are presented in batch, the algorithm can focus of the total coverage of the dataset by the existing set of rules.

- The rules must be evaluated both individually and as a whole. The individual evaluation can be based on either the rule's ability to accumulate high reward values (strength-based) or its ability to predict its reward, regardless of its value (accuracy-based). To evaluate the rule-set as a whole, various criteria can be used, regarding the total coverage of patterns, minization of overlap, fitness sharing, etc.

- Most of the rule-based classifiers rely on crisp memberhip functions. To cover all the patterns of the dataset, they often have to create rules covering very few patterns, with low generalization ability. The employment of fuzzy membership functions resolves this problem to some extent, but is not consistent with most existing evaluation criteria.

3. Outline of the Immune Network Classifier

Based on the biological principles of affinity maturation and immune network theory mentioned in Section 1, a multitude of computational models have been developed (we refer the reader to [17–19] for an extended overview). While each model differentiates from the others in specific aspects, all of them have in common the fact that they address the problem by maintaining a population of antibodies. These antibodies construct a network in the sense that they perform a task in collaboration (while each single member of the network is incapable of producing results), and that the evolution of each antibody depends on specific qualities of other antibodies present in the network. The evolution of each individual antibody is based on criteria concerning its quality, while the evolution of the network as a whole is based on the preservation of diversity, by removing antibodies that are too similar and replacing them by new ones.

Throughout the evolution of the network, antibodies are born, evolve and die. In particular, new antibodies are born when the size of the population is insufficient to confront the antigens. On the contrary, when the population size increases beyond the desired size, the antibodies that do not considerably contribute to the diversity of the network die, leaving space for the fittest and most diverse antibodies to evolve. Antibodies that both exhibit sufficient quality and contribute to the diversity remain in the network. The evolution of these antibodies is based on the clonal selection principle. That is, for each antibody a number of clones (exact copies of the antibody) are created, and the clones go through a mutation process, producing variants of the original antibody. Among these variants, the best ones survive and are inserted to the network.

However, contrary to the computational models, the aim of the biological immune system is not the recognition, but the elimination of the antigens. The recognition ability acquired is a by-product of this process. The suggested algorithm follows this approach which, not only brings it closer to the biological model, but also yields practical benefits, as shown in the following sections. To incorporate that into the algorithm, we introduce a *health* factor for each antigen, described by a variable $h \in [0, h_{max}]$. The use of the term *health* does not imply that the antigen is beneficial to the organism, but quantifies the degree to which it can withstand the damage inflicted by the antibodies before it is dead. This factor is also an indicator of the strengh of the antigen, and consequently the importance assigned to it by the network.

Each of the antibodies composing the network is dedicated to a particular class of antigens. The antibody weakens the antigens of that class to a degree proportional to its affinity to them, having no effect on antigens of other classes. Consequently, the throughout the individual evolution of a rule, the antibody aims at maximizing its affinity to antigens of the same class. The overall evolution of the network is based on the creation and addition of such rules. If the addition of new antibodies results in large degree of similarity or some antibodies presenting lower-than-average recognition ability, these antibodies die and are removed from the network. At each point, the overall effect of the network to an antigen is proportionate to its total affinity to all the antibodies of the same category in the network. The process continues with the addition of new rules, until all antigens are dead or sufficiently weakened.

For the purpose of pattern classification, each antigen encodes a pattern to be recognized, along with its class, and antibodies encode recognition rules. The following chapters explain in detail the form of these rules, the mutation and evaluation process, and the preservation of network quality and diversity by removing unfit antibodies. The combination of these elements results in the proposed system being a strength-based, fuzzy incremental rule learning classifier.

4. Rule Encoding

In constrast to most rule-based classifiers, which encode rules having an **if** $x_i \in [l_i, u_i]$ **and** $x_j \in [l_j, u_j]$ **then** *class* form, producing hyper-rectangles in the problem space, the proposed method employs rules of ellipsoidal form. Such rules have been used in some cases in learning rule systems [20–23]. However, ellipsoidal surfaces are computationally complex, and all of the above algorithms rely on some clustering method to decide the number and center of the ellipsoids in advance, while the evolutionary algorithm is used for micro-tuning of the parameters.

On the contrary, the proposed method is a complete algorithm of producing a set of fuzzy rules based on ellipsoidal surfaces. The system evolves such rules dynamically, defining their number so that they cover all of the dataset, while at the same time, not being too similar or having too much deviation in terms of their quality. To simplify the computations, an alternative form of the ellipsoid is used, which, although not completely equivalent, retains its basic characteristics.

4.1. Ellipsoid Definition

An ellipse is the locus of the points on a plane for which the sum of distances to two constant points focal points f_1, f_2 is constant, that is, the set of all x for which

$$\left\{ x \in \mathbb{R}^2 : \|x - f_1\| + \|x - f_2\| = r \right\} \tag{1}$$

The above locus can also be generated by the linear transform of a circle. As a result, an ellipse can be equivalently defined as

$$\left\{ Ax + b : x \in C(0) \right\} \tag{2}$$

where A is a matrix representing a linear transform (scaling and rotation), b is the translation from the origin of the axes, and $C(0)$ is the unit circle centered at the origin, producing the equivalent definition

$$\left\{ z : (z - b)^T C(z - b) = 1, z \in \mathbb{R}^2 \right\} \tag{3}$$

where $C = (AA^T)^{-1}$ is a symmetric, positive-definite matrix.

If Equation (3) is used to create a set of points in a 3-dimensional space, the resulting locus has the property that its intersection with every plane that passes through point b forms an ellipse. In this sense, it can be regarded as a 3-dimensional equivalent of the ellipse, which is called ellipsoid. Althrough this definition concerns only the 3-dimensional space, similar sets of points in higher dimensions are often also called ellipsoids.

The set of points produced using Equation (1) in 3 dimensions does not have this property, which characterises an ellipsoid in the strict sense. Still, it produces a quadratic surface whose points have the same total distance to two other constant points in that space. In this sense it forms a 3-dimensional generalization of the ellipse, and is used in the current algorithm as the basis for recognition rules. This form constitutes a broad-sense formulation of the ellipsoid, which retains the essential geometric characteristics of the ellipse, while also being significantly simpler computationally than the form described by Equation (3).

4.2. Fuzzy Pseudo-Ellipsoidal Rules

To produce the classification rule, we first re-write Equation (1) as

$$d(x) = \frac{\|x - f_1\| + \|x - f_2\|}{r} \tag{4}$$

which re-defines the ellipsoid as the set of points x for which $d(x) = 1$, regardless of the size of the ellipsoid.

However, all of the above equations describe an $(n-1)$-dimensional closed surface in the n-dimensional vector space. Given that this surface is intended to be used as a classification rule, we are concerned not only with the points on the surface, but also with the ones inside the enclosed volume. This set of points consists of the points for which $d(x) \leq 1$. Equivalently, we could define the volume enclosed by the ellipsoid, as a membership function given by

$$\mu(x) = \begin{cases} 1, & d(x) \in [0,1] \\ 0, & d(x) > 1 \end{cases} \tag{5}$$

where $d(x)$ is the normalized distance of a point x from the two focal points, as defined by Equation (4).

This crisp membership function partitions the space into points inside or outside the space enclosed by the rule. To create a fuzzy rule, this membership function must be transformed to a fuzzy one, so that every point belongs to the rule to some degree. For this purpose, we use the function

$$\mu(x) = \exp\left(-d(x)^f\right) \tag{6}$$

where $f \in [0, +\infty]$ is a parameter defining the steepness of the membership function. It can be seen that for $f \to +\infty$ the above equation reduces to (5). In practice, a typical range for the values of f is $f \in [2,8]$, since for lower values the function becomes almost uniform, while for larger ones it closely resembles the crisp membership function.

5. Mutation Operator

Given the critical role of mutation on the evolution of the network, this section provides a detailed description. We first describe the operator used, specifically the non-uniform mutation operator for real-valued features, defined in [24]. After that, we adapt the mutation range of each feature to the particular characteristics of the proposed rule form, and the mutation probability to achieve its most efficient performance.

5.1. Non-Uniform Mutation Operator

Given a vector $x = \{x_1, \ldots, x_n\}$ to be mutated, the non-uniform mutation operator acts on each of its attributes with probability p_m. Assuming an attribute $x_i \in [l_i, u_i]$ selected for mutation, the operator produces a new value

$$x_i' = \begin{cases} x_i + \Delta(t, u_i - x_i) & , u_1 \leq 0.5 \\ x_i - \Delta(t, x_i - l_i) & , u_1 > 0.5 \end{cases} \tag{7}$$

where

$$\Delta(t, y) = y(1 - u_2^{r(t)}) \tag{8}$$

In the above equations, u_1 and u_2 are random values drawn from the standard normal distribution $u_1, u_2 \sim \mathcal{N}(0,1)$. The quantity $r(t)$ defines the range of the mutation, which is a function of the current generation t. For the operator to function properly, the value $r(t)$ must be confined in $[0,1]$ and its value must decrease as t increases. Given a such $r(t)$, the function $\Delta(t, y)$ returns a value in $[0, y]$ such that the probability that $\Delta(t, y) \to 0$ increases as t increases. As a result, as the training progresses, the produced value x_i' will be closer to the initial value x_i. This property allows the operator to search the problem space globally at first and more locally in later stages of the training.

The originally proposed form of $r(t)$, which is also used here, is

$$r(t) = \left(1 - \frac{t}{T}\right)^b \tag{9}$$

where t is the current generation of the training, T is the total number of generations, and b a parameter defining the decay of $r(t)$ with t. This form has been widely employed in the literature, with typical values of b lying in $b \in [2, 20]$.

5.2. Mutation Range

For the non-uniform mutation to function properly, each attribute x must be confined in a range $[x_{min}, x_{max}]$. To simplify the procedure, all the patterns of the dataset are normalized so that all the values of their attributes lie in $[-1, 1]$. After the normalization, all the attributes of the vectors describing the focal points of the ellipse also lie in $[-1, 1]$, and can take any value in that range.

On the contrary, the distance r of the surface of the ellipsoid from the focal points can not take any value. Its minimum value must be at least equal to the distance between the focal points, that is

$$r_{min} = \|f_1 - f_2\| \tag{10}$$

Regarding its maximum value, there is no constraint. However, is should be large enough so that it can cover the whole problem space. As such value, we choose the largest possible distance in that space, that is

$$r_{max} = \sqrt{\|[1]^n - [-1]^n\|} = 2 \cdot \sqrt{n} \tag{11}$$

where n the number of dimensions.

However, the interval $[r_{min}, r_{max}]$ cannot be use directly as mutation range for the attribute r, since the value of r_{min} changes every time the focal points f_1, f_2 are mutated. For this reason we define a factor $\alpha \in [0, 1]$, which is used for linear mapping from $[0, 1]$ to the current value of $[r_{min}, r_{max}]$. The mutation operator is applied to this quantity, and after the mutation of f_1, f_2 and the evaluation of the resulting r_{min}, the value of r is calculated by

$$r = r_{min} + \alpha \cdot (r_{max} - r_{min}) \tag{12}$$

Finally, the shape of the membership function relies on f. For $f \to 0$ the function becomes almost uniform, while for $f \to +\infty$ the function resembles the crisp membership. To avoid these extremes, it is confined in $f \in [f_{min}, f_{max}]$, where the values f_{min}, f_{max} are selected experimentally (with a typical value range being $f \in [2, 8]$).

5.3. Mutation Probability

A central characteristic of genetic algorithms is that they rely mostly on crossover to evolve the population of candidate solutions [12,25]. Very few members of the population are selected for mutation and, when this happens, it is usually to introduce diversity in the population. For this reason, the algorithms employing mutation usually mutate all the attributes of the solutions. The resulting solution is usually far from optimal, but that is not a concern, because it will be improved with the crossover operator. On the contrary however, immune systems rely solely on mutation to evolve the population, and consequently a different strategy must be used.

The mutation of an attribute of a candidate solution is a random procedure and, as such, it can be beneficial or detrimental to the quality of the individual. When the number of attributes selected for mutation is small, the probability that all, or most or the mutations are beneficial is significant.

However, as the number of selected attributes increases, this probability decreases dramatically, and reduces to random search for a large number of mutated attributes.

For this reason, we select a number n_m of attributes to be mutated at each generation, and, if n is the total number of attributes composing each solution, the mutation probability of each attribute is set to

$$p_m = \frac{n_m}{n} \tag{13}$$

It is noted that this probability concerns only the focal points f_1, f_2 of the pseudo-ellipsoid. The quantities α and f are scalar quantities, and are mutated in every generation of the training.

6. Evaluation Metrics

In this section we give a brief description of some commonly used rule evaluation metrics (we refer the reader to [26–28] for more details), and provide a modified evaluation metric for the proposed fuzzy classifier.

6.1. Common Evaluation Metrics

With the exception of Pittsburg classifiers, all learning systems rely on a criterion that evaluates rules individually. Most criteria are based on the common precision and accuracy metrics. Assuming that P, N is the total number of positive and negative patterns in the dataset, and p, n the number of positive and negative patterns covered by a rule, accuracy is defined as

$$h_{acc} = \frac{p + (N - n)}{P + N} \tag{14}$$

This equation can be reduced to $h_{acc} = c_1 \cdot (p - n) + c_2$, where c_1, c_2 are two constants. Consequently, the main characteristic of this rule is that it assigns equal importance to covering a positive and not covering a negative pattern. As a result, rules covering many patterns can receive a high accuracy score, even if they include a large number of negative patterns, reducing the percentage of correct classifications.

Precision is defined as

$$h_{pr} = \frac{p}{p + n} \tag{15}$$

This quantity evaluates the percentage of correct classifications, but completely ignores the size of the rule, often producing too many rules covering a small number of patterns. Such rules, despite covering only positive patterns, have little or no generalization ability.

As a compromise between the two criteria, the m-estimate has been proposed

$$h_m = \frac{p + m \cdot \frac{P}{P+N}}{p + n + m} \tag{16}$$

This quantity is a modification of precision, requiring that each rules covers at least m patterns. The value of m decides the trade-off between classification percentage and size of the rules, as it is obvious that for $m \to 0$ it converges to precision, while it can be shown that for $m \to +\infty$ it converges to accuracy.

6.2. Fuzzy m-Estimate

The evaluation metric defined by Equation (16) relies on the number p, n of patterns covered by a rule. However, the proposed method uses fuzzy rules, and so every pattern in the dataset is covered by every rule to some degree. As this degree is quantified by the value of the membership function, we can regard the fuzzy equivalent of p, n as

$$p = \sum_{i \in P} \mu_i, \qquad n = \sum_{i \in N} \mu_i \qquad (17)$$

where μ_i is the membership of the i-th antigen to the rule.

Moreover, the algorithm assigns to each pattern importance proportional to the strengh of the antigen that encodes it. Given that this value is given by h_i for the i-th pattern, the above quantities have to be further modified by weighting the patterns by that quantity, resulting in

$$p = \sum_{i \in P} h_i \cdot \mu_i, \qquad n = \sum_{i \in N} h_i \cdot \mu_i \qquad (18)$$

This modification ensures that the network assigns maximum importance to stronger antigens ($h \rightarrow h_{max}$), while weak or dead ($h \rightarrow 0$) antigens have little or no effect to the evolution of the rule. From an algorithmic point of view, this weight factor leads the search of the space to areas that have not yet been covered sufficiently by existing rules, since in already covered areas $h_i \rightarrow 0$ and the value of the evaluation metric will be small, while in uncovered areas $h_i \rightarrow h_{max}$ and the metric receives larger values.

By replacing these terms in the original equation, the evaluation metric becomes

$$e = \frac{\sum_{i \in P} h_i \cdot \mu_i + M \frac{|P|}{|P \cup N|}}{\sum_{i \in P \cup N} h_i \cdot \mu_i + M} \qquad (19)$$

This modified criterion combines the original m-estimate with the fuzzy membership function, and makes the proposed method a fuzzy generalization of the Incremental Rule Learning strategy. In particular, as the steepness of the membership function increases to $f \rightarrow +\infty$, the value of the membership function converges to $\mu_i \rightarrow 1$, and the health of antigens covered by the rule to $h_j \rightarrow 0$. Since the contribution of these patterns to Equation (19) reduces to 0, these patterns can be regarded as effectively removed from the dataset, and the behavior of the algorithm converges to that of a standard Incremental Rule Learning system.

7. Rule Initialization

In traditional learning classifier systems, the rules are randomly initialized [12,14,15], and it is left to the evolution process to lead them to the appropriate areas of the problem space. The same approach can be followed in the proposed system. However, given that the purpose of the training is to cover the problem space to the largest possible extent, it is preferable that the new rules are created in areas that have not been already covered. In our case, these areas are the ones where health h of the antigens has high values.

To detect such areas, each time a new rule is to be created, all the patterns of the dataset are examined as candidate centers of the rule. For each pattern, its nearest neighbors are detected, and the sum of their values is calculated. We note that in this calculation, only the patterns belonging to the same class as the candidate center are included. The value of the sum is given by

$$H_i = \sum_{i \in knn(P)} h_i \qquad (20)$$

The area where H_i has the maximum value is the one that has been covered to the least degree up to that point, and the most suitable for a new rule. However, it is not guaranteed that this rule will have a sufficient fitness value. In this case, the produced rule will be removed, and the system will create a new one. Since the removed rule has no effect on the antigens, if the selection was deterministic, the same rule would be created again, resulting in an endless loop.

To avoid this, the pattern that will be the center of the new rule is not chosen deterministically according to the value H_i, but instead, by using tournament selection. Each pattern can be selected with probability

$$p_i = c \cdot H_i \tag{21}$$

where c is such that

$$\sum_i c \cdot H_i = \sum_i p_i = 1 \Rightarrow c = \frac{1}{\sum_i H_i} \tag{22}$$

Consequently, the selection probability of the i-th pattern is

$$p_i = \frac{H_i}{\sum_i H_i} \tag{23}$$

The above procedure selects the center of a new rule to be created. We note that, since the network is based on ellipsoid rules, each rule has two focal points. Consequently, during the initialization, the two points coincide, since they are given the same initial value. However, this has no effect on the evolution of the rule, since they will be differentiated when the training begins, due to the mutation operator.

The suggested initialization method has a significant impact on the performance of the algorithm. Figure 1 gives an illustrative example, comparing the decay of the average antigen health $\bar{h}$ during the incremental addition of 50 rules, for 3 executions of the algorithm, for both initialization methods. The results shown regard the *libra* dataset (which will be presented in the experimental section), however the effect was similar for all the problems examined.

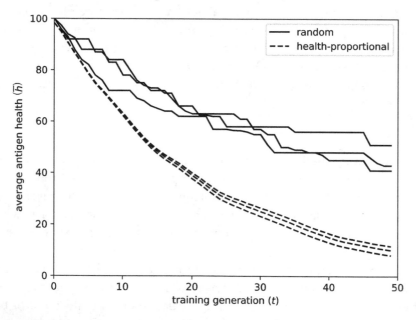

Figure 1. Comparison between the random and health-proportional initialization. The figure displays the decrease of average antigen health $\bar{h}$ with the number of training generations t. As evident from the figure, the proposed method results in faster convergence and smaller deviation between runs.

As shown by the figure, the proposed initialization method has the following advantages in comparison to random initialization:

- The convergence is much faster. Using random initialization, the center of the new rule might be situated in an area that is already covered by other rules, and the mutation operation might fail to lead it to a suitable area. In this case, the rule will be rejected by the network, providing no improvement for that iteration. On the contrary, with the proposed method, it is guaranteed that the new rule will be initialized in an appropriate area.

- To deviation between different runs significantly reduces. As a result, the algorithm achieves more robust behavior.
- The coverage of the dataset, and consequently the final performance of the system, improves. As time progresses and the uncovered areas decrease, it becomes very difficult for the algorithm to detect them, especially in spaces with large number of dimensions. On the contrary, with the proposed initialization, the detection of uncovered areas is almost guaranteed.

8. Antibody Death

An essential property of the immune network is that it regulates its antibody population, by creating new antibodies and removing existing ones. The birth of new antibodies is aimed at fighting antigens than have not been recognized by the existing ones, while the death of existing antibodies aims at maintaining its population fitness and diversity. In particular, antibodies die when they have significantly inferior fitness or large similarity to other antibodies. At this section we define the two corresponding criteria.

8.1. Death Due to Low Fitness

As the network evolves and new antibodies are added, the average fitness of the antibodies that comprise it changes. In most cases, after the training has progressed for a long time and the largest portion of the problem space has been covered by existing rules, it is likely that the new rules will have inferior fitness to the existing ones. In other cases, rules of higher fitness may appear in later stages of the training, increasing the average fitness of the network and rendering some of the existing rules inadequate. In either case, it is desirable that the rules with significantly smaller fitness are removed from the network, so as not to undermine its overall performance. To achieve this, each time a new rule is added, all rules in the network are re-evaluated, and those will significantly smaller fitness are removed.

The evaluation of the fitness of an antibody is indicated by the value of the evaluation metric described in Section 6. To remove the inferior rules, we must look into the distribution of this value among the network antibodies and remove the significantly inferior ones, with some outlier detection criterion. However, the problem is that the fitness values lie in most cases in a small subset of the $[0, 1]$ interval. In such a small interval the value differences are not large enough to consider some points as outliers.

As explained, the evaluation metric evaluates at the same time two features of the rule, namely the number of patterns it covers and the percentage of these belonging to the correct class. Combining these two values in one is suitable choice during the training, because, for a rule to be selected, it must score satisfying values in both these features. On the contrary however, to reject a rule, it suffices that it is inferior in only one of them. Consequently, at this stage we examine each component of the fitness separately for each rule. The advantage of this approach is that these two values have large range of values, and so it is much easier to detect outliers. An illustrative example is given in Figure 2.

The coverage of a rule is given by

$$c = \sum_{i \in P \cup N} \mu_i \tag{24}$$

This quantity presents large deviations between rules, being close to zero for some rules and reaching hundrends of patterns for others, making the outlier detection easier. In a similar manner, the precision of a rule can be described as

$$p = \frac{\sum_{i \in P} \mu_i}{\sum_{i \in P \cup N} \mu_i} \tag{25}$$

In contrast to the coverage, this value is confined in $[0, 1]$. However, for most rules $p \to 1$, so the inferior ones are easy to detect.

To rule out the outliers, we use the common Tukey's range test [29], based on the interquantile distance. In particular, assuming that the values of the distribution lie in the range $[\alpha, \beta]$, we split it in 4 quantiles, $[\alpha, Q_1, Q_2, Q_3, \beta]$, such that, Q_2 is the median value of $[\alpha, \beta]$ and Q_1, Q_3, are the medians of $[\alpha, Q_2], [Q_2, \beta]$ respectively.

The outliers are assumed to be the values for which

$$x \notin [Q_1 - k \cdot IQ, Q_3 + k \cdot IQ] \tag{26}$$

where $IQ = Q_3 - Q_1$ is the interquantile distance (range containing 50% of the values of the distribution), and k is a parameter with a non-negative value, with common values in the interval $[1.5, 2.5]$.

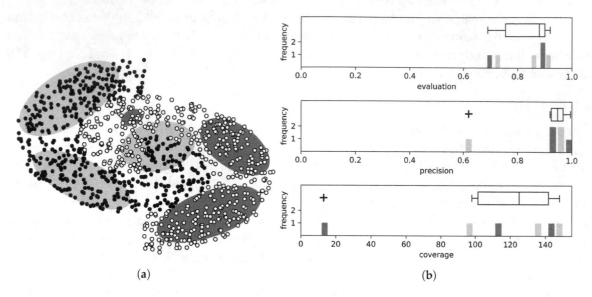

(a) (b)

Figure 2. Removing rules of lower quality. The two rules in the center of (**a**) are inferior to the rest, one of them because it covers many patterns of the wrong class and the other because of its small coverage. Although the value of their evaluation metric, shown in (**b**), is indeed lower, they cannot be easily detected based on that value. However, by breaking the metric down to its coverage and precision components, the differences become much clearer, and the two rules can be rejected as outliers.

8.2. Death Due to High Similarity

In a similar manner, the network retains its diversity by removing rules that are too similar to each other. To a large extend this has been assisted by the incorporation of the health factor h in the evaluation metric, as well as the initialization method described in Section 7. Using these two mechanisms, the network assists the coverage of new areas of the problems space, by initializing rules in uncovered areas, and by giving small rewards to mutated clones moving towards the covered ones.

However, given that the evolution is based on random operators, it is still possible that some rule results in some covered area. This becomes more likely as the training progresses, and the problem space is left with large areas with small values, and small areas with large values, which can yield comparable fitness values. To avoid this phenomenon, during the addition of a rule to the network, it is compared to all existing rules. If the new rule presents high similarity to one of the existing rules, only one of them remains in the network, based on the fitness value.

To apply the above, we must define a similarity metric between two rules. The patterns covered by a rule are reflected by the vector containing the value of its membership function for all patterns in the dataset. If for the i-th rule the membership of the k-th pattern is μ_{ik}, then the vector containing all the values of all the membership of all patterns to the rule is

$$\mu_i = [\mu_{i1}, \ldots, \mu_{in}] \tag{27}$$

Two rules can be regarded as similar if they cover the same patterns, that is, if the vectors of their membership values are similar. We use as similarity metric the inner product of the two vectors, normalized in $[0, 1]$, giving a similarity of

$$s_{ij} = \frac{\mu_i \cdot \mu_j}{\|\mu_i\| \cdot \|\mu_j\|} \tag{28}$$

between rules i and j.

After the training of the i-th rule has been completed, and before it is added to the network, its similarity to all the rules in the network is calculated

$$S = \left\{ s_{ij} | j \in [1, |B|] \right\} \tag{29}$$

and the rule with the maximum similarity is selected

$$j = \arg\max_{j \in [1, |B|]} s_{ij} \tag{30}$$

If the similarity s_{ij} surpasses a threshold S_{max} (which is a parameter of the training) then, only the rule with the higher fitness value remains in the network, that is

$$B = \begin{cases} B \cup \{b_i\} \setminus \{b_j\} & e_i > e_j \\ B & e_i \leq e_j \end{cases} \tag{31}$$

We note that it is sufficient to compare the new rule with the one given by Equation (30). The similarity cannot surpass the threshold for two or more rules, since two such rules would be similar to each other and one of them would have been rejected in a previous stage of the training.

9. Formal Description

Having described in detail the elements that make up the proposed algorithm, we provide in this section a formal description. Let $A = \{a_1, \ldots, a_m\}$ be the set of antigens, with each antigen representing a pattern which is to be classified. The attributes of the antigens are normalized to the interval $[-1, 1]^n$, where n is the number of attributes of each antigen. let $CA = \{ca_1, \ldots, ca_m\}$ be the classes of the corresponding antigens. Regarding the initial health of the antigens, it is set to $h_{max} = 1$ for all antigens. In principle, this value can differ among antigens, since it represents the relative importance the network assigns to each pattern. However, for a classification system with no a priori knowledge of the problem, all patterns are supposed to be of equal importance.

The set of antibodies is initialized to $B = \emptyset$. For the evolution of the network, the following steps are repeated while $\min_{i \in A} h_i \geq h_{min}$.

1. A new antibody is created. Its focal points are set to $f_1 = f_2 = a_j$, where a_j is an antigen selected by the rule initialization procedure described in Section 7. The steepness f of the membership function and radius α receive random values from a uniform distribution in $[f_{min}, f_{max}]$ and $[0, 1]$ respectively. The class of the antigen cb_i receives a random value from the set CA.

2. For a number of T generations, where t is the current generation, the following steps are repeated

   (a) N_C clones (exact copies) of the antibody are created.
   (b) The mutation range is set to $r = \frac{t}{T}$.
   (c) Each attribute of f_1, f_2 is mutated with probability p_m.
   (d) f and α are mutated with probability $p = 1$.

3. Among the mutated clones, the one that maximizes the fuzzy m-estimate, given by Equation (16), is selected and added to the network, producing the candidate set of antibodies B^*.

4. For each antibody, the coverage, precision and maximum pairwise similarity is calculated, as defined by Equations (24), (25) and (29) respectively. Outliers, in terms of any of these values, are removed as described in Section 8, producing the current set of antibodies B.

5. The health of each antigen is reduced by a quantity equal to its membership to each antibody of the same class, until its health drops to zero, giving

$$h_j = \max\left(0, 1 - \sum_{i=1}^{\|B\|} \mu_{ij} \cdot I(i,j)\right) \tag{32}$$

where

$$I(i,j) = \begin{cases} 1, & cb_i = ca_i \\ 0, & cb_i \neq ca_i \end{cases} \tag{33}$$

The loop is repeated until $\min h_i < h_{min}$. At this stage, each pattern is assigned to the class of the rule to which it exhibits the largest membership value. Specifically, the pattern encoded by an antigen a_j will be assigned to the class cb_k of the k-th antibody, where the value of k is given by

$$k = \underset{i \in [1, \|B\|]}{\arg\max} \mu_{ij} \tag{34}$$

10. Experiments

In this section, we present an experimental evaluation of the proposed method by testing it on a number of benchmarks datasets from two well-known sources, LIBSVM [30] and UCI Repository [31]. The datasets are presented in Table 1 where, for each problem, the number of attributes, classes and instances are listed, after removing patterns with missing values. In problems where a separate test set is provided, it is used for the evaluation, while for the rest of the problems we used 5-fold cross-validation.

Table 1. Datasets used for the evaluation of the algorithms. The datasets are ordered in increasing number of attributes, and for each one the number of classes and instances are listed. On problems where a test set is not provided, 5-fold cross-validation was used.

Dataset	Attributes	Classes	Training	Test
iris	4	3	150	
pima	8	2	768	
wisconsin	9	2	683	
wine	13	3	178	
vehicle	18	4	846	
steelplates	27	7	1941	
ionosphere	34	2	351	
satellite	36	6	2000	4435
optdigits	64	10	3823	1797
libra	90	15	360	
musk	166	2	476	
dna	180	3	1400	1186
semeion	256	10	1593	
usps	256	10	7291	2007
protein	357	3	17,766	6621
madelon	500	2	2000	600
isolet	617	26	6238	1559
mfeat	649	10	2000	

The performance of the proposed method is compared against a number of state-of-the-art rule-based classifiers. We have selected one representative algorithm from each major type of learning classifier systems, in particular RIPPER [32] (Incremental Rule Learning), GASSIST [33] (Pittsburg-style classifier), SLAVE [34] (fuzzy rules) and UCS [35] (Michigan-style classifier). These algorithms have been shown to produce the best results in a wide range of comparisons (we refer to reader to [36] for an extended survey).

To test the statistical significance of the results, we employ two groups of tests: The Friedman [37] significance test, as well as its two variations, Aligned ranks [38] and Quade test [39], assume that all the compared classifiers have equal performance, and employ *post-hoc* tests when the null hypothesis is rejected. On the other hand, the two versions of the Wilcoxon test [40], namely the ranked-sum test and the signed ranks test, provide pairwise comparisons of the algorithms. These tests have been shown [41–43] to be more appropriate for comparing classifiers that the widely-used Student t-test and sign-test.

Regarding the training, we used a Matlab implementation of the proposed method. For the training of the classifier, $N_C = 100$ clones where created for each antibody, while the number of generations was set to $T = 20$. The membership function steepness was confined to $f \in [2,8]$, the mutation range decay was set to $b = 5$ and the number of features mutated to $n_m = 10$, resulting in a mutation probability of $p_m = \frac{10}{n}$, where n is the number of features of each particular problem. Based on this value of n, we set of the m-estimate parameter and number of neighbors for rule initialization to $\sqrt{n}$. The outlier threshold parameter was set to $k = 1.5$, and the maximum allowed similarity to $s_{max} = 0.9$. Finally, the termination criterion was set to $h_{min} = \frac{1}{e}$.

To evaluate RIPPER, GASSIST, UCS and SLAVE we used the well-known Keel framework [44,45], which provides Java implementations of a large number of rule based classifiers. The classifiers were trained using the default parameters set by the framework, which co-incide with the ones proposed by the authors of each algorithm, and the most widely used in the literature.

Finally, in addition to the above, we compare the algorithm to Support Vector Machines. We used the well-known library *svmlight* [46], and evaluated SVM by training a binary classifier for each of the $\binom{n}{2}$ class pairs and combining the results by voting, an approach which has been show to produce the best results. We used radial basis functions as kernels, while for the values of C and γ we tried all powers of two in the ranges $C \in [2^{-5}, 2^{15}]$ and $\gamma \in [2^{-15}, 2^3]$, resulting in $21 \times 19 = 399$ experiments, one for each (C, γ) value pair. We refer the reader to [47,48] for more details.

The remaining of the section provides details of the experimental evaluation. We note that for the most of the text, the comments, comparisons and significance tests concern only the rule-based classifiers. The comparison with SVM is given in a separate subsection.

10.1. Overall Performance

To test the algorithms, we calculated the percentage of correct classifications of each algorithm on each problem. The results are listed in Table 2. As evident by the table, AICELL has the best performance in the majority of the problems. In particular, it surpasses GASSIST and RIPPER in 17 out of 18 problems, SLAVE and UCS in 14 out of 18, while it has the best perfomance among all algorithms in 13 out of 18 problems. Moreover, in the problems where is has the best performance, its difference to the second best algorithm is quite noticeable (with the difference having 6.53 mean and 6.16 median value), while on the rest its difference to the best algorithm is significantly smaller (2.82 mean and 1.49 median difference).

Table 2. Precision of the algorithms on the test dataset.

Dataset	RIPPER	GASSIST	UCS	SLAVE	AICELL	SVM
iris	94.67	94.00	91.33	96.67	96.67	97.99
pima	69.78	73.17	74.22	75.12	73.63	76.13
wisconsin	95.73	96.04	96.48	96.03	96.63	96.68
wine	90.49	91.03	92.14	91.59	96.09	96.75
vehicle	67.73	64.77	71.27	63.35	70.36	80.08
steelplates	69.14	61.66	72.43	68.76	68.84	74.79
ionosphere	89.18	92.04	88.61	91.46	92.66	93.37
satellite	84.44	80.11	86.36	80.88	89.72	88.47
optdigits	86.87	53.31	54.98	83.62	97.38	95.26
libra	54.17	26.39	60.28	64.72	75.83	75.27
musk	70.16	79.83	82.56	82.77	74.73	76.67
dna	88.53	87.61	53.79	89.63	89.55	94.26
semeion	73.63	40.87	44.00	75.85	93.38	91.71
usps	84.65	48.38	33.13	77.83	91.13	92.18
protein	58.39	47.00	46.97	52.54	64.33	69.05
madelon	60.17	50.00	60.17	60.83	62.33	61.16
isolet	72.80	3.85	5.26	78.82	89.74	96.21
mfeat	90.80	10.00	63.55	91.11	97.50	98.15

It is also worth pointing out that the performance of the algorithms changes as the number of attributes of the problems increases, practically partitioning the experiments in two groups. The first group consists of datasets with less than 50 features (the first 7 problems examined). These datasets are some of the most well known benchmarks, and have been widely used in algorithms comparisons. In these problems AICELL has the best performance in iris, wisconsin, wine and ionosphere. It is surpassed by two algorithms in pima, and steelplates, and by UCS on vehicle. However, the overall differences between all algorithms are quite small, and none of them appears to be significantly superior.

On the contrary, however, in the rest of the problems, having a larger number of features, the differences between algorithms are much larger. In these problems AICELL has the best performance in all problems, with the exception of musk, where it lacks severely, and dna, where it is marginally surpassed by SLAVE. However, in the rest of the problems it surpasses all other algorithms, and, what's more, with large difference from the second best algorithm, which surpasses 10% in 4 of the problems.

This fact becomes more obvious in the radar plots shown in Figure 3, in which the datasets are listed with the number of attributes increasing clockwise. As obvious, on the right semicircle, where the number of features is relatively small, all algorithms have comparable performances. However, as we move to the left semicircle, the performances of GASSIST and UCS significantly decrease. RIPPER and SLAVE have a more robust performance, but still are significantly behind AICELL in most of the problems.

Finally, the distribution of the classifier accuracy on each problem is shown in the box plots of Figure 4. The distribution of AICELL has the best median value. SLAVE and RIPPER follow, with SLAVE being marginally better. Similarly, the worst-case performance of AICELL is better than the worst performances of SLAVE and RIPPER. On the other hand, GASSIST and UCS have significantly inferior overall performances, in terms of both median and worse-case values, with GASSIST being the worst of the two.

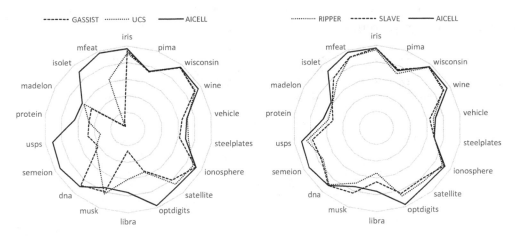

Figure 3. Performance of all classifiers on all problems, ordered clockwise in increasing number of features. As obvious, the performances of GASSIST and UCS significantly decrease as the number of features increases. For RIPPER and SLAVE the differences are significantly smaller, however their overall performance is inferior to that of AICELL.

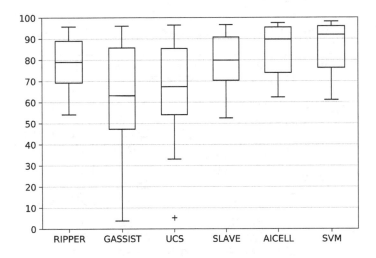

Figure 4. Boxplot of the precision of the algorithms tested on the problems mentioned. GASSIST and UCS fall behind in terms of both mean and median value. RIPPER has comparable distribution to SLAVE, despite not having the best performance in any problem. AICELL has the best overall performance, coming very close to SVM.

10.2. Friedman, Aligned Ranks and Quade Significance Tests.

The values of the significance tests for the Friedman, Aligned ranks and Quade criteria are shown in Table 3. As shown, for the Friedman test, the value of p is in the order of 10^{-6}, while for Quade even smaller. For the aligned ranks metric, the value of p is quite larger, however it remains an order of magnitude below the usual threshold of 0.05. The results of all tests converge to the conclusion that the differences between the algorithms are statistically significant, and a *post-hoc* analysis of the results to find the pairwise differences is required.

Table 3. Results of the Friedman, Aligned ranks and Quade Significance tests. For each test we list the rank of each algorithm, the corresponding z-value, the distributions, and the p-value.

Algorithm	Friedman	Aligned Ranks	Quade
RIPPER	3.3611	41.1944	3.0672
GASSIST	4.2222	67.3888	4.5029
UCS	3.3055	57.9722	3.5964
SLAVE	2.5833	35.25	2.4078
AICELL	1.5277	25.6944	1.4254
value	29.2223	14.8654	12.2959
distribution	$\chi^2(4)$	$\chi^2(4)$	$F(4, 68)$
p-value	7.0454×10^{-6}	4.98852×10^{-3}	1.4048×10^{-7}

The results of the *post-hoc* analysis are shown in Table 4. According to the Friedman criterion, AICELL is better than all algorithms tested. For the comparison to SLAVE, the value of p is marginal, while for the comparisons to the rest of the algorithms the p-value is quite smaller, the differences can safely be regarded as significant. UCS slightly overcomes RIPPER, because of having the best performance of all algorithms in two problems (vehicle and steelplates), while GASSIST has the worst performance among all algorithms.

Table 4. Post-hoc analysis for the Friedman, Aligned ranks and Quade significance tests.

Criterion	Algorithm	Rank	z-Value	p-Value
Friedman	RIPPER	3	3.4785	5.0421×10^{-4}
	GASSIST	4	5.1123	3.1817×10^{-7}
	UCS	2	3.3730	7.4327×10^{-4}
	SLAVE	1	2.0027	4.5201×10^{-2}
Aligned ranks	RIPPER	2	1.7799	7.5088×10^{-2}
	GASSIST	4	4.7879	1.6851×10^{-6}
	UCS	3	3.7065	2.1075×10^{-4}
	SLAVE	1	1.0973	2.7251×10^{-1}
Quade	RIPPER	2	1.9332	5.3208×10^{-2}
	GASSIST	4	3.6237	2.9040×10^{-4}
	UCS	3	2.5563	1.0576×10^{-2}
	SLAVE	1	1.1568	2.4734×10^{-1}

On the contrary, according to Aligned ranks, SLAVE and RIPPER have somewhat better performances, and their differences from AICELL are not statistically significant. On the contrary UCS and GASSIST have much worse performances. The particular criterion, in contrast to the Friedman test, evaluates the overall distribution of the solutions proposed by each algorithm, and not the per-problem relative performances, and for this reason, the overall conclusions are similar to those acquired by the box plots.

Finally, the Quade test combines the characteristics of the two previous tests, correcting the rank of each algorithm on each problem with the performances of the rest of the algorithms on the same problem. As a result, its outcome lies between the conclusions of the two previous tests. With this criterion too, AICELL seems better than all algorithms, but the difference is significant only for the comparisons to UCS and GASSIST.

10.3. Wilcoxon Rank-Sum and Signed-Rank Significance Tests

The values of the significance tests for the rank-sum and signed-rank criteria are given in Table 5. The rank sum test compares the overall distribution of the algorithms' performance. According to this criterion, AICELL has the best performance, followed by SLAVE and RIPPER. UCS and GASSIST have significantly worse performances, with similar results. The difference of AICELL to GASSIST and UCS is statistically significant, being an order of magnitude smaller than the required threshold. The difference to RIPPER is not significant (although it comes close to the threshold), while for the comparison to SLAVE the value of p is quite larger, and the performance of the two algorithms can be regarded as comparable. The overall conclusions of this criterion are similar to those of the boxplots.

Table 5. Wilcoxon rank-sum and signed-rank tests.

Criterion	Algorithm	R^+	R^-	z-Value	p-Value	h
rank sum	RIPPER	394.5	271.5	1.9301	0.0536	0
	GASSIST	421	245	2.7684	0.0056	1
	UCS	424	242	2.8633	0.0042	1
	SLAVE	373.5	292.5	1.2656	0.2056	0
signed rank	RIPPER	170	1	3.68	2.332×10^{-4}	1
	GASSIST	164	7	3.4187	6.292×10^{-4}	1
	UCS	150	21	2.809	0.005	1
	SLAVE	136.5	16.5	2.8407	0.0045	1

On the contrary, according to the signed rank test, the ordering of the algorithms is quite different. RIPPER has the worst performance, overtaking AICELL only on the *steelplates*, and even there with small difference. GASSIST has the second worst performance, being better only in musk, but with bigger difference than RIPPER, while UCS has better performance in 4 problems. However, event with this criterion SLAVE has the second best performance, while AICELL has better performance that all algorithms. Moreover, according to this criterion, the differences are statistically significant for all pairwise comparisons.

10.4. Number of Rules

In Table 6 we list the number of rules of each classifier on each dataset. We omit UCS for which, in contrast to the rest of the classifiers, multiple rules trigger for each pattern, and the class is assigned by voting. However, even if we map its function to that of the other classifiers to render the comparison possible, the number of rules is in general too large, reaching thousands for most of the problems examined.

Table 6. Number of rules of the classifiers on each of the problems examined.

Dataset	RIPPER	GASSIST	SLAVE	AICELL
iris	6.2	4.2	3	6.4
pima	25.6	6.6	15.8	9.4
wisconsin	8.2	4.4	4.6	4.2
wine	6	4.2	3.6	6.2
vehicle	39.4	6.4	29.8	47.2
steelplates	80.4	6.2	50.6	58.2
ionosphere	12.2	4.6	3.2	11.2
satellite	65	9	46	51
optdigits	86	12	62	87
libra	51	10.4	46.4	60.8
musk	15.4	4.8	16.8	20.5
dna	31	5	32	34
semeion	80.2	11.4	71.8	46.4
usps	129	16	96	66
protein	172	2	1390	14
madelon	37	2	47	74
isolet	211	2	138	45
mfeat	37.6	2	41.4	21.8
mean	56.6	8.7	116.9	35.5
median	37.3	4.9	43.7	34

As shown by the table, GASSIST produces, by far, the smallest number of rules. However, this is the greatest problem of the algorithm, since this number of rules is insufficient for larger problems, and consequently the algorithm performs badly on them. The small number of rules is an inherent characteristic of the algorithm, regardless of the training parameters. Among the remaining algorithms, AICELL produces the smallest number of rules, in terms of both mean and median value. The difference is small in terms and median value, and slightly larger in terms of mean, due to the large number of rules produced by SLAVE and RIPPER in some particular problems, however the overall differences are quite small and cannot be considered important.

10.5. Comparison to SVM

Finally, compared to SVMs, AICELL is surpassed in 13 out of the 18 problems examined. However, the difference in small in gereral, having a mean value of 0.88% and a median of 1.87%. This difference is smaller than the difference of AICELL to the second best rule-based algorithm in each problem (mean 2.43 and median 3.57), and even larger than its difference from the overall second best SLAVE, for which the difference surpasses 5% in terms of both mean and median values.

Moreover, as shown by the significance tests listed in Table 7, the differences are statistically significant only for the signed-rank test, and, even for that metric, the p-value is marginally smaller than the critical threshold. The second largest difference appears in the Friedman test which, like the signed-rank test, evaluates the number of problems in which each classifier has the best performance. On the contrary, for all other metrics, which evaluate the overall solution distribution, the differences are negligible, with the value of p being close to 0.5.

Table 7. Comparison to SVM. Although the performance of SVM is better than that of AICELL with all metrics, the difference is statistically significant only for the Wilcoxon signed-rank test, and even for that, with a marginal p-value, while for the rest of the metrics the p-value is an order of magnitude above the critical threshold.

Criterion	R^+	R^-	z-Value	p-Value
Friedman			−1.2917	0.1964
Aligned ranks			−0.6944	0.4874
Quade			−0.5803	0.5616
Rank sum	310	356	−0.7119	0.4765
Signed rank	39	132	−2.2051	0.0429

However, it must be noted that the performance of SVM listed here is produced by a very extensive cross-validation C, γ parameter values, and that for most value pairs, the performance is much worse. On the contrary, AICELL exhibits much more robust behavior in terms of parameter values, while the training duration is also much shorter, by orders of magnitude on some problems. Additionally, the rules produced by AICELL are much simpler.

10.6. Discussion of Results

In this section, the proposed method has been compared with 4 other algorithms that have been widely used in comparisons and are considered state-of-the-art. Among these algorithms, GASSIST and UCS are generally regarded as slightly superior. However, these conclusions have been drawn from experiments on much simpler datasets than the ones examined here, where the number of attributes does not exceed 30, and the number of classes is 2 or 3 (we refer the reader to [36] for detailed comparison). The problems examined here present significantly larger complexity, in terms of both number of attributes and number of classes, the conclusions are considerably different to those presented in the majority of the literature.

In more detail, according to all metrics, GASSIST has the worst performance. Although it achieves satisfying results, while having small number of rules, on the simpler datasets, its performance deteriorates significantly as the number of features and classes increases. These problems have been acknowledged by the creator of the algorithm himself [49]. RIPPER and UCS follow, with UCS having the best performance in some of the problems and very bad in others, especially the more complex ones, while RIPPER, despite not achieving the best performance in any of the problems examined, has satisfactory performance on all of them. SLAVE achieves the best performance, with significant difference, coming first in more problems than the other 3 algorithms, and second in some harder ones. Moreover, the overall distribution of the proposed solutions is much better than that of GASSIST and UCS, and slightly better than that of RIPPER.

According to all the metrics examined, the proposed method achieves the best performance. The difference is statistically significant in all metrics compared to GASSIST, and in most of them compared to UCS. The difference to RIPPER is close to the critical value for most of the tests, while the difference to SLAVE statistically insignificant with most criteria. However, AICELL achieves the best distribution, and has the best performance in larger number of problems than the rest of the algorithms. Moreover, it has consistently good performance in problems with large number of features and classes, achieving large difference from the second best in some of them. Finally, compared to SVM, AICELL is surpassed in most problems, but the difference is marginal and statistically insignificant in most cases, while the training duration and sensitivity to parameter values is much smaller.

11. Conclusions and Future Work

We have proposed in this paper a classification algorithm based on an Artificial Immune Network. The proposed algorithm encodes the patterns to be recognized as antigens, and evolves antibodies representing classification rules of ellipsoidal surface. The antibodies evolve individually, so as to maximize the evaluation metric, resembling in this sense classic Michigan-style classifier rules. Additionally, as happens in most immune networks, antibodies of high similarity or low quality are removed from the network.

However, contrary to most immune algorithms, the aim of the proposed algorithm is not the recognition, but the elimination of the antigens. Antigens that have already been confronted have no further impact on the evolution of the network, which helps minimize the overlap between rules, and guide the new rules towards uncovered areas of the problem space. This brings the algorithm closer to Incremental Rule Learning classifier systems, which have been shown to combine advantages of Pittsburg and Michigan classifiers.

In general, incremental classifiers are not compatible with fuzzy rules, due to the fact that they have to remove patterns that are covered by each new rule, whereas, in fuzzy classifiers, all patterns are covered by all rules. However, the modification employed here enables us to compromise the two approaches, enabling the algorithm to take advantage of the lower number of rules and better generalization ability of fuzzy classifiers. As shown, as the steepness of the membership function increases, the proposed classifier becomes strictly equivalent to an incremental rule classifier.

Regarding more specific algorithm design choices, the recognition rules are based on a quadratic surface, which closely resembles that of an ellipsoid, while being computationally simpler. For the evaluation of the rules a fuzzy generalization of the common m-estimate has been employed. For the removal of unsuitable antibodies from the network, a similarity metric based on the inner product of membership function values has been employed, while antibodies are also removed if the have either lower recognition ability or smaller coverage than the rest of the network population, based on outlier detection criteria. Finally, a rule initialization method was proposed, which further helps the algorithm locate uncovered areas of the problem space.

The proposed method was tested against one representative classifier of each type. On the problems examined, the algorithm had better accuracy than both the Pittsburg and Michigan classifiers. Additionally, it produced much fewer rules than the Michigan classifier, while also performing well in more complex problems, contrary to the Pittsburg classifier, which is limited by its chromosome encoding length. The differences are more obvious in problems with larger number of features and classes, where the proposed method significantly outperformed the competition, maintaining both the robustness and small number of rules exhibited by the incremental rule classifier, and the generalization ability of the fuzzy classifier. Finally, compared to Support Vector Machines, the algorithm was surpassed in the majority of the problems, however the differences are marginal and statistically insignificant, while the proposed method is much more robust to the change of training parameters, and generates much simpler and more interpretable rules.

Regarding possible extensions of the present algorithm, the main area to experiment with is the employment of different geometries of recognition rules and different shapes of membership functions. Since different shapes of surfaces could be more appropriate for covering different areas of the problem space, it would be beneficial to combine multiple forms of rules within the same classifier. Additionally the evaluation metric could be extended so that, during the training of each rule, it also takes into account the existing rules, further assisting cooperation.

Author Contributions: A.L., G.S. and A.S conceived the algorithm. A.L. developed and implemented the model. A.L. and G.S. performed experiments. A.L., G.S. and A.S. analyzed the data. A.L., G.S. and A.S wrote the paper.

References

1. Burnet, F.M. *The Clonal Selection Theory of Acquired Immunity*; Vanderbilt University Press: Nashville, TN, USA, 1959; p. 232.
2. Jerne, N. Towards a network theory of the immune system. *Ann. Immunol.* **1974**, *125*, 373–389.
3. De Castro, L.N.; Timmis, J. *Artificial Immune Systems: A New Computational Intelligence Approach*; Springer: London, UK, 2002.
4. De Castro, L.N.; Von Zuben, F.J. Learning and Optimization Using the Clonal Selection Principle. *IEEE Trans. Evol. Comput.* **2002**, *6*, 239–251.
5. De Castro, L.N.; Zuben, F.J.V. aiNet: An Artificial Immune Network for Data Analysis. In *Data Mining: A Heuristic Approach*; Abbass, H.A., Sarker, R.A., Newton, C.S., Eds.; Idea Group Publishing: Hershey, PA, USA, 2001; pp. 231–259.
6. Karakasis, V.K.; Stafylopatis, A. Efficient Evolution of Accurate Classification Rules Using a Combination of Gene Expression Programming and Clonal Selection. *IEEE Trans. Evol. Comput.* **2008**, *12*, 662–678.
7. Lanaridis, A.; Stafylopatis, A. An Artificial Immune Network for Multiobjective Optimization Problems. *Eng. Optim.* **2013**, *46*, 1008–1031.
8. Magna, G.; Casti, P.; Jayaraman, S.V.; Salmeri, M.; Mencattini, A.; Martinelli, E.; Natale, C.D. Identification of mammography anomalies for breast cancer detection by an ensemble of classification models based on artificial immune system. *Knowl. Based Syst.* **2016**, *101*, 60–70.
9. Martinelli, E.; Magna, G.; Vito, S.D.; Fuccio, R.D.; Francia, G.D.; Vergara, A.; Natale, C.D. An adaptive classification model based on the Artificial Immune System for chemical sensor drift mitigation. *Sens. Actuators B Chem.* **2013**, *177*, 1017–1026.
10. Lanaridis, A.; Stafylopatis, A. An Artificial Immune Classifier Using Pseudo-Ellipsoid Rules. In Proceedings of the 26th International Symposium on Computer and Information Sciences, London, UK, 26–28 September 2011; pp. 395–401.
11. Hyafil, L.; Rivest, R.L. Constructing optimal binary decision trees is NP-complete. *Inf. Proc. Lett.* **1976**, *5*, 15–17.
12. Holland, J.H. *Adaptation in Natural and Artificial Systems: An Introductory Analysis with Applications to Biology, Control and Artificial Intelligence*; University of Michigan Press: Ann Arbor, MI, USA, 1975.
13. Sigaud, O.; Wilson, S.W. Learning classifier systems: A survey. *Soft Comput.* **2007**, *11*, 1065–1078.
14. Smith, S.F. A Learning System Based on Genetic Adaptive Algorithms. Ph.D. Thesis, University of Pittsburg, Pittsburgh, PA, USA, 1980.
15. Holland, J.; Reitman, J. *Cognitive Systems Based on Adaptive Algorithms*; Department of Computer and Communication Science, University of Michigan: Ann Arbor, MI, USA, 1977.
16. Venturini, G. SIA: A Supervised Inductive Algorithm with Genetic Search for Learning Attributes Based Concepts. In *Machine Learning: ECML '93, Lecture Notes on Computer Science*; Springer: London, UK, 1993; pp. 280–296.

17. Garrett, S.M. How Do We Evaluate Artificial Immune Systems? *Evol. Comput.* **2005**, *13*, 145–177.

18. Hart, E.; Timmis, J. Application Areas of AIS: The Past, the Present and the Future. *Appl. Soft Comput.* **2008**, *8*, 191–201.

19. De Castro, L.N.; Timmis, J. *Artificial Immune Systems: A New Computational Intelligence Paradigm*; Springer-Verlag New York, Inc.: Secaucus, NJ, USA, 2002.

20. Abe, S. Dynamic cluster generation for a fuzzy classifier with ellipsoidal regions. *IEEE Trans. Syst. Man Cybern. Part B* **1998**, *28*, 869–876.

21. Yao, L.; Lin, C.C. A fuzzy classifier with evolutionary design of ellipsoidal decision regions. *Proc. World Acad. Sci. Eng. Tech.* **2005**, *1*, 38–44.

22. Abe, S.; Thawonmas, R. A fuzzy classifier with ellipsoidal regions. *Fuzzy Syst. IEEE Trans.* **1997**, *5*, 358–368.

23. Yao, L.; Weng, K.S.; Huang, C.D. Evolutionary design of fuzzy classifier with ellipsoidal decision regions. In Proceedings of the 2005 IEEE International Conference on Systems, Man and Cybernetics, Waikoloa, HI, USA, 12 October 2005; Volume 1, pp. 785–790.

24. Michalewicz, Z. *Genetic Algorithms + Data Structures = Evolution Programs*; Springer: New York, NY, USA, 1996.

25. Goldberg, D.E. *Genetic Algorithms in Search, Optimization, and Machine Learning*; Addison-Wesley: Boston, MA, USA, 1989.

26. Nada Lavrac, P.A.F.; Zupan, B. Rule Evaluation Metrics: A unifying view. In Proceedings of the 9th International Workshop on Inductive Logic Programming, Bled, Slovenia, 24–27 June 1999; pp. 173–185.

27. Furnkranz, J.; Flach, P.A. An Analysis of Rule Evaluation Metrics. In Proceedings of the 20th International Conference on Machine Learning (ICML-2003), Washington, DC, USA, 21–24 August 2003; pp. 202–209.

28. Furnkranz, J.; Flach, P. An Analysis of Rule Learning Heuristics. 2007. Available online: http://citeseer.ist.psu.edu/viewdoc/summary?doi=10.1.1.60.3804 (accessed on 15 June 2017).

29. Tukey, J. Comparing Individual Means in the Analysis of Variance. *Biometrics* **1949**, *2*, 99–114.

30. Chang, C.C.; Lin, C.J. LIBSVM: A Library for Support Vector Machines. *ACM Trans. Intell. Syst. Technol.* **2011**, *2*, doi:10.1145/1961189.1961199.

31. Bache, K.; Lichman, M. UCI Machine Learning Repository. 2013. Available online: http://archive.ics.uci.edu/ml (accessed on 15 February 2017).

32. Cohen, W. Fast Effective Rule Induction. In Proceedings of the Twelfth International Conference on Machine Learning, Tahoe City, CA, USA, 9–12 July 1995; pp. 1–10.

33. Bacardit, J.; Garrell, J. Evolving multiple discretizations with adaptive intervals for a pittsburgh rule-based learning classifier system. In Proceedings of the GECCO 2003 Genetic and Evolutionary Computation Conference, Chicago, IL, USA, 12–16 July 2003; pp. 1818–1831.

34. Gonzalez, A.; Perez, R. Selection of relevant features in a fuzzy genetic learning algorithm. *IEEE Trans. Syst. Man Cybern. Part B* **2001**, *31*, 417–425.

35. Bernado-Mansilla, E.; Garrell, J. Accuracy-Based Learning Classifier Systems: Models and Analysis and Applications to Classification Tasks. *Evol. Comput.* **2003**, *11*, 209–238.

36. Fernandez, A.; Garcia, S.; Luengo, J.; Bernando-Mansilla, E.; Herrera, F. Genetics-Based Machine Learning for Rule Induction: State of the Art, Taxonomy, and Comparative Study. *Evol. Comput. IEEE Trans.* **2010**, *14*, 913–941.

37. Friedman, M. A Comparison of Alternative Tests of Significance for the Problem of *m* Rankings. *Ann. Math. Stat.* **1940**, *11*, 86–92.

38. Hodges, J.L.; Lehmann, E.L. Rank methods for combination of independent experiments in analysis of variance. *Ann. Math. Stat.* **1960**, *6*, 403–418.

39. Quade, D. Using Weighted Rankings in the Analysis of Complete Blocks with Additive Block Effects. *J. Am. Stat. Assoc.* **1979**, *74*, 680–683.

40. Wilcoxon, F. Individual comparisons by ranking methods. *Biom. Bull.* **1945**, *1*, 80–83.

41. Derrac, J.; Garcia, S.; Molina, D.; Herrera, F. A practical tutorial on the use of nonparametric statistical tests as a methodology for comparing evolutionary and swarm intelligence algorithms. *Swarm Evol. Comput.* **2011**, *1*, 3–18.

42. Demvsar, J. Statistical Comparisons of Classifiers over Multiple Data Sets. *J. Mach. Learn. Res.* **2006**, *7*, 1–30.

43. Garcia, S.; Herrera, F.; Shawe-Taylor, J. An extension on statistical comparisons of classifiers over multiple data sets for all pairwise comparisons. *J. Mach. Learn. Res.* **2008**, *9*, 2677–2694.

44. Alcala-Fdez, J.; Sanchez, L.; Garcia, S.; del Jesus, M.; Ventura, S.; Garrell, J.; Otero, J.; Romero, C.; Bacardit, J.; Rivas, V.; et al. KEEL: A software tool to assess evolutionary algorithms for data mining problems. *Soft Comput.* **2009**, *13*, 307–318.

45. Alcala-Fdez, J.; Fernandez, A.; Luengo, J.; Derrac, J.; Garcia, S. KEEL Data-Mining Software Tool: Data Set Repository, Integration of Algorithms and Experimental Analysis Framework. *Mult. Valued Log. Soft Comput.* **2011**, *17*, 255–287.

46. Joachims, T. Making large-Scale SVM Learning Practical. In *Technical Report, SFB 475: Komplexitätsreduktion in Multivariaten Datenstrukturen*; Universität Dortmund: Dortmund, Germany, 1998.

47. Knerr, S.; Personnaz, L.; Dreyfus, G. Single-layer learning revisited: A stepwise procedure for building and training a neural network. In *Neurocomputing*; Springer: Berlin, Germany, 1990; pp. 41–50.

48. Galar, M.; Fernandez, A.; Barrenechea, E.; Bustince, H.; Herrera, F. An overview of ensemble methods for binary classifiers in multi-class problems: Experimental study on one-vs-one and one-vs-all schemes. *Pattern Recognit.* **2011**, *44*, 1761–1776.

49. Bacardit, J. Pittsburgh Genetics-Based Machine Learning in the Data Mining Era: Representations, generalization, and run-time. Ph.D. Thesis, Ramon Llull University, Barcelona, Spain, 2004.

4

Analyzing the Effect and Performance of Lossy Compression on Aeroacoustic Simulation of Gas Injector

Seyyed Mahdi Najmabadi [1,*,†], Philipp Offenhäuser [2,†], Moritz Hamann [1], Guhathakurta Jajnabalkya [1], Fabian Hempert [3], Colin W. Glass [2] and Sven Simon [1]

[1] Institute for Parallel and Distributed Systems, University of Stuttgart, Universitätsstraße 38, 70569 Stuttgart, Germany; moritz.hamann@ipvs.uni-stuttgart.de (M.H.); Jajnabalkya.Guhathakurta@ipvs.uni-stuttgart.de (G.J.); simon@ipvs.uni-stuttgart.de (S.S.)

[2] The High Performance Computing Center Stuttgart (HLRS), Nobelstraße 19, 70569 Stuttgart, Germany; offenhaeuser@hlrs.de (P.O.); glass@hlrs.de (C.W.G.)

[3] Robert Bosch GmbH, Robert-Bosch-Allee 1, 74232 Abstatt, Germany; Fabian.Hempert@de.bosch.com

* Correspondence: mahdi.najmabadi@ipvs.uni-stuttgart.de

† These authors contributed equally to this work.

Academic Editor: Qinjun Kang

Abstract: Computational fluid dynamic simulations involve large state data, leading to performance degradation due to data transfer times, while requiring large disk space. To alleviate the situation, an adaptive lossy compression algorithm has been developed, which is based on regions of interest. This algorithm uses prediction-based compression and exploits the temporal coherence between subsequent simulation frames. The difference between the actual value and the predicted value is adaptively quantized and encoded. The adaptation is in line with user requirements, that consist of the acceptable inaccuracy, the regions of interest and the required compression throughput. The data compression algorithm was evaluated with simulation data obtained by the discontinuous Galerkin spectral element method. We analyzed the performance, compression ratio and inaccuracy introduced by the lossy compression algorithm. The post processing analysis shows high compression ratios, with reasonable quantization errors.

Keywords: adaptive lossy data compression; predictive coding; large-scale simulation; computational fluid dynamics; aeroacoustic simulation; visualization

1. Introduction

Nowadays, with the high availability of computing power, simulation methods have evolved into important tools in many research areas and industry. Current supercomputers such as the Cray XC40 (Hazel Hen) have on the order of 10^5–10^6 computing cores and peak performances of multiple Pflop/s [1]. Many application areas, such as computational fluid dynamics (CFD), have benefited greatly from the massive increase of computing power over the past decades, by specifically developing and implementing parallel codes [2]. On the basis of these codes, it is possible to carry out detailed studies of complex fluid mechanics phenomena, such as turbulent boundary layer effects of a supersonic flow [3] or the flow in the turbine of a helicopter [4]. To ensure that all the relevant characteristics of such complex fluid flow simulations are captured correctly, the simulation domain needs to be discretized with high resolution. Information such as density, momentum and the specific total energy needs to be stored for every discretization point, e.g., in a parallel file system. The combination of huge simulation domains and high temporal and spatial resolution leads to terabytes of simulation results, e.g., for the simulation of the fluid flow in the turbine of a helicopter [4].

This leads to new challenges for high-performance computing. The available bandwidth to the file system is a limiting factor for CFD simulations and can lead to massive performance degradation. In the future, this problem will most likely become even bigger, as it is reasonable to assume that the increase in computing power will be faster than the increase in available I/O-bandwidth. Furthermore, the time to communicate data within the simulation increases, with the increasing amount of data to be communicated.

The large amounts of data are not only a challenge during the simulation, it is also a challenge for post-processing. To analyze and visualize the simulation results, data needs to be accessed from the file system, and again I/O-bandwidth is a limiting factor. Furthermore, archiving the simulation results in itself is a challenge and often, the data has to be stored for years. All these problems scale with the size of data, therefore, the most straight forward remedy is to reduce the amount of data. One way to achieve this would be to reduce the temporal and spatial resolution. However, a reduction of the resolution heavily impacts the accuracy of the results. An alternative is to use data compression techniques. Data compression can be divided in two main categories, lossless or lossy. lossless data compression has more acceptance in scientific field but the compression ratio is limited. In order to increase the compression ratio, Burtscher et al. employed genetic algorithm to find an effective lossless compression algorithm during runtime. To achieve this, they have selected the basic elements that are typically used in compression algorithms and can be implemented to run in linear time. During the runtime they search for the most effective chain of the basic elements [5]. A higher compression ratio can also be obtained by lossy data compression algorithms. Recently, several studies have been analyzing the effects of lossy data compression algorithms in scientific simulations [6–8]. Laney et al. show that the lossy compression is suitable in simulations. Their evaluation method is more realistic due to the observation of physic based metrics other than classical error metrics [7]. Baker et al. show that applying lossy data compression to climate simulation data is both advantageous in terms of data reduction and acceptable in terms of effects on scientific results. They provided both lossy and original data, and challenged climate scientists to examine features of the data relevant to their interests and identify which of the ensemble members have been compressed and reconstructed [8].

In this work, an efficient online lossy compression framework of floating point simulation data is presented, and the effect and performance of lossy compression is analyzed on aeroacoustic simulation data of gas injectors. The presented compression framework provides a capability of dynamically selecting a suitable compression algorithm and also exploiting spatially adaptive quantization to get better compression ratio while still satisfying a maximum relative error tolerance.

Simulation Method

The CFD code used in this work is based on the discontinuous Galerkin spectral element method (DG SEM). The method is well described in the literature, so we restrict ourselves to a short overview of DG SEM. For further reading we refer to [2]. Starting point of DG SEM are the compressible Navier–Stokes equations expressed in conservative form:

$$u_t(x) + \nabla_x \cdot F(u(x), \nabla_x u(x)) = 0 \quad \forall x \in \Omega. \tag{1}$$

where F contains the physical fluxes, Ω is the computational domain, and u is a vector containing the conservative variables that is given by:

$$u = \begin{pmatrix} \rho \\ \rho v_1 \\ \rho v_2 \\ \rho v_3 \\ \rho e \end{pmatrix}. \tag{2}$$

The conservative variables are the density, momentum, and the specific total energy. The simulation domain is divided into hexahedral grid cells. Each grid cell is mapped to the reference element $E = [-1,1]^3$ with coordinates $\boldsymbol{\xi} = (\xi^1, \xi^2, \xi^3)^T$. The actual computation is performed in the reference element and integrated over the reference element, to get the so-called weak formulation. To derive the discontinuous Galerkin (DG) formulation, the transformed conservative law is multiplied with a test function Φ. The solution in each reference element is approximated by tensor products of Lagrangian polynomials of degree N:

$$u(\boldsymbol{\xi}) = \sum_{i,j,k=0}^{N} \hat{u}_{i,j,k}\psi_{i,j,k}(\boldsymbol{\xi}) \quad \text{with } \psi_{i,j,k}(\boldsymbol{\xi}) = l_i(\xi^1)l_j(\xi^2)l_k(\xi^3), \tag{3}$$

where $\hat{u}_{i,j,k} := \hat{u}_{i,j,k}(t)$ are the time dependent degrees of freedom (DOFs), and $l_i(\xi)$ are the Lagrange interpolation polynomials defined by a nodal set $\{\xi_i\}_{i=0}^{N}$. Each element has $(N+1)^3$ nodes, each node contains the five conservative variables. DG schemes are a hybrid of Finite Element schemes and Finite Volume schemes. The solution is approximated by an element-local polynomial basis and the solution is discontinues over element boundaries. This denotes that adjacent elements have different states at the interface. Adjacent elements are coupled by fluxes through their interfaces. For the approximation of the boundary flux $\mathcal{F}^*$, a Riemann solver is used with the information form the state u of an element and the state u^+ of the neighboring element. In the present study, we use the local Lay–Friedrich method [9]. The integration in the DG discretization is solved by Gauss quadrature. The time integration is done with an explicit 3rd-order accurate Runge-Kutta scheme.

2. Related Work

There are several works involving compression of CFD simulation data [10–15]. Wavelet-based compression algorithms is one of the most common techniques used. Sakai et al. proposed a lossy compression method using discrete wavelet transform (DWT) followed by quantization and entropy encoding [12–15]. The main drawback of their approach is that there is no straightway to control the amount of the compression error. However, in this work the accuracy is guaranteed to stay within a certain threshold. Additionally, wavelet transforms produce noise near the rapid signal transition. Therefore, it is not suitable for our simulation data which are generated through the discontinuous Galerkin spectral element method, due to the discontinuities between the neighboring elements. In another work the usefulness of image and video compression technique for compressing CFD data on regular Cartesian grids was investigated [10]. They have compared three main compression algorithms in that domain namely JPEG, JPEG-2000, and MPEG. It was found that JPEG-2000 requires a lot of computing time, mainly because of the wavelet transform, the MPEG compressor requires the input data to be scaled from double floating point to an integer array [0,255], which is time consuming and leads to a very high maximum error of approx. 10% and the main drawback of JPEG compression is that the decompression step takes a lot of time, while giving no possibility to control the generated error on individual data points. Tensor decompositions are another method that is used for compressing multi-dimensional array by reducing the dimension of input data set. This method can provide higher compression ratio than the wavelet transforms or discrete cosine transform (DCT) [16]. However, it cannot guarantee point wise error bound which is the main constraint of this work. Additionally, this method is suffering from computation time but this can be improved by parallel implementation. Austin et al. enhanced the performance by parallelizing the method, and overlapping communication and computation on a Cray XC30 supercomputer [17].

There are several works that support point-wise user defined error bound based on subsequent analysis requirements [18–21]. Iverson et al. investigated a method for grid-based scientific data set. In the proposed approach the value of set of nodes are replaced by a constant value that satisfies the reconstruction error bound, followed by a lossless compression [19]. In comparison to this work they bound the absolute error and not the relative error. Another lossy compression algorithm is ISABELA [18,22], which utilizes B-Splines to approximate the values in the data stream. It divides the continuous stream of floating point numbers into windows of an user-defined length, and then sorts the numbers in every window. This sorting reduces random fluctuations and provides a smoother, monotonically increasing sequence, which is then approximated by a B-Spline. In order to ensure a specific point to point error, the difference between the approximation and the real value is stored in a quantized integer. FPZIP is another compression algorithm that is based on predictive coding and uses three dimensional Lorenzo predictor followed by residual computation and a fast entropy encoder [20,23]. Another algorithm is ZFP [24], which focused on compression of 3D arrays of floating point numbers. The compression algorithm consists of three main steps: conversion to fixed-point, an orthogonal block transform and bit plane encoding. One of the main advantages of ZFP is efficient random-access reads and writes, which is not available in other lossy floating point data compression algorithm. The last compression algorithm that is used for comparison is applying a Lorenzo predictor that exploits the spatial correlation [25]. Three different dimension of Lorenzo predictor is used for comparison by replacing them with the predictor that is used in this work and keeping all other component unchanged. The detailed comparison with the mentioned work is given in Section 5.4.

In this work, a prediction-based compression algorithm is used that exploits the temporal coherence between subsequent simulation frames. The main drawback of this method is that it is not possible to access any time step randomly. It means that to access any of the time step for post processing analysis, all earlier time steps must be decompressed first. Nevertheless, most of the time these data are used for 3D visualization where complete data sets are read sequentially every time some viewing parameter is changed. In such a case the presented method would provide no drawbacks. Another drawback of prediction-based method is that, there should be sufficient memory to buffer one simulation time step. However in our test case each simulation time steps is less than 1 Gbyte. Which is in an acceptable range. For the Cray XC40 (Hazel Hen) supercomputer, each node has 128 Gbyte of memory. Hence the authors feel that the memory problem to buffer only a single time step would not be a major bottleneck in many cases.

3. Data Compression Method

In order to compress the CFD data, a prediction based compression algorithm is applied [26]. The compression is performed on all conservative variables. As it is shown in Figure 1 the compression algorithm consists of four main parts, region of interest (ROI) detection, prediction module, quantization module and lossless compression algorithm module. These parts are explained in the following subsections.

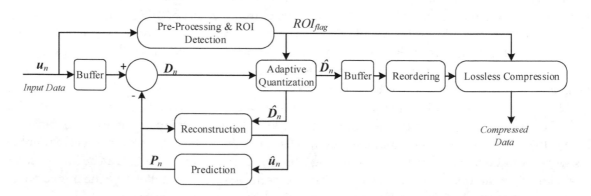

Figure 1. A block diagram of the proposed compression algorithm.

3.1. Pre-Processing and ROI Detection

The main purpose of the region of interest scheme is that all the simulation data are not equally important for the post processing or visualization phase. Therefore, the goal is to detect and identify more relevant regions and compress them with a smaller quantization level to achieve higher decompressed data quality. Those regions can be identified by various criteria such as their position or by the value of specific quantities such as temperature, pressure or turbulence.

In this work, for the investigated simulation case, i.e., natural gas injector, the temperature is a suitable indicator for the ROI. Flow phenomena such as pressure shocks or strong turbulence directly influence the temperature. For instance, Figure 2a shows a snapshot of the temperature of the external flow behind an injector, more specific details about the injector is given in Section 4. Figure 2b shows the ROI that is based on the temperature value, and in this example the ROI is where the temperature value (T) is higher than 300 K. Figure 2c shows the ROI that is based on the position of the simulation elements and was defined before the simulation has started. Figure 2d is the combination of the two previous examples. Figure 2e shows the ROI that is based on the temperature value, and in this example the ROI is where the temperature value (T) is lower than 300 K. There are no implicit advantages or disadvantages between the different ROI. Rather, the ROI should match the actual use case. For instance, Figure 2e is used for sound pressure level analysis, as the observation points are in the region with almost no turbulence which are cooler than the turbulent regions. More detailed information about the ROI is given in Section 5.

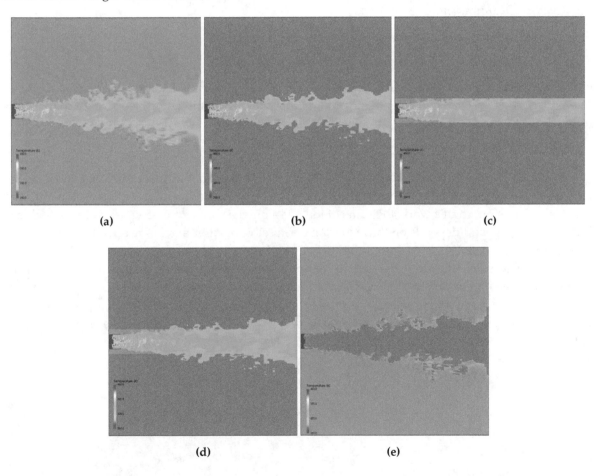

(a) (b) (c)

(d) (e)

Figure 2. A snapshot of the temperature of the external flow flow behind a gas injector: (**a**) without ROI; (**b**) ROI is defined based on the temperature range, ROI condition: $T > 300$ K; (**c**) ROI is defined based on the position of DG-elements; (**d**) ROI is a combination of (b) and (c); (**e**) ROI is defined based on the temperature range, ROI condition: $T < 300$ K.

For each DG-element one ROI_{flag} is defined, where ROI_{flag} is True if one or more nodes in the DG-element satisfy the ROI condition. Hence, only one bit per DG-element is the overhead of the ROI technique, and the process of detecting ROI DG-elements is stopped as soon as the first node in the DG-element satisfies the ROI condition.

3.2. Prediction and Reconstruction

By taking advantage of the prediction based algorithm, the variance and dynamic range of the data is be reduced. The amount of the reduction depends on how well the predictor can predict the next value. In this work, a very simple but fast and effective polynomial predictor is used [27]. The prediction is defined as:

$$P_t = \hat{u}_{t-1}, \tag{4}$$

where $\hat{u}_{t-1}$ is the reconstructed value of the previous simulation time step. The predictor in the compression unit should use the same data that the predictor in the decompression unit will use. Therefore, due to the quantization and lossy compression, the compressed data must be reconstructed in the compression unit. The reconstructed value is derived by:

$$\hat{u}_t = P_t + \hat{D}_t \times \Delta, \tag{5}$$

where Δ is the quantization step vector, and $\hat{D}_t$ is the quantized values of prediction residuals. These two values are explained in the following section.

3.3. Adaptive Quantization

The prediction residual of the polynomial predictor is defined as:

$$D_t = u_t - P_t, \tag{6}$$

which is a floating point variable. By this step the prediction residual, D_t, is converted to an integer. This conversion is done by division of the input amplitude by a quantization step size, Δ, followed by rounding to the nearest integer and is expressed as follows:

$$\hat{D}_t = \text{round}(\frac{D_t}{\Delta}). \tag{7}$$

The quantization is the only source of loss of precision: a small Δ will lead to a higher precision but reduces the compression ratio. Accordingly, Δ has a direct relation both with the compression ratio and the loss of precision. In this work, the value of the Δ is a unique value for each conservative variable in each DG-element, and depends on the requested permissible maximum relative error (PMRE) for ROI and non-ROI regions. With this approach the accuracy is guaranteed to stay within PMRE.

In order to calculate the Δ we need to define the following: Let us assume that the original value A is a vector of size m, $A = \{a_0, a_1, ..., a_{m-1}\}$, the reconstructed value $\hat{A}$ is respectively $\hat{A} = \{\hat{a}_0, \hat{a}_1, ..., \hat{a}_{m-1}\}$, and $I = \{0, 1, ..., m-1\}$. In this work m is the number of nodes in one DG-element. Suppose that maximum absolute error ($|e|_{max}$) and maximum relative error (MRE) due to the quantization are defined as following:

$$
\begin{aligned}
|e|_{max} &= \max_{i \in I} |a_i - \hat{a}_i| \\
&\leq \frac{\Delta}{2},
\end{aligned}
\tag{8}
$$

and:

$$
\begin{aligned}
MRE &= \max_{i \in I} |\frac{a_i - \hat{a}_i}{a_i}| \\
&\leq \frac{|e|_{max}}{|A|_{min}} \\
&\leq \frac{\Delta}{2 \times |A|_{min}}.
\end{aligned}
\tag{9}
$$

We have defined $PMRE$ to be an upper bound for MRE. Therefore, from Equation (9) and by assuming two different values for $PMRE$ at ROI and non-ROI region, namely $PMRE_{ROI}$ and $PMRE_{non-ROI}$, the quantization step size is calculated as follows:

$$\Delta = \begin{cases} 2 \times PMRE_{ROI} \times \mid A \mid_{min}, & \text{if } ROI_{flag} = 1 \\ 2 \times PMRE_{non-ROI} \times \mid A \mid_{min}, & \text{if } ROI_{flag} = 0. \end{cases} \qquad (10)$$

The only unknown variable in Equation (10) is $\mid A \mid_{min}$, which must be calculated for each conservative quantity in each DG-element, and should be transferred to the output stream. Afterward, the decoder can derive the Δ by extracting $\mid A \mid_{min}$, ROI_{flag}, $PMRE_{ROI}$, and $PMRE_{non-ROI}$ from the compressed stream. In case of overflow or division by zero in Equation (9), no quantization is performed on that specific DG-elements.

3.4. Reordering and Lossless Compression

The last chain of the compression algorithm is a lossless compression algorithm that exploits all repetition in the data and achieve a higher compression ratio by representing frequently occurring patterns with few bits and rarely occurring patterns with many bits [28–30]. Additionally, in order to gain a higher compression ratio, the residual of the conservative variables are reordered. It means that the residuals of each conservative quantity are grouped together and then are passed to the lossless compression module.

4. Adaptive Compression Framework

In the context of scientific simulation data compression, traditionally, a single compression algorithm is used, which is selected independently from the environment parameters. However, a fixed compression algorithm prevents dynamic adjustments to changes in the data distribution, data properties or external factors. Therefore, an adaptive compression framework is introduced, which utilizes different compression algorithms, in order to dynamically adjust the compression process to specific conditions. The main task is the adaption to the availability of computing resources, particular the network environments. If the current bandwidth in the network drops, it may be beneficial to change the current compression to an algorithm which achieves better compression ratios at a lower throughput, in order to reduce the overall transmission time of the data in the network.

In order to allow for adaptive compression, the data is divided into multiple windows and each window is divided further into multiple frames. In this work, one frame consists of 100 DG elements. As it is shown in Figure 3, the functionality of the framework can be divided into the three following parts. First, the so called modules, which represents a single algorithm in the compression framework and provide an encoding and decoding function for that algorithm. These modules can be chained together and behave like a pipeline, which allows an implementation of different compression pipelines or even the implementation of an adaptive compression scheme, in which the individual modules are selected at run time. In this work, there are five main modules. Module A (prediction and quantization module) and Module B (reordering module) are fixed for all frames in the compression pipeline and won't change during runtime. However, Modules C, D and E, which are the lossless compression algorithms, may be alternate during runtime. This means that frames can be compressed with different lossless compression algorithms. For instance, by considering that each window has 20 frames, the first 10 frames can be encoded by Module C, while the next nine consecutive frames are encoded by Module D and the last frame is encoded by Module E. The second part is a central monitoring component, which is used to store performance records for every compressed frame, and make these records accessible to the framework. The stored records contain aggregated information over the whole compression, as well as detailed information about the achieved compression ratio and run time duration of each individual module, which was used to compress the corresponding data. The last part of the framework is the central decision unit, which selects the modules, used for the current window. Its strategy is implemented by the user and can range from a simple selection of the same compression modules for each frame in the window, to complex strategies based on information provided by the monitoring component and external information.

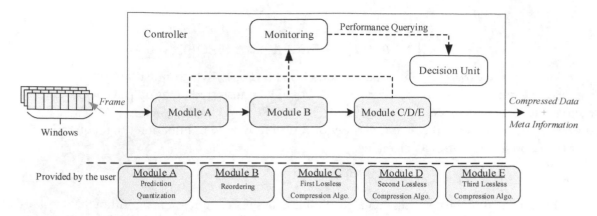

Figure 3. A block diagram of the individual components of the compression framework, and their interaction with each other.

In the next section we describe how to choose the most suitable configuration of different encoding algorithms during run time.

Optimization

The objective of the optimization is to find a proper decision policy with respect to the optimization goals. A goal can be to maximize the total compression ratio (C_{total}) given restrictions on computing time and network bandwidth. Thus, the total output rate (R_{total}) should be slightly higher than the available network throughput (TR_{av}). This goal can be formulated as:

$$\max\{C_{total}|R_{total} > TR_{av}\}. \tag{11}$$

The optimization process is done only once at the beginning, and the decision unit will use the results of the optimization process during run time. To achieve a more adaptive behavior the optimization process can of course be repeated during run time at the cost of computation time.

In order to adjust the output rate, the decision unit changes the ratio between the amount of lossless compression algorithms invocations during run time. Therefore, we define a window size, which represents the number of subsequent frames, for which the output rate of the compression is adjusted. A fraction of those frames in the window is then compressed with different lossless compression algorithms. Therefore window size can be defined as

$$WindowSize = \sum_{i=1}^{n} x_i, \tag{12}$$

where x_i is the number of invocations of the i-th lossless compression algorithm, and n is the number of the lossless compression algorithms. For every lossless compression algorithm we have defined the output rate as:

$$R_i = \frac{CS_i}{t_i}, \tag{13}$$

and the compression ratio obtained by the i-th lossless compression algorithm as:

$$C_i = \frac{DS}{CS_i}, \tag{14}$$

where CS_i is the size of the compressed data obtained by the i-th lossless compression algorithm, DS is the size of one frame, and t_i is the required time to compress one frame. Since the data that are in subsequent frames are very similar, it is assumed that every lossless compression algorithms achieves an almost identical compression ratio and output rate for subsequent frames. The validity of this assumption is proven experimentally in Section 5.4. By considering this assumption the total compression ratio in a window is given by:

$$C_{total} = \frac{WindowSize \times DS}{\sum\limits_{i=1}^{n} x_i \times CS_i}$$

$$= \frac{WindowSize}{\sum\limits_{i=1}^{n} x_i/C_i}, \tag{15}$$

and the total output rate of a window can be calculated from:

$$R_{total} = \frac{x_1 \times CS_1 + x_2 \times CS_2 + \ldots + x_n \times CS_n}{x_1 \times t_1 + x_2 \times t_2 + \ldots + x_n \times t_n}$$

$$= \frac{\sum\limits_{i=1}^{n} (x_i \times CS_i)}{\sum\limits_{i=1}^{n} (x_i \times t_i)}. \tag{16}$$

From Equations (13), (14) and (16), we have:

$$R_{total} = \frac{\sum\limits_{i=1}^{n} (x_i \times DS/C_i)}{\sum\limits_{i=1}^{n} (x_i \times (DS/(C_i \times R_i)))}$$

$$= \frac{\sum\limits_{i=1}^{n} (x_i/C_i)}{\sum\limits_{i=1}^{n} (x_i/(C_i \times R_i))}. \tag{17}$$

According to the Equation (11), the optimization constraint is $R_{total} > R_{av}$. From Equation (17), we have:

$$\frac{\sum\limits_{i=1}^{n} (x_i/C_i)}{\sum\limits_{i=1}^{n} (x_i/(C_i \times R_i))} > TR_{av}, \tag{18}$$

and this can be written as:

$$\sum\limits_{i=1}^{n} \frac{x_i}{C_i}(1 - TR_{av}/R_i) > 0. \tag{19}$$

By considering the Equations (11), (12), (15), and (19), the optimization problem is to find a n-vector, $X = (x_1, \cdots, x_n)^T$, to maximize C_{total}, subject to the following constraints:

$$X \in \mathbb{Z}^n, \quad X \geq 0,$$

$$\sum\limits_{i=1}^{n} x_i = WindowSize, \tag{20}$$

$$AX > b,$$

where $A = ((1/C_1 - TR_{av}/(C_1 \times R_1)), \cdots, (1/C_n - TR_{av}/(C_n \times R_n)))$, and $b = 0$. This problem is solved with the simplex method, which is a method for solving systems of linear inequalities [31].

5. Results and Discussion

In this section, the proposed compression algorithm and adaptive compression framework is evaluated.

5.1. Simulation Case

We have evaluated our compression algorithm and adaptive compression framework based on a use case: simulation of the flow behavior of gas injection. For our simulation we use the original geometry of a natural gas injector (NGI) as shown in Figure 4a. This injector is used in a number of compressed natural gas powered vehicles. For this paper, we focus on the external flow behind the injector. Within this flow, shocks and turbulent shear layers are present, which emit pressure waves. From these pressure signals we can derive sound pressure levels (SPLs) directly from the simulation. The injector has four kidney shaped exits. We apply a direct aeroacoustic simulation, which allows us to calculate the sound pressure level directly from the simulation data. The compressed natural gas exits the four kidney shaped orifices at supersonic conditions and under expanded supersonic jets form. The normal velocity, pressure, density and Mach number are $w = 505$ ms^{-1}, $p = 244$ kPa, $\rho = 1.97$ kg m^{-3} and $Ma = 1.21$. The simulations are performed on 163,691 DG-elements with an order of $N = 4$.

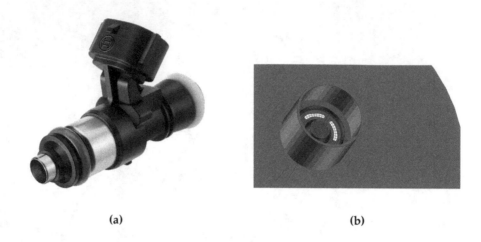

(a)   (b)

Figure 4. The real world use case behind the CFD simulations considered here: (**a**) natural gas injector with the injector outlet at the bottom left and (**b**) the surface mesh of the computational model for the injector outlet [32].

Each element has $(N+1)^3 = 125$ degrees of freedom which leads to 20,461,375 degrees of freedom. For each DOF the conservative variables $\boldsymbol{u} = (\rho, \rho v_1, \rho v_2, \rho v_3, \rho e)^T$ are stored. The surface mesh of the external injector is shown in Figure 4b. For a more detailed description of the geometry and the boundaries we refer to Kraus et al. [33]. The simulation is in excellent agreement with experiential data from [34]. The data compression used here are performed on all conservative variables, which are double precision floating point.

5.2. Compression Ratio

Figure 5 shows the compression ratio comparison at different permissible maximum relative errors and for four different ΔT_f and different framework configurations. ΔT_f indicates the lapsed simulation time between subsequent simulation frames that are stored (measured in number of time steps). In our simulation, a time step corresponds to ≈ 5 ns, and the compression ratio is defined as the ratio of the uncompressed data size to the compressed data size.

Figure 5a shows the compression ratio comparison without considering ROIs. It can be observed that the smaller ΔT_f the higher the compression ratio. The reason is that by having a smaller ΔT_f the prediction module predicts better, which leads to smaller residuals. For instance, when $\Delta T_f = 1$, the compression ratio range from 4.17 to 14.64. For $\Delta T_f = 1000$, the compression ratio decreases significantly, ranging between 2.8 and 6. From the result it can also be observed that after increasing ΔT_f above a certain value, the compression ratios remain almost constant. For instance the compression ratios for $\Delta T_f = 100$ and $\Delta T_f = 1000$ are almost identical. This indicates that, for large gaps between two time steps the predictor module no longer brings any advantages, and the remaining compression ratio is mainly due to the quantization module and the lossless compression algorithm. This is expected and in such cases, the algorithms that exploit spatial correlation or higher degrees predictors are recommended.

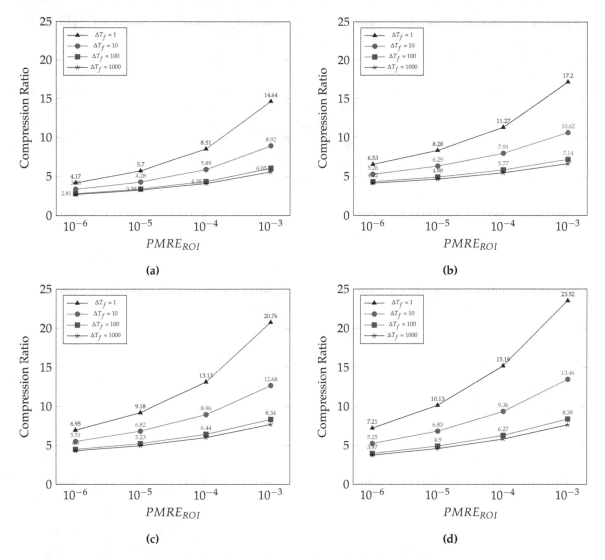

Figure 5. Each sub-figure shows the compression ratio comparison for different $PMRE_{ROI}$ and for various ΔT_f. The configuration of the: (**a**) ROI and Reordering modules are not enabled; (**b**) only ROI module is enabled, ROI condition: $T > 300K$, $PMRE_{non-ROI} = 10^{-2}$; (**c**) both ROI module and Reordering modules are enabled, ROI condition: $T > 300K$, $PMRE_{non-ROI} = 10^{-2}$; (**d**) both ROI module and Reordering modules are enabled, ROI condition: $T < 300K$, $PMRE_{non-ROI} = 10^{-2}$.

Figure 5b shows the compression ratio comparison considering ROIs. In this evaluation, the ROI is defined based on the temperature range. The temperature of all the nodes in one DG-element is measured, and if one of them has a temperature over 300 K, that DG-element is considered within the ROI. The $PMRE_{non-ROI}$ is equal to 10^{-2}, and the $PMRE_{ROI}$ varies from 10^{-3} to 10^{-6}. In this evaluation almost 50% of the DG-elements are in the region of interest, and the comparison with the previous configuration shows an average improvement of 30%. Figure 5c shows the compression ratio comparison considering ROIs and activating the reordering module. It can be seen that by reordering the nodes of each DG-elements and grouping the prediction residual of each parameter together, leads to an average improvement of 10% compared to the previous configuration. Figure 5d shows the compression ratio comparison considering ROIs with the condition being a temperature of less than 300 K. In this case, the ROI data values have much smaller variance and are more predictable than the previous ROI, which has more turbulences, leading to higher compression ratios.

5.3. Compression Performance

Figure 6 shows the relation between compression throughputs and compression ratio by applying different lossless compression algorithms. For this evaluation the throughput is defined as the original size divided by the required time to compress the data. Three different lossless compression algorithms namely, Bzip2 [28], Zlib [29] and FSE [30] are used in the compression framework. The Zlib library uses the LZ77 algorithm followed by a Huffman coding, whereas the Bzip2 algorithm first applies a Burrows–Wheeler transform on the data, followed by a run length encoding and also a Huffman coding. Finite state entropy (FSE) is a fast entropy encoder that has the same level of performance as Arithmetic coder, but only requires additions, masks, and shifts. Therefore, it is much faster than the other lossless compression algorithms. Our results show that it is almost 10 times faster than Bzip2 and six-times faster than Zlib. This benchmark is highly dependent on the data sets and requires online monitoring of the performance and compression ratio which is done by the proposed adaptive compression framework.

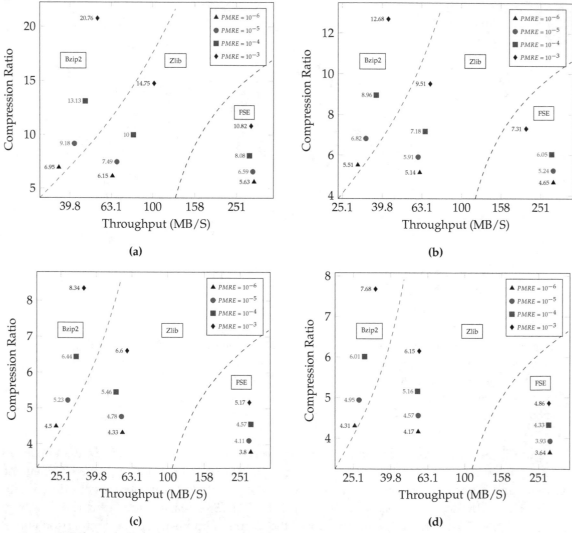

Figure 6. Relation between compression throughputs and compression ratios for different configurations while considering three different lossless compression algorithms. ROI condition: $T > 300\ K$, $PMRE_{non-ROI} = 10^{-2}$. (a) $\Delta T_f = 1$; (b) $\Delta T_f = 10$; (c) $\Delta T_f = 100$; (d) $\Delta T_f = 1000$.

5.4. Compression Algorithm Comparison

In order to evaluate the compression efficiency of this work, we have made comparisons with five lossy compression algorithms, which are applicable to floating point simulation data. The following tests were conducted on a Core i7-3520M CPU @ 2.9GHz. For these comparisons, the throughput is defined as the amount of original size divided by the required time to compress the data. Tables 1 and 2 list the compression ratio and the throughput comparison between the proposed algorithm and seven other lossy compression algorithms. In order to have a fair comparison, no ROI was considered for these comparisons. This means that $PMRE_{ROI}$ is equal to $PMRE_{non-ROI}$. All algorithms exploit the correlations of nearby values either spatial or temporal, and all of them are performed on structured $5 \times 5 \times 5$ DG-element.

Table 1. The comparison of the compression ratio for three different *PMRE*.

PMRE	10^{-3}	10^{-4}	10^{-5}
Proposed Algorithm $_{\Delta T_f = 1000, 100, 10, 1}$	6.4, 7, **10.7**, 17.8	4.6, 4.8, **6.7**, 10.3	3.4, 3.6, **4.7**, 6.4
Lorenzo Predictor-1D	8.1	5.4	3.9
Lorenzo Predictor-2D	9	5.9	4.2
Lorenzo Predictor-3D	**9.48**	**6.28**	**4.5**
FPZIP	6.7	5.4	4
ZFP *	7.9	4.1	2.6
ISABELA	3.9	2.9	2.4

* mean relative error is considered instead of *PMRE*.

Table 2. The throughput comparison for three different *PMRE*. Throughput unit is MB/s.

PMRE	10^{-3}	10^{-4}	10^{-5}
Proposed Algorithm $_{\Delta T_f = 1000, 100, 10, 1}$	30.9, 33.1, 37.2, 47.1	24.2, 25.4, 32.7, 36.2	22.3, 22.9, 25.3, 31.8
Lorenzo Predictor-1D	32.3	28.8	23.1
Lorenzo Predictor-2D	36.2	30.4	23.6
Lorenzo Predictor-3D	36.9	30.3	25.6
FPZIP	**89.1**	**73.1**	**63.5**
ZFP *	63.97	54.21	40.1
ISABELA	3.7	4.4	5.1

* mean relative error is considered instead of *PMRE*.

The first three comparisons involved changing the temporal predictor with three types of Lorenzo predictor while keeping all the other aspects of the algorithm unchanged for fair comparison. Three categories of Lorenzo predictors are shown in Figure 7. The value of the corner "p" should be predicted by adding the value of the green corners and subtracting to the value of the red corners. In case of 1D Lorenzo only a neighboring value is considered as the predicted value, in this case $p(x,y,z,t) = a(x-1,y,z,t)$ and if $x = 0$ then $p(0,y,z,t) = 0$. The variable $a(x,y,z,t)$ indicates the value of the point (x,y,z) at the time t. The proposed method is also in one dimension but in time, i.e., $p(x,z,y,t) = a(x,z,y,t-1)$. The 2D Lorenzo is applied in xy plane, where $p(x,y,z,t) = a(x-1,y,z,t) + a(x,y-1,z,t) - a(x-1,y-1,z,t)$. Similarly, the 3D Lorenzo predictor uses full 3D spatial prediction. For the boundary samples to be predicted, one layer of zero is padded in each dimension as proposed by [20]. Due to the lossy compression, all predicted values are updated by reconstructed values since these values are only ones available to the decompressor [20]. In this evaluation, Bzip2 [28] is used as a lossless compression algorithm for all compression algorithm. By comparing the compression ratios it can be observed that the three dimensional Lorenzo predictor has the highest compression ratio among the other algorithms. The proposed algorithm can only outperforms it when ΔT_f is less than 100.

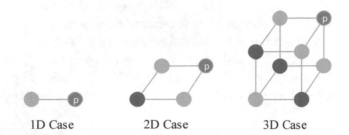

Figure 7. Three different types of Lorenzo predictor [25] that are applied for comparison.

FPZIP is the next algorithm which is considered in our benchmarking list [20,23]. FPZIP also applies the three dimensional Lorenzo predictor, however the compression is less than three dimensional Lorenzo that is discussed earlier. In the previous case we used the adaptive quantization method that is explained in Section 3.3 followed by Bzip2 which is a complex and slow lossless compression algorithm, while FPZIP performs different residual computation. However, due to the fast and optimized entropy encoder, FPZIP has the highest throughput among the other compression algorithms which are listed in Table 2.

ZFP is another compression algorithm that is considered for comparison [24]. ZFP handles three dimensional structure, therefore no dimension conversion is required. However, ZFP cannot bound the maximum relative error, therefore mean relative error instead of PMRE were ensured experimentally by varying the precision. The results shows that ZFP is among the fastest compression algorithms and has the second rank after FPZIP, and it is almost two times faster than the proposed compression algorithm in combination with Bzip2.

The last algorithm which is used for comparison is ISABELA, in which the relative error can be bounded [18]. In the first step each three dimensional DG-element is converted to a single dimension. Therefore, the ISABELA window size has 125 double precision floating point data. These data are sorted before performing the compression by B-spline interpolation. We have considered 10 points for B-spline curve fitting algorithm. In order to gain more compression ratio, Bzip2 is performed in the last step. The results shows that neither compression ratio nor throughput are comparable with other compression techniques. The main reason is that the ISABELA is originally designed for the data set which are random and noisy, which is not the case for the considered simulation data. Furthermore, sorting algorithm and B-splines curve fitting significantly degrade the throughout.

The combined information of Tables 1 and 2 gives a holistic view on the interplay between compression ratio, throughput and quality (PMRE) and equips simulation experts with a greater degree of freedom. In case of the proposed algorithm, the compression ratio and the throughput is dependent on ΔT_f as evident from both Tables 1 and 2. It can be observed that the proposed algorithm performs better than the other algorithms when the $\Delta T_f < 100$. As ΔT_f increases the performance of the proposed algorithm drops in comparison to most other compression algorithms discussed in this work, however, even at $\Delta T_f = 1000$ the proposed algorithm is still able to outperform state of the art compressor like ZFP for $PMRE \leq 10^{-4}$.

5.5. Adaptive Compression

The ability of the framework to optimize the dynamic selection of the lossless compression algorithm during run time is shown in Figure 8. In this example three lossless compression algorithms are considered. *WindowSize* is equal to 20, which represents the number of subsequent frames in each windows, and $DS = 50,000$ bytes. A fraction of the frames in each window is then compressed with Zlib, a fraction of them is compressed with Bzip2 and the rest with FSE encoder. In this evaluation the optimization algorithm was performed only once at the very beginning. The available throughput increases up to 50 MB/s. It can be seen that by invoking different lossless compression algorithms the total output rate follows the available throughput. If the total output rate is greater than the available throughput, the compressed data will be buffered.

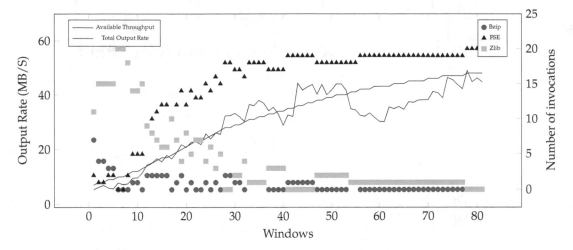

Figure 8. Dynamic adaptation of the compression algorithm to available throughput by varying the number of the lossless compression algorithm invocations for each window.

In order to derive Equations (15) and (16) we assumed that each lossless compression algorithm has almost identical output rate and compression ratio in one window. To prove these assumption we calculated the relative standard deviation (RSD) of the compression ratio and output rate of each lossless compression algorithm in each window. Let C_{ij} be the compression ratio of the i-th algorithm at the j-th frame of a window, and s_i the frame position that the i-th algorithm start compressing the data . Then the relative standard deviation of the compression ratio of the i-th compression algorithm is given by:

$$RSD_{C,i} = 100\% \times \frac{\sqrt{\frac{1}{x_i} \sum_{j=s_i}^{x_i} (C_{ij} - \overline{C_i})^2}}{\overline{C_i}}, \tag{21}$$

where $\overline{C_i}$ denotes the average compression ratio of all the frames in a window that are compressed with i-th compression algorithm. The same equation also holds for output rate, the relative standard deviation of the output rate of the i-th compression algorithm is given by:

$$RSD_{R,i} = 100\% \times \frac{\sqrt{\frac{1}{x_i} \sum_{j=s_i}^{x_i} (R_{ij} - \overline{R_i})^2}}{\overline{R_i}}, \tag{22}$$

where $\overline{R_i}$ denotes the average output rate of all the frames in a window that are compressed with i-th compression algorithm. $RSD_{C,i}$ and $RSD_{T,i}$ are calculated for 80 windows, where each window contains 20 frames. The results are shown in Figure 9a for compression ratio and Figure 9b for output rate respectively. It can be observed that the maximum deviation from the average value in the worst case is around 15% for the compression ratios and almost 10% for the output rates. This is an indication that we can assume that each lossless compression algorithm provides almost identical compression ratio and output rate in one window.

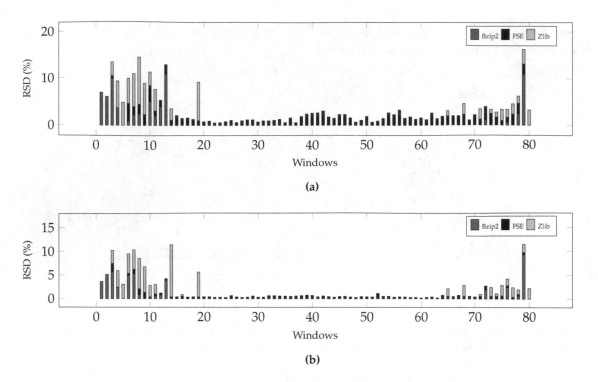

(a)

(b)

Figure 9. (a) The relative standard deviation of the compression ratio of each lossless compression algorithm in each window; (b) the relative standard deviation of the output rate of each lossless compression algorithm in each window.

5.6. Temperature Analysis

In this section, the effect of lossy compression on the temperature (T) is investigated. The Temperature unit is Kelvin and is computed as:

$$T = \frac{p}{\rho R_s},\tag{23}$$

where the R_s is the specific gas constant, ρ is the density, and pressure (p) is given by:

$$p = (\kappa - 1)(\rho e_{tot} - \frac{1}{2}\rho v^2),\tag{24}$$

where κ is the heat capacity ratio and the velocity is computed as:

$$v = \sqrt{v_1^2 + v_2^2 + v_3^2}.\tag{25}$$

In order to assess the quality of the decompressed data, three quality measures are considered: maximum relative error (MRE), maximum absolute error ($| e |_{max}$) and root mean square error (RMSE); where,

$$MRE = \max(\frac{| T_i - \hat{T}_i |}{T_i}),\tag{26}$$

$$| e |_{max} = \max(| T_i - \hat{T}_i |),\tag{27}$$

and:

$$RMSE = \sqrt{\frac{1}{i - n}\sum_{i=1}^{n}(| T_i - \hat{T}_i |)^2},\tag{28}$$

where T_i refers to the temperature of each point with the scale of Kelvin and, $\hat{T}_i$ is the corresponding reconstructed value. Table 3 lists the MRE, $|e|_{max}$, RMSE and compression ratio (C) for ROI and non-ROI with respect to the various $PMRE_{ROI}$ and $PMRE_{non-ROI}$ of the conservative variables. In this evaluation, a DG-element is considered in the ROI if it has a temperature above 300 K. The $PMRE_{non-ROI}$ is taken to be one order of magnitude larger than $PMRE_{ROI}$. It can be seen that in the first evaluation where $PMRE_{ROI} = 10^{-2}$, the achieved compression ratio is very high. However, the quality of the decompressed data is low. In this case the maximum absolute error of almost 10 degrees for the ROI should be expected. It can be observed that the accuracy of the temperature improves by the same factor as the conservative PMRE improvement. A decent trade off between compression ratio and decompressed data quality can be seen in the third evaluation, where $PMRE_{ROI} = 10^{-4}$ and the maximum absolute error is almost 0.1 K. In this case a compression ratio of around 11 is achievable. Another fact is that the relative error of the temperature value is increased by four times compared to the relative error of the conservative values. The reason is that the relative error will be increased by arithmetic operations that are required to calculate the temperature value. For a more detailed description of error propagation we refer to [35].

Table 3. Comparison of the decompressed data quality for ROI and non-ROI, as well as corresponding compression ratios.

Cons. Var.				Temperature				Compression Ratio
PMRE		MRE		$|e|_{max}$		RMSE		
ROI	non-ROI	ROI	non-ROI	ROI	non-ROI	ROI	non-ROI	$\Delta T_f = 1$
10^{-2}	10^{-1}	0.0397	0.34	14.60	149.4	2.7	2.07	38.77
10^{-3}	10^{-2}	0.0043	0.032	1.43	14.57	0.28	1.42	20.76
10^{-4}	10^{-3}	0.00042	0.0030	0.13	1.4	0.0277	0.22	11.88
10^{-5}	10^{-4}	0.00004	0.0003	0.014	0.14	0.0027	0.023	7.54

Figure 10 shows the influence of the lossy data compression for the visualization of the temperature distribution. Figure 10b illustrates that by setting $PMRE_{ROI}$ to 10^{-3} and $PMRE_{non-ROI}$ to 10^{-2}, a compression ratio of up to 20.76 can be achieved and the decompressed data are visually identical to the original data. However, by introducing more loss, as it it can be observed in Figure 10c, the data can be compressed almost two times more than the previous case, but an absolute error of up to 14.6 K in region of interest can occur.

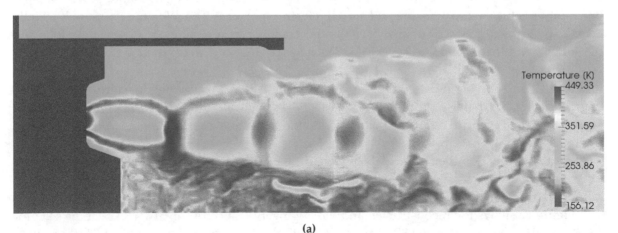

(a)

Figure 10. *Cont.*

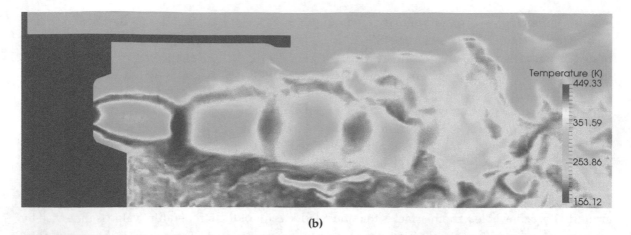

(b)

(c)

Figure 10. Influence of the data compression on the visualization of the temperature distribution, ROI condition: $T > 300$. (a) Original data; (b) decompressed data, $PMRE_{ROI} = 10^{-3}$, $PMRE_{non-ROI} = 10^{-2}$, C = 20.76; (c) decompressed data, $PMRE_{ROI} = 10^{-2}$, $PMRE_{non-ROI} = 10^{-1}$, C = 38.77.

5.7. Sound Pressure Level Analysis

The sound pressure level (SPL) is used for measuring the magnitude of sound. SPL is the ratio between the actual sound pressure and a fixed reference pressure. The reference pressure is usually taken to be 20 micro pascals. For analyzing the effect of lossy compression on SPLs we have followed the simulation set–up proposed by [33,34], which has been shown to reproduce experimental data very accurately.

As is depicted in Figure 11, four observation areas, P1-P4, are considered for calculating the SPL, each consisting of 20 points. The pressure signals for each point are recorded at every time step and are averaged over 20 evenly distributed points around the center line axis. Afterwards, a transformation from the pressure signals to a SPL spectra is performed.

For this evaluation the regions which have the temperature less than 300 K are considered as ROIs, and compression ratio of up to 23.5 is achieved. Figure 5d shows the obtained compression ratios under different configurations.

Figure 12 shows the reconstructed and the original SPL spectra for P1-P4. As can be seen for $PMRE \leq 10^{-4}$, the reconstructed SPL are almost identical to the original SPL. In case of $PMRE = 10^{-3}$, the reconstructed SPL follows the trend of the original SPL but has a maximum absolute deviation of 5 db. However, if the peak value of the SPL spectrum is the value of interest, which is the case for some applications [36], the reconstructed SPL shows nearly the same peak values as the original SPL. This is an indication that even highly compressed data can be used effectively for SPL analysis.

It is worth to mention that averaging over 20 points reduces the inaccuracy which may be caused by the quantization.

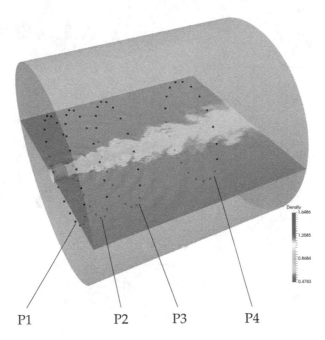

Figure 11. The kidney-shaped orifices and the simulation domain behind the injector with a cutting surface. The cutting surface shows a snapshot of the density. Four sets of observation points (P1 to P4) with different distances to the orifice are defined.

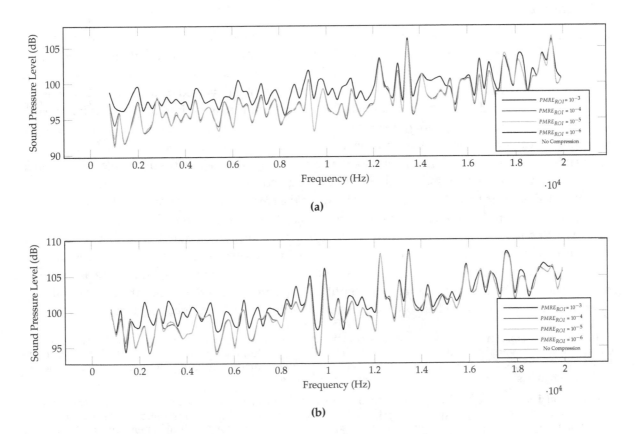

Figure 12. *Cont.*

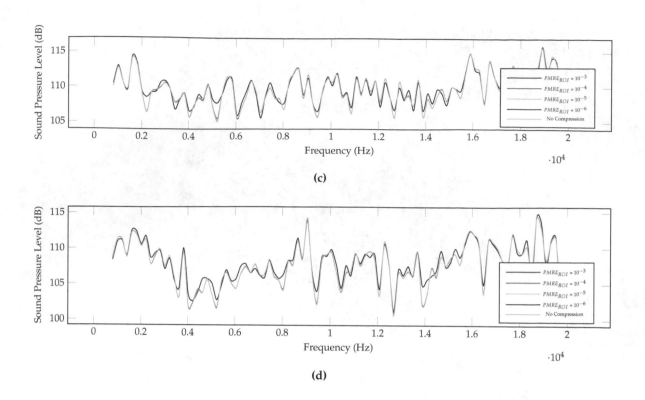

Figure 12. Shows sound pressure level spectrum with various $PMRE_{ROI}$ at four different areas: (**a**) P1; (**b**) P2; (**c**) P3; (**d**) P4.

6. Conclusions

In this work, an adaptive prediction-based lossy compression scheme for compressing CFD simulation data is introduced to overcome storage requirements and I/O bandwidth limitation. In the proposed method, the inaccuracy caused by the lossy compression is adjustable and depends on the post processing requirements and ROI. In this work, the ROIs are indicated by a specified temperature range and are detected at run time. Additionally, by introducing an adaptive compression framework, the compression modules can adapt to the available network throughput. The proposed compression algorithm and adaptive compression framework are evaluated by the investigation of the flow behavior of gas injection. For our simulation, we use the original geometry of a natural gas injector, which is used in a number of compressed natural gas-powered vehicles. The compression ratios depend on the requested accuracy and the time interval between the stored simulation frames. The experimental results have shown that the compression ratio can easily vary from 2.8 to 23.5, and an average of 90% reduction in the data size is achievable. As a primary contribution of this work, we have shown that with reasonable choices for the permissible maximum relative error due to compression, the accuracy of post processing analysis such as sound pressure level and temperature measurements remain reliable. The lossless compression algorithms that are used in this paper are general purpose; more advanced and suitable lossless compression algorithms are considered as a future work.

Acknowledgments: The authors would like to thank the German Research Foundation (DFG), the SimTech Cluster of the University of Stuttgart and the Federal Ministry of Education and Research (BMBF) within the HPCIII project HONK "Industrialisierung von hochauflösender Numerik für komplexe Strömungsvorgänge in hydraulischen Systemen" for the financial support of this project.

Author Contributions: Seyyed Mahdi Najmabadi and Moritz Hamann contributed to the design and development of the data compression algorithm. Philipp Offenhäuser contributed to the CFD simulation and post processing. Guhathakurta Jajnabalkya performed the comparison of the compression algorithm. Fabian Hempert provided the simulation model. Colin W. Glass formulated the original approach and supervised the work together with Sven Simon.

Abbreviations

The following abbreviations are used in this manuscript:

ROI	Region of interest
CFD	Computational fluid dynamics
SPL	Sound pressure level
PMRE	Permissible maximum relative error
MRE	Maximum relative error
RMSE	Root mean square error
DWT	Discrete wavelet transform
FSE	Finite state entropy
MB	Mega bytes
DG	Discontinuous Galerkin
DG SEM	Discontinuous Galerkin spectral element method
DOF	Degrees of freedom
RSD	Relative standard deviatio
DCT	Discrete cosine transform
NGI	Natural gas injector

References

1. Strohmaier, E.; Dongarra, J.; Simon, H.; Meuer, M. Top500 List—June 2016. Available online: https://www.top500.org/list/2016/06/ (accessed on 5 June 2016).

2. Hindenlang, F.; Gassner, G.J.; Altmann, C.; Beck, A.; Staudenmaier, M.; Munz, C.D. Explicit discontinuous Galerkin methods for unsteady problems. *Comput. Fluids* **2012**, *61*, 86–93.

3. Atak, M.; Beck, A.; Bolemann, T.; Flad, D.; Frank, H.; Munz, C.D. High Fidelity Scale-Resolving Computational Fluid Dynamics Using the High Order Discontinuous Galerkin Spectral Element Method. In *High Performance Computing in Science and Engineering, Transactions of the High Performance Computing Center, Stuttgart (HLRS) 2015*; Nagel, E.W., Kröner, H.D., Resch, M.M., Eds.; Springer: Cham, Switzerland, 2016; pp. 511–530.

4. Cetin, M.O.; Pogorelov, A.; Lintermann, A.; Cheng, H.J.; Meinke, M.; Schröder, W. Large-Scale Simulations of a Non-Generic Helicopter Engine Nozzle and a Ducted Axial Fan. In *High Performance Computing in Science and Engineering, Transactions of the High Performance Computing Center, Stuttgart (HLRS) 2015*; Nagel, E.W., Kröner, H.D., Resch, M.M., Eds.; Springer: Cham, Switzerland, 2016; pp. 389–405.

5. Burtscher, M.; Mukka, H.; Yang, A.; Hesaaraki, F. Real-Time Synthesis of Compression Algorithms for Scientific Data. In Proceedings of the International Conference for High Performance Computing, Networking, Storage and Analysis, SC '16, Salt Lake City, UT, USA, 13–18 November 2016; IEEE Press: Piscataway, NJ, USA, 2016; pp. 23:1–23:12.

6. Treib, M.; Bürger, K.; Wu, J.; Westermann, R. Analyzing the Effect of Lossy Compression on Particle Traces in Turbulent Vector Fields. In Proceedings of the 6th International Conference on Information Visualization Theory and Applications, Berlin, Germany, 11–14 March 2015; pp. 279–288.

7. Laney, D.; Langer, S.; Weber, C.; Lindstrom, P.; Wegener, A. Assessing the Effects of Data Compression in Simulations Using Physically Motivated Metrics. In Proceedings of the International Conference on High Performance Computing, Networking, Storage and Analysis, SC '13, Denver, CO, USA, 17–22 November 2013; ACM: New York, NY, USA, 2013; pp. 76:1–76:12.

8. Baker, A.H.; Hammerling, D.M.; Mickelson, S.A.; Xu, H.; Stolpe, M.B.; Naveau, P.; Sanderson, B.; Ebert-Uphoff, I.; Samarasinghe, S.; de Simone, F.; et al. Evaluating lossy data compression on climate simulation data within a large ensemble. *Geosci. Model Dev.* **2016**, *9*, 4381–4403.

9. Toro, E.F. *Riemann Solvers and Numerical Methods for Fluid Dynamics—A Practical Introduction*, 3rd ed.; Springer: Berlin/Heidelberg, Germany, 2009.

10. Schmalzl, J. Using standard image compression algorithms to store data from computational fluid dynamics. *Comput. Geosci.* **2003**, *29*, 1021–1031.

11. Kang, H.; Lee, D.; Lee, D. A study on CFD data compression using hybrid supercompact wavelets. *KSME Int. J.* **2003**, *17*, 1784–1792.

12. Sakai, R.; Sasaki, D.; Nakahashi, K. Parallel implementation of large-scale CFD data compression toward aeroacoustic analysis. *Comput. Fluids* **2013**, *80*, 116–127.

13. Sakai, R.; Sasaki, D.; Obayashi, S.; Nakahashi, K. Wavelet-based data compression for flow simulation on block-structured Cartesian mesh. *Int. J. Numer. Methods Fluids* **2013**, *73*, 462–476.

14. Sakai, R.; Sasaki, D.; Nakahashi, K. Data Compression of Large-Scale Flow Computation Using Discrete Wavelet Transform. In Proceedings of the 48th AIAA Aerospace Sciences Meeting Including the New Horizons Forum and Aerospace Exposition, Orlando, FL, USA, 4–7 January 2010; Volume 1325.

15. Sakai, R.; Onda, H.; Sasaki, D.; Nakahashi, K. Data Compression of Large-Scale Flow Computation for Aerodynamic/Aeroacoustic Analysis. In Proceedings of the 49th AIAA Aerospace Sciences Meeting Including the New Horizons Forum and Aerospace Exposition, Orlando, FL, USA, 4–7 January 2011.

16. Ballester-Ripoll, R.; Pajarola, R. Lossy volume compression using Tucker truncation and thresholding. *Vis. Comput.* **2016**, *32*, 1433–1446.

17. Austin, W.; Ballard, G.; Kolda, T.G. Parallel Tensor Compression for Large-Scale Scientific Data. In Proceedings of the 2016 IEEE International Parallel and Distributed Processing Symposium (IPDPS), Chicago, IL, USA, 23–27 May 2016; pp. 912–922.

18. Lakshminarasimhan, S.; Shah, N.; Ethier, S.; Ku, S.H.; Chang, C.S.; Klasky, S.; Latham, R.; Ross, R.B.; Samatova, N.F. ISABELA for effective in situ compression of scientific data. *Concurr. Comput. Pract. Exp.* **2013**, *25*, 524–540.

19. Iverson, J.; Kamath, C.; Karypis, G. Fast and Effective Lossy Compression Algorithms for Scientific Datasets. In *Lecture Notes in Computer Science, Processings of the Euro-Par 2012: Parallel Processing Workshops, Rhodes Island, Greece, 27–31 August 2012*; Kaklamanis, C., Papatheodorou, T., Spirakis, P.G., Eds.; Springer: Berlin/Heidelberg, Germany, 2012; pp. 843–856.

20. Lindstrom, P.; Isenburg, M. Fast and Efficient Compression of Floating-Point Data. *IEEE Trans. Vis. Comput. Graph.* **2006**, *12*, 1245–1250.

21. Chen, Z.; Son, S.W.; Hendrix, W.; Agrawal, A.; Liao, W.K.; Choudhary, A. NUMARCK: Machine Learning Algorithm for Resiliency and Checkpointing. In Proceedings of the International Conference for High Performance Computing, Networking, Storage and Analysis, SC '14, New Orleans, LA, USA, 16–21 November 2014; IEEE Press: Piscataway, NJ, USA, 2014; pp. 733–744.

22. Lakshminarasimhan, S.; Shah, N.; Ethier, S.; Klasky, S.; Latham, R.; Ross, R.; Samatova, N.F. Compressing the Incompressible with ISABELA: In-Situ Reduction of Spatio-Temporal Data. In *Lecture Notes in Computer Science, Processings of the 17th International European Conference on Parallel and Distributed Computing Euro-Par 2011, Bordeaux, France, 29 August–2 September 2011*; Jeannot, E., Namyst, R., Roman, J., Eds.; Springer: Berlin/Heidelberg, Germany, 2011; pp. 366–379.

23. Lindstrom, P. FPZIP Version 1.1.0. Available online: https://computation.llnl.gov/casc/fpzip (accessed on 10 March 2017).

24. Lindstrom, P. Fixed-Rate Compressed Floating-Point Arrays. *IEEE Trans. Vis. Comput. Graph.* **2014**, *20*, 2674–2683.

25. Ibarria, L.; Lindstrom, P.; Rossignac, J.; Szymczak, A. Out-of-core compression and decompression of large n-dimensional scalar fields. *Comput. Graph. Forum* **2003**, doi:10.1111/1467-8659.00681.

26. Sayood, K. *Introduction to Data Compression*, 2nd ed.; Morgan Kaufmann Publishers: San Francisco, CA, USA, 2000.

27. Fout, N.; Ma, K.L. An Adaptive Prediction-Based Approach to Lossless Compression of Floating-Point Volume Data. *IEEE Trans. Vis. Comput. Graph.* **2012**, *18*, 2295–2304.

28. Seward, J. bzip2. Available online: http://www.bzip.org/ (accessed on 20 October 2016).

29. Gailly, J.; Adler, M. zlib. Available online: http://www.zlib.net/ (accessed on 20 October 2016).

30. Collet, Y. New Generation Entropy Codecs: Finite State Entropy. Available online: https://github.com/Cyan4973/FiniteStateEntropy (accessed on 20 October 2016).

31. Schrijver, A. *Theory of Linear and Integer Programming*; John Wiley & Sons, Inc.: New York, NY, USA, 1986.

32. Boblest, S.; Hempert, F.; Hoffmann, M.; Offenhäuser, P.; Sonntag, M.; Sadlo, F.; Glass, C.W.; Munz, C.D.; Ertl, T.; Iben, U. Toward a Discontinuous Galerkin Fluid Dynamics Framework for Industrial Applications. In *High Performance Computing in Science and Engineering' 15*; Heidelberg, S.B., Ed.; Springer: Heidelberg, Geramny, 2015; pp. 531–545.

33. Kraus, T.; Hindenlang, F.; Harlacher, D.; Munz, C.D.; Roller, S. Direct Noise Simulation of Near Field Noise during a Gas Injection Process with a Discontinuous Galerkin Approach. In Proceedings of the 33rd AIAA Aeroacoustics Conference, Colorado Springs, CO, USA, 4–6 June 2012.

34. Hempert, F.; Hoffmann, M.; Iben, U.; Munz, C.D. On the simulation of industrial gas dynamic applications with the discontinuous Galerkin spectral element method. *J. Therm. Sci.* **2016**, *25*, 250–257.

35. Ku, H.H. Notes on the use of propagation of error formulas. *J. Res. Natl. Bur. Stand. C Eng. Instrum.* **1966**, *70*, 263–273.

36. Robinson, M.; Hopkins, C. Effects of signal processing on the measurement of maximum sound pressure levels. *Appl. Acoust.* **2014**, *77*, 11–19.

5

Using an Interactive Lattice Boltzmann Solver in Fluid Mechanics Instruction

Mirjam S. Glessmer [1,*,†] and Christian F. Janßen [2,†]

[1]   Physics Education, Leibniz Institute for Science and Mathematics Education, Olshausenstraße 62, 24118 Kiel, Germany

[2]   Institute for Fluid Dynamics and Ship Theory, Hamburg University of Technology, Am Schwarzenberg-Campus 4, 21073 Hamburg, Germany; christian.janssen@tuhh.de

*   Correspondence: glessmer@ipn.uni-kiel.de

†   These authors contributed equally to this work.

Abstract: This article gives an overview of the diverse range of teaching applications that can be realized using an interactive lattice Boltzmann simulation tool in fluid mechanics instruction and outreach. In an inquiry-based learning framework, examples are given of learning scenarios that address instruction on scientific results, scientific methods or the scientific process at varying levels of student activity, from consuming to applying to researching. Interactive live demonstrations on portable hardware enable new and innovative teaching concepts for fluid mechanics, also for large audiences and in the early stages of the university education. Moreover, selected examples successfully demonstrate that the integration of high-fidelity CFD methods into fluid mechanics teaching facilitates high-quality student research work within reach of the current state of the art in the respective field of research.

Keywords: fluid mechanics; engineering education; interactive simulation; inquiry-based learning

1. Introduction

The highlight of fluid mechanics instruction is often time spent at wind tunnels or wave tanks, where students can observe phenomena in action that they typically only encounter using complex mathematical tools and abstract theories. Ideally, those facilities would be accessible to students for self-guided inquiry and experiments, so that they can experience how researchers of fluid mechanics historically come to form their theories. However, time at such research facilities is, for typical teaching contexts, prohibitively expensive for more than fleeting visits, and time away from the university campus always implies logistical challenges. With the exponential increase of calculating power over recent years, an attractive alternative to classical fluid mechanics experiments has emerged for both research and teaching purposes. Nowadays, simulations can provide physically-accurate results in (or near) real-time and, additionally, interactively respond to user input, under the condition that a sufficiently accurate and fast numerical method is used. This presents a great opportunity for instruction in diverse fields like mechanical engineering, water management, energy management or geophysical fluid dynamics. We here present the successful application of an interactive lattice Boltzmann-based simulation tool for a wide range of teaching purposes such as lectures, tutorials or self-study. The lattice Boltzmann method (LBM) is a viable alternative to conventional computational fluid dynamics approaches that approximate continuum physics equations, mostly Navier–Stokes. Thanks to a number of model-specific advantages, particularly concerning data locality and parallel computing, the method scales very well on recent high-performance computing hardware and provides numerical solutions in a very competitive computational time. This is beneficial for numerous scientific and industrial applications and at the same time enables innovative and interactive ways of teaching, primarily in the field of fluid mechanics. After a brief review of the state of the art in fluid mechanics instruction in Section 2, the basics of the employed LBM solver ELBE are presented in Section 3. In Section 4, the use of ELBE for instructional purposes is discussed within an inquiry-based learning framework; in Section 5 in light of student feedback; and finally, in Section 6 conclusions are drawn and an outlook is given.

2. Motivation

The science of fluid mechanics studies the behavior of liquids and gases if subjected to forces or displacements and their interaction with their surroundings. Typically, problems considered in fluid mechanics are large-scale problems in violent environments, like the impact of wave action on coastlines or the interaction between a ship and an ice-covered ocean. Observations of these phenomena in situ might be possible in some cases, but even for very simple flow problems, for example, a cylinder in a flow shedding eddies (Figure 1, top left panel), precisely measuring the acting forces is extremely difficult. Furthermore, reproducing conditions in situ in order to run repeated measurements is impossible.

2.1. Laboratory Experiments for Fluid Mechanics Instruction

Laboratory experiments, which are easier to control than measurements in situ, have therefore always been an important method of knowledge generation in fluid mechanics. Elaborate experiments are being conducted in research facilities around the world. For scaling reasons, experiments often require very large wave tanks, wind channels or water tunnels. For example, models of container ships have to be several meters long, and the towing tanks to investigate their behavior moving through water have to be accordingly long and wide: the large towing tank at The Hamburg Ship Model Basin (HSVA) is 300 m long, 18 m wide and 6 m deep. Research questions on static structures in moving water are arguably as difficult to represent in a laboratory. For example, the problem of a cylinder shedding eddies in a flow requires large volumes of water (especially if dye is added to visualize the flow field; see Figure 1, middle left panel) in a very well-controlled flow field throughout the experimental chamber.

Because of their importance in research, laboratory experiments play an important role in instruction in science, technology, engineering and mathematics subjects (STEM) [1], where they can accommodate many desirable learning outcomes [2]. Ideally, one would expose students of fluid mechanics to real research facilities and let them run self-guided, inquiry-based experiments, thereby providing realistic research contexts and preparing them for future research careers [3,4]. However, due to the issues sketched above, fluid mechanics research facilities are prohibitively expensive to use in fluid mechanics instruction for more than the occasional visit during a field day, where students look at carefully-prepared experiments, rather than having the opportunity to plan and conduct experiments themselves, making and learning from their own mistakes. Many of the experiments run at large research facilities are documented and shared, for example via videos shared on online platforms, in addition to conventional publication channels to the scientific community. Presenting experiments in teaching, however exciting, always leaves something to be desired, since students are restricted to passively watching and have no way of interacting with the experiment.

In some cases, it is possible to run very simplified versions of experiments in teaching labs or even at home. For example, in the case of the cylinder in a flow, the problem could be turned upside down by moving the cylinder relative to the water, rather than the water relative to the cylinder (see Figure 1d). However, for obvious reasons, such simplified experiments can only ever give a qualitative taste of what could be observed and never provide the opportunity to engage with real instrumentation or achieve authentic measurements that can be used in further analysis. This deprives students of the opportunity to learn many of the skills they could acquire working with "real" experiments.

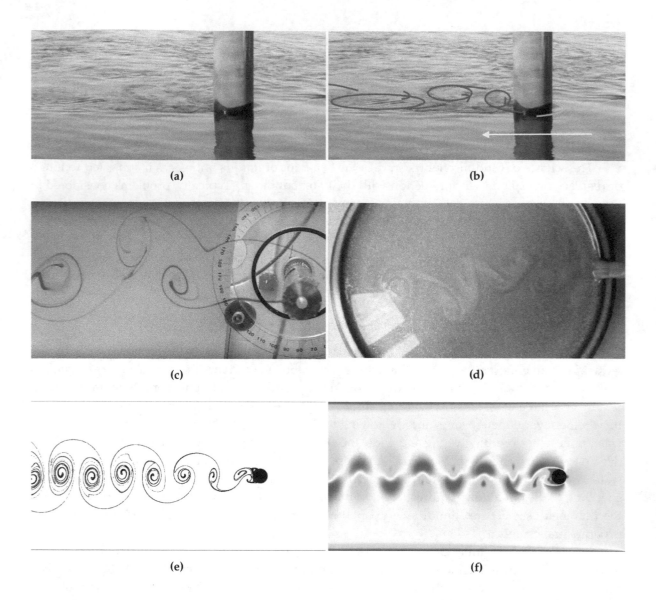

Figure 1. Comparison of a fluid mechanics problem, a Kármán vortex street, in situ, in two different laboratory realizations and in an ELBE simulation. (**a**) Periodically shedding, alternating eddies downstream of a cylinder in the Elbe river. (**b**) Same as (a), but the direction of flow (yellow) and the structures of eddies (red) are indicated. (**c**) Vortex shedding behind a cylinder in a water tunnel. The flow field is visualized using food coloring diluted in water. Picture by courtesy of Sarwesh Narayan Parbat. (**d**) "Kitchen experiment" of the same situation as in the other figures. A paint brush is moved through sugar water dyed with metallic water colors to simulate the above situation. (**e,f**) ELBE simulation results of a similar situation: (**e**) adding "dye" yields a visualization similar to the water tunnel; (**f**) velocity magnitude.

2.2. (Interactive) Simulations for Fluid Mechanics Instruction

Luckily, a new alternative has emerged over the last couple of years, made possible by the exponential increase of computing power: numerical simulations. An interactive simulation can give students the opportunity to manipulate the experiment and experience in real time how the system reacts to their interventions. This way, classical, as well as novel fluid mechanics experiments can be simulated, but with many advantages over the laboratory experiment: fewer resources are needed; the experiment can be repeated as often as desired; and the experiment can be conducted in a lecture theater, as well as in an office instead of only at specialized facilities. Figure 1e and Figure 1f show examples of this: an obstacle of any shape, in this case representing a cylinder as in the other examples above, was drawn into a homogeneous flow field by a student, and the flow interactively adjusted to this disturbance in real time. Watching this simulation is therefore much like observing what happens when putting a physical obstacle into a stream of water, except that simulations provide the opportunity for extended visualizations that are extremely difficult or impossible in physical experiments. Simulations therefore are a highly beneficial addition to conventional teaching. Successful examples include, e.g., the software packages TeachFlow [5], CFD Studio [6], FlowLab [7,8], VirtualFlowLab [9] (http://users.metu.edu.tr/csert/virtualFlowLab) and jFlowSim (https://github.com/ChristianFJanssen/jflowsim). More recently, implementations based on high-performance hardware have emerged, as discussed in the next section on LBMs. When embedded in blended-learning scenarios, i.e., integrated in face-to-face learning, simulations or remote experiments can lead to similar learning gains as laboratory experiments [10].

When designing learning opportunities using blended scenarios, as is the case in all instructional designs, the desired characteristics of the learning process (see for example [11]) have to be adequately addressed. In general, experiments are most beneficial in student-centered teaching scenarios, where students take on the responsibility for their learning and follow their interests: inquiry-based learning aims at designing learning situations in which students experience the research process, as a whole or in parts. One characteristic of inquiry-based learning is therefore that new knowledge is gained which is interesting not only to the student/researcher himself/herself. However, this does not mean that inquiry-based learning has to lead to cutting-edge research results. Knowledge is also considered as "new", even though not new to the scientific community, if it is new and interesting to the students' peer group, i.e., other students of the same course or of other courses, where the results might be presented [12]. Indeed, it is important to include presenting and other typical social practices and norms in authentic science learning [13].

3. LBM for Interactive Monitoring and Steering

Compared to other fields of numerical simulations, simulation of fluid mechanical problems is computationally very demanding. Due to the large scale of the problems under consideration and the highly turbulent nature of the flows that require a high temporal and spatial resolution, a large number of operations is required. Efficient software and hardware concepts have to be harmonized in order to obtain numerical results in a reasonable amount of time. Concerning the numerical back-end, this motivates the use of lattice Boltzmann methods, mainly due to the following four reasons: 1. The LBM is a valid discretization and approximation of the weakly compressible Navier–Stokes equations. 2. The LBM features solver-specific advantages in terms of data locality and parallel computing, which allow for very efficient simulations on massively-parallel hardware. 3. The LBM allows for a parallelization on GPUs, bringing massive computing power to the lecture room, as one single GPU offers the performance of approximately 4–5 recent CPUs, but with a significantly higher energy efficiency and a lower price. 4. Grid generation is rather simple, as it does not involve a change in topology, and wall boundary conditions can be adapted easily, opposite to, e.g., finite-volume-based solvers.

3.1. State of the Art

Real-time rendering and interactive simulations in the realm of scientific high performance computing (HPC) and computational fluid dynamics (CFD) are comparably young fields of research. The complexity of most fluid mechanics problems with engineering relevance requires such detailed simulations of both time and space that an apparent change in intermediate results, obtained by current methods that simulate viscous flows, occurs in time frames that do not coincide with the human time frame defined by practicality and patience.

A very early approach to visualize and interact with a computational fluid dynamics simulation in real time was implemented by Kreylos et al. [14]. It included rudimentary 2D visualization, but also allowed for a dynamic remeshing of the fluid domain, as required for potentially interactive simulations. Höfler [15] presented a real-time visualization technique for unstructured data employing a shading language to program graphics cards. A more recent implementation by De Vuyst et al. [16] showcases the current processing and visualization capabilities of modern graphics cards. With the recent advances of GPU computing and its application in the field of computational fluid dynamics, it is possible to compute complex simulations of reasonable resolution even in a time frame that relates to the human perception of real time. Mawson et al. [17] present an interactive LBM solver that, on top of the conventional input of 2D geometry using a mouse or stylus, offers input based on the Kinect sensor, yielding 2D silhouettes or even 3D topologies. Harwood and Revell [18] take another step forward and develop an interactive LBM flow solver on Android-powered mobile devices.

3.2. LBM Bulk Scheme

The visualization suite that is used in our work utilizes the highly parallelized ELBE [19] code, which is optimized for execution on graphics processing units (GPUs). Tölke and Krafczyk [20] among others [21–23] have already demonstrated the immense performance capabilities and, therefore, the suitability for real-time visualization of LBM implementations on GPUs. The method's inherently explicit character in time allows unlimited parallelization and yields simulation times that fit the human time frame. For some engineering problems, computations in real-time are possible, even on one single GPGPU board only.

ELBE is based on the second author's PhD thesis work at Braunschweig University of Technology, where he developed first GPU-accelerated free surface flow kernels [23]. Since the completion of his PhD, he is leading the development of ELBE, an object-oriented and efficient C++ and CUDA-based framework for GPU-accelerated free surface flow simulations, first at the University of Rhode Island (2011) and since 2012 at Hamburg University of Technology. ELBE supports 1D, 2D and 3D simulations of shallow water flows, single-phase flows, flows with a free surface and fluid-structure interactions. For the bulk flow solution, both conventional single-relaxation-time (SRT) and multiple-relaxation-time (MRT) collision operators and more sophisticated, very low-diffusive Cumulant operators are applied, as elaborately discussed for turbulent channel flows in [24]. Rigid-body motions are modeled with quaternion-based motion solvers or a collision-resolving physics engine, as detailed in [25,26]. The code permits simulations on $\mathcal{O}(10{,}000)$ CUDA cores on multiple GPUs in a shared memory system. The code was carefully validated, e.g., for sloshing and slamming, wave run-up [27], internal floodwater dynamics in partly filled tanks [28] and for three-dimensional free-surface flows with fluid-structure interactions [29,30]. Several applications related to ocean engineering were also addressed, e.g., wave propagation and wave run-up [27], steady streaming in boundary layers of progressive waves [31] and air-sea interaction and sea spray generation [32–34]. An efficient on-device grid generator serves to map complex geometries to the computational grid [30] and was recently extended to second-order accuracy [35].

ELBE is using mainly weakly compressible lattice Boltzmann models, for which single-precision arithmetics have been shown to be sufficiently accurate. The following performance estimates were obtained on an NVIDIA Quadro M6000 device. Performance is reported in terms of million node updates per second (MNUPS). For 2D single-phase flows, the performance is in the order of 1000 MNUPS and above, e.g., for a lid-driven cavity simulation on a 512×512 grid. With additional consideration of fluid-structure interactions, e.g., for the simulation of an oscillating cylinder in a transient flow, the performance is slightly reduced and in the order of 700–800 MNUPS, for a 1024×512 node grid. In case the VOF free surface tracking is activated, the resulting performance is further reduced. For a 2D numerical wave tank with inlet and outlet boundary conditions on a 1300×218 node grid, we end up with node update rates in the order of 550 MNUPS. In 3D, performance naturally is slightly lower. For 3D lid-driven cavity flows (on a 100^3 grid and finer), we obtain node update rates in the order of 700 MNUPS. If again free surface capturing and the bidirectional fluid-structure interaction interface are activated, we end up with 450 MNUPS, as tested for the simulation of the water entry of a solid cube on a $300 \times 195 \times 121$ node grid. All in all, the performance is found to be very competitive and sufficiently high for the application of ELBE as a tool for interactive teaching.

3.3. Online Visualization: The Key to Success for Teaching Purposes

For the teaching applications presented in this work, the ELBE solver is used in combination with the visualizer interface ELBE*vis* [36]. The primary objective of all added functionality for visualization and interaction purposes is to maintain the high update rates of the main computation. The resulting tool uses CUDA and OpenGL interoperability to avoid the bottleneck of device-to-host data transfers and to visualize the results directly from the GPU memory. The visualization features are realized directly on the GPU so that no additional and comparatively slow data transfer have to be performed. The easy and direct control of these features is realized with a graphical user interface that can be started as a separate process and communicates with ELBE*vis* through a shared memory segment. The details of ELBE*vis* are elaborately discussed in [36]. The performance of the fully-coupled ELBE-ELBE*vis* solver yields still more than 90% of the performance of the standalone ELBE simulation for both 2D and 3D simulations (Tables 1 and 2 in [36]). Only for two very compute-intensive visualizer features, the performance is significantly reduced, down to 76% for the isolines filter and down to 38% for the streamline filter (which requires a time-integration of a frozen velocity field).

Selected visualizer features are shown in the following, for two standard fluid dynamics test cases, the Kármán vortex street and a dam break setup. The Kármán vortex street is simulated as a two-dimensional single phase channel flow around a cylinder. A dam break test case is used to demonstrate the three-dimensional visualizer features. Figure 2 shows the colored-slice feature applied to both test cases. The local distribution of flow velocities in the whole computational domain can be observed. Figure 3a shows the reconstructed free water surface for the dam break case. The isosurface feature can not only be used to reconstruct the free surface, but can also be applied to the velocity or density field to acquire information about the values within the fluid. Thanks to the GPU acceleration, the surface can be reconstructed with almost no computational overhead, while a similar reconstruction on the CPU would significantly slow down the simulations. For complex three-dimensional fluid flow problems, the visualization of field values throughout the entire domain can be very useful, as similar information would not be accessible with experiments at all. Figure 3b shows the dam break's velocity magnitude distribution. Lattice nodes are transparently blended with their opacity and color adjusted in accordance with the applied data range and color map. Lattice nodes with vanishing velocities are discarded entirely.

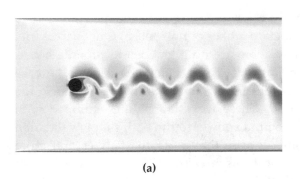
(a)

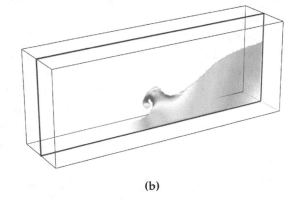
(b)

Figure 2. Colored slice applied to (**a**) a flow around a cylinder and (**b**) the dam break test case.

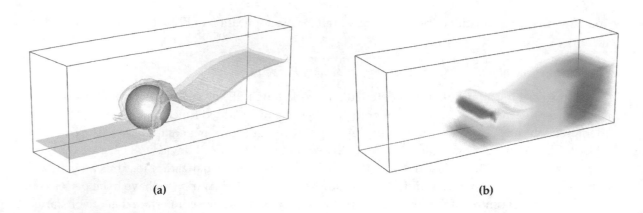

Figure 3. Two sophisticated three-dimensional visualizer features: (a) a free-surface dynamically computed with the marching cubes algorithm; (b) volume rendering applied to the dam break's velocity magnitude field.

3.4. Hardware Concepts: Bringing the Computing Power to the Lecture Room

The usage of GPUs is essential for the interactive monitoring environment of ELBE. Moreover, running computations on GPUs allows to run computationally-expensive simulations on the desktop, without tedious access to remote supercomputers. This also allows to bring HPC-based simulations to the lecture room, e.g., with GPU-accelerated laptops and workstations or remote access to local GPU-based HPC hardware. The hardware that is used for the simulations presented here is summarized in Table 1, and selected devices are depicted in Figure 4. In addition to its portability, the hardware is found to be rather inexpensive, in comparison to other state of the art high-performance computing hardware. The hardware demonstrator ELBE2go (Figure 4a), which is used for interactive live demos in lectures, at exhibitions, or science nights, costs only around 1500 Euros (approximately 1680 USD). The machine can be connected to any projector, smart board or conventional screen, as required by the particular audience. Note that the machine is equipped with the most powerful NVIDIA gaming GPU, which allows for very demanding simulations. In case that slightly less computing power and even more portability is required, a laptop solution can be used: the ELBEbook; see Figure 4b. The device formally cannot be distinguished from a conventional office laptop. As it is equipped with a portable NVIDIA GTX 970M GPU, it can, however, be used to run ELBE and ELBE*vis*, with approximately half the performance of its stationary equivalent. This is more than sufficient for most of the live demos and the interactive test cases.

Note that this sort of portable performance is available to the teaching personnel only. The hardware that is commonly used by students (standard tablets or notebooks) is not necessarily equipped with (efficient) GPU hardware. Right now, there are no intentions to provide access to GPUs to a broad range of students. If students already have achieved a reasonable base knowledge of ELBE and are able to run their own simulations, they typically get access to the institute's standard workstations in the student pool. These workstations are equipped with recent NVIDIA gaming GPUs that provide sufficient compute power to run both simple validation cases and one's own, more demanding, simulations. In case that in-depth analyses and more time-/memory-consuming simulations are needed, the students can also access our in-house server infrastructure, with professional NVIDIA Tesla boards (C2075, K40 and K80 configurations). For a more interactive solution, we are currently discussing porting ELBE to a tablet-based version using NVIDIA's own tablet series. From an economical point of view, the use of less scientific tools (such as apps for conventional cell phones) would also be an appealing alternative, even though they do not offer the possibility of scientific, research-oriented simulations at all.

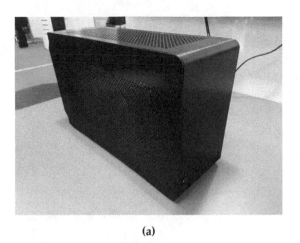

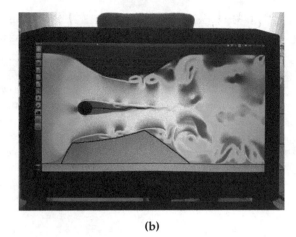

(a)   (b)

Figure 4. Hardware used for the present work. (**a**) ELBE2go, portable Mini-ITX machine with an NVIDIA GTX Titan GPU, mainly used for lectures, science nights and presentations. (**b**) ELBEbook, gaming notebook with a portable NVIDIA GTX 970M device.

Table 1. Hardware resources that were used for the results presented here.

Form Factor	GPU	Scope of Application	Level
Laptop	NVIDIA GTX 970 M	Live demos during presentations	Consumption
Small workstation	NVIDIA GTX Titan X	Live demos at exhibitions, science nights, etc.	Consumption
Standard workstation	NVIDIA GTX Titan X	Student research assistant work, theses work	Application
Rack server (small)	4x NVIDIA Tesla C2075	Overnight runs	Research
Rack server (large)	4x NVIDIA K80 GPUs	Overnight runs	Research

4. Inquiry-Based Learning Scenarios with the LBM Solver ELBE

We use the Rueß (2013, [37]) framework to describe how a tool like ELBE can be used in student-centered teaching as successfully demonstrated at Hamburg University of Technology (TUHH). In this framework, different inquiry-based learning activities are presented as a function of the student activity (i.e., consuming, applying or researching) and the topic of the activity (scientific results, scientific methods or scientific processes; Table 2). Student activity can range from more or less passive consumption of the application, to active engagement in different kinds of research activities. The type of content can be broken down into content with a focus on research results ("learning about research"), research methods ("learning for research") or the research process itself ("learning through research") [38]. Depending on the desired learning outcomes, each of the nine fields, or any combination thereof, can inform design choices for any part of an instructional unit, for all of it or even for a whole course or study program. We present examples of different teaching scenarios and explain how they let students gain familiarity with aspects of the research process and, combined with each other, prepare students for active participation in the research process.

Table 2. Example tasks for different flavors of inquiry-based learning (based on Rueß (2013, [37]) and personal communication with Klaus Vosgerau and Timo Lüth (2014)).

Activity	Topic of the Task		
	Scientific Results	Scientific Methods	Scientific Processes
Consumption	Students consume research results.	Students consume research methods.	Students receive explanations of scientific processes.
Examples:	*Attend lectures or presentations at science nights on recent CFD results.*	*Listen to a presentation on numerical methods.*	*Listen to a presentation on the history of ELBE.*
	Watch animated results of numerical simulations on YouTube.	*Attend a lecture on fluid mechanics with a live demo.*	*Participate in an excursion to a model basin to compare experimental results with numerical results.*
Application	Students discuss or transfer research results.	Students discuss or practice existing methods.	Students discuss or develop research processes.
Examples:	*Read literature to write a wiki article on turbulent mixing.*	*Determine if the grid resolution that meets the computational constraints is sufficient to answer a question.*	*Decide for/against higher grid resolution (vs. duration of calculation) for a numerical simulation.*
	Learn from an ELBE simulation of wing profiles in a wind tunnel to improve personal sailing skills.	*Replicate a predefined ELBE test scenario in order to practice running the code.*	*Figure out a research design to answer questions on nonlinear flow physics using ELBE.*
Research	Students systematically study the literature on a scientific topic	Students apply existing methods to a research question.	Students apply the full scientific research cycle.
Examples:	*Find a suitable parametrization for an array of wind turbines for a simulation in ELBE.*	*Figure out a way to determine the influence of the shape of a blade on the efficiency of mixing of a gas into a liquid using ELBE simulations.*	*Address own research questions using ELBE.*
	Find the state of the art knowledge on parametrizations of turbulent mixing to consider modifications to the ELBE code.	*Suggest a parametrization from literature to parametrize the shape of pools and tanks subject to violent sloshing.*	*Extend ELBE with novel algorithms to be able to address the new problem.*

☐ Instruction based on precomputed scenarios or interactive demos on light-weight hardware in the teaching room (Section 4.1)

☐ Instruction based on results of a simulation, not on the simulation itself (Section 4.2)

☐ Instruction based on intermediate hardware for numerical simulations on the desktop, mainly student theses at the bachelor's and master's level (Section 4.3)

☐ Instruction based on heavy-duty hardware for long-term simulations in a HPC environment, research mainly on PhD and professional level (Section 4.4)

Colors indicate the use of ELBE.

The research process consists of many individual steps that are conducted in a distinct sequence (Figure 5). Sometimes, it becomes necessary to repeat one or several of those steps, while maintaining their order. When educating future researchers, the final goal for students is to be able to independently conduct a full research process. This can be scaffolded by first teaching about research processes, then discussing and practicing the design of research questions and then, finally, conducting research, now using skills learned on all other aspects of research mentioned in Table 2. Consequently, fluid mechanics teaching can either focus on one of the key ingredients or address the full loop. ELBE is used as a tool to support the situatedness of learning, demonstrating the relevance of each individual task to the larger research questions of the ELBE community. In order for this to work well, it is important to communicate where each task fits, and where it is relevant and important in the large research process.

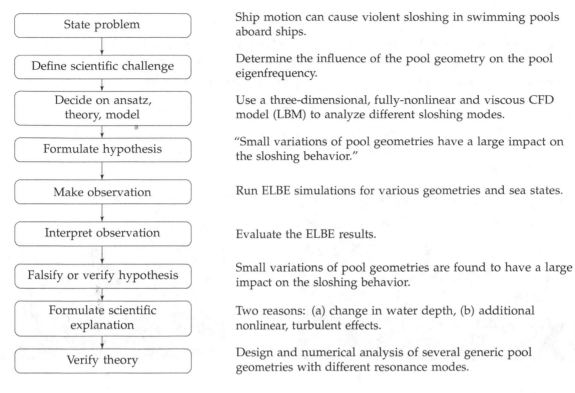

State problem	Ship motion can cause violent sloshing in swimming pools aboard ships.
Define scientific challenge	Determine the influence of the pool geometry on the pool eigenfrequency.
Decide on ansatz, theory, model	Use a three-dimensional, fully-nonlinear and viscous CFD model (LBM) to analyze different sloshing modes.
Formulate hypothesis	"Small variations of pool geometries have a large impact on the sloshing behavior."
Make observation	Run ELBE simulations for various geometries and sea states.
Interpret observation	Evaluate the ELBE results.
Falsify or verify hypothesis	Small variations of pool geometries are found to have a large impact on the sloshing behavior.
Formulate scientific explanation	Two reasons: (a) change in water depth, (b) additional nonlinear, turbulent effects.
Verify theory	Design and numerical analysis of several generic pool geometries with different resonance modes.

Figure 5. Schematic view of a scientific process. Shown is a linear model; in practice, it often is necessary to repeat one or several steps. On the right, an example is given, based on a master thesis project with ELBE that is aiming at analyzing violent pool sloshing aboard cruise ships.

Whether tasks then resemble authentic research can be evaluated using the Chinn and Malhotra (2015, [39]) framework. One drawback that they typically find with computer simulated experiments used in teaching is, for example, that students are asked to make choices about variables that they would otherwise not consider and that they are limited to the theories included in the model and cannot invent and include theories or variables on their own. While this is likely true for many instances, we suggest how to overcome this specific limitation and let students experience authentic research in the ELBE framework.

Even though the presentation in the following might seem to imply a preferred sequence of instructional activities, the different aspects of the research process are presented in only one of many feasible orders. However, any other order might be more appropriate for planned overarching learning progressions. Arranging by topic of the student task and increasing level of student activity is, most generally speaking, an order that makes sense in terms of scaffolding and is traditionally followed (more or less closely) in teaching. Learning about results, then methods, then processes can be a sensible progression, as well, if a context is first motivated, and students then dig into the topic more and more deeply. Additionally, many of the tasks will lead to students wanting to expand on them, leading to new questions that extend into different fields of the Rueß (2013, [37]) framework, towards conducting a full research process. However, even addressing only selected fields of the matrix in individual lessons or even courses might be most suitable for a given learning outcome as long as care is taken that interested students are not hindered from pursuing goals larger than the learning outcomes of that course.

In the following, we have grouped aspects of the Rueß (2013, [37]) matrix together under four headings to draw a picture from getting a taste of fluid mechanics and CFD (Section 4.1), of working with literature (Section 4.2) and learning aspects of simulation (Section 4.3) to authentic, full research processes (Section 4.4).

4.1. Getting a Taste of Fluid Mechanics and CFD

ELBE provides a great opportunity to give a first taste of fluid mechanics, as well as CFD to both students and the general public: its easy visualization and interactivity make it hugely attractive to use in introductory lectures or for demonstration and PR purposes at conferences, fairs, open days and numerous other events when faced with large groups of dozens to hundreds of people to be taught simultaneously with one or very few instructors (compare Figure 6). Even though large lecture theaters or online learning scenarios are, at first glance, not conducive to actively experiencing the research process, inquiry-based learning can still happen in those settings and in a way that is similar to the parts of the research process as described above.

(a)   (b)

Figure 6. Two examples of students (and other interested audience) consuming scientific results: (**a**) Preparations for a lecture in the Audimax II, the TUHH's second-largest lecture theater. ELBE2go can be seen standing on the desk. (**b**) ELBE in action at the TUHH science night. Again, the computations are run on ELBE2go, this time in combination with the smart board interface.

4.1.1. Students Consume Scientific Results

When the desired learning outcome is to familiarize an audience with scientific results, ELBE is used to visualize and explain basic fluid mechanics phenomena that would otherwise not be presented at all or as purely theoretical constructs (e.g., turbulence, drag, vortex shedding, boundary layers, and so on). By varying parameters in the input to the simulation, the influence of those parameters on given properties can be directly "experienced" by way of real-time simulation rather than just calculated. Streamlines around bodies or dispersion of tracer particles become tangible, and scientific results therefore approachable and much more easily recognized when later encountered "in the wild". In such teaching scenarios, the interaction with the ELBE tool is mainly done by the lecturer or one or a few volunteers, possibly reacting to audience's suggestions. If interactive input devices (such as smart boards) are used with the ELBE tool, the interested audience can get in touch with a real CFD simulation easily, e.g., by writing or drawing shapes that act as obstacles to the flow and observing the real-time changes in the flow fields, and depending on group size, as many as possible of the participants are encouraged to try and gain first-hand experience.

As a concrete example, such a teaching scenario was used in the lecture Fluid Mechanics and the corresponding exercise. The course is scheduled for the fourth semester of the bachelor degrees in Naval Engineering and Mechanical Engineering. Weekly lectures are accompanied by weekly exercises to practice solving actual fluid mechanics problems. This mostly involves analytical solutions of the previously-introduced equations. In this context, ELBE was tested in the lecture room as an alternative to conventional equation-solving. The question that the students had to answer was, which of the two wings of a double-decker airplane (the upper or the lower one) generates more lift. Typically, this question is answered by a theoretical analysis with the help of inviscid potential flow theory. After a quick introduction to ELBE and showing standard live simulations of, e.g., vortex shedding behind cylindrical obstacles (see Figure 1), the audience was asked to answer this question with an interactive analysis. The group size was approximately 25. A couple of volunteers drew simple profile-like shapes in the numerical ELBE wind-tunnel. ELBE generated the resulting velocity and pressure fields on the fly. By analyzing the pressure distribution along the two NACA profiles, the students finally were able to answer the question: the upper NACA profile creates significantly more lift than the lower one. Instead of a conventional analysis based on equations, a more playful, interactive and memorable explanation was obtained. On the technical side, the simulation was addressed with a 2D LBM single-phase simulation with MRT collision operator and LES turbulence closure. Standard results of a predefined simulation are shown in Figure 7. This scenario was used after the students interactively drew their own test shapes.

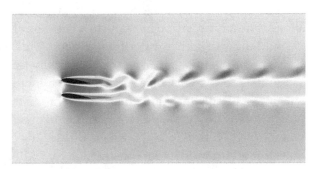

Figure 7. ELBE simulation of two NACA profiles to answer the question which of the two profiles generates more lift. The flow is coming from the left (velocity boundary condition). 512 times 256 lattice nodes were used, yielding a total of 131,072 lattice nodes.

4.1.2. Students Consume Scientific Methods

A learning outcome that focuses on familiarizing students with scientific methods can, in the spirit of inquiry-based learning, mean many different things, for example students attending presentations on methodological topics or watching videos explaining a specific method. ELBE can be used here to demonstrate the influence of different resolutions on run speeds that change from real time to visually slower or that have effects on the solution the simulation findings. Doing this, students experience an important part of the scientific process: participation in scientific conferences and browsing of scientific presentations, which are common occurrences in the life of a scientist and where being part of a large, mainly passive, audience is part of the experience. Moving from passive consumption to active engagement with the topic can be supported by interactive formats that engage students in discussions or quizzes.

4.1.3. Students Consume Scientific Process

Consuming the scientific process will, as consuming in the two previously mentioned fields, likely mean listening to a presentation, for example on the history of ELBE. However, it can also mean to go on a field trip to a fluid mechanics research facility where experiments are presented and the results compared to results of ELBE simulations. Even though this counts as "consuming" the scientific processes, this should not be a passive endeavor. Even though they are not producing scientific results themselves, students should still be actively engaging in the learning process.

4.2. Working with the Literature

Reading articles written by authors personally known to the students (e.g., their professors, instructors, even fellow students at master's or Ph.D. level) is highly motivating, as is working with literature in order to solve an authentic problem of the ELBE community. Therefore, practicing skills related to literature search in the context of ELBE provides situatedness of learning. This refers to the gray-shaded cells of Table 2.

4.2.1. Students Apply Scientific Results

When the desired learning outcome for students is to be able to apply scientific results, a task could be to search the scientific literature for specific topics of interest, to discuss scientific results critically and then to add a synthesis to the ELBE wiki, corresponding to early steps in the research process concerned with reviewing the literature for state of the art solutions. Alternatively, students can analyze results of ELBE simulations to draw conclusions about related, real-life problems they are interested in: They can for example use simulations of rigid wing profiles in a flow field to improve their own sailing skills by considering the difference between lift and drag and different downwind turbulence fields or simulations of tracer dispersion in a flow to determine at which location relative to a source of pollution they would draw drinking water from a creek. This would correspond to the "formulating a hypothesis" step in the scientific process. This organically leads to students wanting to conduct other steps of the scientific process, as well, e.g., testing the hypothesis they just generated.

Although it is more difficult to instruct this kind of tasks when audiences are large, it is possible to make this kind of learning available to the public, for example by having interfaces to the tools available online and then collecting answers via social media and engaging participants in discussions there. An interactive web interface is currently under construction for ELBE, but successful examples include the dispersion of surface drifters in the world oceans (adrift.org.au) or a simple climate model (http://mscm.dkrz.de).

4.2.2. Students Research Scientific Results

When students are asked to research scientific results, this can mean a classical literature study, as well as interviewing experts on a topic. This is motivated by the direct relevance to the further development of ELBE and the contribution to the ELBE community, and questions can be given by the instructor or developed by the students themselves. A current example is project work on the topic of wind turbines in the form of a literature study. This study will directly influence the ELBE community's future research directions and is therefore in itself an important part of an authentic research process.

This kind of task is easiest to implement in the form of students working on their own projects or with small groups in which students can share and discuss the results of their literature searches with others. Getting large groups of people to engage in such a task requires high levels of motivation on the participants' part and will most likely occur as self-directed rather than instructed, unless extrinsically-motivating mechanisms like homework and feedback are in place.

4.3. *Learning about (Aspects of) Simulation*

In many study programs, important learning outcomes are skills in applying, sometimes predefined, scenarios of simulations as a prerequisite for future independent work with numerical models. The following two sections refer to the orange cells of Table 2.

4.3.1. Students Apply Scientific Methods

When students "apply scientific methods", they use one specific scientific method to carry out a given task. Applying scientific methods in an inquiry-based learning sense can mean, for example, to run a predefined ELBE test scenario. In those scenarios, sensible parameters are suggested, and the setup is guaranteed to work; however, students can practice running a numerical model in a low-stakes environment and gain experience applying this specific scientific method. Furthermore, the discussion of the advantages and disadvantages of scientific methods is an application that is a very real part of the research process and an important part of the learning process.

Current examples of students applying scientific methods related to the ELBE project, e.g., include project tasks in several lectures at TUHH (InnoCFD and ASM; see Section A.1), where students are asked to determine the relationship between the frequency with which vortices are shed and the Reynolds number. This task is addressed by each participant by running individual numerical simulations and developing individual routines to analyze the flow field to extract the vortex shedding frequency. Another example, currently part of a master's project, is the design of the aerodynamics package of an electronic race car using ELBE simulations of wings (master thesis of Reichert, `elbe-2015-17`, Table 3).

A typical example for such an application-oriented example is the ASM project task on flooding (Budde, Conradi and Lüke, 2014). The students were asked to validate ELBE for flooding and sloshing scenarios of ships and were provided with a set of experimental data (free surface elevations and force time series). The group started using ELBE, implemented several minor code extensions and, finally, validated the code with the help of experimental data; see Figure 8.

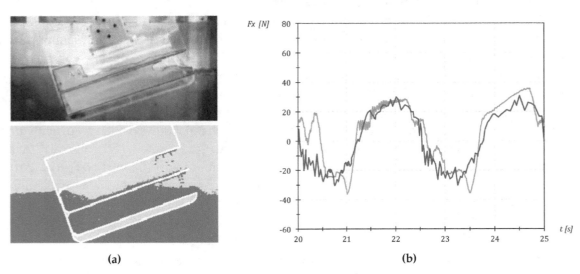

(a)　　　　　　　　(b)

Figure 8. Selected figures from the ASM project work of Budde, Conradi and Lüke on flooding simulations with ELBE: (**a**) comparison of experimental (top) and numerical (bottom) results for a damaged car deck; (**b**) comparison of fluid forces of experiment (red) and simulation (blue). A grid with 1280 times 256 nodes was used. Twenty six seconds of real-time sloshing were simulated in less than one hour on a single GPU.

Adapting this setup for large groups is challenging, but can, as discussed in Section 4.2.1, be managed through web-based or app-based approaches. It is important to give participants a reason to participate, for example by letting them contribute to discussions with experts.

4.3.2. Students Apply Scientific Processes

When the aim is for students to apply scientific processes, they can be asked to discuss research designs or practice developing research questions or designs. This can, for example, mean making decisions on questions like which grid resolution is suitable for a given research question or how to design an experiment for another question; or, as currently in the seminar InnoCFD/ASM (see Section A.1), students can do analyses of the convergent behavior in space and time for a simple, two-dimensional academic test case. With large groups, it can mean discussing research designs and actively encouraging suggestions.

4.4. Research

The goal of academic education is to enable students to do independent research, whether in industry, in academia or elsewhere. The corresponding cells in Table 2 are colored in red.

4.4.1. Students Research Scientific Methods

When students "research scientific methods", they are very active in the way a researcher would be, except that they are only doing one specific part of the research process: they do literature searches, talk to colleagues or attend presentations, all with the goal to find a scientific method that can be used to address a specific question. This question can both be their own or prescribed; however, students' own questions usually are better motivators. Current examples of students researching their own questions in the ELBE team include master's projects on finding and implementing a new LBM model for the simulation of turbulent channel flows, finding and implementing an overset grid model in ELBE and the implementation of a suitable visualization.

The latter is essentially the basis of the current work: Koliha (`elbe-2013-06`, Table 3) implemented and validated the basic ELBE visualizer interface, which is now the basis of the present publication and most of the ELBE applications in teaching. He started with a sound literature review, followed by a technical analysis of the requirements and technical options for a visualizer interface In the second part of his work, he implemented and validated the visualization environment.

Similarly, much progress was made with ELBE in the actual LBM- and CFD-based research. Gehrke presented a new model for simulations of turbulent channel flows, which is currently part of an international, peer-reviewed journal publication (`elbe-2015-12`, Table 3, [24]). Similarly, Asmuth very recently implemented and tested a new overset grid approach for LBM methods (`elbe-2016-21`, Table 3). Both theses would not have been possible without proper and fast online visualization and GPU acceleration of the code.

4.4.2. Students Research Scientific Processes

When "students research scientific processes" in the sense of the inquiry-based learning framework, they are actively participating in the full research process. It is not difficult to see that this is inquiry-based learning in its most obvious sense. This happens in many different scenarios ranging from courses where ELBE is used to answer smaller research questions, over bachelor's and master's theses, to fully-developed research projects and Ph.D. theses on very challenging topics, such as three-dimensional ship-ice interactions, tsunami propagation and inundation modeling and transition from laminar to turbulent flow.

A typical example for the full implementation of the research cycle (as depicted in Figure 5) is the master's project of Budde (`elbe-2016-22`, Table 3). Focusing on pool-sloshing onboard of mega-yachts, the first part of his thesis was concerned with analyzing the actual problem by field observations and evaluating experimental field data taken from model tests. He then came up with a hypothesis on the influence of the shape of the pool on the eigenfrequency and sloshing behavior, which then was tested with a whole set of ELBE simulations (Figure 9). In the end, he was able to derive simple relations of swimming pool shapes aboard mega yachts on the sloshing behavior. The numerical simulations of the complex three-dimensional sloshing process were run overnight on one of the ELBE rack servers (see Table 1). Also note that he first got in touch with ELBE in the scope of the ASM lectures and the related project tasks that were mentioned in Section 4.3.1.

Table 3. List of completed ELBE thesis projects: bachelor theses (B.Sc.), master theses (M.Sc.) and project theses (P.Th.). Note that most of the titles were translated from German to English. An up-to-date list can also be found online: https://www.tuhh.de/elbe/education/thesis-projects.html.

Author	Title	Date	Type	ID
Steinert, A.	Numerical simulation of wave propagation and wave run-up	Jul 2012	B.Sc.	elbe-2012-01
Gralher, S.	Numerical simulation of sloshing and slamming	Jul 2012	B.Sc.	elbe-2012-02
Bengel, S.	An LB method for the numerical simulation of sloshing in partly filled tanks	Dec 2012	B.Sc.	elbe-2012-03
Marckmann, H.	Entwicklung und Implementierung eines Simulationsverfahrens zur effizienten Berechnung von Körpern in Seegang	Apr 2013	M.Sc.	elbe-2013-04
Nagrelli, H.	Numerical Analysis of Fluid-Structure-Interaction with an LBM-VOF solver on GPGPU hardware	Aug 2013	P.Th.	elbe-2013-05
Koliha, N.	Computation and Real-Time Rendering of Complex Multiphase Flows on GPGPU Clusters	Oct 2013	M.Sc.	elbe-2013-06
Bieler, C.	Numerical analysis and fluid-mechanical optimization of a formula student racer	Jun 2014	B.Sc.	elbe-2014-07
Nagrelli, H.	Simulation of Fluid-Structure Interactions with a GPGPU-accelerated lattice Boltzmann Method	Jul 2014	M.Sc.	elbe-2014-08
Schimonek, P.	On the applicability of the flow solver ELBE to aircraft ditching	Nov 2014	P.Th.	elbe-2014-09
Mierke, D.	Coupling of a GPU-based lattice Boltzmann solver to a physics engine for the simulation of colliding multi-body systems	Dec 2014	P.Th.	elbe-2014-10
Überrück, M.	Development of a numerical towing tank for the analysis of wave loads on partly and fully submerged bodies	Dec 2014	P.Th.	elbe-2014-11
Gehrke, M.	Validation of a GPU-accelerated, non-uniform Lattice-Boltzmann solvers for turbulent flows	Jan 2015	M.Sc.	elbe-2015-12
Huisman, M.	Numerical modeling of ship-ice interactions with physics engines under the consideration of ice breaking	Jul 2015	M.Sc.	elbe-2015-13
Mierke, D.	An Efficient and Accurate Simulation Procedure for Modelling coupled Fluid-Ice-Ship-Interaction on Graphics Processing Units	Oct 2015	M.Sc.	elbe-2015-14
Überrück, M.	Alternative advection schemes and outlet boundary conditions for numerical towing tanks	Oct 2015	M.Sc.	elbe-2015-15
Richter, M.	Implementation of a seaway boundary condition into a GPU-accelerated lattice Boltzmann solver	Nov 2015	B.Sc.	elbe-2015-16
Reichert, L.	Fluiddynamic Analysis of Front- and Rear Wings of a Formula Student Racing Car	Nov 2015	M.Sc.	elbe-2015-17
Hartmann, M.C.N.	Development of a cavitation model for Lattice-Boltzmann-Methods	Nov 2015	P.Th.	elbe-2015-18
Angerbauer, R.	Numerical Simulation of Propeller Flows with a GPU-accelerated Lattice-Boltzmann solver	Dec 2015	P.Th.	elbe-2015-19
Metzner, A.	Performance Analysis of CUDA-aware MPI for a 2D Laplace Solver	Apr 2016	P.Th.	elbe-2016-20
Asmuth, H.	Development of Overset Strategies for LBM-Based Flow Solvers	Oct 2016	M.Sc.	elbe-2016-21
Budde, A.	Pool-Sloshing aboard of mega yachts	Oct 2016	M.Sc.	elbe-2016-22
Faulkner-Harding, P.	Multi-GPU parallelization techniques for the acceleration of LBM-type flow solvers	Oct 2016	M.Sc.	elbe-2016-23
Brüdigam, N.	Implementation and Validation of a RANS model for Lattice-Boltzmann models with local grid refinement	Jan 2017	M.Sc.	elbe-2017-24
Angerbauer, R.	A hybrid RANS/LES method for LBM-based simulations of propeller flows	Feb 2017	M.Sc.	elbe-2017-25
Boelle, T.	Implicit Large Eddy Simulation with the Cumulant lattice Boltzmann Method: A theoretical Analysis	Feb 2017	P.Th.	elbe-2017-26
Hartmann, M.	Development of a numerical method for the prediction of ice loads on vessels traveling in pre-broken ice.	Jul 2017	M.Sc.	elbe-2017-27
Rodriguez, A.	Volume Rendering extension and general enhancements for the TUHH-ELBE visualization tool	Mar 2016	P.Th.	ext-2016-01
Bach, C.	Extending a panel code for deformed airplane sections with the help of viscous CFD	May 2016	P.Th.	ext-2016-02
Conradi, H.	Optimization of the hull shape of the Flying Dutchman dinghy with CFD simulations	Aug 2016	P.Th.	ext-2016-03

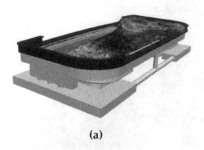 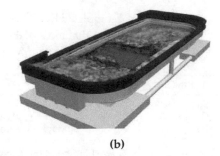

(a)   (b)

Figure 9. Two different pool geometries that were part of the analysis of Budde: (**a**) original pool with large sloshing amplitudes; (**b**) optimized pool with an irregular bottom elevation in the form of a bump with significantly lower sloshing amplitudes. Each simulation took only two hours on a single GPU.

5. Feedback and Evaluation

In order to give an impression of the success of ELBE in the instructional context at TUHH, we have added information on the amount of student research projects at our institute, which can serve as approximation for the attractiveness of the tool, and we have additionally asked selected ELBE team members, who attended the ELBE lectures years ago, for personal feedback.

5.1. Statistics

The Institute for Fluid Dynamics and Ship Theory (FDS) is responsible for research and teaching in the field of fluid dynamics in general and ship hydrodynamics specifically. The team of approximately 40 Ph.D. students is led by two professors that are supported by 2–3 postdoctoral researchers (https://www.tuhh.de/fds/staff.html). The development of ELBE and the visualizer interface ELBE*vis* was initiated and led by the second author (C.F.J.) and is associated with the team of Prof. Rung. Martin Gehrke, the first regular ELBE Ph.D. student, joined the team in 2015. Since then, the team is growing continuously. Currently, as of July 2017, the ELBE team consists of five employees, corresponding to $\approx$12.5% of the whole team size. In the last five years, a total of 150 theses at the bachelor's and master's level were advised by members of the FDS. Thirty of these 150 theses were associated with ELBE (see Table 3), approximately 20% of the total lab contribution, despite having significantly lower human resources. This gives a strong indication that the actual teaching style and the interactive, versatile combination of ELBE and ELBE*vis* is at least one of the reasons for the high popularity and mid-term success.

5.2. Personal Feedback

In addition, we have asked three selected ELBE team members for detailed personal feedback. All three team members have experienced ELBE and ELBE*vis* during their university education and are now permanent members of the ELBE research team at the FDS.

> After attending the lecture "Application of Numerical Methods in Marine Engineering" (ASM) and the project that was part of the course, I had a clear overview of the research code ELBE and its application spectrum. The possibility of quick implementation of new code snippets and the fast computation and post-processing times enables the user to get a fast response to his own code developments. This makes it possible to quickly generate working simulations, even for beginners without distinct programming skills. When I started my master thesis (simulation of fluid-ship-ice interaction) I already had a good sense of the functionalities and possibilities of ELBE. Now I am working as part of the ELBE developer team in a research project following my master degree. This project is based on the topic of my master thesis and therefore good example for student work leading to new research activities.

Michael Huisman, Ph.D. student, TUHH

Huisman is working for the European research project PRICE. He joined the team in 2016 and already attended a couple of international conferences and published his work with ELBE in peer-reviewed conference proceedings [40,41].

> My first contact with the lattice Boltzmann Method was in a lecture during my master program. During the practical part of the course, I was impressed by the performance and simplicity of the code, also in the case of flow problems with a free surface, which are very important for me as a naval architect. I decided to write my project thesis and also later on my master thesis in this research field. Moreover, I was involved in a research project as student research assistant. The project was concerned with the analysis of the sloshing behavior in LNG tanks and was funded by a big aircraft manufacturer. I ran all the simulations on campus and later on presented the results at the customer's site, including a live demo of ELBE*vis*. All in all, the research on this method and the cooperation with the company motivated me to become a research assistant at the FDS.

Micha Überrück, Ph.D. student, TUHH

Überrück joined the FDS in 2016. Even though he is not part of the ELBE team anymore, he's occasionally using ELBE for gaining additional fluid mechanical insight for his current research project, or for demonstration purposes. Moreover, he published his work for the above-mentioned research project in three different journal publications [30,42,43]. On top, he presented the results in front of a large audience at an international conference.

> I had the chance to participate in the lecture ASM in summer 2013. From the very beginning, I was fascinated by the innovative style of teaching. Advantages and disadvantages, as well as challenges of fluid simulation approaches based on the lattice Boltzmann method (LBM) were demonstrated in a modern and playful way. Furthermore, the development and implementation of the new algorithms on many-core hardware systems like GPUs together with other students resulted in very efficient simulation tools. This has allowed us to visualize the numerical results and even to interact with the fluid simulation during runtime, which was very interesting, fascinating and helpful to understand complex fluid mechanics. Later on, my curiosity for the LBM increased even more. In my project and my master thesis at the FDS, I've focused on algorithmic and numerical details of the LBM and developed a valuable new method that I later presented on a notable LBM conference as well as in a publication. Thanks to the inspiring ASM lecture, which has caught my attention and triggered my interest in LBM, I'm now working as a Ph.D. student at the FDS, focusing on numerical and algorithmic details of complex LBM schemes for large engineering applications.

Dennis Mierke, Ph.D. student, TUHH

Mierke is working as a Ph.D. student for the ProEis project. He also contributed to a couple of papers already [25,26,30,35]. Moreover, he won the "Best GPU-related talk" award at the 13th International Conference for Mesoscopic Methods in Engineering and Science (ICMMES 2016, 18–22 July, Hamburg, Germany) and was awarded a recent NVIDIA GPU.

6. Conclusions

In this article, we presented a variety of inquiry-based learning activities using the ELBE simulation tool. Thanks to innovative hardware and software concepts and an inquiry-based approach to teaching and learning, even complex numerical simulations were successfully embedded into various teaching and learning activities at TUHH and beyond. This presents an alternative to conventional laboratory experiments and gives students the opportunity to actively experience (parts of) research processes. Since teaching activities are often part of the larger ELBE research strategy, this provides situated learning opportunities, which are highly motivating to students. The long list of successful ELBE research projects (Table 3) shows that the integration of high-fidelity CFD methods into fluid mechanics teaching facilitates high-quality student research work within reach of the current state of the art in the respective field of research. Moreover, interactive live demonstrations on portable hardware enable new and innovative teaching concepts for fluid mechanics, also for large audiences and in the early stages of the university education.

Future work will address further increased levels of student participation and student interest-led inquiry-based learning. On the technical side, further improvements of the visualizer interface ELBE*vis* will allow enriched interactions and self-study. In this context, an open-source release of the ELBE*vis* framework is currently up for discussion.

Acknowledgments: The authors would like to thank NVIDIA for supporting the ELBE-related research in the scope of the Academic Partnership Program and the more recent GPU Research Center initiative. The authors would also like to thank Sarwesh Narayan Parbat for permission to use a screenshot of his video in this article.

Author Contributions: M.S.G. is a physical oceanographer and researcher in physics education and ocean/climate outreach. C.F.J. is the chief developer of the efficient lattice Boltzmann environment (ELBE), which is the basis for the numerical simulations presented here. Both authors contributed equally to this manuscript.

Appendix A   List of ELBE Teaching Activities

Appendix A.1. List of ELBE-related lectures and presentations

Lecture "Application of Numerical Methods in Marine Engineering (ASM)"
Application of ELBE for individual student research projects. Lecture given by C. Janßen, 2012 – 2015.

Lecture "Innovative Numerical Methods for Computational Fluid Mechanics (InnoCFD)"
Application of ELBE for demos in the lecture room and individual student research projects. Lecture given by T. Rung and C. Janßen, since 2015.

Lecture "Fluid Mechanics"
Application of ELBE for interactive demos in the lecture room. Lecture given by T. Rung, since 2015.

Event "TUHH Science Night"
Application of ELBE for interactive demos with smart board input for a public audience. Demos given by T. Rung and C. Janßen. November 2015 and November 2017 (scheduled).

Appendix A.2. List of ELBE-Related Project Works in ASM

"LBM, VOF, FSI and GPU", Detlefsen, Gäbler, Nagrelli, Schimonek. 2012.

"Analysis of a stirring unit", Feder, Kömpe, Tobies, 2013.

"Sloshing in partly filled tanks", Gehrke, Huisman, Willing, 2013.

"Analysis of a waterbike in the numerical towing tank", Herting, v. Meyerinck, Überrück, 2013.

"Cavitation Modeling", Brüdigam and Hartmann, 2014.

"Flooding of generic ship sections", Budde, Conradi and Lüke, 2014.

"Sloshing Simulations for various testcase setups", Rudaa and Olivucci, 2015.

"The Potsdam Propeller Test Case (PPTC)", Angerbauer, 2015.

"LBM for aeroacoustics", Worst, 2016.

References

1. Hart, C.; Mulhall, P.; Berry, A.; Loughran, J.; Gunstone, R. What is the purpose of this experiment? Or can students learn something from doing experiments? *J. Res. Sci. Teach.* **2000**, *7*, 655–675.

2. Feisel, L.D.; Rosa, A.J. The role of the laboratory in undergraduate engineering education. *J. Eng. Educ.* **2005**, *1*, 121–130.

3. Weaver, G.C.; Russell, C.B.; Wink, D.J. Inquiry-based and research-based laboratory pedagogies in undergraduate science. *Nat. Chem. Biol.* **2008**, *4*, 577–580.

4. Crouch, C.; Fagen, A.P.; Callan, J.P.; Mazur, E. Classroom demonstrations: Learning tools or entertainment? *A. J. Phys.* **2004**, *6*, 835–838.

5. Krafczyk, M. *Gitter-Boltzmann-Methoden: Von der Theorie zur Anwendung*; Technical University of Munich (TUM): München, Germany, 2001.

6. Pieritz, R.A.; Mendes, R.; da Silva, R.F.A.F.; Maliska, C.R. CFD studio: An educational software package for CFD analysis and design. *Comput. Appl. Eng. Educ.* **2004**, *12*, 20–30.

7. LaRoche, R.; Muralikrishnan, R.; Hutchings, B. FlowLab: Computational fluid dynamics (CFD) framework for undergraduate education. In Proceedings of the 2002 ASEE/SEFI/TUB Colloquium, Montreal, Canada, 16–19 June 2002; pp. 1235–1238. Available online: https://peer.asee.org/10204 (accessed on 28 July 2017).

8. Parihar, A.; Kulkarni, A.; Stern, F.; Xing, T.; Moeykens, S. Using FlowLab: An educational computational fluid dynamics tool: To perform a comparative study of turbulence models. *Comput. Fluid Dyn. J.* **2006**, *15*, 175.

9. Nakiboglu, G. Development of an Educational CFD Software for Two-Dimensional Incompressible Flows. Master's thesis, Department of Mechanical Engineering, METU, Ankara, Turkey, 2007.

10. Corter, J.E.; Esche, S.K.; Chassapis, C.; Ma, J.; Nickerson, J.V. Process and learning outcomes from remotely-operated, simulated, and hands-on student laboratories. *Comput. Educ.* **2011**, *57*, 2054–2067.

11. Reinmann-Rothmeier, G.; Mandl, H. Unterrichten und Lernumgebungen gestalten. In *Pädagogische Psychologie. Ein Lehrbuch*; Krapp, A.W., Ed.; Beltz Psychologie Verlags Union: Weinheim, Germany, 2001; pp. 601–646.

12. Huber, L.; Hellmer, J.; Schneider, F. *Forschendes Lernen im Studium*, 2nd ed.; UVW Universitäts Verlag: Bielefeld, Germany, 2009.

13. Edelson, D.C. Realising authentic science learning through the adaptation of scientific practice. *Int. Handb. Sci. Educ.* **1998**, *1*, 317–331.

14. Kreylos, O.; Tesdall, A.; Hamann, B.; Hunter, J.; Joy, K. Interactive visualization and steering of CFD simulations. In Proceedings of the Symposium on Data Visualisation 2002, Barcelona, Spain, 2002; pp. 25–34.

15. Höfler, M. Real-time visualization of unstructured volumetric CFD data sets on GPUs. 2006. Available online: https://pdfs.semanticscholar.org/9ab5/9f46c79fc5ae214a43bd04692bd9673c8c57.pdf (accessed on 28 July 2017).

16. De Vuyst, F.; Labourdette, C.; Rey, C. GPU-accelerated real-time visualization and interaction for coupled fluid dynamics. 2013. Available online: http://documents.irevues.inist.fr/handle/2042/52817 (accessed on 28 July 2017).

17. Mawson, M.; Leaver, G.; Revell, A. Real-time flow computations using an image based depth sensor and GPU Acceleration. In Proceedings of the NAFEMS World Congress 2013, Salzburg, Austria, 9–12 June 2013.

18. Harwood, A.; Revell, A. Parallelisation of an interactive Lattice-Boltzmann method on an Android-powered mobile device. *Adv. Eng. Softw.* **2017**, *104*, 38–50.

19. Janßen, C.F. The efficient lattice boltzmann environment ELBE. Available online: http://www.tuhh.de/elbe (accessed on 28 July 2017).

20. Tölke, J.; Krafczyk, M. TeraFLOP computing on a desktop PC with GPUs for 3D CFD. *Int. J. Comput. Fluid Dyn.* **2008**, *22*, 443–456.

21. Linxweiler, J.; Krafczyk, M.; Tölke, J. Highly interactive computational steering for coupled 3D flow problems utilizing multiple GPUs. *Comput. Vis. Sci.* **2010**, *13*, 299–314.

22. Delbosc, N.; Summers, J.; Khan, A.; Kapur, N.; Noakes, C. Optimized implementation of the lattice Boltzmann Method on a graphics processing unit towards real-time fluid simulation. *Comput. Math. Appl.* **2014**, *67*, 462–475.

23.   Janßen, C.; Krafczyk, M. Free surface flow simulations on GPUs using the LBM. *Comput. Math. Appl* **2011**, *61*, 3549–3563.

24.   Gehrke, M.; Janßen, C.F.; Rung, T. Scrutinizing Lattice Boltzmann methods for direct numerical simulations of turbulent channel flows. *Comput. Fluids* **2017**, doi:10.1016/j.compfluid.2017.07.005.

25.   Mierke, D.; Janßen, C.; Rung, T. GPU-accelerated large-eddy simulation of ship-ice interactions. In Proceedings of the 6th International Conference on Computational Methods in Marine Engineering (MARINE 2015), Rome, Italy, 15–17 June 2015; pp. 229–240.

26.   Janßen, C.F.; Mierke, D.; Rung, T. On the development of an efficient numerical ice tank for the simulation of fluid-ship-rigid-ice interactions on graphics processing units. *Comput. Fluids* **2017**, doi:10.1016/j.compfluid.2017.05.006.

27.   Janßen, C.F.; Grilli, S.; Krafczyk, M. Efficient simulations of long wave propagation and runup using a LBM approach on GPGPU hardware. In Proceedings of the 22nd International Offshore and Polar Engineering Conference, Rhodes, Greece, 17–22 June 2012; pp. 145–152.

28.   Janßen, C.; Bengel, S.; Rung, T.; Dankowski, H. A fast numerical method for internal flood water dynamics to simulate water on deck and flooding scenarios of ships. In Proceedings of the 32nd International Conference on Ocean, Offshore and Arctic Engineering, Nantes, France, 9–14 June 2013.

29.   Janßen, C.; Nagrelli, H.; Rung, T. GPGPU-accelerated simulation of wave-ship interactions using LBM and a quaternion-based motion modeler. In Proceedings of the 5th International Conference on Computational Methods in Marine Engineering (MARINE 2013), Hamburg, Germany, 29–31 May 2013; pp. 229–240.

30.   Janßen, C.F.; Mierke, D.; Überrück, M.; Gralher, S.; Rung, T. Validation of the GPU-accelerated CFD solver ELBE for free surface flow problems in civil and environmental engineering. *Computation* **2015**, *3*, 354–385.

31.   Janßen, C.; Grilli, S. Modeling of wave breaking and wave-structure interactions by coupling of fully nonlinear potential flow and Lattice-Boltzmann models. In Proceedings of the 20th International Offshore and Polar Engineering, Beijing, China, 20–25 June 2010.

32.   Banari, A.; Janßen, C.; Krafczyk, M.; Grilli, S.T. Efficient GPGPU implementation of a lattice Boltzmann Model for multiphase flows with high density ratios. *Comput. Fluids* **2014**, *93*, 1–11.

33.   Banari, A.; Janßen, C.; Grilli, S. An efficient lattice Boltzmann multiphase model for 3D flows with large density ratios at high Reynolds numbers. *Comput. Math. Appl.* **2014**, *68*, 1819–1843.

34.   Banari, A.; Mauzole, Y.; Hara, T.; Grilli, S.T.; Janßen, C.F. The simulation of turbulent particle-laden channel flow by the lattice Boltzmann method. *Int. J. Numer. Methods Fluids* **2015**. *79*, 491–513.

35.   Mierke, D.; Rung, T.; Janßen, C.F. An effcient algorithm for the calculation of sub-grid distances for higher-order LBM boundary conditions in a GPU simulation environment. *Comput. Math. Appl.* **2017**, under review.

36.   Koliha, N.; Janßen, C.F.; Rung, T. Towards online visualization and interactive monitoring of real-time CFD simulations on commodity hardware. *Computation* **2015**, *3*, 444–478.

37.   Rueß, J.; Gess, C.; Deicke, W. Schärfung des Konzepts Forschenden Lernens im Kontext forschungsorientierter Lehre. 2013. Available online: https://www.hu-berlin.de/de/einrichtungen-organisation/verwaltung/bolognalab/aktuelles/archiv/wiss_beitrag/schaerfung-des-konzeptes-forschenden-lernen (accessed on 28 July 2017).

38.   Reinmann, G. Gestaltung akademischer Lehre: semantische Klärungen und theoretische Impulse zwischen Problem- und Forschungsorientierung. 2016. Available online: http://www.zfhe.at/index.php/zfhe/article/view/983 (accessed on 28 July 2017).

39.   Chinn, C.A.; Malhotra, B.A. Epistemologically authentic inquiry in schools: A theoretical framework for evaluating inquiry tasks. *Sci. Educ.* **2002**, *86*, 175–218.

40.   Huisman, M.; Janßen, C.F.; Rung, T.; Ehlers, S. Numerical simulation of ship-ice interactions with physics engines under consideration of ice breaking. In Proceedings of the 26nd Offshore and Polar Engineering Conference, Rhodes, Greece, 26 June–2 July 2016.

41.   Ehlers, S.; Leira, B.; Hahn, M.; Dankowski, H.; Ergec, S.; Rung, T.; Huisman, M.; Sjoblom, H.; Chai, W. Numerical Prediction of Ship-Ice Interaction (OMAE2017 61814). In Proceedings of the 36th International Conference on Ocean, Offshore & Arctic Engineering (OMAE), Trondheim, Norway, 25–30 June 2017.

42.   Janßen, C.F.; Überrück, M.; Rung, T.; Behruzi, P. Real-time simulation of impact waves in LNG ship tanks with Lattice Boltzmann single-phase models. In Proceedings of the 26nd Offshore and Polar Engineering Conference, Rhodes, Greece, 26 June–2 July 2016.

43.   Überrück, M.; Janßen, C.F. On the applicability of Lattice Boltzmann single-phase models for the simulation of wave impact in LNG tanks. *Int. J. Offshore Polar Eng.* **2017**, accepted.

6

CFD-PBM Approach with Different Inlet Locations for the Gas-Liquid Flow in a Laboratory-Scale Bubble Column with Activated Sludge/Water

Le Wang [1], Qiang Pan [1], Jie Chen [2] and Shunsheng Yang [1],*

[1] School of Civil Engineering, Southwest Jiaotong University, Chengdu 610031, China;
    lewang@my.swjtu.edu.cn (L.W.); pqiang1985@my.swjtu.edu.cn (Q.P.)
[2] School of Energy and Power Engineering, Xi'an Jiaotong University, Xi'an 710049, China;
    Chenkm705@stu.xjtu.edu.cn
* Correspondence: yss@home.swjtu.edu.cn

Abstract: A novel computational fluid dynamics-population balance model (CFD-PBM) for the simulation of gas mixing in activated sludge (i.e., an opaque non-Newtonian liquid) in a bubble column is developed and described to solve the problem of measuring the hydrodynamic behavior of opaque non-Newtonian liquid-gas two-phase flow. We study the effects of the inlet position and liquid-phase properties (water/activated sludge) on various characteristics, such as liquid flow field, gas hold-up, liquid dynamic viscosity, and volume-averaged bubble diameter. As the inlet position changed, two symmetric vortices gradually became a single main vortex in the flow field in the bubble column. In the simulations, when water was in the liquid phase, the global gas hold-up was higher than when activated sludge was in the liquid phase in the bubble column, and a flow field that was dynamic with time was observed in the bubble column. Additionally, when activated sludge was used as the liquid phase, no periodic velocity changes were found. When the inlet position was varied, the non-Newtonian liquid phase had different peak values and distributions of (dynamic) liquid viscosity in the bubble column, which were related to the gas hold-up. The high gas hold-up zone corresponded to the low dynamic viscosity zone. Finally, when activated sludge was in the liquid phase, the volume-averaged bubble diameter was much larger than when water was in the liquid phase.

Keywords: CFD-PBM; numerical simulation; non-Newtonian/Newtonian liquid; bubble column

1. Introduction

The bubble column, which is a reactor that is widely applied in chemical engineering and biochemical industrial processes, can be used in the activated sludge process to treat industrial sewage and municipal wastewater. Due to the complex nature of two-phase flow in bubble columns, researchers have studied two-phase hydrodynamic behavior experimentally [1–3] and using numerical simulations [4]. However, the fundamental properties of two-phase hydrodynamics, such as the liquid-gas two-phase flow with a non-Newtonian liquid, remain incompletely understood.

Because of its cost-effective nature and ability to conveniently predict behavior, such as liquid-phase velocities and gas hold-up values, at different positions in a bubble column, numerical simulation has been extensively applied. The models used for numerical simulations of the gas-liquid two-phase flow in bubble columns mainly include the Euler-Euler two-fluid model [5], Euler-Euler two-fluid model coupled with a population balance model (PBM) [6–8] and discrete particle model (DPM) [4]. The PBM accounts for the effects of bubble coalescence and breakup and can predict the local bubble size distribution [9]. The methods of solving the PBM include the discrete homogenous method [10], discrete inhomogeneous method [11], quadrature method of moments [12], and direct quadrature method of moments [13]. The Euler-Euler two-fluid model coupled with PBM has the potential for higher accuracy than the Euler-Euler two-fluid model and therefore can potentially predict the gas-liquid exchange area more accurately. Although simulations of multi-phase flow in the bubble column are based on the fundamental physics, the drag force coefficient model [8] and turbulence model [14–16] must be considered in the simulation to determine an appropriate numerical simulation model.

Many studies of the gas-liquid two-phase flow in bubble columns are based on the use of water, which is a Newtonian fluid, as the liquid phase. However, little research has focused on non-Newtonian fluids, such as activated sludge. Due to the opacity of activated sludge, researchers have been unable to use particle image velocimetry (PIV) or laser Doppler velocimetry (LDV) to study the velocity field, flow regime type and gas hold-up distribution in bubble columns. Instead, the experimental research on activated sludge (i.e., a non-Newtonian fluid) as the liquid phase focuses on its rheological behavior, hydrodynamics (mean shear rate) and volumetric oxygen transfer coefficient [17]; the velocity field, gas hold-up distribution, and bubble diameter in bubble columns have not been studied.

Currently, the commonly used liquid phases in simulation studies are other transparent non-Newtonian fluids, such as sodium carboxymethyl cellulose (CMC) aqueous solution [18,19]. The selected mathematical models include the Euler-Euler framework-based Euler-Euler two-fluid model and the Euler-Lagrange framework-based DPM model [20–23]. Most of the reported numerical simulations focus on single-bubble diameter and neglect the bubble coalescence and breakup effects in the non-Newtonian liquid phase because of the lack of research on the coalescence and breakup kernel function in the non-Newtonian liquid phase. Furthermore, the gas-liquid numerical simulation model used for a non-Newtonian liquid phase differs from that used for a Newtonian liquid phase. The mathematical model for the drag force coefficient and dynamic viscosity of a non-Newtonian liquid phase is very different from that of a Newtonian liquid phase [24–26]. Few numerical simulation studies have considered the rheological properties of activated sludge (i.e., a non-Newtonian fluid) in biochemical installations. Dapelo et al. [21] simulated the gas-liquid two-phase flow in an anaerobic digestion installation under the Euler-Lagrange framework and found that the model reproduces the experimental data robustly and accurately. By simulating the gas-liquid two-flow in an anaerobic aeration installation with a non-Newtonian liquid, Wu [23] showed that the gas-liquid mixing efficiency is decided by the mixing mechanism and pump transport period.

However, the existing numerical simulations of a non-Newtonian liquid phase (i.e., activated sludge) in bubble columns rarely considered the rheological properties of activated sludge, the bubble breakage or coalescence processing and the effects of different gas inlet positions. In this work, a Euler-Euler two-fluid model coupled with PBM was used for the first time to simulate the liquid-gas two-phase flow with an opaque non-Newtonian liquid. Comparing the results of simulations and experiments [3,21], we simulated the gas-liquid two-phase flow with different gas inlet positions and liquid-phase properties in a laboratory-scale bubble column and analyzed the hydrodynamic behavior of gas-liquid two-phase flow. We aim to develop an appropriate numerical simulation model and provide guidance for the optimized design and gas inlet position selection for opaque non-Newtonian liquid phase in bubble columns.

2. Mathematical Models

An Euler-Euler two-fluid model was used to simulate gas-liquid two-phase flow, and PBM was used to simulate the bubble coalescence and breakage processes. During the simulations, the gas-liquid interphase heat transfer was ignored, and the two phases were considered incompressible fluids. We assumed that the mixture of the activated sludge and water is a single-phase liquid [27].

2.1. Euler-Euler Two-Fluid Model

Mass conservation equation:

$$\frac{\partial}{\partial t}(\alpha_q \rho_q) + \nabla \cdot (\alpha_q \rho_q \boldsymbol{u}_q) = 0 \tag{1}$$

Momentum conservation equation:

$$\frac{\partial}{\partial t}(\alpha_q \rho_q \boldsymbol{u}_q) + \nabla \cdot (\alpha_q \rho_q \boldsymbol{u}_q \boldsymbol{u}_q) = -\alpha_q \nabla p + \nabla \alpha_q \tau_q + \alpha_q \rho_q \boldsymbol{g} + \boldsymbol{F} \tag{2}$$

where α is the volume fraction; ρ is the density, kg/m^3; p is the pressure, Pa; g is the acceleration due to gravity, 9.8 m/s^2; q is the phase division, with g being the gas phase and l being the liquid phase; and τ_q is the shear stress tensor computed as follows:

$$\tau_q = \mu_{eff,q}(\nabla \boldsymbol{u}_q + (\nabla \boldsymbol{u}_q)^T - \frac{2}{3}(\nabla \cdot \boldsymbol{u}_q)I) \tag{3}$$

where $\mu_{eff,q}$ is the effective viscosity. The effective viscosity of the liquid phase consists of three terms—molecular viscosity, turbulent viscosity and bubble-induced turbulence—as shown below:

$$\mu_{eff,l} = \mu_l + \mu_{T,l} + \mu_{B,l} \tag{4}$$

We adopted the Sato and Sekoguchi model [28] that has been widely used in the bubble column numerical simulations to address bubble-induced turbulence [29–31]. The formulation of viscosity due to the induced turbulence can be expressed as:

$$\mu_{B,l} = \rho_l C_{\mu,B} \alpha_g d |\boldsymbol{u}_g - \boldsymbol{u}_l| \tag{5}$$

where $C_{\mu,B}$ is a constant: 0.6. The magnitude of the drag force was more than 100 times greater than those of the other forces, such as the virtual mass force and turbulent dispersion force. Therefore, we neglected the turbulent dispersion forces, virtual mass force, and wall lubrication force during our numerical simulations and considered only the drag and lift force [15]. $\boldsymbol{F}$ is the interphase force, which is calculated as follows:

$$\boldsymbol{F} = \boldsymbol{F}_D + \boldsymbol{F}_l \tag{6}$$

The drag force $\boldsymbol{F}_D$ and the lift force $\boldsymbol{F}_l$ are considered in this work. The lift force is given by:

$$\boldsymbol{F}_l = C_l \alpha_g \rho_l (\boldsymbol{u}_g - \boldsymbol{u}_l) \times \nabla \boldsymbol{u}_g \tag{7}$$

where C_l is the lift coefficient: 0.5 [3,32]. The drag force can be determined as follows:

$$\boldsymbol{F}_D = \frac{3}{4} \alpha_g \alpha_l \rho_l \frac{C_D}{d} |\boldsymbol{u}_g - \boldsymbol{u}_l|(\boldsymbol{u}_g - \boldsymbol{u}_l) \tag{8}$$

where d is the bubble diameter, m. The drag force coefficient model C_D considering the effects of the rheological properties of non-Newtonian fluids can be expressed as follows [24]:

$$C_D = \begin{cases} \dfrac{16}{\mathrm{Re}_t}\left(1 + 0.173\mathrm{Re}_t^{0.657}\right) + \dfrac{0.413}{1 + 16300\mathrm{Re}_t^{-1.09}} & \mathrm{Re}_t < 135 \\ 0.95 & \mathrm{Re}_t > 135 \end{cases} \tag{9}$$

Since Newtonian and non-Newtonian fluids exhibit different flow behaviors, the definition of the Reynolds number for Newtonian fluids is invalid for non-Newtonian fluids [33]. Therefore, the Reynolds number of spherical bubbles for non-Newtonian fluids Re_t is calculated as follows [34]:

$$Re_t = \frac{\rho_l d^n u_t^{2-n}}{K} \tag{10}$$

where K is the consistency coefficient, kg/(m·s^n); n is the is the power-law index. The drag force coefficient model of the Newtonian fluid is calculated based on the literature [35].

2.2. Turbulence Modeling

Turbulent effects are modeled by the standard $k - \varepsilon$ model. This turbulence model is typically applied to predict the liquid flow pattern and gas hold-up under a low superficial gas velocity due to its simple algorithm and relatively low computational cost [5,36,37]. The standard $k - \varepsilon$ model can be expressed as follows:

$$\frac{\partial(\alpha_q \rho_q k_q)}{\partial t} + \nabla \cdot (\alpha_q \rho_q u_q k_q) = \nabla \cdot \left(\alpha_q \frac{\mu_{eff,q}}{\sigma_k} \nabla k_q \right) + \alpha_q G_{k,q} - \alpha_q \rho_q \varepsilon_q \tag{11}$$

$$\frac{\partial(\alpha_q \rho_q \varepsilon_q)}{\partial t} + \nabla \cdot (\alpha_q \rho_q u_q \varepsilon_q) = \nabla \cdot \left(\alpha_q \frac{\mu_{eff,q}}{\sigma_\varepsilon} \nabla \varepsilon_q \right) + \alpha_q \frac{\varepsilon_q}{k_q} (C_1 G_{k,q} - C_2 \rho_q \varepsilon_q) \tag{12}$$

where k is the turbulent kinetics energy; ε is the turbulent kinetics energy dissipation rate; C_1 and C_2 are constant.

2.3. Non-Newtonian Fluid Rheological Model

The liquid dynamic viscosity is constant (0.001003 kg/(m·s)) for water, which is a Newtonian fluid. The existing models describing the rheology of a non-Newtonian fluid such as activated sludge include the Ostwald de Vaele model, Herschel-Bulkley model, and Bingham model. In particular, Hasar et al. [25] found that the low-shear-speed Ostwald de Vaele model was suitable for practical purposes in studying the flow characteristics of activated sludge. The fitted results obtained by Mohapatra et al. [26] indicate that the Ostwald de Vaele model for wastewater sludge has a higher confidence level than the Bingham or Casson models. The equation for the molecular viscosity can be expressed as:

$$\mu_l = K \dot{\gamma}^{n-1} \tag{13}$$

where $\dot{\gamma}$ is the shear rate, s^{-1}. It should be noted that the effects of temperature on the rheological properties of the sludge were ignored. In this article, the data from Durán et al. [16] were used to characterize the high-concentration activated sludge, where the activated sludge concentration was 7.9 g/L, K was 0.0741 kg/(m·s^n) and n was 0.49.

2.4. Population Balance Model

To consider the bubble breakup and coalescence phenomena in bubble columns, a PBM can be applied to calculate the bubble size distribution as follows:

$$\frac{\partial n(v,t)}{\partial t} + \nabla \cdot (u n(v,t)) = B_a - D_a + B_b - D_b \tag{14}$$

$$B_a = \frac{1}{2} \int_0^v n(v-v',t) n(v',t) a(v-v',v') dv' \tag{15}$$

$$D_a = \int_0^\infty n(v,t) n(v',t) a(v,v') dv' \tag{16}$$

$$B_b = \int_v^\infty \beta(v,v')g(v')n(v',t)dv' \qquad (17)$$

$$D_b = g(v)n(v,t) \qquad (18)$$

where $n(v,t)$ is the bubble size distribution function; Ba, Da, Bb and Db are the births due to coalescence, death due to aggregation, birth due to breakage, and death due to breakage, respectively. Equation (14) is solved using the discrete method solution [38]. The terms for the breakup phenomena are estimated using the Luo and Svendsen model [39]. The model described by Luo is used to model the coalescence processes [40]. The bubble diameter is discretized into 10 sub-classes ranging from 1.45 mm to 9.55 mm [3].

For a non-Newtonian liquid phase, we used the same breakage and coalescence kernel function, primarily based on the following reasons: (1) in the Navier-Stokes equation, we considered the non-Newtonian liquid rheological properties that are a partial influence on the coalescence and breakage processing. (2) It is very difficult to accurately measure the bubble diameter and establish the breakage and coalescence kernel model because of the opacity of activated sludge. (3) We further verified this assumption in Section 4.3.

3. Model Setup and Calculation Algorithm

3.1. Model and Mesh

3.1.1. Physical Model

We adopted the physical three-dimensional (3D) model described by Díaz et al. [3] as shown in Figure 1a, with model height = 0.45 m, length = 0.2 m, and width = 0.04 m. As shown in Figure 1b, the gas inlet is modeled as a rectangular area with dimensions of 0.018×0.006 m at the bottom of the central domain, which represents the experimental sparger setup. As shown in Table 1 and Figure 1c, we modeled eight different cases that varied according to the distance from the gas inlet center to the bottom center of the bubble column and the liquid properties.

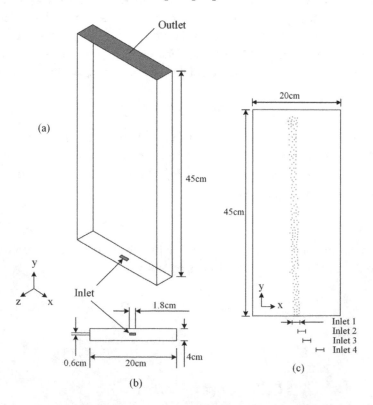

Figure 1. (**a**) 3D physical model, (**b**) inlet parameter, and (**c**) different inlet positions.

Table 1. Parameters of different calculation cases.

No. of Case	1	2	3	4	5	6	7	8
Distance from inlet center to bubble column's bottom center (m)	0	0.025	0.045	0.06	0	0.025	0.045	0.06
Liquid property	Newtonian				Non-Newtonian			

Note: NEW-0/Non-0 mentioned in the title of graph means that the liquid property is Newtonian/Non-Newtonian and the distance from inlet center to the center of the bubble column's base is 0 m.

3.1.2. Mesh

To obtain adequate simulation results compared with experimental data (Section 4.1), different numerical simulations were conducted using four meshes of structured cells (i.e., 1872, 3360, 10,395 and 22,185) to determine an ideal mesh, and a total of 10,395 cells was chosen for computational modeling (Section 4.1). As shown in Figure 2, the meshes in the x-, y- and z-directions were 21, 45 and 11, respectively.

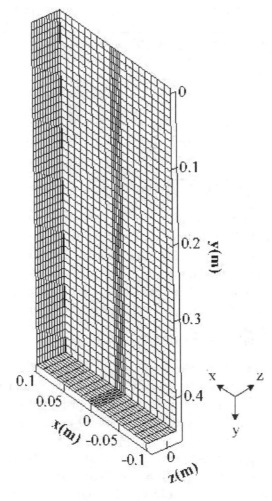

Figure 2. Mesh of case No. 1.

3.2. Calculation Methods

The equations in Section 2 were discretized via the finite volume method, and the volume fractions were differentiated using the QUICK scheme. The time term was treated by a first-order scheme, whereas other terms were treated via a second-order upwind discretization scheme. The pressure and speed were coupled via the semi-implicit method for pressure-linked equation (SIMPLE). The inlet was set as a single-gas phase. The speed inlet boundary conditions were used: the superficial gas velocity was 0.0024 m/s, the outlet was set as a degassing boundary condition [30,41], and the other physical boundaries were set as solid-wall boundary conditions. The residual error was 10^{-5}, the time step was 0.01 s, and the maximum iteration number was 30. Prior to obtaining the unsteady state numerical simulation results, we set the simulation result obtained from 1000 steady-state steps as the initial field of the unsteady state computation. The initial diameter is 5.95 mm. Numerical simulations were performed using the computational fluid dynamics (CFD) commercial code ANSYS Fluent 14.5.

4. Validation

4.1. Mesh Validation

As for the physical model of case 1 (Table 1) under four different grid dimensions, we simulated the aeration of pure water (i.e., a Newtonian fluid) and obtained simulation data for the average gas hold-up in the bubble column. The maximum iteration number and time step length at each step are given in Table 2.

Table 2. Gas hold-up values with different parameters.

Elements Number	Time Step Size (s)	Max Iterations	Gas Hold-Up *
1872	0.01	30	0.0058
3360	0.01	30	0.0060
10,395	0.01	30	0.0065
22,185	0.01	30	0.0057
10,395	0.01	10	0.0064
10,395	0.01	50	0.0065
10,395	0.02	30	0.0064
10,395	0.005	30	0.0065

* The gas hold-up in the experiments was 0.0069.

Table 2 shows that increasing the grid density did not improve the comparability of the simulation results and the experimental data. This finding is in agreement with those reported by Díaz et al. [3] and Buwa et al. [42] and is attributable to the turbulent spectrum. The time step size and maximum iterative step influenced the simulation result but only very slightly. Thus, for the simulations, we selected the grid quantity at which the gas hold-up value was similar to the experimental result: 10,395. Further validation of the gas hold-up distribution was conducted as described in Section 4.2.

4.2. Flow Visualization: Experimental versus Simulated Results

The simulations of the gas hold-up distribution with the above physical model and mathematical method are shown in Figure 3, where the total number of mesh elements is 10,395. The bubble plume oscillates periodically over time. We picked out the most consistent result to the experimental result from the different instantaneous gas hold-up distribution simulation results. Comparing the simulation results with experimental observations reveals that the instantaneous simulated gas hold-up distribution (i.e., the plume) is S-shaped and that the maximum gas hold-up occurs near the inlet area. The simulated gas plume gradually widens from the bottom to the top, and all the simulated phenomena relating to the gas hold-up distribution were basically consistent with the experimental observations.

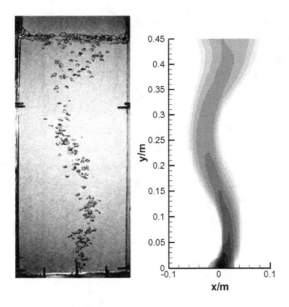

Figure 3. Comparison of the experimental and computational instantaneous gas hold-up results.

4.3. Non-Newtonian Velocity Field Verification

We performed numerical simulations of gas-liquid mixing during the anaerobic digestion in a non-Newtonian liquid phase (i.e., CMC solution) and compared our results with the experimental results reported by Dapelo et al. [21]. The CMC solution had a consistency coefficient of 0.209 kg/(m·s^n) and a power-law index of 0.730. The equations, numerical methods, boundary conditions and bubble particle size distribution used for the numerical simulations were described in Sections 2 and 3. The inlet velocity was 2.05 mL/s. The mesh division method is shown in Figure 4. Figure 4a presents the bottom mesh division, Figure 4b presents the inlet mesh, and Figure 4c presents the axial cross-sectional mesh division when the total number of mesh elements was 108,720.

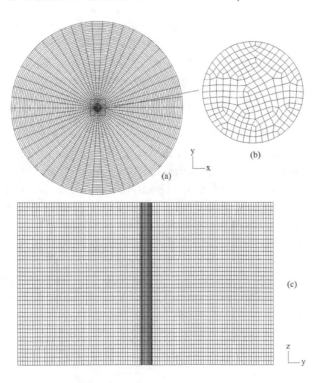

Figure 4. Grid used in the computational fluid dynamics (CFD) simulations: (**a**) bottom, (**b**) inlet, and (**c**) axial cross-section.

Figure 5 presents the comparison of the simulation results for the time-averaged liquid-phase velocity magnitude distributions at different r/R ratios with the simulation results of Dapelo et al. [21] and the experimental results [21]. In the simulation described in this paper, the measured bubble diameter was 5.65 mm, lower than the experimental result (7.94 mm). The bubble diameter relative error between the experimental and simulation data is 28%, possibly because the bubble was assumed to be spherical and to undergo binary collision and breakup processes in the numerical simulations. Furthermore, comparing the velocity magnitudes at different r/R ratios revealed that the simulation results in this paper were better than those of Dapelo et al. [21] and that the numerical simulation method described here could reproduce the velocity magnitude, indicating that the assumptions of the non-Newtonian drag force, lift force, Newtonian coalescence and breakage kernel used for the low-velocity non-Newtonian liquid phase were rational.

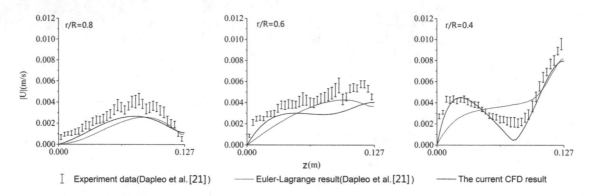

Figure 5. Comparison of the time-averaged velocity magnitude results along a vertical axis between the numerical simulation and particle image velocimetry (PIV) [21].

5. Results and Discussion

5.1. Flow Field

Figure 6 shows the time-averaged liquid-phase streamline at the cross section ($z = 0$ m) in the rectangular bubble column. The position of the inlet determines the form of the liquid-phase flow field. When the inlet was located in the middle of the bottom of the bubble column, two symmetric vortices were formed in the bubble column, and their centers were located in the lower part of the bubble column, as shown in Figure 6a. By contrast, when the inlet was shifted from the middle of the bottom of the bubble column, one main vortex was formed in the middle-left of the bubble column, and two small eddies were formed above the left and right sides of the bubble column, as shown in Figure 6b,c.

When the inlet was the farthest from the middle of the bottom of the bubble column, one large vortex encompassing the bubble column and one eddy were formed above the right side of the bubble column because the liquid phase was influenced by the boundary conditions at the top and the wall, as shown in Figure 6d. The flow field structure changed as the position of the inlet changed.

For the same inlet position, the liquid rheological properties also influenced the flow field in the bubble column. Comparing Figure 6a and Figure 6e shows that symmetric vortices were formed in the bubble column, but their centers were in different positions because of the different liquid-phase velocities in the bubble column (see Section 5.2). These differences also led to the difference between Figure 6d and Figure 6h. In addition, comparing Figure 6b and Figure 6c, and Figure 6f and Figure 6g reveals that when activated sludge was in the liquid phase, the influence area of the main vortex changed, and more small eddies were formed in the bubble column.

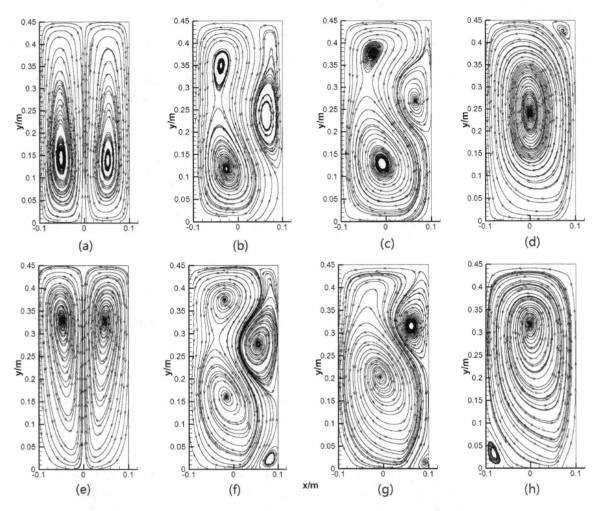

Figure 6. Time-averaged streamline at $z = 0$ m in the bubble column: (**a**) case 1 (NEW-0), (**b**) case 2 (NEW-0.025), (**c**) case 3 (NEW-0.045), (**d**) case 4 (NEW-0.06), (**e**) case 5 (NON-0), (**f**) case 6 (NON-0.025), (**g**) case 7 (NON-0.045), and (**h**) case 8 (NON-0.06).

5.2. Velocity

5.2.1. Liquid-Phase Velocity in the y-Direction

The velocities of a liquid phase in the y-direction at heights 0.09 m and 0.22 m at $z = 0$ m (i.e., at the bubble column centerline) in the bubble column were compared, as shown in Figure 7. As the inlet gradually shifted to the right from the middle of the bottom of the bubble column, the liquid-phase velocity peak value in the y-direction increased. Examination of Figure 7a,b shows that the velocity was much higher at 0.22 m than at 0.09 m from the bottom; at this point, the liquid phase was in the acceleration phase. Moreover, Figure 7a,b indicate that the maximum liquid-phase velocity occurred above the inlet of the bubble column, whereas the minimum velocity occurred at the two sides, indicating that the liquid was driven by the gas phase to flow up through the column to the top and then down to the column bottom along the column wall.

The two liquid phases (water and non-Newtonian sludge) showed different liquid velocity distributions in the y-direction. This difference was one of the reasons for the difference between the liquid-phase streamlines in the bubble column. In Figure 7a, as the inlet gradually shifted from the middle of the bubble column, the difference in the maximum velocity in the y-direction between water and activated sludge decreased gradually until a negative value was reached. In calculation cases 1 and 5 and calculation cases 2 and 6, the activated sludge exhibited larger liquid-phase maximum velocities in the y-direction than water. In contrast, when the inlet was close to the right wall (i.e., in calculation cases 4 and 8 and calculation cases 3 and 7), the maximum velocity in the y-direction of activated sludge was smaller than that of water, possibly because the viscosity was higher in the middle and upper parts of the right side in the column (see Section 5.4); this velocity change also influenced the gas hold-up. Figure 7b shows the liquid-phase velocity in the y-direction showed similar behavior.

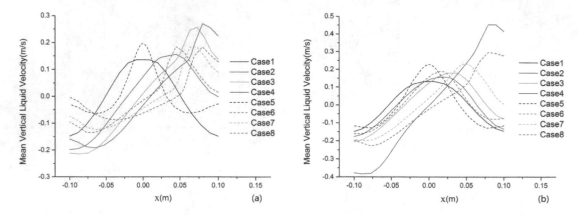

Figure 7. Liquid velocity in the y-direction at $z = 0$ m at different heights in the bubble column: (**a**) 0.09 m and (**b**) 0.22 m.

5.2.2. Liquid-Phase Velocities at Different Monitoring Points

Figure 8 shows the instantaneous horizontal velocities of the liquid phase at the monitoring points: 0 m, 0.225 m, and 0 m. When the liquid phase was water, the oscillation period of the velocity in the x-direction increased as the inlet was shifted farther from the middle of the bottom of the bubble column, as shown in Figure 8a. When the inlet was the farthest from the middle of the bottom of the column (case 4), the liquid-phase velocity in the x-direction did not change over time, indicating that the plume did not periodically oscillate over time, mainly because the gas phase drove the liquid phase to form one quasi-steady-state vortex in the bubble column when the inlet was very close to the wall. Figure 6d shows the form of this vortex; the monitoring points were also near the vortex center. This arrangement is consistent with the lower velocity in the x-direction tending toward zero, as shown in Figure 8a, and with the stable vortex in the bubble column found in the simulation and experimental studies of the corner inlet [4].

The velocity of activated sludge as the liquid phase in the x-direction was constant, while the velocity of water as the liquid phase in the x-direction periodically oscillated, as shown in Figure 8b, because quasi-steady-state vortices were formed, and the velocities in the x-direction at the monitoring points did not change over time in the bubble column. Böhm et al. [43] experimentally studied the bubble upflow in a non-Newtonian liquid (xanthan solution), and their results showed that when the inlet was located in the middle of the bottom of the bubble column, the bubbles did not oscillate from side to side. Passos et al. [20] also found no periodical oscillations of the plume at low velocity during their experimental study of gas-liquid two-phase flow in the xanthan solution as the non-Newtonian liquid in the bubble column. The above studies show that the simulation results and experimental observations in this paper are consistent. In summary, the change in the velocity in the x-direction at the monitoring points was related to the inlet position and liquid rheological properties. The flow field velocity in the bubble column was constant due to the higher overall viscosity of the non-Newtonian liquid phase. For further analysis, we refer the reader to Section 5.4.

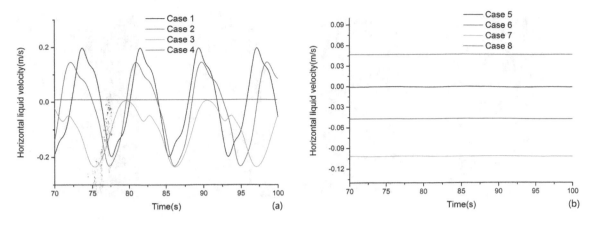

Figure 8. Instantaneous horizontal velocity of the liquid phase at the monitoring points: (**a**) cases 1–4 and (**b**) cases 5–8.

5.3. Gas Hold-Up

5.3.1. Gas Hold-Up Distribution

Figure 9 shows the time-averaged gas hold-up distribution at $z = 0$ m in the bubble column. The calculation cases for the different inlet positions indicated a smaller gas hold-up distribution area at the bottom and a larger gas hold-up distribution area at the top. When the inlet position was farther from the middle of the bottom of the bubble column, the gas-phase distribution area at the bottom gradually decreased, and one extremely low gas hold-up zone was found on the bottom and the walls at the two sides of the bubble column. For different liquid phases and inlet positions, the gas hold-up distribution in the bubble column varied. The gas hold-up distribution was symmetric at $x = 0.1$ m because the inlet position and physical model were symmetric at $x = 0.1$ m, as shown in Figure 9a. By contrast, the gas hold-up distribution was S-shaped in Figure 9b,c; the high-gas hold-up zone was close to the right wall of the bubble column and was cylindrical in the middle of the lower part of bubble column, as shown in Figure 9d.

Varying the liquid-phase properties affected the gas hold-up distribution. When activated sludge was in the liquid phase, the gas hold-up distribution was symmetric and exhibited a V shape, with very low gas hold-up values in the axial area in the middle and upper part of the bubble column, as shown in Figure 9e. In contrast, in Figure 9f,g, the gas hold-up distribution was S-shaped, but the gas hold-up distribution zones were very narrow in the middle and lower part of the bubble column. A low gas hold-up zone was found on the top of the right side of the bubble column, as shown in Figure 9h, possibly because of the high-dynamic viscosity at this location. This finding will be discussed in Section 5.4.

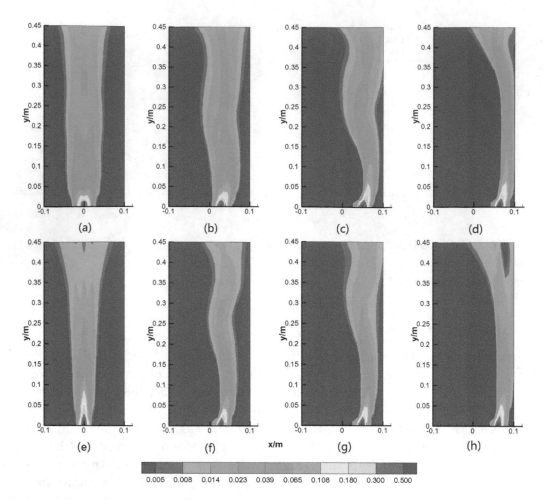

Figure 9. Gas hold-up distribution at $z = 0$ m in the bubble column: (**a**) case 1 (NEW-0), (**b**) case 2 (NEW-0.025), (**c**) case 3 (NEW-0.045), (**d**) case 4 (NEW-0.06), (**e**) case 5 (NON-0), (**f**) case 6 (NON-0.025), (**g**) case 7 (NON-0.045), and (**h**) case 8 (NON-0.06).

5.3.2. Global Gas Hold-Up

The global gas hold-ups in the bubble column for the different cases were compared, as shown in Figure 10. When water was in the liquid phase, calculation cases 1, 2, and 3 showed similar gas hold-ups. Case 4 had the smallest gas hold-up because the high gas velocity in the bubble column led to a shorter residence time of the gas in the liquid phase. The liquid was driven by the gas to flow through the bubble column, and thus, the liquid velocity indirectly reflected the gas velocity shown in Figure 7b. In contrast, when activated sludge was in the liquid phase, the gas hold-up was much lower than that of water in the bubble column. This finding was consistent with the results of Durán et al. [17], Mineta et al. [44] and Fransolet et al. [45] because an increase in the gas-phase upflow velocity led to a shorter residence time of the gas in the bubble column. Furthermore, in calculation case 4, water and activated sludge exhibited similar gas hold-up values in the bubble column because the higher dynamic viscosity of the non-Newtonian liquid at the top of the bubble column led to a large gas hold-up distribution zone.

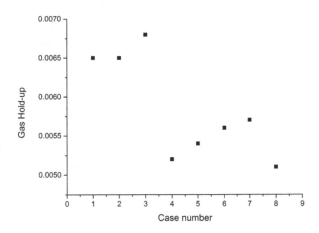

Figure 10. Global gas hold-up.

5.4. Non-Newtonian Liquid Dynamic Viscosity

The higher dynamic viscosity of the non-Newtonian liquid led to lower flowability. Thus, the flowability was studied further by comparing the dynamic viscosity of the non-Newtonian liquid in the bubble column at different inlets, which helped elucidate the origins of the velocity and gas hold-up distribution. Figure 11 presents the dynamic viscosity distribution of the non-Newtonian liquid at $z = 0$ m in the bubble column. The maximum dynamic viscosity peak value of the non-Newtonian liquid occurred when the inlet was located in the middle of the bottom of the bubble column. The low-dynamic viscosity zone distribution was V-shaped and symmetrical at $x = 0$ m, and the peak values were found at the two sides at the bottom of the bubble column, indicating that in this zone, the flowability of the non-Newtonian liquid is lower. When the inlet was located between the middle and the right wall of the bubble column, the dynamic viscosity distribution and peak value were found on the bottom of the left side of the bubble column, while low-dynamic viscosity was observed on the right of the bubble column, as shown in Figure 11b,c. When the inlet was the farthest from the middle of the bottom of the bubble column, the non-Newtonian liquid its minimum dynamic viscosity peak value and much lower dynamic viscosity and high flowability at the zone close to the right wall from the bottom to the middle; however, a visible high-dynamic viscosity zone in the middle and upper part of the right side blocked the non-Newtonian liquid flow, as shown in Figure 11d. Lower gas hold-up was also found in this zone, as shown in Figure 9h. This phenomenon may explain why water (i.e., the Newtonian liquid phase) had a much higher velocity in the y-direction in the right side of the bubble column than the activated sludge (i.e., a non-Newtonian liquid).

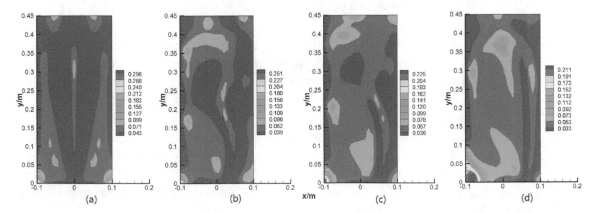

Figure 11. Dynamic viscosity distribution of non-Newtonian liquid at $z = 0$ m in the bubble column: (**a**) case 5 (NON-0), (**b**) case 6 (NON-0.025), (**c**) case 7 (NON-0.045), and (**d**) case 8 (NON-0.06).

Comparing the gas hold-up distributions and dynamic viscosity distributions of the non-Newtonian liquid revealed that these distributions are interrelated. Figure 9e shows the V-shaped hold-up distribution, and Figure 11a presents the V-shaped low-dynamic viscosity zone distribution. Figure 9f and Figure 11b, Figure 9g and Figure 11c, Figure 9h and Figure 11d revealed that high-gas hold-up zones always correspond to low-dynamic viscosity zones. This finding indicated that the liquid phase had strong flowability in the low-dynamic viscosity zone and that the gas phase always flowed up in this zone. Moreover, the instantaneous velocity did not change periodically, as shown in Figure 8b, possibly because of the influence of the dynamic viscosity of the liquid. The viscosity was small in the low-dynamic viscosity zones, and thus, the gas phase flowed up along these zones to form a gas upflow path in the bubble column.

5.5. Volume-Average Bubble Diameter

As an important bubble column parameter, the bubble diameter is highly meaningful for the prediction of the gas-liquid mass transfer in the bubble column. As shown in Figure 12, when water was the Newtonian liquid phase, the volume-averaged bubble diameter was small: 0.0057 m and 0.0042 m in cases 3 and 4, respectively, when the inlet was far from the middle of the bottom of bubble column. Larger values—0.0067 m and 0.0059 m—were found in cases 1 and 2, respectively, when the inlet was close to the middle of the bottom of bubble column. As shown in Figure 12, when activated sludge was the non-Newtonian liquid phase, the volume-averaged bubble diameter in the bubble column was similar to the values reported above, with case 6 showing the highest bubble diameter: 0.0062 m.

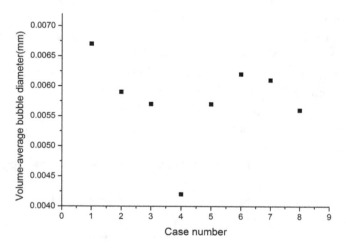

Figure 12. Comparison of the volume-averaged bubble diameter.

Moreover, we found that the activated sludge as the liquid phase exhibited slightly higher volume-averaged bubble diameters than water as the liquid phase, except in cases 1 and 5; these findings were in accordance with the experimental observations of Fabiyi and Novak [46].

6. Conclusions

We aimed to measure the gas mixing in the hydrodynamic behavior of activated sludge (i.e., an opaque non-Newtonian liquid), which has been difficult to measure experimentally in previous research. An Euler-Euler two-fluid model coupled with the PBM model was developed for numerical simulations of different liquid phases and inlet positions in the bubble column in this work. The following conclusions were obtained:

The inlet position and liquid rheological properties influenced the number of vortices, vortex distribution and vortex center in the flow field in the bubble column. Using water as the liquid phase provided some velocity fields in the bubble column that differed from those obtained using activated sludge as the liquid phase; i.e., as the inlet gradually shifted from the center of the bubble column, the difference in the maximum velocity in the y-direction between activated sludge and water decreased until a negative value was reached in the bubble column.

The inlet position influenced the gas hold-up. When water was in the liquid phase, the inlet position deviated farther from the bubble column, resulting in a larger gas hold-up; the lowest gas hold-up was observed when the inlet position was the farthest from the center of the bubble column. In contrast, when activated sludge was in the liquid phase, the gas hold-up was much lower than that of water, and as the inlet position moved farther from the center of the bubble column, the gas hold-up in the bubble column decreased.

When activated sludge was in the liquid phase, the liquid dynamic viscosity distribution influenced the gas hold-up distribution, and high-gas hold-up zones always corresponded to low-dynamic viscosity zones. The volume-averaged bubble diameter varied nonlinearly with the inlet position in the bubble column; i.e., as the inlet position moved farther from the center of the bubble column, the volume-averaged bubble diameter decreased. In contrast, when pure water was in the liquid phase, the volume-averaged bubble diameters were lower than when activated sludge was used in the simulations.

The study in this paper was based on the assumption that bubbles coalescence and breakup effect of in the non-Newtonian liquid phase was consistent with that in Newtonian liquid phase. This assumption is still defective. The future study focuses on (1) experimental study on bubble distribution in non-Newtonian liquid phase; and (2) accurate determination of bubbles coalescence and breakup kernel function in the non-Newtonian liquid phase.

Author Contributions: Le Wang carried out the model simulations, data analysis and writing of the manuscript. Qiang Pan contributed analysis tools. Jie Chen contributed to the interpretation of the results. Shunsheng Yang conceived the simulation process. All the authors participated and contributed to the manuscript.

References

1. Ali, B.A.; Kumar, C.S.; Pushpavanam, S. Analysis of liquid circulation in a rectangular tank with a gas source at a corner. *Chem. Eng. J.* **2008**, *144*, 442–452. [CrossRef]

2. Sun, H.; Mao, Z.S.; Yu, G. Experimental and numerical study of gas hold-up in surface aerated stirred tanks. *Chem. Eng. Sci.* **2006**, *61*, 4098–4110. [CrossRef]

3. Díaz, M.E.; Montes, F.J.; Galán, M.A. Experimental study of the transition between unsteady flow regimes in a partially aerated two-dimensional bubble column. *Chem. Eng. Process.* **2008**, *47*, 1867–1876. [CrossRef]

4. Ali, B.A.; Pushpavanam, S. Analysis of unsteady gas-liquid flows in a rectangular tank: Comparison of Euler-Eulerian and Euler-Lagrangian simulations. *Int. J. Multiph. Flow* **2011**, *37*, 268–277. [CrossRef]

5. Pfleger, D.; Becker, S. Modelling and simulation of the dynamic flow behaviour in a bubble column. *Chem. Eng. Sci.* **2001**, *56*, 1737–1747. [CrossRef]

6. Wang, T.; Wang, J. Numerical simulations of gas-liquid mass transfer in bubble columns with a CFD-PBM coupled model. *Chem. Eng. Sci.* **2007**, *62*, 7107–7118. [CrossRef]

7. Gupta, A.; Roy, S. Euler-Euler simulation of bubbly flow in a rectangular bubble column: Experimental validation with radioactive particle tracking. *Chem. Eng. J.* **2013**, *225*, 818–836. [CrossRef]

8. Liang, X.F.; Pan, H.; Su, Y.H.; Luo, Z.H. CFD-PBM approach with modified drag model for the gas-liquid flow in a bubble column. *Chem. Eng. Res. Des.* **2016**, *112*, 88–102. [CrossRef]

9. Xing, C.; Wang, T.; Wang, J. Experimental study and numerical simulation with a coupled CFD-PBM model of the effect of liquid viscosity in a bubble column. *Chem. Eng. Sci.* **2013**, *95*, 313–322. [CrossRef]

10. Hounslow, M.J.; Ryall, R.L.; Marshall, V.R. A discretized population balance for nucleation, growth, and aggregation. *AIChE J.* **1988**, *34*, 1821–1832. [CrossRef]

11. Tomiyama, A.; Shimada, N. (N+2)-field modeling for bubbly flow simulation. *Comput. Fluid Dyn. J.* **2001**, *9*, 418–426.

12. McGraw, R. Description of aerosol dynamics by the quadrature method of moments. *Aerosol Sci. Technol.* **1997**, *27*, 255–265. [CrossRef]

13. Marchisio, D.L.; Fox, R.O. Solution of population balance equations using the direct quadrature method of moments. *J. Aerosol Sci.* **2005**, *36*, 43–73. [CrossRef]

14. Tabib, M.V.; Roy, S.A.; Joshi, J.B. CFD simulation of bubble column—An analysis of interphase forces and turbulence models. *Chem. Eng. J.* **2008**, *139*, 589–614. [CrossRef]

15. Laborde-Boutet, C.; Larachi, F.; Dromard, N.; Delsart, O.; Schweich, D. CFD simulation of bubble column flows: Investigations on turbulence models in RANS approach. *Chem. Eng. Sci.* **2009**, *64*, 4399–4413. [CrossRef]

16. Liu, Y.; Hinrichsen, O. Study on CFD-PBM turbulence closures based on k–ε and Reynolds stress models for heterogeneous bubble column flows. *Comput. Fluids* **2014**, *105*, 91–100. [CrossRef]

17. Durán, C.; Fayolle, Y.; Pechaud, Y.; Cockx, A.; Gillot, S. Impact of suspended solids on the activated sludge non-Newtonian behaviour and on oxygen transfer in a bubble column. *Chem. Eng. Sci.* **2016**, *141*, 154–165. [CrossRef]

18. Esmaeili, A.; Guy, C.; Chaouki, J. Local hydrodynamic parameters of bubble column reactors operating with non-Newtonian liquids: Experiments and models development. *AIChE J.* **2016**, *62*, 1382–1396. [CrossRef]

19. Godbole, S.P.; Schumpe, A.; Shah, Y.T.; Carr, N.L. Hydrodynamics and mass transfer in non-Newtonian solutions in a bubble column. *AIChE J.* **1984**, *30*, 213–220. [CrossRef]

20. Passos, A.D.; Voulgaropoulos, V.P.; Paras, S.V.; Mouza, A.A. The effect of surfactant addition on the performance of a bubble column containing a non-Newtonian liquid. *Chem. Eng. Res. Des.* **2015**, *95*, 93–104. [CrossRef]

21. Dapelo, D.; Alberini, F.; Bridgeman, J. Euler-Lagrange CFD modelling of unconfined gas mixing in anaerobic digestion. *Water Res.* **2015**, *85*, 497–511. [CrossRef] [PubMed]

22. Bandyopadhyay, T.K.; Das, S.K. Non-Newtonian and gas-non-Newtonian liquid flow through elbows-CFD analysis. *J. Appl. Fluid Mech.* **2013**, *6*, 131–141.

23. Wu, B. CFD simulation of gas and non-Newtonian fluid two-phase flow in anaerobic digesters. *Water Res.* **2010**, *44*, 3861–3874. [CrossRef] [PubMed]

24. Dewsbury, K.; Karamanev, D.; Margaritis, A. Hydrodynamic characteristics of free rise of light solid particles and gas bubbles in non-Newtonian liquids. *Chem. Eng. Sci.* **1999**, *54*, 4825–4830. [CrossRef]

25. Hasar, H.; Kinaci, C.; Ünlü, A.; Toğrul, H.; Ipek, U. Rheological properties of activated sludge in a sMBR. *Biochem. Eng. J.* **2004**, *20*, 1–6. [CrossRef]

26. Mohapatra, D.P.; Brar, S.K.; Tyagi, R.D.; Picard, P.; Surampalli, R.Y. Ferro-sonication and partial ozonation pre-treatment and biotransformation of wastewater sludge for degradation of bisphenol a: Rheology studies. *Chem. Eng. Sci.* **2012**, *81*, 20–27. [CrossRef]

27. Gresch, M.; Armbruster, M.; Braun, D.; Gujer, W. Effects of aeration patterns on the flow field in wastewater aeration tanks. *Water Res.* **2011**, *45*, 810–818. [CrossRef] [PubMed]

28. Sato, Y.; Sadatomi, M.; Sekoguchi, K. Momentum and heat transfer in two-phase bubble flow-I. Theory. *Int. J. Multiph. Flow* **1981**, *7*, 167–177. [CrossRef]

29. Pourtousi, M.; Sahu, J.; Ganesan, P. Effect of interfacial forces and turbulence models on predicting flow pattern inside the bubble column. *Chem. Eng. Process.* **2014**, *75*, 38–47. [CrossRef]

30. Li, G.; Yang, X.; Dai, G. CFD simulation of effects of the configuration of gas distributors on gas-liquid flow and mixing in a bubble column. *Chem. Eng. Sci.* **2009**, *64*, 5104–5116. [CrossRef]

31. Silva, M.K.; d'Ávila, M.A.; Mori, M. Study of the interfacial forces and turbulence models in a bubble column. *Comput. Chem. Eng.* **2012**, *44*, 34–44. [CrossRef]

32. Zhang, D.; Deen, N.G.; Kuipers, J.A.M. Numerical simulation of the dynamic flow behavior in a bubble column: A study of closures for turbulence and interface forces. *Chem. Eng. Sci.* **2006**, *61*, 7593–7608. [CrossRef]

33. Wu, B.X.; Chen, S.L. CFD simulation of non-Newtonian fluid flow in anaerobic digesters. *Biotechnol. Bioeng.* **2008**, *99*, 700–711. [CrossRef] [PubMed]

34. Lali, A.M.; Khare, A.S.; Joshi, J.B.; Nigam, K.D.P. Behaviour of solid particles in viscous non-Newtonian solutions: Settling velocity, wall effects and bed expansion in solid-liquid fluidized beds. *Powder Technol.* **1989**, *57*, 39–50. [CrossRef]

35. Grace, J.R.; Wairegi, T.; Nguyen, T.H. Shapes and velocities of single drops and bubbles moving freely through immiscible liquids. *Trans. Inst. Chem. Eng.* **1976**, *54*, 167–173.

36. Ranade, V.V.; Tayalia, Y. Modelling of fluid dynamics and mixing in shallow bubble column reactors: Influence of sparger design. *Chem. Eng. Sci.* **2001**, *56*, 1667–1675. [CrossRef]

37. Pourtousi, M.; Ganesan, P.; Sahu, J.N. Effect of bubble diameter size on prediction of flow pattern in Euler-Euler simulation of homogeneous bubble column regime. *Measurement* **2015**, *76*, 255–270. [CrossRef]

38. Ramkrishna, D. *Population Balances: Theory and Applications to Particulate Systems in Engineering*; Academic Press: San Diego, CA, USA, 2000.

39. Luo, H.; Svendsen, H.F. Theoretical model for drop and bubble breakup in turbulent dispersions. *Chem. Eng. Sci.* **1996**, *66*, 766–776. [CrossRef]

40. Luo, H. *Coalescence, Breakup and Liquid Circulation in Bubble Column Reactors*; Norwegian Institute of Technology: Trondheim, Norway, 1993.

41. Masood, R.M.A.; Khalid, Y.; Delgado, A. Scale adaptive simulation of bubble column flows. *Chem. Eng. J.* **2015**, *262*, 1126–1136. [CrossRef]

42. Buwa, V.V.; Ranade, V.V. Dynamics of gas-liquid flow in a rectangular bubble column: Experiments and single/multi-group CFD simulations. *Chem. Eng. Sci.* **2002**, *57*, 4715–4736. [CrossRef]

43. Böhm, L.; Kurita, T.; Kimura, K.; Kraume, M. Rising behaviour of single bubbles in narrow rectangular channels in Newtonian and non-Newtonian liquids. *Int. J. Multiph. Flow* **2014**, *65*, 11–23. [CrossRef]

44. Mineta, R.; Salehi, Z.; Yoshikawa, H.; Kawase, Y. Oxygen transfer during aerobic biodegradation of pollutants in a dense activated sludge slurry bubble column: Actual volumetric oxygen transfer coefficient and oxygen uptake rate in p-nitrophenol degradation by acclimated waste activated sludge. *Biochem. Eng. J.* **2011**, *53*, 266–274. [CrossRef]

45. Fransolet, E.; Crine, M.; Marchot, P.; Toye, D. Analysis of gas holdup in bubble columns with non-Newtonian fluid using electrical resistance tomography and dynamic gas disengagement technique. *Chem. Eng. Sci.* **2005**, *60*, 6118–6123. [CrossRef]

46. Fabiyi, M.E.; Novak, R. Evaluation of the factors that impact successful membrane biological reactor operations at high solids concentration. *Proc. Water Environ. Fed.* **2007**, 503–512. [CrossRef]

7

Performance Comparison of Feed-Forward Neural Networks Trained with Different Learning Algorithms for Recommender Systems

Mohammed Hassan [1,2,*,†] **and Mohamed Hamada** [1,†]

[1]   Software Engineering Lab, Graduate School of Computer Science and Engineering, University of Aizu, Aizuwakamatsu 965-8580, Japan; hamada@u-aizu.ac.jp

[2]   Department of Software Engineering, Bayero University Kano, Kano 700231, Nigera

*   Correspondence: d8171104@u-aizu.ac.jp

†   These authors contributed equally to this work.

Abstract: Accuracy improvement is among the primary key research focuses in the area of recommender systems. Traditionally, recommender systems work on two sets of entities, *Users* and *Items*, to estimate a single rating that represents a user's acceptance of an item. This technique was later extended to multi-criteria recommender systems that use an overall rating from multi-criteria ratings to estimate the degree of acceptance by users for items. The primary concern that is still open to the recommender systems community is to find suitable optimization algorithms that can explore the relationships between multiple ratings to compute an overall rating. One of the approaches for doing this is to assume that the overall rating as an aggregation of multiple criteria ratings. Given this assumption, this paper proposed using feed-forward neural networks to predict the overall rating. Five powerful training algorithms have been tested, and the results of their performance are analyzed and presented in this paper.

Keywords: recommender systems; artificial neural network; genetic algorithm; simulated annealing; back-propagation; Adaline; Levenberg-Marquardt

1. Introduction

Recommender systems are fast becoming essential instruments for both industries and academic institutions in addressing decision-making problems, such as choosing the most appropriate items from a large group of items. They play important roles in helping users to find items that might be relevant to what they want [1,2]. Nowadays, many definitions have been suggested for the term recommender system, but the most common one is to define it as an intelligent system that predicts and suggests items to the users that might match their choices. Another simple way to explain it is to assume there are two sets (*Users* and *Items*) consisting of the users of the system and the items that will be recommended to them respectively. A recommender system uses a utility function f to measure the likeness of an item i by a user u, where $i \in Items$ and $u \in Users$. This relationship can be represented as: $f(u,i) \mapsto r_o$, where r_o is a rating, which measures the degree to which the user may accept the item. Recommender systems seek to estimate r_o for each $user \times item$ relationship and recommends items with higher rating values to the users [3].

Several forms of supervised learning algorithms have been applied to predict users' preferences of unseen items from a vast catalog of products using datasets of numerical preferences within some closed interval (e.g., 1 to 10). The most commonly used algorithms are content-based filtering, collaborative filtering, knowledge-based, and hybrid-based which combines two or more algorithms in different ways [4]. However, these kinds of the systems have some fundamental issues such as sparsity, cold start, and scalability problems. These problems have significantly affected the performance of the recommender systems. Artificial neural networks can be used to handle some of these problems as proposed by Zhao et al. [5], where contextual information are incorporated into the systems and modeled as a network of substitutable and complementary items. Another major drawback with these kinds of recommender systems is the of a single rating r_0 to decide whether the user is interested in the item or not. There is a considerable amount of research that establishes the limitations of single rating traditional recommender systems [6]. This is because there are many attributes of items used by users to decide on the usefulness of the items. Recent developments in the domain of recommender systems have heightened the need for considering some of these major attributes of items to make more accurate recommendations.

Multi-criteria recommender systems have invoked some of the most remarkable current discussions for solving some of the difficult problems of traditional recommendation systems. This area has been studied by many researchers [6,7], and it shows more reasonable recommendation accuracy over the traditional techniques. However, the central question is how to model the criteria ratings to estimate the overall rating that can be used in making the final recommendation. Consequently, Gediminas et al. [6] challenge the recommender systems community to use some of the sophisticated machine learning algorithms (especially artificial neural networks) to predict overall ratings based on the ratings given to the criteria. Even though a lot of research has been carried out on multi-criteria recommender systems, what is not yet clear is the impact of other sophisticated machine learning algorithms such as artificial neural networks in improving recommendation accuracy for multi-criteria recommendation problems. These challenges are currently quite open. This paper seeks to pursue this challenge by proposing different learning algorithms to train artificial neural networks using movie recommendation data sets. The aim of the study is to examine the emerging performance of some learning algorithms such as backpropagation (gradient descent-based), Levemberg-Marquardt, simulated annealing, Delta rule, and genetic algorithms in training artificial neural networks to shed more light on which option to pursue when using neural networks to improve the accuracy of multi-criteria recommender systems. This research will provide a significant opportunity to advance our understanding of the better algorithms to use for training neural networks, especially when modeling multi-criteria recommendation problems. The paper is composed of five themed sections, including this introduction section. Section 2 begins by laying the theoretical background of multi-criteria recommender systems, artificial neural networks, and the training algorithms used. Section 3 contains the details of the experiments conducted, while results and discussion of the study are provided in Section 4. Finally, the conclusion in Section 5 gives a summary of the work and identifies potential areas for future research.

2. Background

This study covers many independent research domains within the area of computational science. Therefore, at this point, it is considered necessary to give a brief panorama of the topics concerned. The most important areas to understand are the multi-criteria recommender systems and artificial neural networks, followed by the training algorithms.

2.1. Multi-Criteria Recommender Systems (MCRSs)

MCRSs were proposed principally to overcome some of the shortcomings of traditional recommendation techniques by taking into consideration the users' preferences based on multiple characteristics of items to possibly provide more accurate recommendations [8]. This technique has been applied in many popular recommendation domains such as product recommendations [9], tourism and travel domains[10], restaurant recommendation problems [11], research paper recommendations [12], e-learning [13] and many others.

The *MCRSs* technique extends traditional recommender systems by allowing the users to give ratings to several items' characteristics known as criteria. Each criteria rating r_i for $i = 1, 2, ..., k$, provides additional information about users' opinions on the items; for instance, in a movie recommendation problem, users may like a movie based on action, story, visuals, or the direction of the movie. Therefore, users are expected to give ratings for those criteria and possibly with an additional rating called the overall rating. Hence, the utility function of traditional recommender systems introduced briefly in the introduction section needs to be extended to account for multiple criteria ratings as presented in (1) below:

$$f : Users \times Items \rightarrow r_1 \times r_2 \times r_3 \times ... \times r_k \qquad (1)$$

Because of the nature of the utility function (see (1)), it becomes necessary to introduce a new technique that can use all the ratings for making more accurate predictions. There are two main approaches used for calculating user preferences in *MCRSs*. One of them is the heuristic-based approach that uses multidimensional similarity metrics to calculate similarity values on each criterion together with the overall rating r_o, and the second one is the model-based approach in which a model is built to estimate the r_o. An aggregation function model is a perfect example of the model-based approach that computes r_o as a function of other criteria (see (2)).

$$r_o = f(r_1, r_2, r_3, ..., r_k) \qquad (2)$$

2.2. Artificial Neural Networks (ANNs)

ANNs are coordinative intelligent systems consisting of neurons as the essential elements. They are powerful algorithms initially inspired by the goal of implementing machines that can imitate the human brain [14]. *ANNs* strive to simulate, in a great fashion, the network of neurons (nerve cells) of the biological nervous system. The physical structure and information processing of the human brain are partially imitated with collections of interconnected neurons to model nonlinear systems [15]. Neurons are cells in the brain that contain input wires to other neurons called dendrites and output wires from a neuron to other neurons called axons.

Neurons are computational units that accept inputs via dendrites and sends the result to another neuron after the computations through the axon. Neurons are organized in *ANNs* in the form of layers. A layer that receives inputs from the external environment is called an input layer and the one that presents the computational results is referred to as the output layer. Between the input and output layers, there may be other layers called hidden layers. Every neuron in the network belongs to exactly one layer, and there may be several neurons in one layer. *ANNs* architecture is referred to as a feedforward network if the flow of signal is in a direction in which the input values are fed directly into the input layer, then to the next layer after the computation. *ANNs* that contain at least three layers (input, output, and one or more hidden layers) are called multi-layer *ANNs* (or *MANNs* for short). The underlying architecture of *MANNs* is given in Figure 1, containing one hidden layer. *ANNs* are fully connected, which means that each neuron at every layer is attached to all neurons in the adjacent layer [16].

The output of *ANNs* is a computational result of an activation function $f_\omega(\chi)$ where ω is a vector of synaptic weights between neurons and χ is a vector of the input values. ω contains important parameters that the *ANNs* need to learn for determining an accurate output value for any input values in χ. The $f_\omega(\chi)$ can be of different types such as a sigmoid (logistic) activation function $\left(f_\omega(\chi) = \frac{1}{1+e^{-\omega^T \chi}} \right)$, linear activation function $\left(f_\omega(\chi) = \omega^T \chi \right)$, tangent hyperbolic activation function $\left(f_\omega(\chi) = \frac{1-e^{-\omega^T \chi}}{1+e^{-\omega^T \chi}} \right)$, etc. In working with the *ANNs*, an appropriate activation function must be defined at each layer that receives signals from the previous layer to scale the data output from the layer. The choice of the kind of activation function to use depends on the nature of the output the neuron is expected to provide.

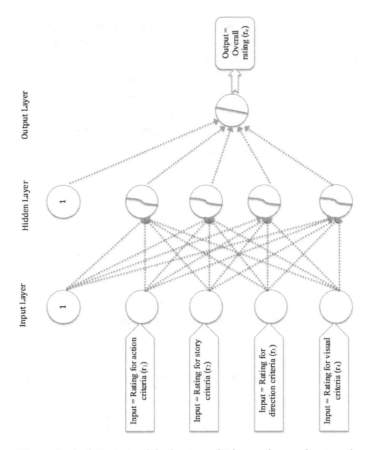

Figure 1. Architecture of the basic multi-layered neural network.

However, as the output of the network depends on the synaptic weights and bias, the central question in using *ANNs* to solve any machine learning problem is to think about how the networks will be trained in learning the appropriate connection weights to produce optimal outputs. The target is to find a value $\Delta\omega$ that can be used to update the weights based on some given criteria. Several algorithms can be used to find $\Delta\omega$ to train *ANNs*. In the subsequent sections, we briefly explain some of the possible algorithms for training *ANNs*.

2.3. Delta Rule Algorithm (DRA)

The *DRA* is a popular and efficient algorithm for training *ANNs* that does not contain hidden layers. It is based on a gradient descent algorithm that was developed to train two-layer networks which deal with a nonlinearly separable data set. It uses a constant learning rate η, which is a parameter that controls how much the updating steps can affect the current values of the weights. It also contains the derivative of the activation functions $f_\omega(\chi)$, the error between real and estimated outputs, and the current features to compute $\Delta\omega$ (see (3), y_j is the actual value from the data set) so that the updated weights that can be used in the $n+1$ iteration will be computed using $\Delta\omega$ (see (4)). Note that in this experiment, the *DRA* algorithm may be referred to as ADAptive Linear Neuron (Adaline) algorithm.

$$\Delta\omega_i = \eta(y_j - f_\omega(\chi))f'_\omega(\chi_i)x_i \qquad (3)$$

$$\omega(n+1) = \omega(n) + \Delta\omega \qquad (4)$$

2.4. Backpropagation Algorithm (BPA)

Section 2.2 explained the basic architecture of *MANNs*, and how features are forward propagated from the input to the output layer. Although the algorithm described in Section 2.3 works quite well for

ANNs having only two layers, this algorithm can not be applied to *ANNs* with more than two layers. To solve this problem, *BPA* is one of the algorithms used to determine the optimal values of weights in *MANNs*. There are two versions of back-propagation algorithms employed in this experiment: the gradient descent-based, and Levenberg-Marquardt-based *BPA*. For simplicity, this study refers to gradient descent-based algorithm simply as "*BPA*" (discussed here) and the Levenberg-Marquardt algorithm-based as "*LMA*". *BPA* works by training the networks to produce the estimated output $f_\omega(\chi)$. As each feature set is presented to the network, errors are calculated between the outputs of the networks y_j for $j's$ feature sets. The weights' matrix is then modified to minimize the errors. In an experiment with training data containing N features, the average error E_{av} is determined as follows:

$$E_{av} = \frac{1}{2N} \sum_{j=1}^{N} (y_j - f_\omega(\chi))^2 \tag{5}$$

The following steps explained how BPA works according to some of the recent implementations of the algorithm [17].

1. Define the training sets and randomly generate the synaptic weights.
2. Advance the training data set from the input to the output layer via the hidden layers to obtain the estimated output.
3. Calculate the error using (5).
4. Terminate the training if the error satisfies the given criteria or if the maximum number of iteration is reached.
5. Update the synaptic weights of the networks according to the layers.
6. Go to step 2.

Calculating $\Delta\omega$ using BPA is a bit lengthy compared to doing so with Adaline. It requires someone to have a basic mathematical background, especially the rules of differential calculus. We therefore skip the derivation, but the reader can find a detailed explanation of this derivation in [16].

2.5. Levenberg-Marquardt Algorithm (LMA)

LMA was proven to be among the most efficient optimization algorithms for solving various minimization problems than conjugate gradient techniques like the dog-leg algorithm, the double dog-leg algorithm, the truncated conjugate gradient, two-dimensional search methods, as well as the gradient descent algorithm [18]. It is used to solve nonlinear least square optimization problems that look exactly like the error function in (5).

To highlight how the *LMA* computes the error function and updates the weights, let $d_j = (y_j - f_\omega(\chi))$; we can rewrite the error function over the feature set x as $E(x) = \frac{1}{2N} \sum_{j=1}^{N} d_j^2(x)$ where x contains the elements $x_1, x_2, ..., x_k$. d_j is a function $\mathbb{R}^k \mapsto \mathbb{R}$ which is an error for $j's$ feature set where $N \geq k$. To put it in a simpler form, we can take the error function E as a vector of errors $d : \mathbb{R}^k \mapsto \mathbb{R}^N$ defined by $d(x) = (d_1(x), d_2(x), d_3(x), ..., d_N(x))$ so that the error E can be written as $E(x) = \frac{1}{2} \| d(x) \|^2$. Let's define a Jacobian matrix $M(x)$ as a matrix of the derivatives of the error function with respect to x as $M(x) = \frac{\partial d_j}{\partial x_i}$ for $j \in [1, N]$ and $i \in [1, k]$. The weight update $\Delta\omega$ can be obtained using (6), and for the new weights, we go back to (4).

$$\Delta\omega = (M^T M + \eta I)^{-1} M^T d \tag{6}$$

2.6. Genetic Algorithm (GA)

GA is a very prominent non-traditional optimization technique which resembles the theory of evolution. It is an adaptive search algorithm that works based on the methods of natural selection. Unlike the previous algorithms, *GA* works based on logic, not derivatives of a function and it can search for a population of solutions, not only one solution set. The logic it uses is based on the concept of 'Survival of the fittest' from Darwin's theory [19] which means only the most competent individual will survive and generate other individuals that might perform better than the current generation.

While a variety of explanations can be found about this algorithm in the literature, the most common way to explain GA is to look at it as a replica of biological chromosomes and genes, where the chromosome is a solution set or an individual containing the set of parameters to be optimized, and a gene represents single components of those parameters. New generations of chromosomes can be generated by manipulating the genes in the chromosomes. A collection of chromosomes is known as a population, and the population size is the exact number of chromosomes in the experiment. Two basic genetic operators 'mutation' and 'crossover' are used to manipulate genes in the chromosomes.

The crossover operation combines genes from two parents to form an offspring, while the mutation operation is used to bring new genetic material into the population by interchanging the genes in the chromosome [20]. The following steps summarize how GA works in solving optimization problems.

1. Generate n population of chromosomes at random.
2. Compute the fitness ($E(x)$ in our case) of each chromosome.
3. Generate a new population using the selected GA operator.
4. Run the algorithm using the newly generated population.
5. Stop if a particular stopping condition is satisfied or
6. Go back to step 2.

Chromosomes are selected as parents for step (3) based on some selected rule (GA operator) to produce new chromosomes for the next iteration. In this experiment, the stochastic universal sampling technique was adopted. This method chooses potential chromosomes according to their calculated fitness value in step (2) [15]. Both mutation and crossover were applied concurrently to reproduce the fittest offspring.

2.7. Simulated Annealing Algorithm (SMA)

The SMA is a non-traditional optimization algorithm that uses some probabilistic laws to search for an optimal solution. In science and engineering, the word 'annealing' is defined as a thermal method of getting low energy states of a solid in a heat bath by initially changing the temperature of the heat bath to the melting state of the solid and then lowering it down gently for the particles to organize themselves as in the initial state of the solid [21]. The SMA mimics the adaptive metropolis algorithm [22], which is a procedure used for sampling a specified distribution of a large data set. In 1953, Metropolis et al. [23] introduced an algorithm based on Monte Carlo methods [24] to simulate the change of states of a solid in a heat bath to thermal equilibrium in the following way. Let e_i be the energy of the solid at a state i, any subsequent energy e_j of the same solid at state j can be generated by transforming e_i using a perturbation mechanism. If the difference $e_j - e_i \leqslant 0$, then e_j will be accepted directly, otherwise, e_i will be accepted with a certain probability $\exp^{\frac{(e_i - e_j)}{cT}}$, where the parameter c is called a Boltzmann constant and T is the temperature of the heat bath. Similarly, the SMA generates sequence of solutions to optimization problems by replacing a state in the Metropolis algorithm to serve as one solution, and the energy of the state as a result produced by the activation/error function E. Therefore, if we have two solutions a_1 and a_2, then the values produced by functions can be written as $E(a_1)$ and $E(a_2)$ respectively. Accepting a_2 to replace a_1 depends on the probability distribution given in (7), where k is a real number called a control parameter (similar to the Boltzmann constant, c). This result can be generalized to any two solutions (a_i) and (a_j) for $i \neq j$.

$$P_k(accepta_2) = \begin{cases} 1, & \text{if } E(a_2) \leqslant E(a_1) \\ \exp^{\frac{(E(a_1) - E(a_2))}{kT}}, & \text{otherwise} \end{cases} \tag{7}$$

Updating the weights in SMA-based networks requires a vector $\vec{V}$ of step lengths of the weights matrix W, with $v_i \in \vec{V}$ and $w_i \in W$. The error $E(W)$ produced by W is calculated in a manner similar to (5), and the subsequent weights can be computed by changing the individual weight w_i (see (8)). r is a random number between -1 and 1.

$$w_i' = w_i + r * v_i \qquad (8)$$

Similarly, $E(W')$ will be calculated and compared with $E(W)$. Accepting W' instead of W depends on the result of whether $E(W') \leqslant E(W)$. This decision will be taken by applying the Metropolis algorithm in (7). The T in (7) will be updated to $T' = TQ$, where Q is another random number between a given interval.

2.8. Randomized and Ensemble Methods

Another training approaches that even though have not been experimented in this study are the randomized and ensemble approaches. We briefly mention them here to serve as additional guides to someone who might be interested in improving the accuracy of the approaches we analyzed. Similar to SMA and GA, both randomized and ensemble methods are optimization techniques that have been studied extensively for improving the performance of $ANNs$. A Random Neural Networks (RNN) was introduced in the inaugural RNN paper [25], which has found to be capable of providing excellent performance in various areas of application [26] and has motivated many theoretical papers [27]. A recent survey of randomized algorithms for training neural networks conducted by [14] provides an extensive review of the use of randomization in kernel machines and related fields. Furthermore, Ye et al. [28] provide a systematic review and the state-of-the-art of the ensemble methods that can serve as a guideline for beginners and practitioners. They discussed the main theories associated with the ensemble classification and regression. The survey reviewed the traditional ensemble methods together with the recent improvements made to the traditional methods. Additionally, the survey outlined the applications of the ensemble methods and the potential areas for future research.

3. Experimental Section

The experiment was carried out by using object oriented programming techniques with Java [29] to develop the ANNs [17] and to use five training algorithms to train the models. The skeleton of the class diagram implemented for carrying out the study is shown in Figure 2. Note that the diagram did not constitute all the classes used in the experiment; for instance, the genetic algorithm alone contains additional classes such as the chromosomes class, individual class, and so on. Lee et al. [30] gave a straightforward explanation of the classes required to implement genetic algorithms in Java. Nevertheless, the figure just gives an abstract architecture of the model. Additionally, the simulation of the five algorithms is undertaken using a Windows personal computer (NCC, Abuja, Nigeria) with system configuration as Intel® Core™ i7-3612QM CPU @2.10 GHz 2.10 GHz and installed memory (RAM) of 4.00 GB.

Furthermore, in all five experiments, the weights of the neural network were randomly generated to form a matrix of weights as arrays of floating point numbers between some given interval (mostly between 0 and 1. Sometimes the range is determined by values of other variables like the starting temperature as in the case of simulated annealing). Two or more weights can have the same real value since weights of neural networks are independent of one another. The progress of the five algorithms was monitored based on the series of training cycles.

Figure 2. Class diagram of the model.

Moreover, analogous to the case of the *SMA*, *GA* also requires some parameters for the algorithm to work efficiently. The population of the candidate solution was first randomly generated to begin the training. Individuals in the population known as chromosomes contain floating point numbers called genes. The number of chromosomes to participate in the training needs to be specified. Also, the experiment requires a parameter that determines the percentage of chromosomes to mate based on the fitness values and reproduced offspring that will be used for future iterations. Mating in this context means pairing of two chromosomes to exchange some of their genes to generate new chromosomes that are expected to have higher fitness than the parents. The experiment requires the percentage of the number of genes that two pairs of chromosomes can exchange randomly as a parameter. Several values of those parameters were tested to choose an optimal solution.

On the other hand, the remaining three algorithms (Adeline, *BPA*, and *LMA*) share many things in common. Their basic requirements are to define activation functions at each layer of the network (except at the input layer), and also to set the learning rate to a real number to control the speeds of which the networks produced optimal solutions. Different values have been tested to prevent the networks from oscillating between solutions, or to prevent the networks from diverging completely, or to prevent longer convergence time. In the same manner, as in the previous algorithms, the number of training cycles and the target error value were also specified. The activation functions used are the linear activation function for the output layers and the sigmoid logistic function for the hidden layers in *BPA* and *LMA*. Each of the four *MANNs* consists of three layers: input, hidden and output layers (see Figure 1), with five neurons in the input layer.

Moreover, a data set extracted from *Yahoo!Movies* [31] was used in the experiments. It consists of multi-criteria ratings obtained from users who rate movies based on four different characteristics. The criteria ratings $r_{i's}$ are considered as to determine the preferences of users on movies. The criteria ratings are for the action, the story, the direction and the visual effects of the movies, represented by r_1, r_2, r_3, and r_4 respectively. The ratings were measured using a 13-fold quantifiable scale from A^+ to F representing the highest and the lowest references for each criterion r_i, for $1 < i < 4$ as in Table 1, where r_0 is the overall rating.

Table 1. Sample of the *Yahoo!Movies* data det for multi-criteria recommender systems.

User ID	Acting (r_1)	Story (r_2)	Direction (r_3)	Visual (r_4)	Overall (r_o)	Movie ID
	C	C	B^-	A	B^-	1
1	B	A^-	B^+	B	B^+	2
	A^+	C	C^-	B^-	C^-	47
	A^+	A^+	A^+	A^+	A^+	3
2	B^-	A	A^-	B	A^+	4
	C^-	C	A^+	A^+	A^+	5
	A	B^+	A	B^+	B^+	6
3	B^+	B	B^+	B^+	B^+	4
	B	B^+	B	B^+	B^+	3

To obtain numerical ratings that can be suitable for the experiments, the ratings in Table 1 were transformed to numerical ratings (see Table 2). The most preferred rating (A^+) is represented by an integer number 13, and the least preferred rating (F) is replaced by 1. The same changes have been made to all other ratings ($A, A^-, B^+, ...$).

Table 2. Modified sample of the *Yahoo!Movies* data set for multi-criteria recommender systems.

User ID	Acting (r_1)	Story (r_2)	Direction (r_3)	Visual (r_4)	Overall (r_o)	Movie ID
	6	6	8	12	8	1
1	9	11	10	9	10	2
	13	6	5	8	5	47
	13	13	13	13	13	3
2	8	12	11	9	13	4
	5	6	13	13	13	5
	12	10	12	10	10	6
3	9	9	10	10	10	4
	9	10	9	10	10	3

Data cleaning was performed after the transformation to remove cases that have missing ratings either among the four criteria or the overall rating. Likewise, movies rated by few users were taken out of the experimental data. The resulting data set used for the study contains approximately 62,000 ratings from 6078 users to about 1000 different movies.

Furthermore, when training *ANNs*, for various reasons such as the type of activation function used, it is important to perform other preliminary treatments on the data set before the training [32]. For instance, when using a logistic sigmoid function as the activation function of the neurons, which produces an output between 0 and 1, then the interval of the output values from the activation function has to be respected. Although data normalization has been used by many researchers and shows significant improvements in the results and reduction of the length of the training period, no particular method is recommended for data normalization. However, the most important thing is to normalize the data with respect to the range of values given by the candidate activation function [32,33]. For this reason, we considered taking the ratio between each entry in the data set to the maximum number of all the entries. Recall that all the entries in Table 2 are between 1 and 13, then dividing each r_i by 13 gives the desired result in a normalized form $0 < r_i/13 \leqslant 1\ \forall i$. For example, the first row of Table 2 will be in the form $[0.461538462, 0.461538462, 0.615384615, 0.923076923, 0.615384615]$ for the action, the story, the direction, the visuals, and the overall ratings respectively.

We used statistical data analysis techniques to compute the linear relationships between the criteria ratings and the overall rating, and also to find the statistical significance of each criteria rating with respect to the overall rating. The Pearson correlation coefficient was used for computing the linear relationships while the significance was obtained using P-Value by setting the significance level to 5% ($p = 0.05$). Table 3 displays the results which indicate that all the correlations are statistically significant.

Table 3. Statistical analysis of the data.

Measure	Acting	Story	Direction	Visual
Correlation	0.904645	0.865350	0.910920	0.833844
Covariance	0.065629	0.058301	0.065686	0.055819
p-Value	0.00000	1.44×10^{-15}	0.00000	3.73×10^{-29}

Additionally, the experiment was conducted, and the results were analyzed using two types of data sets: the training and testing set. The two sets are in the ratio of 3:1 (75% and 25%) of the entire data set for training and testing respectively.

3.1. Parameter Settings

The first step necessary to achieve an accurate performance of the algorithms was to select appropriate parameter values required by each algorithm. Consequently, the experiment started by choosing a constant positive number between 0 and 1 to serve as the learning rate. Several values were tested to find the one that provided the minimum *MSE* and also allowed the networks to converge. Therefore, we started with a relatively high value (0.4) and monitored the performance of the algorithms. The same process was repeated many times by decreasing the value as the training continued. Figure 3 shows the errors for different learning rates. We decided to choose 0.01 as a good value for the experiments. The same procedure was followed to choose the population size, the mutation rate, and the starting temperature for the genetic and simulated annealing algorithms respectively. We considered relevant literature and used comparable methods of selecting the experimental parameters [34] and taking various precautions to avoid premature convergence [35]. The target training error used in all the experiments was set to 0.001. In *SMA*, setting the T was done carefully to ensure that the initial probability of accepting the solutions be close to 1. However, too high T may result in bad performance and long training computation time. According to Bellio et al. [36] choosing T in the interval $[1, 40]$ and $Q \in [0.99, 0.999]$ was confirmed to provide better performance of the *SMA*. Therefore we initialized $T = 30$, and Q was generated randomly within the above interval. Furthermore, to prevent accepting bad solutions, the minimum value that T can take was set to 1, and the was epoch 500 iterations. The stopping condition depends on attaining the target error, $T < 1$, or the number of iteration equals 500.

Similarly, in the *GA* experiment, the elitism number was set to 5, epoch to 100 iterations, and population size to 100 chromosomes. Other relevant parameters are the mutation and crossover probabilities. After conducting a sensitivity analysis, we select the crossover probability to be 85%, and the mutation probability to 9%. The stopping condition depends on the epoch and the target error.

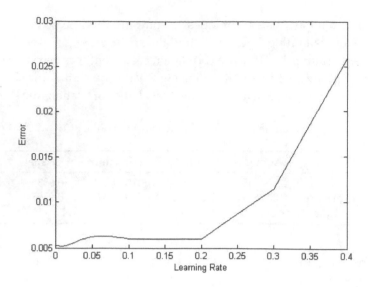

Figure 3. MSE against different values of the learning rate.

4. Results and Discussion

Mean square error (*MSE*) was proposed as the criteria for evaluating the performance of the learning algorithms during training and testing phases of the study. It was used to measure how close the outputs of the networks were to the real values from the data set. It was explained in Section 2.4 when discussing (5), which for every output, the *MSE* takes the vertical distance between the actual output and the corresponding real value and squares the value. Then for each iteration, it adds up all the values and divides by the number of the input sets from the data set. This metric was chosen due to its non-negative characteristics and suitable statistical properties.

Furthermore, the result of the experiment for comparing the effectiveness of the algorithms is shown in Table 4. It contains the total number of iterations required by the algorithms for training, the training and test errors, the correlation between the estimated and actual outputs in the test data set, as well as the p-value which is a function that measures how close the predicted outputs are relative to the actual values. Moreover, the correlation coefficients between the actual outputs of the five experiments and the real values are presented in Table 5.

Table 4. Statistical Analysis of the Experimental result.

Algorithms	Number of Training Cycles	Average Training MSE	Average Test MSE	p-Value
Adaline	10	0.0054	0.0053	8.7×10^{-59}
SMA	460	0.0075	0.0069	2.3×10^{-57}
GA	70	0.0145	0.0138	1.4×10^{-55}
LMA	750	0.0514	0.0389	5.4×10^{-52}
BPA	2197	0.0509	0.0437	8.6×10^{-49}

The results in Tables 4 and 5 are supported by graphs in Figures 4–9 that show the relationships between the actual values (see Figure 4) and those of the five algorithms in Figure 6, while Figures 5–9 contain pairs of curves of the actual values and the output of the individual training algorithm. The findings show the advantages and disadvantages of the five algorithms used, in particular between the ones used for training the *MANNs*. The rest of this section discusses the findings of the study. Subsequently, some issues that determined the predictive performance of the five networks were identified. The explanation begins by first considering the architectural differences between the networks regarding the differences in accuracy of the four algorithms used to train the *MANNs*.

To begin with, it is interesting to note that among the two architectures (single and *MANNs*) and five algorithms employed in this study, the Adaline network performs better than the *MANNs* trained with any of the other four algorithms. According to Table 4, the *MSE* of Adaline was observed to be better than *MANNs* training algorithms, which also confirmed the efficiency of single layer networks [37], and consequently, it is not necessary to implement *MANNs* trained with any of the remaining algorithms for improving the prediction accuracy of *MCRSs*. This observation is consistent with the result shown in Table 5 and Figures 5 and 6 that showed that the neural network trained using Adeline has the strongest linear relationships with the actual values from the test data. Another strong piece of evidence of the efficiency of the Adaline network is the computation speed and the number of training cycles required for the algorithm to converge. This can be seen from the second column in Table 4 where it was reported that Adaline requires significantly fewer iterations than the other four algorithms.

Table 5. Correlations between Experimental results.

	Actual	**Adeline**	**LMA**	**BPA**	**SMA**	**GA**
Actual	1.00	0.97	0.82	0.80	0.96	0.94
Adaline	0.97	1.00	0.86	0.85	0.99	0.96
LMA	0.82	0.86	1.00	0.97	0.88	0.90
BPA	0.80	0.85	0.97	1.00	0.86	0.87
SMA	0.96	0.99	0.88	0.86	1.00	0.97
GA	0.94	0.96	0.90	0.87	0.97	1.00

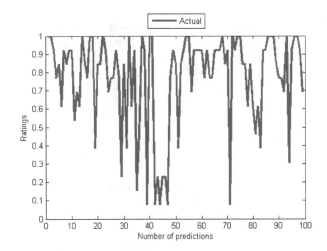

Figure 4. Curve of actual rating from the data set.

However, the performances of the training algorithms for *MANNs* are not all that bad. Together, these results provide significant insights into choosing the appropriate algorithm for training *MANNs*. Although the *LMA* and *BPA* have high computation speeds compared to the *GA* and the *SMA*, the study reveals that *BPA* and *LMA* have slow convergence rates. By comparing the five results, it can be seen that the convergence of the *BPA* is extremely slow. Moreover, the training and test errors of the two back-propagation algorithms are the highest. This became apparent after performing several computations of the derivatives of the error functions that can make their outputs to be maximally wrong since strong errors for adjusting the weights during the training can not be produced. In respect to this, the graphs of their predicted values in Figures 7 and 8 did not show reasonable correlations with the actual values from the data set. A comparison of the two results reports that the *LMA* outperforms and achieves faster convergence than the *BPA*. Another problem of back-propagation algorithms that may contribute to their poor performance is their inability to provide global solutions since they can get stuck in local minima. On the other hand, the *GA* and the *SMA* have the potential to produce global search of neurons' weights by avoiding local minima.

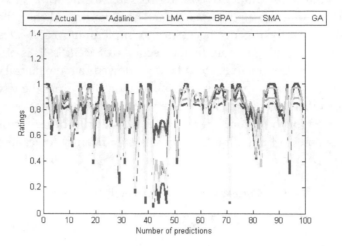

Figure 5. Graph of actual ratings and the predicted ratings of the experimented algorithms.

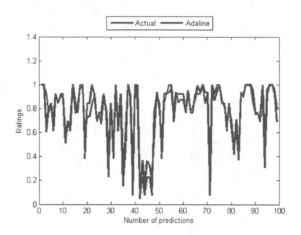

Figure 6. Curves of actual ratings and predicted ratings of Adaline.

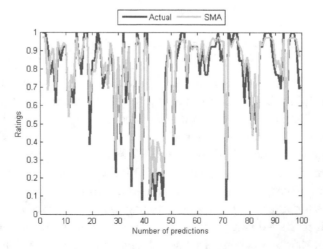

Figure 7. Curves of actual ratings and predicted ratings of SMA.

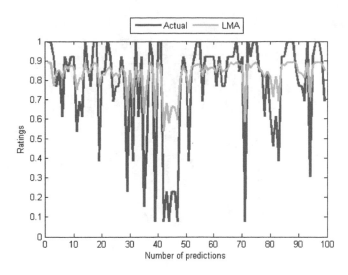

Figure 8. Curves of actual ratings and predicted ratings of LMA.

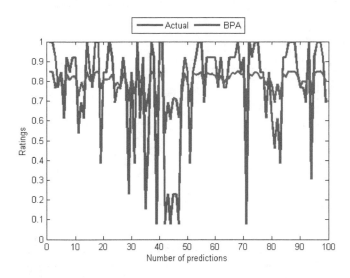

Figure 9. Curves of actual ratings and predicted ratings of BPA.

Although the *GA* does not require many training cycles (see Table 4), its outstanding problem is long computation time which is related to the population size and several operations like evaluating fitness and sorting the population based on fitness. Turning also now to the experimental evidence, the results in Tables 4 and 5, and that of Figures 6 and 9 indicate that the *GA*-based network has outperformed the two back-propagation algorithms. In the final part of the discussion, the single most striking observation to emerge from the data comparison was the ability of the *SMA*-based network to provide better prediction than all the remaining three *MANNs*. The performance of the *SMA* is close to that of Adaline except for the number of training cycles, which was higher compared to Adaline and the *GA*. However, when using the *SMA*, it is important to bear in mind that the error performance curve during training was not completely smooth unlike the case of the *BPA* and the *LMA*, which means that the same error value could be repeated many times before convergence. This is illustrated in Figure 11, which is the error versus the number of iterations (epoch) curve that shows the nature of its performance during the training. Overall, it can be seen from Table 4 and Figures 5, 6 and 11 that Adaline and *SMA*-based models have the lowest *MSE* values and provide more accurate estimations of the target values. Their performance on training and test data indicates that the two models have good predictive potentials.

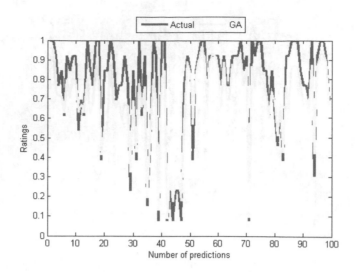

Figure 10. Curves of actual ratings and predicted ratings of GA.

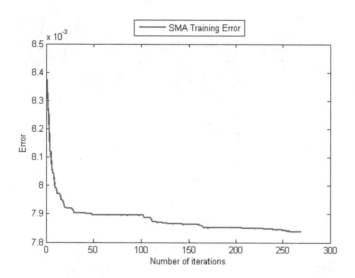

Figure 11. Error Performance measure during training with the SMA.

Finally, as both *BPA* and Adaline used partial derivatives to update the weights (see (3) for example), the results indicate that additional hidden layer increases the number of iterations and the test errors, proving that the simple network is enough to estimate the overall rating in multi-criteria recommendation problems, and hence more complex network that contains hidden layers is not required.

5. Conclusions and Future Work

Recently, Adomavicius et al. [6,38] challenged the recommender systems research community to use artificial neural networks in modeling *MCRSs* for improving the prediction accuracy while predicting the overall rating. Based on our knowledge, up to the present, no one has attempted to pursue this challenge. This paper presented a comprehensive comparison between the experimental results of five different neural network models trained with five machine learning algorithms.

This study aimed at addressing the problems of choosing an optimal neural networks architecture and efficient training algorithms to train the networks for modeling the criteria ratings to compute an overall rating in *MCRSs* using an aggregation function approach. Two types of neural network models were designed and implemented, one of them consisting of only the input and output layers and the other four models containing hidden layers. The study used five different powerful training algorithms to train the networks. The advantages and disadvantages of each algorithm regarding prediction accuracy, the length of training time, and the number of iterations required for the networks to converge were investigated and analyzed. This experiment produced results which support the findings of a large amount of some of the previous work in the field of computational intelligence.

The study makes significant contributions not only to the recommender system research community but also to other industrial and academic research domains that are willing to use neural networks in solving optimization problems. The results of the experiment can serve as recommendations and guidelines to the reader when choosing a better architecture and suitable training algorithms for building and training neural network models.

The research findings admit several future research topics that need to be taken to investigate other possibilities of improving the prediction accuracy of *MCRSs*. For instance, the study shows that some of the algorithms are more efficient than othersregarding prediction accuracy, speed, the number of training iterations, and so on. Future research work needs to investigate the possibility of improving the accuracy through hybridization of two or more algorithms. For instance, a hybrid between the *BPA* and the *LMA* might improve the faster convergence ability, and with the *SMA* or the *GA* approach could improve the searching capacity and avoidance of getting trapped at local optima. Köker and Çakar [39] observed that hybrids with those algorithms could reduce the number of iterations, minimize the error, ease the difficulty in choosing parameters, and might produce a better result. More information on their performance using other evaluation metrics would help us to establish a greater degree of accuracy on this matter.

As the research was conducted with only one data set, future studies on the current topic that could use additional multi-criteria data sets to extend our understanding of the kind of architecture and the training algorithm that are suitable for modeling the criteria ratings are therefore recommended. Moreover, we suggest future studies on the current topic that would consider randomized algorithms and ensemble methods.

Acknowledgments: The authors would like to offer special thanks to the Editors of the Journal of Computational Engineering and the anonymous reviewers for their useful comments and recommendations, which helped significantly in improving the quality of this article.

Author Contributions: The experiments and writing the first version of the paper were done by Mohammed Hassan under the supervision of Mohamed Hamada. Hamada also proposed the structure of the paper and helped in proofreading and improving the quality of the article.

References

1. Zhang, D.; Simoff, S.; Aciar, S.; Debenham, J. A multi agent recommender system that utilises consumer reviews in its recommendations. *Int. J. Intell. Inf. Database Syst.* **2008**, *2*, 69–81.

2. Hassan, M.; Hamada, M. A Framework for Recommending Learning Peers to Support Collaborative Learning on Social Networks. *Int. J. Simul. Syst. Sci. Technol.* **2016**, *17*.

3. Hassan, M.; Hamada, M. Performance Comparison of Featured Neural Network Trained with Backpropagation and Delta Rule Techniques for Movie Rating Prediction in Multi-Criteria Recommender Systems. *Informatica* **2016**, *40*, 409.

4. Hassan, M.; Hamada, M. Recommending Learning Peers for Collaborative Learning Through Social Network Sites. In Proceedings of the 7th International Conference on Intelligent Systems, Modelling and Simulation (ISMS), Bangkok, Thailand, 25–27 January 2016; pp. 60–63.

5. Zhao, T.; McAuley, J.; Li, M.; King, I. Improving recommendation accuracy using networks of substitutable and complementary products. In Proceedings of the International Joint Conference on Neural Networks (IJCNN), Anchorage, AK, USA, 14–19 May 2017; pp. 3649–3655.

6.   Adomavicius, G.; Manouselis, N.; Kwon, Y. Multi-criteria recommender systems. In *Recommender Systems Handbook*, 2nd ed.; Springer: New York, NY, USA, 2015; pp. 854–887.

7.   Hassan, M.; Hamada, M. Enhancing learning objects recommendation using multi-criteria recommender systems. In Proceedings of the International Conference on Teaching, Assessment, and Learning for Engineering (TALE2016), Bangkok, Thailand, 7–9 December 2016; pp. 62–64.

8.   Hassan, M.; Hamada, M. A Neural Networks Approach for Improving the Accuracy of Multi-Criteria Recommender Systems. *Appl. Sci.* **2017**, *7*, 868.

9.   Palanivel, K.; Sivakumar, R. A study on collaborative recommender system using fuzzy-multicriteria approaches. *Int. J. Bus. Inf. Syst.* **2011**, *7*, 419–439.

10. Jannach, D.; Gedikli, F.; Karakaya, Z.; Juwig, O. Recommending Hotels Based on Multi-Dimensional Customer Ratings. In *Information and Communication Technologies in Tourism 2012*; Springer: Vienna, Austria, 2012; pp. 320–331.

11. Sanchez-Vilas, F.; Ismoilov, J.; Lousame, F.P.; Sanchez, E.; Lama, M. Applying multicriteria algorithms to restaurant recommendation. In Proceedings of the 2011 IEEE/WIC/ACM International Conferences on Web Intelligence and Intelligent Agent Technology, Lyon, France, 22–27 August 2011; pp. 87–91.

12. Zarrinkalam, F.; Kahani, M. A multi-criteria hybrid citation recommendation system based on linked data. In Proceedings of the 2nd International eConference on Computer and Knowledge Engineering (ICCKE), Mashhad, Iran, 18–19 October 2012; pp. 283–288.

13. Weng, M.M.; Hung, J.C.; Weng, J.D.; Shih, T.K. The recommendation mechanism for social learning environment. *Int. J. Comput. Sci. Eng.* **2016**, *13*, 246–257.

14. Zhang, L.; Suganthan, P.N. A survey of randomized algorithms for training neural networks. *Inf. Sci.* **2016**, *364*, 146–155.

15. Göçken, M.; Özçalıcı, M.; Boru, A.; Dosdoğru, A.T. Integrating metaheuristics and Artificial Neural Networks for improved stock price prediction. *Expert Syst. Appl.* **2016**, *44*, 320–331.

16. Haykin, S.S.; Haykin, S.S.; Haykin, S.S.; Haykin, S.S. *Neural Networks and Learning Machines*, 3rd ed.; Pearson: Upper Saddle River, NJ, USA, 2009.

17. Souza, A.M.; Soares, F.M. *Neural Network Programming with Java*; Packt Publishing Ltd: Birmingham, UK, 2016.

18. Ranganathan, A. The levenberg-marquardt algorithm. *Tutor. LM Algorithm* **2004**, *11*, 101–110.

19. Michalewicz, Z. GAs: What are they? In *Genetic Algorithms+ Data Structures= Evolution Programs*; Springer: Berlin/Heidelberg, Germany, 1994; pp. 13–30.

20. Heaton, J. *Introduction to Neural Networks with Java*, 2nd ed.; Heaton Research, Inc.: St. Louis, MO, USA, 2008.

21. Aarts, E.; Korst, J. *Simulated Annealing and Boltzmann machines: A Stochastic Approach to Combinatorial Optimization and Neural Computing*; John Wiley: Hoboken, NJ, USA, 1990.

22. Beichl, I.; Sullivan, F. The metropolis algorithm. *Comput. Sci. Eng.* **2000**, *2*, 65–69.

23. Metropolis, N.; Rosenbluth, A.W.; Rosenbluth, M.N.; Teller, A.H.; Teller, E. Equation of state calculations by fast computing machines. *J. Chem. Phys.* **1953**, *21*, 1087–1092.

24. Gilks, W.R. *Markov Chain Monte Carlo*; Wiley Online Library: Hoboken, NJ, USA, 2005.

25. Gelenbe, E. Random neural networks with negative and positive signals and product form solution. *Neural Comput.* **1989**, *1*, 502–510.

26. Igelnik, B.; Pao, Y.H. Stochastic choice of basis functions in adaptive function approximation and the functional-link net. *IEEE Trans. Neural Netw.* **1995**, *6*, 1320–1329.

27. Georgiopoulos, M.; Li, C.; Kocak, T. Learning in the feed-forward random neural network: A critical review. *Perform. Eval.* **2011**, *68*, 361–384.

28. Ren, Y.; Zhang, L.; Suganthan, P.N. Ensemble classification and regression-recent developments, applications and future directions. *IEEE Comput. Intell. Mag.* **2016**, *11*, 41–53.

29. Kendal, S. *Object Oriented Programming Using Java*; Bookboon: Copenhagen, Denmark, 2009.

30. Jacobson, L.; Kanber, B. *Genetic Algorithms in Java Basics*; Springer: New York, NY, USA, 2015.

31. Lakiotaki, K.; Matsatsinis, N.F.; Tsoukias, A. Multicriteria user modeling in recommender systems. *IEEE Intell. Syst.* **2011**, *26*, 64–76.

32. Sola, J.; Sevilla, J. Importance of input data normalization for the application of neural networks to complex industrial problems. *IEEE Trans. Nucl. Sci.* **1997**, *44*, 1464–1468.

33. Ioffe, S.; Szegedy, C. Batch normalization: Accelerating deep network training by reducing internal covariate shift. *arXiv* **2015**, arXiv:1502.03167. Available online: https://arxiv.org/abs/1502.03167 (accessed on 12 September 2017).

34. Haupt, R.L. Optimum population size and mutation rate for a simple real genetic algorithm that optimizes array factors. In Proceedings of the 2000 IEEE Antennas and Propagation Society International Symposium, Salt Lake City, UT, USA, 16–21 July 2000; Volume 2, pp. 1034–1037.

35. Pandey, H.M.; Chaudhary, A.; Mehrotra, D. A comparative review of approaches to prevent premature convergence in GA. *Appl. Soft Comput.* **2014**, *24*, 1047–1077.

36. Bellio, R.; Ceschia, S.; Di Gaspero, L.; Schaerf, A.; Urli, T. Feature-based tuning of simulated annealing applied to the curriculum-based course timetabling problem. *Comput. Oper. Res.* **2016**, *65*, 83–92.

37. Jeong-Hwan, K.; Park, S.E.; Jeung, G.W.; Kim, K.S. Detection of R-Peaks in ECG Signal by Adaptive Linear Neuron (ADALINE) Artificial Neural Network. In Proceedings of the MATEC Web of Conferences, EDP Sciences, Melbourne, Australia, 3–4 March 2016; Volume 54.

38. Adomavicius, G.; Manouselis, N.; Kwon, Y. Multi-criteria recommender systems. In *Recommender Systems Handbook*, 1st ed.; Springer: New York, NY, USA, 2011; pp. 769–803.

39. Köker, R.; Çakar, T. A neuro-genetic-simulated annealing approach to the inverse kinematics solution of robots: a simulation based study. In *Engineering with Computers*; Springer: London, UK, 2016; pp. 1–13.

8

Multiresolution Modeling of Semidilute Polymer Solutions: Coarse-Graining Using Wavelet-Accelerated Monte Carlo

Animesh Agarwal [1,*], Brooks D. Rabideau [2] and Ahmed E. Ismail [3,*]

[1]   Institute for Mathematics, Freie Universität Berlin, Berlin 14195, Germany

[2]   Department of Chemical and Biomolecular Engineering, University of South Alabama, Mobile, AL 36688, USA; brabideau@southalabama.edu

[3]   Department of Chemical and Biomedical Engineering, West Virginia University, Morgantown, WV 26506, USA

*   Correspondence: animesh.agarwal@fu-berlin.de (A.A.); ahmed.ismail@mail.wvu.edu (A.E.I.)

Abstract: We present a hierarchical coarse-graining framework for modeling semidilute polymer solutions, based on the wavelet-accelerated Monte Carlo (WAMC) method. This framework forms a hierarchy of resolutions to model polymers at length scales that cannot be reached via atomistic or even standard coarse-grained simulations. Previously, it was applied to simulations examining the structure of individual polymer chains in solution using up to four levels of coarse-graining (Ismail et al., *J. Chem. Phys.*, 2005, 122, 234901 and Ismail et al., *J. Chem. Phys.*, 2005, 122, 234902), recovering the correct scaling behavior in the coarse-grained representation. In the present work, we extend this method to the study of polymer solutions, deriving the bonded and non-bonded potentials between coarse-grained superatoms from the single chain statistics. A universal scaling function is obtained, which does not require recalculation of the potentials as the scale of the system is changed. To model semi-dilute polymer solutions, we assume the intermolecular potential between the coarse-grained beads to be equal to the non-bonded potential, which is a reasonable approximation in the case of semidilute systems. Thus, a minimal input of microscopic data is required for simulating the systems at the mesoscopic scale. We show that coarse-grained polymer solutions can reproduce results obtained from the more detailed atomistic system without a significant loss of accuracy.

Keywords: multiscale simulations; structure-based coarse-graining; wavelet transform; Monte Carlo simulation of self-avoiding polymer chains

1. Introduction

Despite rapid advances in computational power in recent decades, realistic simulation of polymers remains a major scientific challenge because of the enormous range of time and length scales that must be accessed. To address this challenge, numerous solution paradigms have been introduced. One approach has been through so-called multiresolution simulation, in which a single computational routine that is capable of consistently simulating a system at different length scales is developed. In this manner, different simulations can be studied at a common length scale by appropriately coarse-graining a given model without switching between the different simulation methods. These methods are different from common coarse-graining techniques, which are adequate for studying the large-scale features of a system, but usually address the system at just two different levels of detail [1–9].

Recently, several approaches have been proposed that use a single computational routine to model the system using a hierarchy of different resolutions. Pandiyan and co-workers [10] devised a hierarchical multiscale scheme where high temperature polyimide HFPE-30 was coarse-grained at three different levels of detail, and the structural properties were reproduced at each of the resolutions. Lyubarstev et al. [11] formulated a hierarchical multiscale approach that covered three different levels of description by using inverse Monte Carlo (IMC). Yang et al. [12,13] developed structure- and relative-entropy-based coarse-graining methods for homopolymer melts and compared the structural and thermodynamic properties of the original and the coarse-grained (CG) systems at various coarse-graining levels. Zhang et al. [14] developed an elegant hierarchical coarse-graining and reverse-mapping strategy to model high molecular weight polymer melts, mapping the atomistic chains onto a model of soft spheres with fluctuating size.

The wavelet-accelerated Monte Carlo (WAMC) method developed by Ismail et al. [15–19] is a multiresolution approach capable of forming a sequence of resolutions of a system within one computational scheme, allowing for feasible computation without distorting the large-scale structural features of the system. As the wavelet transform is recursive, it produces averaged objects, which can be further averaged to provide a much coarser representation of a given system; therefore, the explicit construction of mapping from atomistic to CG representation is not required [19]. Thus, it is a systematic strategy that can model a system with an arbitrary number of length scales and may be particularly useful for systems that are so large that modeling with only two levels of coarse-graining remains insufficient. The WAMC technique was successfully applied to freely jointed and self-avoiding chains using up to four stages of coarse-graining. It was shown that the method preserves sensitive measures from the fine-grained calculations such as the mean end-to-end distance and the radius of gyration. Furthermore, as a result of the reduction in the number of degrees of freedom, independent configurations could be generated with a speedup of up to seven orders of magnitude.

A similar approach was used by Chen et al. [20] to simulate DNA molecules by fitting the CG potentials to analytical functions for additional computational efficiency. Maiolo et al. [21] formulated the wavelet-based MSCG approach and demonstrated its robustness through studies modeling liquid water and methanol. In addition to the aforementioned sequential multiscale methods, concurrent multiscale simulation approaches have also been developed in the last decade, where the coupling between the atomistic and CG regions allows for "on-the-fly" particle exchange [22,23].

Our goal in this paper is to extend the work on topological coarse-graining of polymer chains to a fully-functional and hierarchical approach for coarse-graining polymers solvated by good solvents in the semidilute regime. This is done by determining the potentials between coarse-grained units using simulations at one length scale and deriving new potentials at different resolutions through the use of scaling laws. This allows one to tune the WAMC algorithm so that the potentials are not recalculated when changing the resolution, something that would not be possible for algorithms operating at fixed levels of coarse-grained resolution. Thus, using the results of single chain statistics (zero-density simulations), we develop potentials that are transferable to finite densities in the semi-dilute regime. The major advantage of such an approach is that a minimal input of microscopic data or fine-grained simulation is required to simulate polymer chains at different coarse-grained resolutions.

The remainder of the paper is organized as follows: In the first section, we give an overview of the wavelet transform and WAMC algorithm. In the second section, we derive bonded and non-bonded (intramolecular) potentials and parameterize the potentials for different levels of coarse-graining for off-canticle polymer systems. In the third section, we formulate the modified WAMC algorithm for multiple polymer chains and make an approximation to compute the intermolecular potential. In the last section, we report the technical details of the simulations and compare the results obtained with the WAMC algorithm to reference off-lattice simulations. The Results and Discussion section is divided into two parts. The first deals with the simulation of single polymer chains (zero-density limit), while the second part deals with multiple polymer chains (finite density). In the zero-density limit case, we have considered two different scenarios: polymer chains both in an athermal solvent, where the interaction beads are defined by a hard sphere potential, and in a good solvent, where the interaction beads are defined by a Lennard–Jones potential.

2. Methods

2.1. The WAMC Method

2.1.1. Wavelet Transform Representation of a Polymer Chain

A one-dimensional wavelet transform is comprised of two functions: a scaling function α and a wavelet function β. A mathematical object is decomposed into two components that represent averages and differences, using the functions α and β. Suppose there is a "signal" $u = [u(1), u(2), u(3), \ldots, u(n)]$. If the functions α and β are applied to this signal, then one obtains a set of averages $s(i)$ and a set of differences $\delta(i)$ [24,25]:

$$s(i) = \sum_{k=0}^{r-1} \alpha(k)u(i+k),$$

$$\delta(i) = \sum_{k=0}^{r-1} \beta(k)u(i+k), \qquad (1)$$

where r defines a length scale where α and β are nonzero functions with compact support in the range $[0, r-1]$. The coefficients of α and β are usually in the range $[-1, 1]$, and both α and β can assume negative values [24]. In the previous work [15,16], the Haar wavelet was used, with $r = 2$, $\alpha = [\alpha(0), \alpha(1)] = (1/\sqrt{2}, 1/\sqrt{2})$ and $\beta = [\beta(0), \beta(1)] = (-1/\sqrt{2}, 1/\sqrt{2})$ [26]. The application of the wavelet transform is straightforward for polymer chains, as they are inherently topological in structure [2,27]. The coarse-grained representations can be easily created using the connectivity of the polymer chains as a template. If the input data are the set of positions of the beads within the polymer chain, $R = \{r_1, r_2, \ldots, r_N\}$, then the following variables are obtained:

$$r_n^{(k)} = \frac{1}{2}[r_{2n-1}^{(k-1)} + r_{2n}^{(k-1)}],$$

$$w_n^{(k)} = \frac{1}{2}[r_{2n-1}^{(k-1)} - r_{2n}^{(k-1)}]. \qquad (2)$$

$r_n^{(k)}$ denotes a set of averages $\{r_i^{(k)}\}_{i=1}^{N/2^{(k)}}$, and $w_n^{(k)}$ denotes a set of differences $\{w_i^{(k)}\}_{i=1}^{N/2^k}$, where the superscript notation (k) denotes the number of times that the Haar wavelet transform has been applied. The averaging operator in Equation (2) creates a new coarse-grained bead $r_n^{(k)}$ at the center of mass of the beads at $r_{2n-1}^{(k)}$ and $r_{2n}^{(k)}$, and the differencing operator returns the distance between the position of one of the original particles and the center of mass. Figure 1 shows the coarse-graining of a self-avoiding random walk in two dimensions, as described by the wavelet transform method. After two iterations, four sites are created that lie on quarter-integer lattice points. We neglect the contributions of the differencing variables in the remainder of this work.

2.1.2. Wavelet-Accelerated Monte Carlo Algorithm

The main idea behind the wavelet-accelerated Monte Carlo (WAMC) algorithm is the division of the full-atomistic simulation into different stages, where each stage is treated separately at coarse-grained resolution [15,16]. The algorithm is detailed as follows:

- The WAMC algorithm starts with a full-atomistic simulation of a smaller segment of the initial chain with $N_{b,1} \ll N$ beads. A simulation of a much shorter segment of the fully-atomistic chain helps cut down on the computational cost. Thus, each bead still has an effective size $N_{e,1} = 1$, where the subscript "1" indicates the simulation stage.
- The subsystem is sampled using the pivot algorithm [28].
- The wavelet transform is applied K_1 times to obtain the positions $r^{(K_1)}$ of each coarse-grained bead at regular intervals of $O(N_{b,1})$ steps. The effective size of the coarse-grained bead corresponds to

$N_{e,2} = 2^{K_1}$ beads in the fully-atomistic representation. The distribution representing interactions between these "virtual" coarse-grained beads, which are also referred to as "superatoms", is calculated.

- The probability distributions obtained from the the first stage are then used in the second stage of the (real) simulation that consists of a chain of length $N_{b,2}$ beads ($N_{b,2} = N/N_{e,2}$). The effective size of the coarse-grained bead is $N_{e,2}$, and the total effective chain length is $N_{b,2} \times N_{e,2}$.
- If desired, further coarse-graining of the system occurs by transferring the probability distributions obtained from the current stage to the next stage of resolution as discussed above.

Figure 2 is the schematic representation of the original WAMC method.

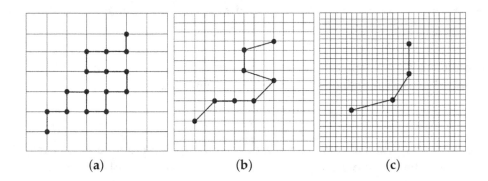

(a)	(b)	(c)

Figure 1. Coarse-graining of a random walk in two dimensions using the wavelet-transform method. (a) Random walk on a lattice representing the "atomistic" polymer chain ($N_{e,1} = 1$ and $N_{b,1} = 16$); (b) coarse-grained chain after one level of coarse-graining ($N_{e,2} = 2$ and $N_{b,2} = 8$); (c) coarse-grained chain after two levels of coarse-graining ($N_{e,3} = 4$ and $N_{b,3} = 4$). $N_{e,k}$ corresponds to the No. of beads in the full-atomistic chain that are coarse-grained, and $N_{b,k}$ corresponds to the total No. of beads at the k-th simulation level. Although the figure shows the application of the wavelet transform on a lattice, our simulations are performed off-lattice.

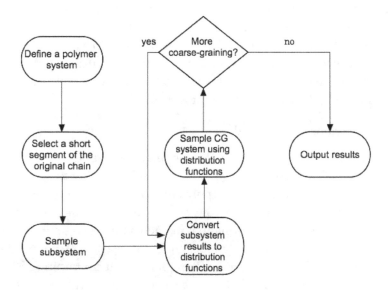

Figure 2. Schematic representation of the original WAMC method.

2.1.3. Translate-Jiggle Algorithm

The translate-jiggle algorithm [29] is used to generate trial conformations of the coarse-grained chain since the length of an individual bond does not change if the pivot algorithm is used, which makes the pivot algorithm non-ergodic for sampling chains where the bond-length is variable. Thus, a different algorithm is required to simulate a coarse-grained polymer chain, which requires correct sampling of the probability distributions obtained from the original level. In the translate-jiggle algorithm, a bead is selected randomly (k) and is given a random displacement. As a consequence, the bond between between beads k and bead $k-1$ will be either stretched or compressed, which ensures that the previous bond lengths between remain constant. After defining the displacement vector for bead k, all the remaining beads ($k+1, k+2,..., N$) undergo the same vector transformation. The resulting chain is then tested for energy differences using the Metropolis Monte Carlo algorithm [30] to determine if the proposed configuration is either accepted or rejected. Since the internal coordinate distributions were already calculated in the preceding stage of the WAMC algorithm, a new bond length and orientation (r_i, ϕ_i, θ_i) are selected from these distributions to be used in the translate-jiggle algorithm. This ensures that the coarse-grained model reproduces the aforementioned distributions given sufficient sampling.

2.2. Potentials in a Coarse-Grained System

The complete set of CG interaction functions can be separated into bonded and non-bonded interactions, which are each obtained separately. The potential energy of a coarse-grained chain can be written as:

$$U_{CG} = U_{CG}^B + U_{CG}^{NB}, \tag{3}$$

where the superscripts B and NB refer to the bonded and non-bonded interactions, respectively [31]. First, we discuss the non-bonded potentials, with a discussion of the bonded interactions following later.

2.2.1. Non-Bonded Potentials

There are various methods available in the literature for constructing non-bonded (intramolecular) potentials between CG beads. One notable approach is to consider the polymer coils as soft particles and to replace the detailed interactions between the segments with an effective interaction acting between the center-of-mass of polymer coils [32,33]. This effective interaction is equivalent to the potential of mean force obtained by Boltzmann inversion of the center of mass distribution of the polymer chains. The resulting potential is finite at all distances and has a range on the order of the radius of gyration. In this work, we use a method similar to the method developed by Dautenhahn and Hall [34]. This method was designed to calculate the potential to a high degree of accuracy, which is desirable in our work as we want to correlate the potential for different polymer sizes. In the next sections, we report the technical aspects of this method, and how we obtain a universal potential function from the functions calculated for different values of N_e.

Construction of Coarse-Grained Force Fields

A self-avoiding polymer chain of length N_e monomers, where N_e is the number of monomers coarse-grained in the original chain of length $N_b \times N_e$, is simulated using the pivot algorithm and used to generate two sets of 500 conformations of the polymer chain. In this work, the hard-sphere radius is taken as $\sigma = 0.5$. Therefore, two monomers are considered to overlap if they are separated by a distance less than $r_{cut} = 2\sigma = 1$. Independent conformations are generated each time the number of accepted pivot algorithm moves is equal to the chain length [35]. In this way, 1000 independent conformations are generated, and two sets of single-chain conformations, each containing 500 conformations for $N_e = 32, 64$ and 128, are used in calculating $U(r)$. One conformation from each set is placed with its center of mass a given distance at a random orientation. The distance between the centers of mass of two chains is varied from 0–5-times the average radius of gyration R_g of the chain with spacing equal to $0.2R_g$. The following relation is used to calculate the statistical weight of each configuration at a given separation:

$$W_i^{(r)} = \exp\left(\frac{-\phi_i(r)}{k_B T}\right), \tag{4}$$

where $W_i(r)$ is the weighting of the two-chain configuration i, r is the distance between the centers of mass of the two chains and $\phi_i(r)$ is the potential between the two chains in configuration i. The potential of mean force between the chains, $U(r)$, is calculated as a function of the distance between the two centers of mass using the following relation [34]:

$$\frac{U(r)}{k_B T} = -\ln \frac{\sum_{i=1}^{M} W_i(r)}{M} \qquad (5)$$

where M is the total number of two-chain configurations used at that particular distance. For self-avoiding chains with no overlap between the conformations, the potential is $\phi_i(r) = 0$, and the statistical weight of the configuration is $W_i(r) = 1$. If the two chains overlap, then $\phi_i(r) = \infty$ and $W_i(r) = 0$.

Figure 3 shows the potential obtained for three different polymer chains of length $N_e = 32, 64$ and 128. As expected, the potential is short-ranged and finite even at small separations. There is no attractive potential between the chains. There is a weak repulsion at very small distances indicating that some of the conformations are able to interpenetrate without monomer overlap when the centers of mass of the two chains coincide. As the chain length increases, there is an increase in the number of such conformations since the chains can arrange themselves in an increasing number of different ways. According to Equation (5), the repulsive potential decreases as the number of such configurations increases. As we are only working with a two-chain system or an infinitely-diluted system, the potential of mean force calculated above represents the true potential between the polymer "soft particles", since entropy has a negligible contribution to the free energy of the interaction. At finite densities however, the many-body interactions produce a nonzero entropic contribution, and this relation no longer holds.

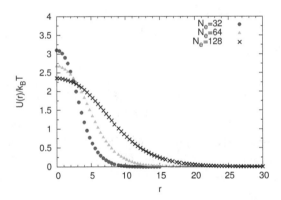

Figure 3. Non-bonded potential $U(r)$ for CG beads of size $N_e = 32$, $N_e = 64$ and $N_e = 128$.

Universal Scaling

The motivation for using wavelet-accelerated Monte Carlo (WAMC) is to analyze the polymer system on different length scales, without the need for recomputing the potentials as the scale is changed. Hence, it is important to have a universal function that gives the potential function at any length scale using scaling laws. Since the radius of gyration is a measure of the size of the polymer chain and is often used to scale results for the different chains, we normalize the distance by the root mean square radius of gyration of the coarse-grained bead of size N_e. Figure 4a shows the potentials for athermal chains of length $N_e = 32, 64$ and 128 with the normalized distance. It can be seen that the potential functions for different chain sizes are considerably different for $r/r_g < 2$. Figure 4b shows that the different potentials can be collapsed onto a single function by scaling the energy by $N_e^{-0.19}$. Consequently, we do not need to recalculate the potential. The exponent -0.19 was determined by using trial and error. A plot of the variance in the values of $U(0)$ for the three chains after scaling is shown in Figure 5.

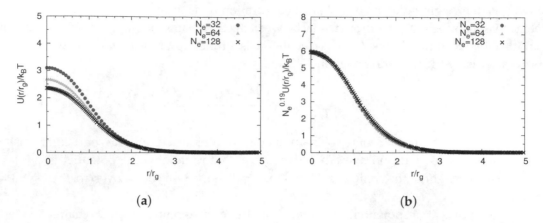

(a)   (b)

Figure 4. "Universal" functions for the CG non-bonded potential. (**a**) Coarse-grained non-bonded potential obtained from chains of length $N_e = 32, 64$ and 128, with distance normalized by the radius of gyration R_g; (**b**) Collapse of coarse-grained non-bonded potential obtained from chains of length $N_e = 32, 64$ and 128 showing an $N_e^{0.19}$ dependence on the magnitude of the potential.

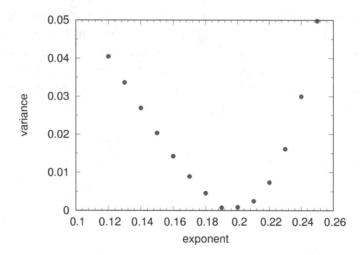

Figure 5. Variance in the potential $U(0)$ for chains with $N_e = 32, 64$ and 128 as a function of the exponent ζ used to fit a scaling relation of the form $N_e^{-\zeta}$.

2.2.2. Bonded Potentials

While non-bonded potentials act between pairs of CG beads separated by three or more intervening beads, we assume that nearest, next-nearest and next-next-nearest neighbor pairs are governed by separate interaction potentials:

$$U_{\text{bonded}} = U_{i,i+1} + U_{i,i+2} + U_{i,i+3}, \tag{6}$$

where the three terms indicate nearest neighbor (or 1–2), next-nearest neighbor (1–3) and next-next-nearest neighbor (1–4) interactions, respectively. These interactions are computed in such a way that the distributions of the 1–2, 1–3 and 1–4 distances are identical in the atomistic and coarse-grained cases. If the distributions computed from the atomistic simulation are $P_{\text{atom}}(r_i)$ and the distributions from the coarse-grained system are $P_{\text{CG}}(r_i)$, then the potentials should be such that $P_{\text{atom}}(r_i) = P_{\text{CG}}(r_i)$. We note that bond, angle and torsion potentials are not used to calculate the energy of chains. However, as discussed earlier, during the "translate-jiggle" moves, when a bead is randomly displaced, the values of (r, θ, ϕ) can be taken from the distributions of the bond length, bond angle and torsion angle calculated from the atomistic simulations. This ensures that lower energy states are adequately sampled with respect to angle and dihedral energy functions. The total potential energy of a single polymer chain can be written as:

$$U_{\text{intra}} = \sum_{i=1}^{N-1} \phi_{i,i+1}^{\text{bonded}}(r_{ij}) + \sum_{i=1}^{N-2} \phi_{i,i+2}^{\text{bonded}}(r_{ij}) + \sum_{i=1}^{N-3} \phi_{i,i+3}^{\text{bonded}}(r_{ij}) + \sum_{i=1}^{N-4} \sum_{j=i+4}^{N} \phi_{i,j}^{\text{non-bonded}}(r_{ij}) \quad (7)$$

The neighbor distributions, as well as the cumulative bond length, angle and dihedral angle distributions, which are used in the translate-jiggle moves, are calculated using a self-avoiding polymer chain of length $N = 1024$ for different values of N_e. The potentials are determined through the use of an iterative procedure known as reverse Monte Carlo [6,36], which can compute the interactions when there are interdependent distributions and the entropic contributions cannot be neglected in the free energy of the interaction. In the following sections, we give an overview of the method and find the common functions for the potentials obtained for different values of N_e. Figure 6 shows the various distributions that have been obtained for use in the reverse Monte Carlo routine.

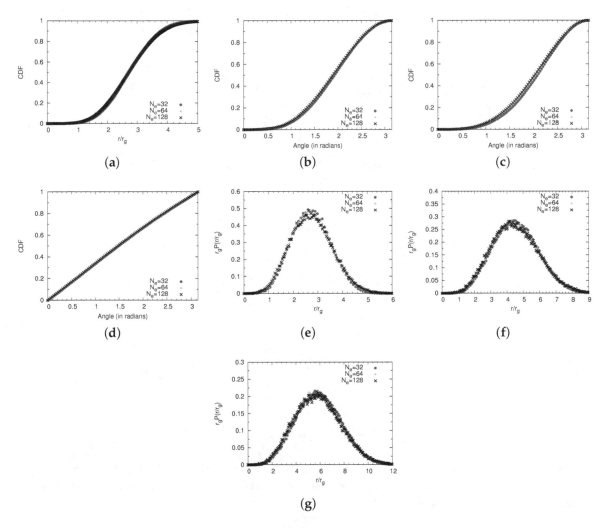

Figure 6. Distribution functions between the CG beads of size $N_e = 32$, 64 and 128 required for reverse Monte Carlo. (**a**) Bond-length distributions; (**b**) bond-angle distributions for $r < 1.5N_e^{1/2}$; (**c**) bond-angle distributions for $r > 1.5N_e^{1/2}$; (**d**) torsion-angle distributions; (**e**) 1–2 neighbor distributions; (**f**) 1–3 neighbor distributions; (**g**) 1–4 neighbor distributions.

Reverse Monte Carlo Simulations

A reverse Monte Carlo simulation of a coarse-grained system updates the potential according to:

$$\phi_{\text{new}}(r) = \phi_{\text{old}}(r) + fk_BT \ln\left(\frac{P(r)_{\text{measured}}}{P(r)_{\text{target}}}\right) \tag{8}$$

where $f = 0.2$ is chosen to ensure stable convergence. In this method, an initial guess of the potential is first used, and the simulation yields a probability distribution function $P(r)_{\text{measured}}$, which may be different from the target distribution function $P(r)_{\text{target}}$, but can also be used to obtain a first correction to the potential. This process can be iterated until the distribution function and the potential are self-consistent. This method has been used to calculate the 1–2, 1–3 and 1–4 interactions, with target distributions calculated from the atomistic system. In this work, the initial guess for the potential is taken to be $\phi(r) = 0$. This proved to be a reasonable assumption as the measured distributions converged to the target distributions in just a few iterations. The potentials obtained after this procedure are shown in Figure 7 for $N_e = 32$, 64 and 128. In the next section, we find common functions for the potentials obtained by polynomial fitting, to avoid further RMC calculations when changing the scale of coarse-graining.

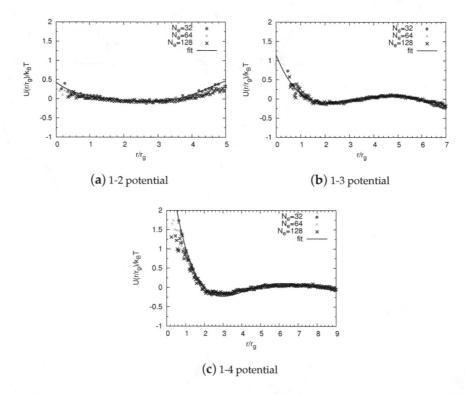

(a) 1-2 potential

(b) 1-3 potential

(c) 1-4 potential

Figure 7. Potentials for bonded interactions between (a) 1–2 neighbors, (b) 1–3 neighbors and (c) 1–4 neighbors, as obtained from nine iterations of reverse Monte Carlo. Simulation results are shown in black, polynomial fits in red.

Universal Scaling

To obtain the universal functions, we parameterize these potentials by normalizing the distance with the radius of gyration of the CG bead. Thus, the bonded and non-bonded potentials both have common functions, which can be tuned for different sizes of the coarse-grained bead. This ensures that the potentials need not be recalculated as the scale of the system is changed. We fit the 1–2 potential to a quadratic polynomial and the 1–3 and 1–4 potentials to a sixth-degree polynomial (see Figure 7). If the probability of finding the neighbors at a certain distance is zero, then the potential at that distance is not calculated. Hence, the softness of these potentials as $r \to 0$ remains unclear due to the absence of data at these distances. It can be seen in Figure 7c that below $r/R_g < 0.5$, the potential goes to infinity, which corresponds to zero probability of finding the next-nearest neighbors in Figure 6g. This assumption works well, giving accurate results and retaining the distributions in the coarse-grained model. The 1–2 potential shows a very small attractive well $(-0.1k_BT)$ at $r/R_g \approx 0.5$. Overall, the potential varies from $-0.1k_BT$ to $0.4k_BT$, which is quite small. However, as mentioned earlier, during the translate-jiggle moves, we used the values of r, θ and ϕ from the distributions calculated from the atomistic simulation. This ensures that the bond length distributions are sampled effectively, leading to a lower bond energy. The 1–3 and 1–4 potentials show an oscillatory behavior, with a strong repulsive core followed by a small attractive well. The 1–3 potential ranges from $0.2k_BT$ at $r/R_g = 1$ to $-0.1k_BT$ around $r/R_g = 1.7$, while the 1–4 potential varies from k_BT at $r/R_g = 1$ to $-0.7k_BT$ around $r/R_g = 2.7$. The 1–2 and 1–3 neighbors pay a significantly lower energy penalty compared to 1–4 neighbors for $r/R_g \sim 1$. Since the 1–4 potential has a much higher energy penalty for $r/R_g \sim 1$, it makes it highly unlikely that the 1–4 pairs approach each other. The range of the repulsive core in the 1–4 potential is comparable to that of the non-bonded potential.

3. Extension to Semidilute Systems

In the semidilute regime, additional interactions must be added to the coarse-grained representation when compared with the single-chain model, which have to be evaluated separately. To compute these interactions, a few approximations are introduced. Our aim is to develop these potentials from the knowledge of single-chain statistics so as to enable transferability of the force field to different densities.

3.1. Semidilute Solutions

The coarse-grained representation of many-chain systems consists of intramolecular interactions between coarse-grained beads in a single chain and intermolecular interactions between beads in different chains:

$$U_{total} = U'_{intra} + U'_{inter}, \tag{9}$$

where

$$U'_{intra} = \sum_{i=1}^{M} U_{intra}, \tag{10}$$

and

$$U'_{inter} = \sum_{i=1}^{M-1} \sum_{a=1}^{N_b} \sum_{j=i+1}^{M} \sum_{b=1}^{N_b} U_{inter}, \tag{11}$$

where U_{inter} is the pairwise potential between two beads on different chains, M is the total number of chains in the system and N_b is number of coarse-grained beads in each chain. The intermolecular potential acts between all the beads of one particular chain and all the beads in the other chains.

There are different ways to construct the intermolecular potential. The most obvious way is to simulate the fully-atomistic system and construct an inter-segment distance distribution function, which can then be used to obtain the potential through Boltzmann inversion. This is a particularly useful approach for simulating the system on one length scale, although it becomes cumbersome if the scales of the system are continuously changed, as is done in this work.

As mentioned earlier, our goal is a potential that can be easily transferred to different densities and resolutions. In light of this requirement, we assume that the intermolecular potential is equal to the non-bonded potential calculated in the previous section, so that $U_{inter} = \phi_{nb}$. This assumption holds for dilute systems, where many-body interactions can be neglected, and the potential of mean force represents the actual potential. Furthermore, as shown by Pierleoni et al. [37,38], this assumption works well even for semidilute systems. If the number N_b of coarse-grained beads per chain is such that the coarse-grained bead density is below the overlap density of the coarse-grained beads, then it is expected that zero-density potentials between different chains can be safely used (see the Appendix for a justification of the conditions under which the zero-density potentials can be used). Under such assumptions, the total energy can be written as:

$$U_{total} = \sum_{i=1}^{M} U_{intra} + \sum_{i=1}^{M-1} \sum_{a=1}^{N_b} \sum_{j=i+1}^{M} \sum_{b=1}^{N_b} \phi_{nb}. \tag{12}$$

With the distributions from the single chain, we can simulate a coarse-grained semidilute polymer system. We expect the force field to work for all polymer volume fractions satisfying Equation (A3) under athermal conditions. The force field has to be recalculated for different temperatures; however, at different densities and levels of coarse-graining at a given temperature, it should yield the correct results.

3.2. Modified WAMC Algorithm for Semidilute Solutions

The WAMC algorithm has been previously employed to model a single freely-jointed chain [15,16]. In this work, we have modified the algorithm to simulate semi-dilute solutions of polymer chains. The algorithm is outlined as follows:

- We define a dilute/semi-dilute polymer system containing M polymer chains, where each polymer chain consists of N beads.
- The first stage is an atomistic simulation in the limit of zero density to calculate intermolecular and intramolecular potentials discussed in the previous sections. The number of atomistic beads represented by a coarse-grained bead is $N_e = 1$ in the first stage, by definition.
- Next, the finite density polymer system is coarse-grained by iterating Equation (2) K_1 times, so that the size of each coarse-grained bead is $N_e = 2^{K_1}$ in the second stage. We then calculate the true potentials from the universal functions shown in Figures 4 and 7.
- If the level of coarse-graining is sufficient, then we can stop after this coarse-grained simulation. Otherwise, we apply the wavelet transform (Equation (2)) again K_2 times to obtain coarse-grained beads with an effective size of $N_e = 2^{K_2}$.

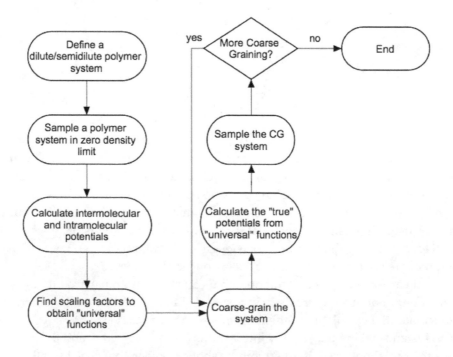

Figure 8. Schema of the modified WAMC algorithm.

Figure 8 shows a flowchart describing the various steps of the modified algorithm.

4. Results and Discussion

4.1. Single Chains

4.1.1. Technical Details

We perform simulations of off-lattice polymer chains of varying lengths using the atomistic freely-jointed model and the coarse-grained model under two levels of coarse-graining $N_e = 32$ and 64. The trial conformations of the freely-jointed chain model are generated using the pivot algorithm, and the Metropolis criterion is subsequently used to accept or reject the trial conformation. In an athermal solvent, a trial conformation is rejected if any two monomers appear closer than one distance unit. We test the WAMC model for polymer chains in good solvents. Although our simulations do not explicitly include solvent molecules, their interaction with the polymer chains is effectively accounted for by considering a Lennard–Jones type of potential between the monomers that has a small attractive well.

By changing the well depth $\epsilon/k_B T$, the interaction of the solvent with the polymer chains is taken into account. Thus, $\epsilon/k_B T$ can be viewed as the polymer-polymer potential modified by polymer-solvent and polymer-polymer interactions. We assume that there is no energetic interaction between covalently connected beads, while all other neighbors interact with a truncated LJ potential:

$$
\begin{aligned}
U(r_{ij}) &= 4\epsilon \left(\left(\frac{\sigma}{r_{ij}} \right)^{12} - \left(\frac{\sigma}{r_{ij}} \right)^{6} \right) && \text{for} \quad r_{ij} < r_o \\
&= 0 && \text{for} \quad r_{ij} > r_o
\end{aligned}
\tag{13}
$$

where r_{ij} is the distance between two monomers, ϵ and σ are the energy and distance parameters associated with the potential model and r_o is the distance at which the potential is truncated.

The parameters in this study are taken from a study of polyethylene [39], in which a single sphere constituted 3.5 methylene units where $\epsilon = 400$ and $\sigma = 4.6$ Å. The cutoff radius r_o was taken to be 2.5 σ. Furthermore, the important physical quantity in our simulation is the well depth $\epsilon/k_B T$, which defines the attractive part of the LJ potential. The greater $|\epsilon/k_B T|$ is, the greater the attraction. We simulate the polymer chains for three values of $|\epsilon/k_B T|$: 0.0 (athermal system), 0.10 and 0.15. This represents the good solvent regime, which was determined by calculating the theta point, which lies around $\epsilon/k_B T \approx -0.25$. We simulate freely-jointed chains of length $N = 2^5 = 32$ to $N = 2^{13} = 8192$ for $\epsilon/k_B T = 0.0, -0.10, -0.15$ and determine the scaling factor for each system: $\nu = 0.604, 0.599$ and 0.590 for $\epsilon/k_B T = 0.0, -0.10$ and -0.15, respectively.

Using these scaling relations, we determine the size of the chains of length $N = 2^{14}$ and 2^{15}. The second set of simulations is performed on the coarse-grained model of a freely-jointed chain at three different values of $\epsilon/k_B T$ under two levels of coarse-graining: $N_e = 32$ and 64, where N_e represents the size of the CG bead or number of monomers coarse-grained. The total number of beads in the coarse-grained model was $N_b = N/N_e$. For the coarse-grained simulations, the "translate-jiggle" algorithm described in Section 2.1.3 was used. The potential functions for different N_e were extracted from the fitted functions for the force field derived.

4.1.2. Comparison of Coarse-Grained and Atomistic Results

We compare the atomistic model and the coarse-grained model by calculating the mean squared radius of gyration and the Flory exponent ν in the polymer scaling law, $R \sim N^\nu$. The calculation of the radius of gyration provides a good platform to compare the original "atomistic" and coarse-grained models, as the size of the polymer coil should be similar in the two models. Table 1 shows the mean-squared radius of gyration obtained from the atomistic and coarse-grained models under different solvent conditions, as a function of $\epsilon/k_B T$. It can be seen from these results that the values obtained from the coarse-grained models agree quite well with the results from the atomistic simulation. The values obtained from the CG simulation lie within 3% of the values obtained from the freely-jointed chain simulations.

Table 1. Radius of gyration for polymer chains of different lengths calculated using the atomistic model and coarse-grained model under two levels of coarse-graining, for $\epsilon/k_B T = 0.0, -0.10$ and -0.15.

N	$\epsilon/k_B T = 0.0$			$\epsilon/k_B T = -0.10$			$\epsilon/k_B T = -0.15$		
	$N_e = 1$	$N_e = 32$	$N_e = 64$	$N_e = 1$	$N_e = 32$	$N_e = 64$	$N_e = 1$	$N_e = 32$	$N_e = 64$
256	177	184	165	143	142	139	133	132	125
512	410	422	378	322	325	316	298	299	283
1024	957	990	916	755	759	716	659	697	641
2048	2198	2283	2130	1732	1737	1657	1493	1591	1481
4096	5052	5151	4895	3973	3932	3772	3583	3618	3373
8192	11,767	11,858	11,243	9006	8935	8548	7864	8070	7613
16,384	27,184	27,240	26,190	20,662	20,468	19,500	17,818	18,282	17,249
32,768	62,799	62,582	61,009	47,404	46,893	44,490	40,370	41,424	39,083

As $\epsilon/k_B T$ decreases, the mean-squared radius of gyration decreases, due to the increased attractive interactions between monomers. While the general agreement is quite good, some discrepancies occur for large chains, particularly for $N_e = 64$. The discrepancy is due to end effects induced by the coarse-graining procedure. We expect the observed radius of gyration, $\langle R_g^2 \rangle_{CG}$, of a chain of length N for a coarse-grained simulation to be smaller than the value obtained without coarse-graining, $\langle R_g^2 \rangle_{atomistic}$, because the chain's "tails", representing the distance between the beginning of the atomistic chain and the first coarse-grained bead and between the end of the atomistic chain and the last coarse-grained bead, are effectively excluded. As the eliminated length increases with the level of coarse-graining, thus the disagreement in the results should increase, as well. The Flory exponent ν for each system was obtained by fitting this data to the power law $\langle R_g^2 \rangle \sim N^{2\nu}$, as shown in Table 2. The scaling factors are almost identical in the three models for a given value of $\epsilon/k_B T$. This again shows that the behavior of the polymer is correctly predicted using coarse-grained models, although there can be a small discrepancy in the actual values.

Table 2. Flory exponent obtained using atomistic and coarse-grained models.

$\epsilon/k_B T$	ν		
	Atomistic	CG, $N_e = 32$	CG, $N_e = 64$
0.0	0.604	0.601	0.610
-0.10	0.599	0.598	0.595
-0.15	0.590	0.595	0.593

4.2. Semidilute Solutions

4.2.1. Technical Details

To demonstrate the applicability of the wavelet-accelerated Monte Carlo method for semidilute solutions, we perform off-lattice simulations of a freely-jointed chain model and coarse-grained models at polymer volume fractions $\phi = 0.69$ and 1.72, representing both dilute and semidilute regimes. We consider chains of length $N = 512$ under athermal conditions in all simulations and do not allow individual monomers to overlap.

The trial conformations of the "atomistic" system are generated using a combination of pivot and translation moves. As the system has a finite density, the polymer chain can be translated by some distance to generate a new conformation. A total of one hundred million MC cycles is performed, where one MC cycle refers to a sweep of M chains one by one. After the chain is translated or rotated (using the pivot algorithm), it is checked for overlaps with the other chains and also with itself in the case of pivot moves. To generate independent confirmations, we store a confirmation after every one thousand accepted moves. The coarse-grained system is constructed analogous to the full monomer system at the same polymer volume fraction.

We consider three coarse-grained models, with $N_e = 16, 32$ and 64 in both cases. The trial conformations of the coarse-grained system are generated using "translate-jiggle" and translation moves. Unlike the atomistic system, whose energy function is just a hard-sphere potential, the coarse-grained potential is nontrivial and thus requires the Metropolis criterion to accept or reject the proposed configurations. A total of ten million MC cycles was performed on the system. In both systems, periodic boundary conditions were employed in all the directions. Table 3 shows the specific details of the systems studied in this work.

Table 3. Specific details of the systems studied in this work. Here, N denotes the size of a single chain, M the No. of chains and L the size of the box.

ϕ	N	L	M
0.69	512	100	20
1.72	512	100	50

4.2.2. Comparison of Coarse-Grained and Atomistic Models

To compare the coarse-grained and the atomistic models, we calculated the intra-segment distribution functions, the center-of-mass radial distribution functions and the inter-segment radial distribution functions. The intra-segment distribution function is defined as the pairwise distance distribution between segments of length N_e in a single chain, averaged over all M chains in the system. For a coarse-grained system, this would just be the pairwise distribution function between coarse-grained beads in a single coarse-grained chain, averaged over all of the chains. The inter-segment radial distribution function describes, on average, how the segments of size N_e in the system are radially packed around each other. In the coarse-grained representation, this is the same as calculating the pair correlation function between a coarse-grained bead of one chain and all of the coarse-grained beads on the other chains, averaging over all beads that are present in the system. In addition to the above quantities, the average radius of gyration:

$$R_g^{av} = \frac{\sum_{i=1}^{M} R_g^{(i)}}{M} \tag{14}$$

was determined, where $R_g^{(i)}$ is the radius of gyration of chain i.

Figure 9 compares the intra-segment distribution functions for $\phi = 0.69$ and 1.72 using both the fully-atomistic and the coarse-grained models. It can be seen that the results from CG simulations are in good agreement with the fully-atomistic simulations for both $\phi = 0.69$ and 1.72. Furthermore, increasing the density has no major effect on the coarse-grained distribution functions with only slight discrepancies between the two models at short distances due to the approximations introduced while computing the potentials. As discussed in the previous section, the actual intramolecular function is quite complex, and at higher densities, these approximations are likely to break down due to many-body correlations. As we move towards higher coarse-graining levels, from $N_e = 16$–64, there is no change in the results aside from an increase in the probability of finding a segment within a chain. The agreement between the coarse-grained model with $N_e = 64$ and the non-coarse-grained model is quite consistent.

Figure 10 shows the inter-segment radial distribution functions obtained from the atomistic and with coarse-grained simulations for $\phi = 0.69$ and 1.72. Again, the inter-segment distributions from the coarse-grained simulations are in extremely close agreement with the atomistic distribution for all values of N_e, showing that the coarse-grained model reproduces the center-of-mass pair correlation functions obtained from atomistic model with great precision. This further justifies the use of the intermolecular potential as the potential of mean force between two polymer chains of size N_e at these densities. Provided that the entropic contribution to the free energy of this interaction is negligible, this can be used as the intermolecular potential between the coarse-grained beads of different chains. These findings are in agreement with the results obtained by Pierleoni et al. [37,38], who found that many-body correlations are absent provided that the coarse-grained bead density is below the overlap density of the coarse-grained beads.

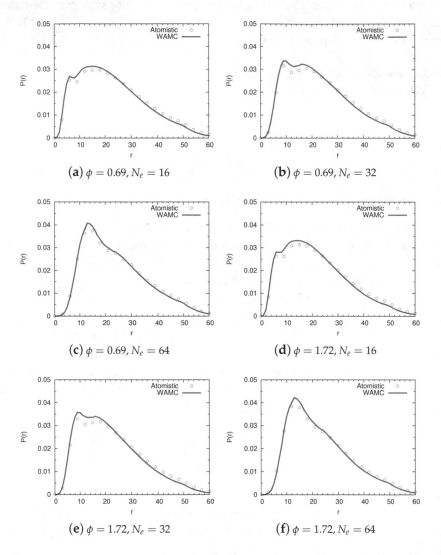

Figure 9. Intra-segment distribution functions showing the comparison between atomistic and coarse-grained models: for $\phi = 0.69$ with (**a**) $N_e = 16$; (**b**) $N_e = 32$; (**c**) $N_e = 64$; and $\phi = 1.72$ with (**d**) $N_e = 16$; (**e**) $N_e = 32$; and (**f**) $N_e = 64$.

The results of the intra-segment distributions and inter-segment RDF's prove that the allowed moves in the coarse-grained simulation adequately sample the phase space of the underlying atomistic model. Furthermore, the CG force field is clearly transferable to different densities. It should be noted that we have only sampled a single freely-jointed chain to obtain the probability distributions used to simulate semidilute solutions at different resolutions. The center-of-mass radial distribution functions are shown in Figure 11. This result is of considerable importance as the center-of-mass radial distribution function can be used to obtain the second virial coefficient of the system. The figure shows that there is a satisfactory agreement between the atomistic and coarse-grained systems. As the density of the system increases, however, the assumption breaks down, and discrepancies at low r/r_g begin to appear, as shown in Figure 11b.

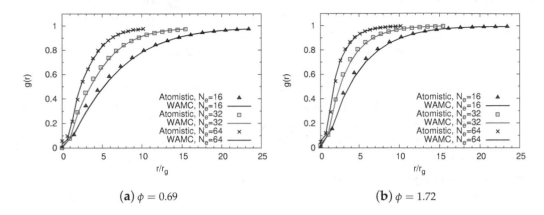

(a) $\phi = 0.69$　　　　　　**(b)** $\phi = 1.72$

Figure 10. Inter-segment RDF's showing the comparison between atomistic and coarse-grained models for **(a)** $\phi = 0.69$ and **(b)** $\phi = 1.72$.

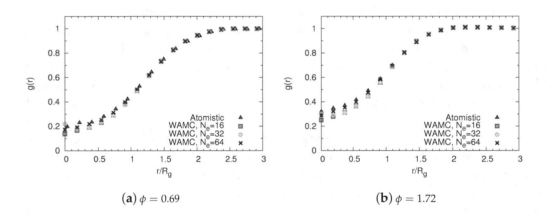

(a) $\phi = 0.69$　　　　　　**(b)** $\phi = 1.72$

Figure 11. Center-of-mass RDF's showing the comparison between atomistic and coarse-grained models for **(a)** $\phi = 0.69$ and **(b)** $\phi = 1.72$.

Table 4 shows the average radius of gyration obtained from the atomistic and coarse-grained simulations. In the zero-density limit, the radius of gyration of a chain with $N = 512$ monomers obtained is 20.2. As the density of polymer chains increases, the average radius of gyration of a single chain decreases due to additional correlations with the other chains. This reduction in the radius of gyration is captured precisely in the coarse-grained model at all resolutions. As discussed in the previous section, however, the coarse-grained values will be slightly underestimated when compared with the atomistic results.

Table 4. Average radius of gyration obtained from the atomistic and coarse-grained system, at different polymer volume fractions ϕ.

	Model			
2–5 ϕ	Atomistic	CG, $N_e = 16$	CG, $N_e = 32$	CG, $N_e = 64$
0.0	20.23	20.08	19.87	19.57
0.69	17.12	16.98	16.75	16.59
1.72	16.61	16.24	16.04	15.98

5. Conclusions and Outlook

We have extended the wavelet-accelerated Monte Carlo approach to a semi-dilute system of polymer chains under athermal conditions. It was demonstrated that such a coarse-graining scheme is effective and that one can access different length scales conveniently within a single computational routine. The bonded and non-bonded potentials were obtained from zero density simulations, which were then parameterized using different scaling factors. This enables one to use the same potential functions at each of the different simulation scales, circumventing the need for recalculation when moving from one scale to the next.

To extend the wavelet transform approach to semidilute system of polymer chains, a significant approximation was made in which the intermolecular potential was assumed to be equal to the non-bonded potential. We show that this approximation is quite reasonable provided that the coarse-grained bead density is below the overlap density of the coarse-grained beads. Thus, using the results of the single chain statistics, we are able to simulate semidilute systems at different densities and length scales. The results from the coarse-grained and atomistic simulations were compared and showed that the coarse-grained polymer systems can reproduce results to a reasonable degree of accuracy.

Future works might extend the above approach for polymer solutions in concentrated regimes. The major challenge here would be to compute intermolecular potentials that are "universal" and can be transferred to different densities. One option would be to use the iterative Boltzmann inversion (BI) approach to derive an effective coarse-grained potential for a given (nonzero) density. Then, at each coarse-grained stage, one could use the potential from the previous stage as the starting approximation and then perform a few additional BI iterations to reach the final potential at that particular resolution. A somewhat similar method known as multi-state iterative Boltzmann inversion was developed by McCabe et al. [40]. One can also introduce a reverse-mapping scheme within the WAMC framework in precisely the same way. Using the probability distributions for the bond, angle, dihedral and non-bonded terms obtained during the coarse-graining procedure, one can reconstruct the fine details of the polymer that are consistent with both the geometric constraints and energetic considerations.

We would also like to extend the method to study chain dynamics using molecular dynamics simulations. The recent work by Hsu et al. [41,42], which shows that parameterizing non-bonded interactions allow for the good approximation of chain dynamics, could be used as the basis for such a study.

Acknowledgments: We are thankful to the high-performance computing service at RWTHAachen for providing the computational resources.

Author Contributions: Animesh Agarwal performed the computations, and all the authors developed the idea. Animesh Agarwal and Ahmed E. Ismail designed the research plan, and all the authors wrote the paper.

Appendix A. Validity of Using Zero-Density Potentials for the Intermolecular Potential

The concentration of polymer chains is

$$\rho_b = \frac{M}{V},$$ (A1)

and the overlap concentration is

$$\rho^* = \frac{3}{4\pi R_g^3},$$ (A2)

where $R_g = bN^\nu$ is the radius of gyration. The semidilute regime exists when

$$\phi = \frac{\rho_b}{\rho^*} = \frac{4\pi M R_g^3}{3V} > 1.$$ (A3)

We can think of this system as composed of superatoms or coarse-grained beads, where the local bead density permits use of the non-bonded potential as the inter-chain potential. If a chain of L monomers is partitioned into N_b CG beads with N_e monomers per bead, the local concentration of the beads is

$$\rho_{CG,b} = \frac{MN_b}{V},$$ (A4)

and the bead overlap concentration is given by

$$\rho^*_{CG} = \rho^* = \frac{3}{4\pi R_g^3}.$$ (A5)

If the radius of gyration is taken to be $R_g = bN_e^\nu$, where b is the Kuhn length that appears in the scaling of radius of gyration, then:

$$\phi_{CG} = \frac{\rho_{CG,b}}{\rho^*_{CG}} = \frac{MN_b 4\pi b^3 N_e^{3\nu}}{3V}$$ (A6)

and therefore

$$\frac{\phi_{CG}}{\phi} = \frac{N_b b^3 N_e^{3\nu}}{b^3 N^{3\nu}} = N_b \left(\frac{N_e}{N}\right)^{3\nu} = N_b^{1-3\nu}.$$ (A7)

Thus,

$$\phi_{CG} = \phi N_b^{1-3\nu}.$$ (A8)

For athermal and good solvents, the Flory exponent $\nu \approx 0.588$. Upon substitution in the above equation, this yields:

$$\phi_{CG} = \phi N_b^{-0.76}$$ (A9)

Thus for any polymer volume fraction $\phi > 1$ which is a semidilute regime, N_b can be chosen such that the coarse-grained bead overlap volume fraction $\phi_{CG} < 1$, and hence the beads do not overlap. It is therefore reasonable to neglect many-body interactions among the coarse-grained beads and to represent intermolecular interactions by the zero-density pair potential. Thus, the total energy now becomes:

$$U_{total} = \sum_{i=1}^{M} U_{intra} + \sum_{i=1}^{M-1} \sum_{a=1}^{N_b} \sum_{j=i+1}^{M} \sum_{b=1}^{N_b} \phi_{nb}.$$ (A10)

References

1. Akkermans, R.; Briels, W. Coarse-grained interactions in polymer melts: A variational approach. *J. Chem. Phys.* **2001**, *115*, 6210–6219.

2. Baschnagel, J.; Binder, K.; Doruker, P.; Gusev, A.; Hahn, O.; Kremer, K.; Mallice, W.; Muller-Plathe, F.; Murat, M.; Paul, W.; et al. Bridging the gap between atomistic and coarse-grained models of polymers: Status and perspectives. *Adv. Polym. Sci.* **2000**, *152*, 41–156.

3. Lyubarstev, A.; Karttunen, M.; Vattulainen, I.; Laaksonen, A. On coarse-graining by the inverse Monte Carlo method: Dissipative particle dynamics simulations made to a precise tool in soft matter modeling. *Soft Matter* **2003**, *1*, 121–137.

4. Tan, R.; Petrov, A.; Harvey, S. YUP: A molecular simulation program for coarse-grained and multi-scaled models. *J. Chem. Theory Comput.* **2006**, *2*, 529–540.

5. Clementi, C. Coarse-grained models of protein folding: Toy models or predictive tools? *Curr. Opin. Struct. Biol.* **2008**, *18*, 10–15.

6. Ashbaugh, H.; Patel, H.; Kumar, S.; Garde, S. Mesoscale model of polymer melt structure: Selt consistent mapping of molecule correlations to coarse-grained potentials. *J. Chem. Phys.* **2005**, *122*, doi:10.1063/1.1861455.

7. Fukunaga, H.; Takimoto, J.; Doi, M. A coarse-graining procedure for flexible polymer chains with bonded and nonbonded interactions. *J. Chem. Phys.* **2002**, *116*, 8183–8190.

8. Harmandaris, V.; Adhikari, N.; Van der Vegt, N.; Kremer, K. Heirarchical modeling of polystyrene: From atomistic to coarse-grained simualtions. *Macromolecules* **2006**, *39*, 6708–6719.

9. Kamio, K.; Moorthi, K.; Theodorou, D. Coarse grained end bridging Monte Carlo simulations of poly(ethylene terephthalate) melt. *Macromolecules* **2007**, *49*, 710–722.

10. Pandiyan, S.; Parandekar, P.V.; Prakash, O.; Tsotsis, T.K.; Basu, S. Systematic coarse graining of a high-performance polyimide. *Macromol. Theory Simul.* **2015**, *24*, 513–520.

11. Lyubartsev, A.P.; Naome, A.; Vercauteren, D.P.; Laaksonen, A. Systematic hierarchical coarse-graining with the inverse Monte Carlo method. *J. Chem. Phys.* **2015**, *143*, doi:10.1063/1.4934095.

12. Yang, D.; Wang, Q. Systematic and simulation-free coarse graining of homopolymer melts: A relative-entropy-based study. *Soft Matter* **2015**, *11*, 7109–7118.

13. Yang, D.; Wang, Q. Systematic and simulation-free coarse graining of homopolymer melts: A structure-based study. *J. Chem. Phys.* **2015**, *142*, doi:10.1063/1.4906493.

14. Zhang, G.; Moreira, L.A.; Stuehn, T.; Daoulas, K.C.; Kremer, K. Equilibration of high molecular weight polymer melts: A hierarchical strategy. *ACS Macro Lett.* **2014**, *3*, 198–203.

15. Ismail, A.E.; Rutledge, G.C.; Stephanopoulos, G. Topological coarse-graining of polymer chains using wavelet-accelerated Monte Carlo. I. Freely jointed chains. *J. Chem. Phys.* **2005**, *122*, doi:10.1063/1.1924480.

16. Ismail, A.E.; Rutledge, G.C.; Stephanopoulos, G. Topological coarse-graining of polymer chains using wavelet-accelerated Monte Carlo. II. Self-avoiding chains. *J. Chem. Phys.* **2005**, *122*, doi:10.1063/1.1924481.

17. Ismail, A.E.; Rutledge, G.C.; Stephanopoulos, G. Multiresolution analysis in statistical mechanics. I. Using wavelets to calculate thermodynamic properties. *J. Chem. Phys.* **2003**, *118*, doi:10.1063/1.1543581.

18. Ismail, A.E.; Stephanopoulos, G.; Rutledge, G.C. Multiresolution analysis in statistical mechanics. II. The wavelet transform as a basis for Monte Carlo simulations on lattices. *J. Chem. Phys.* **2003**, *118*, doi:10.1063/1.1543582.

19. Rinderspacher, B.; Bardhan, J.; Ismail, A. Theory of wavelet-based coarse-graining hierarchies for molecular dynamics. *Phys. Rev. E* **2017**, *96*, doi:10.1103/PhysRevE.96.013301.

20. Chen, J.; Teng, H.; Nakano, A. Wavelet-based multi-scale coarse graining approach for DNA molecules. *Finite Elem. Anal. Des.* **2007**, *43*, 346–360.

21. Maiolo, M.; Vancheri, A.; Krause, R.; Danani, A. Wavelets as basis functions to represent the coarse-graining potential in multiscale coarse graining approach. *J. Comput. Phys.* **2015**, *300*, 592–604.

22. Praprotnik, M.; Delle Site, L.; Kremer, K. Adaptive resolution molecular-dynamics simulation: Changing the degrees of freedom on the fly. *J. Chem. Phys.* **2005**, *123*, doi:10.1063/1.2132286.

23. Wang, H.; Hartmann, C.; Schütte, C.; Delle Site, L. Grand-canonical-like molecular-dynamics simulations by using an adaptive-resolution technique. *Phys. Rev. X* **2013**, *3*, doi:10.1103/PhysRevX.3.011018.

24. Daubechies, I. Ten lectures on wavelets. In *CBMS-NSF Regional Conference Series in Applied Mathematics: Ten Lectures on Wavelets No. 61 by Ingrid Daubechies*; Society for Industrial and Applied Mathematics: Philadelphia, PA, USA, 1992.

25. Strang, G.; Nguyen, T. *Wavelets and Filter Banks*; Wellesley-Cambridge Press: Wellesley, MA, USA, 1996.

26. Haar, A. Zur Theorie der orthogonalen Funktionensysteme, (Erste Mitteilung). *Math. Ann.* **1910**, *69*, 331–369.

27. Muller-Plathe, F. Coarse-graining in polymer simulation: From the atomistic to the mesoscopic scale and back. *Chem. Phys. Chem.* **2002**, *3*, 754–769.

28. Lal, M. 'Monte Carlo' computer simulations of chain molecules. *Mol. Phys.* **1969**, *17*, 57–64.

29. Dickman, R.; Hall, C. Equation of state for chain molecules: Continuous space analog of Flory theory. *J. Chem. Phys.* **1986**, *85*, doi:10.1063/1.450881.

30. Metropolis, N.; Rosenbluth, A.W.; Rosenbluth, M.N.; Teller, A.H.; Teller, E. Equation of state calculations by fast computing machines. *J. Chem. Phys.* **1953**, *21*, 1087–1092.

31. Peter, C.; Kremer, K. Multiscale simulation of soft matter systems-from the atomistic to the coarse-grained level and back. *Soft Matter* **2009**, *5*, 4357–4366.

32. Bolhuis, P.; Louis, A.; Hansen, J.; Meijer, E. Accurate effective pair potentials for polymer solutions. *J. Chem. Phys.* **2001**, *114*, 4296–4311.

33. Bolhuis, P.; Louis, A.; Hansen, J. Many-body interactions and correlations in coarse-grained descriptions of polymer solutions. *Phys. Rev. E* **2001**, *64*, doi:10.1103/PhysRevE.64.0218011.

34. Dautenhahn, J.; Hall, C. Monte Carlo simulation of off-lattice polymer chains: Effective pair potentials in dilute solution. *Macromolecules* **1994**, *27*, 5399–5412.

35. Kremer, K.; Binder, K. Monte Carlo simulation of lattice models for macromolecules. *Comput. Phys. Rep.* **1988**, *7*, 259–310.

36. Lyubartsev, A.; Laaksonen, A. Calculation of effective interaction potentials from radial distribution functions: A reverse Monte Carlo approach. *Phys. Rev. E* **1995**, *52*, 3730–3737.

37. D'Adamo, G.; Pelissetto, A.; Pierleoni, C. Coarse-grained strategies in polymer solutions. *Soft Matter* **2012**, *8*, 5151–5167.

38. D'Adamo, G.; Pelissetto, A.; Pierleoni, C. Consistent and transferable coarse-grained model for semidilute polymer solutions in good solvent. *J. Chem. Phys.* **2012**, *137*, doi:10.1063/1.4732851.

39. Kumar, S.; Vacatello, M.; Yoon, D. Offlattice Monte Carlo simulations of polymer melts confined between two plates. *J. Chem. Phys.* **1988**, *89*, doi:10.1063/1.455611.

40. Moore, T.; Iacovella, C.; McCabe, C. Derivation of coarse-grained potentials via multistate iterative Boltzmann inversion. *J. Chem. Phys.* **2014**, *140*, doi:10.1063/1.4880555.

41. Hsu, D.; Xia, W.; Arturo, S.; Keten, S. Systematic method for thermomechanically consistent coarse-graining: A universal model for methacrylate-based polymers. *J. Chem. Theory Comput.* **2014**, *10*, 2514–2527.

42. Hsu, D.; Xia, W.; Arturo, S.; Keten, S. Thermomechanically consistent and temperature transferable coarse-graining of atactic polystyrene. *Macromolecules* **2015**, *48*, 3057–3068.

9

Deformable Cell Model of Tissue Growth

Nikolai Bessonov [1] and Vitaly Volpert [2,*]

[1] Institute of Problems of Mechanical Engineering, Russian Academy of Sciences,
199178 Saint Petersburg, Russia; nickbessonov@yahoo.com

[2] Institut Camille Jordan, UMR 5208 CNRS, University Lyon 1, 69622 Villeurbanne, France

* Correspondence: volpert@math.univ-lyon1.fr

Abstract: This paper is devoted to modelling tissue growth with a deformable cell model. Each cell represents a polygon with particles located at its vertices. Stretching, bending and pressure forces act on particles and determine their displacement. Pressure-dependent cell proliferation is considered. Various patterns of growing tissue are observed. An application of the model to tissue regeneration is illustrated. Approximate analytical models of tissue growth are developed.

Keywords: deformable cells; tissue growth; pattern formation; analytical approximation

1. Introduction

Mathematical and computer modelling of tissue growth is used in various biological problems such as wound healing and regeneration, morphogenesis, tumor growth, etc. Tissue growth can be described with continuous models: partial differentiation equations for cell concentrations (reaction–diffusion equations), Navier–Stokes or Darcy equations for the velocity of the medium, and elasticity equations for the distribution of mechanical stresses. There is a vast literature devoted to these models (see, e.g., [1–5] and references therein). Another approach deals with individual-based models where cells are considered as individual objects. It allows a more detailed description at the level of individual cells though analytical investigation of such models becomes impossible and their numerical simulations are often more involved than for the continuous models. There are various lattice and off-lattice cell-based models which can be regrouped as spherical particle models, cellular automata and deformable cell models.

Spherical particle models originate from molecular dynamics. Each cell is considered as a sphere which can interact with the surrounding cells. The force acting between them depends on the distance between their centers. Additional random and dissipative forces can be introduced, as is the case in dissipative particle dynamics [6]. The motion of particles is determined by Newton's second law. Moreover, cells can divide, die and change their type. Different cell types can have different behavior from the point of view of their motion, division, and death. Already in the 1980s, a similar model, with the equation of motion replaced by some algorithm of cell displacement, was used to study embryogenesis [7]. The spherical particle method to model morphogenesis was developed in a recent work [8]. In [9], one-cell layered tissues were studied under the assumption that there were additional adhesion forces between cells. Hematopoiesis and leukemia development were investigated in [10–13]. Consecutive cell proliferation and differentiation allowed the description of normal and leukemic hematopoiesis in the bone marrow. Dynamics of cell populations and the conditions of leukemia development were studied. In more complex models, cells can be represented as two connected spherical particles [14].

In the cell-center models, cells are considered as polygons with their centers connected by springs, and cell shape determined by Voronoi tessellation. This approach was used for crypt modelling in [15,16] and brain cancer in [17,18]. Particle models can be combined with continuous models, ordinary and partial differential equations for various intracellular and extracellular concentrations. This hybrid method was used for modelling of cancer [19,20], hematopoiesis and blood diseases [21–24] and blood clotting in flow [25,26]. In some cases, it is possible to justify transition from particle models to continuous models [27–29].

Another approach to tissue growth is based on cellular automata (see [5,30,31] and references therein). This method can be easier to implement and it is better adapted for the transition from discrete to continuous models. On the other hand, it imposes a square lattice geometry which can influence the results. This method is used to study tumor growth [32,33] and cell invasion [34,35], angiogenesis [36,37], tissue engineering [38], and development of avian gut tissue [39]. This approach was further developed in the cellular Potts model [30,40] (see also [41,42] and references therein).

Deformable cell models take into account cell geometry and possible deformation due to mechanical forces. The cell membrane can be considered as an ensemble of particles with various forces acting on them (Section 2). This approach is developed for modeling blood flows where blood cells are considered as individual objects (see [43] and references therein). It is close to the spherical particle models though the particles here do not correspond to individual cells. This method gives more detailed information about cell geometry, adhesion and deformation but it is more difficult to realize, especially in the case of cell division (not considered in the works on blood flows). The questions about the direction of cell division and the mechanical properties of the cell wall become of primary importance here. If they are not sufficiently well described, then the model will fail because of geometrical constraints or because of an accumulation of mechanical stresses.

There are various realizations of the deformable cell model, including the immersed boundary method [44], the subcellular element method [45], and the level set method [46] (see [30] and references therein). The deformable cell model coupled with Navier–Stokes equations was used to study the development of epithelial acini [47,48] and ductal tumor [49]. The interaction of cell geometry and migration for the development of cancer was studied in [50]. A phase field model for collective cell migration was developed in [51]. Deformable cell models for plant growth were developed in [52,53]. Growing shoots and roots have a particular cell organization where dividing cells are located in outer layers of the meristem. Differentiated cells do not divide. The direction of cell division depends on cell location. A precise description of the location of dividing cells and of the direction of their division allowed us to reproduce a self-similar growing structure of the plant root [52]. Directions of cell division and visco-elasto-plastic properties of cell walls are important in modelling root growth with a deformable cell model.

In this work, we continue to develop the deformable cell model of tissue growth. The main assumptions of the model are similar to those in [52] except for the location of dividing cells and the direction of their division. Instead of a particular cell structure and division specific for root and shoot meristem, we consider uniform tissue growth where dividing cells can be located everywhere. The direction of their division is determined by a special algorithm described in the next section. We will describe the deformable cell model in Section 2. Some properties of growing tissues and applications are discussed in Section 3. Section 4 is devoted to an approximate analytical model of tissue growth.

2. Deformable Cell Model

2.1. Forces

We begin the description of the model with mechanical forces acting in cellular structures. An individual cell at its mechanical equilibrium (without deformation) represents a regular polygon with n vertices. Initially, it has an area S_0, the length of the sides l_0 and the angle between any neighboring sides α_0. These parameters can be different for different cells. We place a particle of mass m at each vertex of the polygon.

If the polygon changes its shape, then there are three forces which tend to return it to its original configuration. They depend on the change of side length, angles and volume. Similar to other deformable cell models, we define them as follows. If the length l of a side changes, then there is a force acting on each of the two vertices located at this side:

$$\vec{f}_1 = \left(k_1 \left(\frac{l}{l_0} - 1 \right) + \mu_1 \frac{dl}{dt} \right) \vec{\tau}, \quad \vec{f}_2 = -\vec{f}_1 \tag{1}$$

(Figure 1b). Here, $\vec{\tau}$ is the unit vector along the side. If the angle α between two sides changes (Figure 1c), then there is momentum

$$M = k_2 \left(1 - \frac{\alpha}{\alpha_0} \right) - \mu_2 \frac{d\alpha}{dt} \tag{2}$$

which creates a pair of forces applied to the vertices and acting on each side in the direction perpendicular to it, $\alpha_0 = 180°$. Finally, if the cell area S changes, then there is a force (pressure)

$$P = k_3 \left(1 - \frac{S}{S_0} \right) - \mu_3 \frac{dS}{dt} \tag{3}$$

applied to each side and acting in the direction perpendicular to it (Figure 1d). Let us note that the first terms in (1)–(3) describe elastic force and the second term viscous dissipation. They correspond to visco-elastic properties of biological cells. The problem is considered in dimensionless variables. Coefficients k_i are material parameters which determine the resistance to stretching, bending and compression. Parameters μ_i represent artificial viscosity introduced in order to avoid numerical instability.

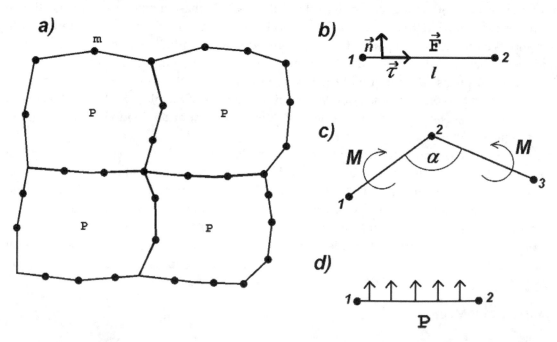

Figure 1. Schematic representation of the model: a structure which consists of four deformable cells (**a**); stretching force acts between two neighboring vertices along the line connecting them (**b**); bending force acts on neighboring sides as the angle between them differs from the angle α_0 (**c**); pressure acts on all sides in the direction perpendicular to them (**d**).

The total force $\vec{F}_i$ acting on the i-th vertex is a sum of these three forces. The position $\vec{r}_i$ of this vertex is determined by the equations

$$\frac{d\vec{r}_i}{dt} = \vec{v}_i, \quad m_i \frac{d\vec{v}_i}{dt} = -\mu \vec{v}_i + \vec{F}_i, \tag{4}$$

where $\vec{v}_i$ is the vertex velocity, μ is the coefficient which determines viscous friction from the surrounding medium.

For further description of the model, we denote by l_0 the side length at mechanical equilibrium and by l its length in the process of cell growth and deformation. Due to plastic deformations, l_0 can change. So, we will distinguish the initial value l_0^i which corresponds to the moment of cell appearance, and the current value l_0, which can be different from l_0^i. We introduce two additional features in the model:

1. If the length of a side becomes twice as large as its initial length l_0^i, then an additional vertex is introduced in the middle of the side. At the moment of side division, the stretching force is preserved. Hence the number of vertices depends on cell deformation. This allows us to better describe cell shape in the case of large deformations.

2. If the length l of a side becomes sufficiently large, that is $l_0^i/l \leq \gamma$, with some γ, $0 < \gamma < 1$, then the initial length l_0 increases irreversibly in such a way that it satisfies the equality $l_0 = \gamma l$. In this case, if the stretching force is removed, then the spring will not return to its initial length but to some greater length. This corresponds to the irreversible deformation of the cell wall when it grows. Here, γ is a material parameter characterizing plastic deformation observed for biological tissues. In the simulations presented below, we set $\gamma = 0.8$.

2.2. Cell Growth and Division

2.2.1. Cell Growth

The cell area S_0 (without deformation) of growing cells changes in time with the rate:

$$\frac{dS_0}{dt} = \sigma(t),$$

where $\sigma(t)$ is some given function. We set $\sigma = 0$, if a cell does not grow and $\sigma(t) = \text{const}$ in the case of linear growth. Other growth rates can also be considered [52]. When S_0 increases two-fold, the cell divides. The area of the daughter cell (without deformation) returns to the two-fold lower value. When studying root growth, we also introduced cell growth without division [52].

2.2.2. Cell Division

One of the important characteristics of growing tissue is the directions of cell division. If these directions are not coordinated, then cells can become strongly deformed. This contradicts biological observations and can result in failure of the numerical method. We will choose the direction of cell division according to the algorithm explained below. This algorithm is specific for unpolarized cells [47].

Let us recall that cells are represented as polygons. They grow, increasing their volume, and divide into two cells with approximately equal areas. Cell division occurs along a section connected to vertices (diagonal) of the polygon. Only such sections are considered. For each cell, the algorithm of choice of the section consists of two steps. In the first step, we choose all sections which divide the polygon into two parts with approximately equal area. Since these two areas are determined by the vertices of the polygon, in general they are not exactly equal to each other. Therefore, we introduce a maximal possible difference ϵ. Hence we choose all sections such that the areas S_1 and S_2 of two resulting post-division polygons satisfy the condition $|S_1 - S_2| < \epsilon$. Here, $S_1 + S_2 = S_0$. In the second step of the algorithm, we choose the shortest section among all of those chosen in the first step. Let us note that this algorithm depends on the location of cell nodes.

Thus, we can summarize this algorithm as a choice of the shortest section by dividing the polygon into two subpolygons with approximately equal areas. Due to this algorithm of cell division, cells cannot be strongly deformed (elongated). We will see that it provides stable tissue growth in a wide range of parameters. Other approaches to the direction of cell division were used in [52] in order to model plant root growth and other polarized cells in [47].

3. Numerical Modelling of Tissue Growth

3.1. All Cells Grow and Divide

Modelling of tissue growth with a deformable cell model implies certain restrictions on the location of dividing cells and on the direction of their division. If these condition are not satisfied, then it will lead to a rapid accumulation of mechanical stresses and to failure of the cellular structure. One possible cell organization was suggested in [52] for the description of root growth. According to the biological observations, dividing cells are located in this case close to the outer surface of the growing root. Directions of cell division are also precisely determined. In this work, we consider a uniform tissue growth where all cells of the tissue can divide.

Let us recall that each cell is characterized by its equilibrium area S_0 and current area S. The equilibrium area grows here as a linear function of time. An example of a growing tissue is shown in Figure 2. Each cell grows and divides. The direction of division is determined by the shortest diagonal algorithm described above. Initially, there are 20 nodes at the surface of the cell in this simulation. Other nodes can be added if the distance between two neighboring nodes exceeds some given value. We will use the values of parameters $k_1 = 40, k_2 = 0.1, k_3 = 100, dS_0/dt = 0.1$, $\mu = 30, dt = 0.04$ (time step), $S_0(0) = 20, \mu_1 = 1, \mu_2 = 0.01, \mu_3 = 1, \gamma = 0.8$, unless other values are specified.

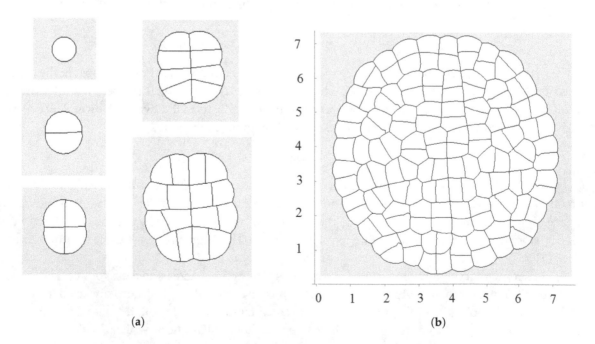

(a)   (b)

Figure 2. Example of simulations where all cells grow and divide; S_0 is a linear function of time; direction of cell division is chosen along the shortest diagonal. First divisions are shown in (a); and a snapshot of the growing cell structure is shown in (b).

The first division occurs along a diameter of the circular cell. The second division takes place along the perpendicular diameter. These first two divisions form the axis of the growing cell structure. They determine the next several divisions. However, during further growth of the tissue, the axes are not preserved and radial structure begins to emerge. The outer cells divide either in the direction parallel to the outer surface or perpendicular to it. This cell organization becomes more obvious during further growth (Figures 3 and 4a). Let us also note that the shapes of the cells represent mostly polygons with four or five vertices. The cell structure symmetry is lost after several divisions because cells have approximately equal area but not exactly equal. Therefore, even after the first division, the two daughter cells are slightly different.

3.2. Pressure-Dependent Proliferation

Cell division leads to cells' compression and to internal pressure growth. Initially, internal pressure in a separate cell equals zero because the cell has its equilibrium shape. When it grows, its equilibrium area S_0 increases linearly in time. Its actual area also grows but slower because the cell membrane resists elongation. This difference creates internal cell pressure. When the cell divides, its equilibrium area S_0 is divided by 2 and its actual area is divided approximately by 2. Therefore, the value of pressure remains approximately the same. Moreover, since cells are attached to each other, they cannot return to the circular shape for which the area is maximal. Cell deformation increases the pressure.

Maximal pressure (among all cells) is reached at the center of the domain filled by cells. It grows exponentially in time (Figure 5a) because cells at the center need to push surrounding cells more and more in order to expand. This is related to the exponential growth of cell number (Section 4). For a fixed time, the maximal pressure depends on parameters. It grows approximately as a linear function of viscosity (Figure 5b). It can be compared with fluid flow in a porous medium where pressure difference is proportional to the viscosity (Section 4).

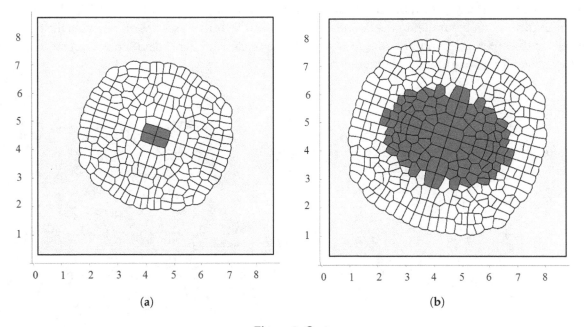

(a)   (b)

Figure 3. *Cont.*

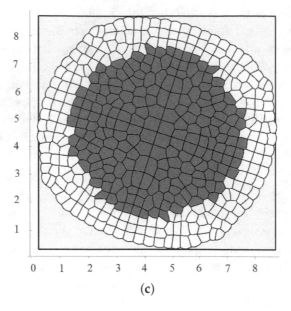

(c)

Figure 3. Snapshots of growing tissue with the maximal division pressure $p_{max} = 15$ in the consecutive moments of time. Non-dividing cells with pressure greater than p_{max} are shown in dark grey.

Biological cells cannot divide when they are too compressed (see [54] and references therein). In order to describe this effect, we introduce the maximal pressure beyond which cells do not divide. Let us recall that pressure P inside cells is determined by Equation (3). We impose an additional condition that if P is greater than some critical value p_{max}, then the cell does not divide. Figure 4a shows a snapshot of the growing cells' structure for the maximal division pressure $p_{max} = 10$. We obtain a regular structure close to a circle with radial cell organization near its outer border. Cells there divide either in the direction parallel to the boundary or perpendicular to it. The latter increases the number of cells in the outer layer and provides growth of the perimeter. Similar cell structures can be observed in the cross-section of growing plant branches.

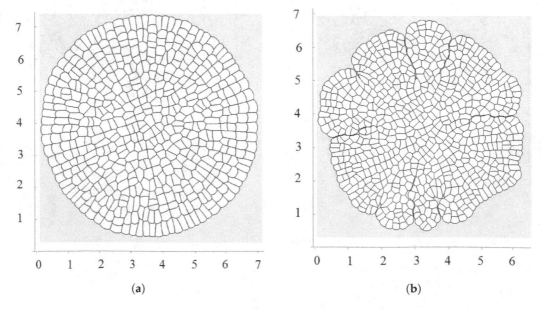

(a)   **(b)**

Figure 4. *Cont.*

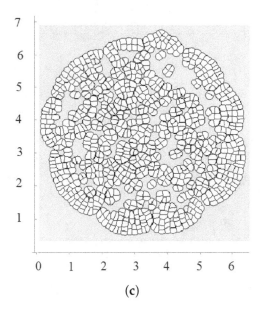

(c)

Figure 4. A snapshot of the growing cell structure with the maximal division pressure $p_{max} = 10$ (**a**); $p_{max} = 4$ (**b**) and with the disappearance of non-dividing cells (**c**).

The value of the maximal division pressure can influence the properties of the growing cell structure. Another example is shown in Figure 4b. Here, the maximal division pressure is set at $p_{max} = 4$ after a short initial period when $p_{max} = 5$ (otherwise, the first divisions do not occur). In this case, there are cells which do not divide even at the outer surface. This results in the appearance of the specific asymmetric structure with a curved surface and "leaves" separated by an interface. Cells at the interface do not divide since the pressure there is greater than the critical value p_{max}.

The appearance of curved structures can be considered as instability of symmetric circular structures. This instability results from cell competition for space. More compressed cells do not grow, and less compressed cells grow and take even more space. As happens in many other examples, the instability occurs near the extinction limit where the cell structure stops growing because of the excessively high pressure.

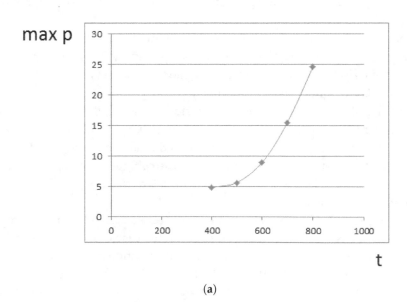

(a)

Figure 5. *Cont.*

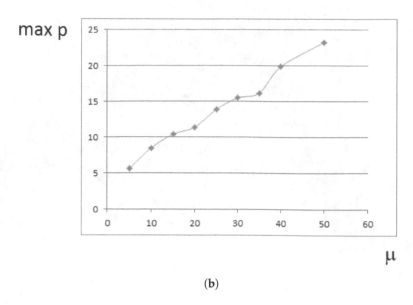

(b)

Figure 5. Maximal pressure in the growing cell tissue. (a) maximal pressure as a function of time; (b) maximal pressure at time $t = 700$ for different values of viscosity coefficient μ. Dimensionless time and pressure units are used.

We consider one more example where cells die by apoptosis if they do not divide during some time. This is related to the check points during the cell cycle. In this case, they are removed from the computational domain. In this case, there is a curved front of cells slowly propagating outwards and numerous cell clusters inside (Figure 4c). This is a non-stationary structure where cells divide and expand if they have enough space; they stop dividing and disappear if there is not enough space.

3.3. External Supply of Nutrients

If nutrients come from outside of the growing tissue, as is the case for tumor growth, then exterior cells have more nutrients than the cells inside the tissue. They will grow and divide faster than cells inside the tissue. They will also compete for nutrients. This competition can lead to nonuniform tissue growth and to the emergence of asymmetric structures. This effect was also observed in hybrid models of tumor growth [55].

In this section, we illustrate it with the deformable cell model. We assume that the growth rate of exterior cells is proportional to the length of their exterior boundary. This assumption implies that the concentration of nutrients in the medium surrounding the tissue is constant and their consumption by cells is proportional to the length of the cell boundary.

If we assume that nutrients can be transported inside the tissue, then interior cells will also have some nutrients. In order to simplify the model, we will suppose that the concentration of nutrients in the extracellular matrix at some point inside the tissue is the same as in the cell located at this point. The flux of nutrients q between cells is proportional to the difference of concentrations c_1 and c_2 in the neighboring cells and to the length L of the boundary between them, $q = \lambda(c_1 - c_2)L$. Here, λ is a parameter which determines the flux intensity.

Figure 6 shows examples of numerical simulations of tissue growth with an external supply of nutrients only to the outer cells and to the interior cells in the case of nutrient diffusion in the tissue. We observe asymmetric growth which results from cell competition for nutrients. A cell which has a longer exterior boundary will grow and divide faster and will compress surrounding cells, reducing their exterior boundary and growth rate. Moreover, the pressure-dependent proliferation increases this competition because compressed cells can stop their growth completely. Emerging structures are more pronounced here than in the model without nutrients (Section 3.2).

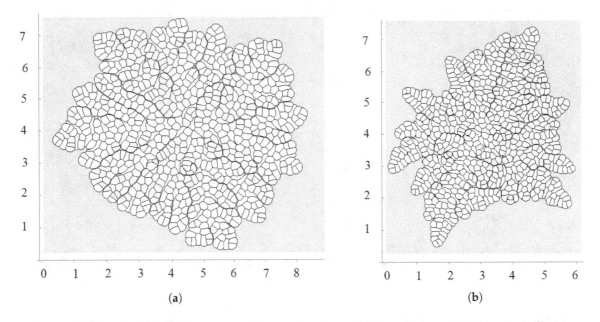

Figure 6. A snapshot of growing tissue with an external supply of nutrients only to the outer cells (**a**) and with nutrient diffusing inside the tissue (**b**).

3.4. Wound Healing

Together with tumor growth, wound healing is one of the main applications of tissue growth models. An extensive literature review on this subject can be found in [56]. A conventional approach to study wound healing consists in the analysis of travelling wave solutions of the reaction–diffusion system of equations for the cell density and for the concentration of some substances which influence cell proliferation (e.g., oxygen). The wave of cell proliferation fills the spatial domain, which corresponds to the wound and which is surrounded by the remaining tissue. In this section, we illustrate modelling of wound healing with the deformable cell model. We will see that pressure-dependent proliferation is an appropriate mechanism to control wound closure.

Figure 7 shows an example of numerical simulations of tissue regeneration. The original tissue (left image) is obtained from a single cell as described above. The cells of this tissue are fixed—they do not grow or divide any more. After that, we remove the internal part of the tissue. The cells at the boundary of the removed tissue can grow and divide. They fill the available place. They stop growing and divide when the tissue is regenerated due to pressure-dependent proliferation. Cells push each other, internal pressure grows and they no longer grow and divide. The new tissue fits the form of the wound well. However, some damage remains at the place where two parts of the tissue meet each other. Its size depends on the mechanical properties of cells. It decreases if cells are more deformable and better fit each other.

Another example of tissue regeneration is shown in Figure 8. The main difference here in comparison with the previous example is that the region where a part of the tissue is removed is not bounded by the remaining tissue (Figure 8b). If we use the same approach as in the previous case, we obtain a different form of the regenerated tissue compared with the initial tissue (Figure 8c). In order to reproduce the form of the original tissue, we need to introduce different growth rates for different cells. Consider cells located at the wound surface in Figure 8b. We impose a particular growth rate for each of these cells. Their descendants will preserve these growth rates. The cells located closer to the outer surface grow and divide slowly. The growth rate and division increase as much as the cells go deeper into the damaged tissue. The maximal growth rate is reached at the center. Such distribution of the growth rate allows us to approximate the initial tissue form by the regenerated tissue (Figure 8d). It should also be noted that this tissue continues to grow even when the initial form is regenerated. Therefore, there are additional mechanisms which control the size of the tissue [57–59].

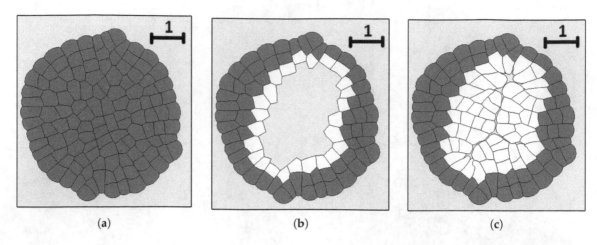

(a)   (b)   (c)

Figure 7. Numerical simulations of wound healing. Original tissue (**a**); damaged tissue (**b**); tissue regeneration (**c**). Grey cells are fixed, while white cells divide and fill the missing part of the tissue.

Let us note that if the critical value p_{max} is high enough, it will not influence cell division. On the other hand, there is a biochemical regulation of the cell division rate, implying that some cells divide faster than others. This regulation is not explicitly introduced in the model but it acts implicitly through the cell location.

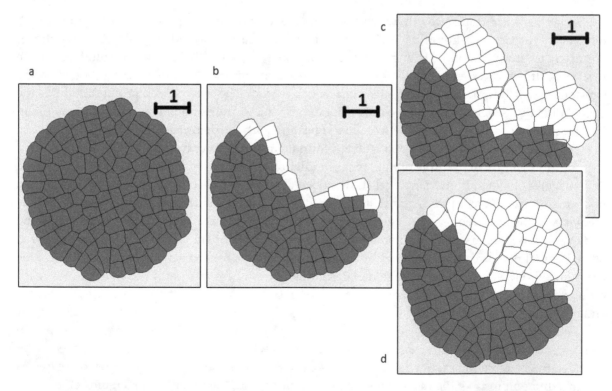

Figure 8. Numerical simulations of wound healing. Original tissue (**a**); damaged tissue (**b**); tissue regeneration with equal rates of cell growth (**c**); cell growth rate depends on the initial position of the first dividing cell in its lineage (**d**).

4. Analytical Approximation of the Growth Rate

4.1. Approximate Model

Passing from the equation of motion of individual particles to an approximate averaged equation of motion of the medium, we get

$$\frac{\partial v}{\partial t} + \mu v + k \frac{\partial p}{\partial x} = 0, \tag{5}$$

where v is the velocity of the medium and p is the pressure (see [27] for more detail). We consider this equation in the one-dimensional case in order to obtain an approximate analytical solution. It corresponds to the two-dimensional case with plane geometry or to the circular tissue with a sufficiently large radius. Equation (5) is a macroscopic analogue of Equation (4) with an average force proportional to the pressure gradient. It should be noted, however, that force in (4) also contains other components. So, the analytical continuous model is an approximation. Parameter μ in both equations corresponds to viscous friction.

We will consider this equation in the quasi-stationary approximation,

$$\mu v = -k \frac{\partial p}{\partial x}, \tag{6}$$

which takes the form of the Darcy equation for the porous medium. Next, we will assume that the medium is incompressible. This assumption is justified for sufficiently large values of the pressure force coefficient k_3 in the cell model. In this case, cells preserve their volume and, in the limit of large coefficients, the medium becomes incompressible. In this case, the mass conservation (or continuity) equation can be written as follows:

$$\text{div } v = W, \tag{7}$$

where W is the rate of production of mass. In the one-dimensional case, divergence is the space derivative $\partial v / \partial x$. Production of mass is determined by the rate of cell division $W = f(p)$. We will suppose that it depends on the pressure. When biological cells are strongly compressed, they do not divide. This assumption is consistent with pressure-dependent proliferation in the cell model (Section 3), which can be considered as discretization of the continuous model.

From Equations (6) and (7), we get

$$kp'' + \mu f(p) = 0, \tag{8}$$

where prime denotes the space derivative.

4.2. Constant Proliferation

If the proliferation rate does not depend on pressure, then we set $f(p) = b$, where b is some positive constant. We solve Equation (8) in the interval $-\xi < x < \xi$ with the boundary condition $p(\pm\xi) = p_0$. We obtain

$$p(x) = -\frac{\mu b}{2k} \left(x^2 - \xi^2 \right) + p_0.$$

Since $d\xi/dt = v(\xi)$, then taking into account (6), we have

$$\frac{d\xi}{dt} = b\xi.$$

Hence the length of the interval grows exponentially. If we consider a circular tissue with the radius ξ, then neglecting the influence of the curvature on the growth rate, we get the formula for the tissue area $A = \pi\xi^2$:

$$A(t) = e^{2bt} A_0,$$

where A_0 is the initial area.

Figure 9a shows an example of numerical simulations of tissue growth with a constant proliferation rate. The linear dependence of the logarithm of tissue area on time, $\log A(t)$, shows that the growth rate is exponential. Three different proliferation rates are considered, $dS_0(t)/dt = 0.1, 0.05, 0.025$. The slopes of the straight lines are in the same proportions. For large amounts of time, the assumptions of the model may not be satisfied, and the growth rate slows down in comparison with the exponential one.

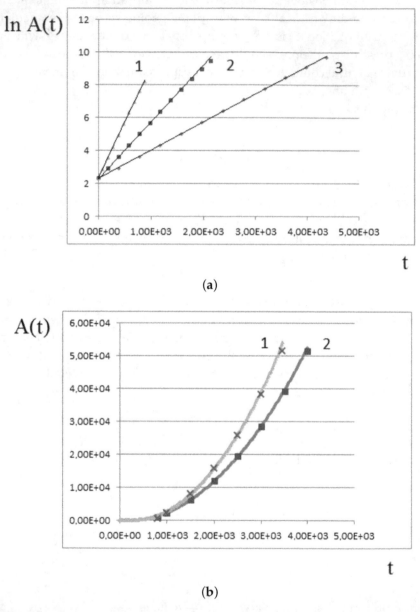

(a)

(b)

Figure 9. Comparison of numerical simulations (continuous curves) with the analytical model (dots) for different values of parameters. (a) tissue growth with a constant proliferation rate in logarithmic coordinates. Linear dependence corresponds to the exponential growth. 1. $dS_0(t)/dt = 0.1$, 2. $= 0.05$, 3. $= 0.025$; (b) quadratic growth for pressure-dependent proliferation, 1. $p_m = 6$, 2. $p_m = 5$. Dimensionless time and area units are used.

4.3. Pressure-Dependent Proliferation

We will consider a piece-wise constant function $f(p)$:

$$f(p) = \begin{cases} b & , \quad 0 < p < p_m \\ 0 & , \quad \quad p \geq p_m \end{cases}.$$

Let us suppose that the medium fills the half-axis $x \leq \xi$. We should complete the formulation of the problem by the boundary condition for the pressure

$$p(\xi) = p_0, \tag{9}$$

where p_0 is some non-negative constant, $p_0 < p_m$.

We can now solve problem (8) and (9). Suppose that the value $p = p_m$ is reached at $x = 0$. Taking into account the continuity of pressure and of its first derivative at $x = 0$, we obtain

$$p(x) = \begin{cases} p_0 & , \quad x \leq 0 \\ p_m - \alpha x^2/2 & , \quad 0 < x \leq \xi \end{cases},$$

where $\alpha = b\mu/(2k)$. From the boundary condition (9), we find the value of ξ:

$$\xi = \sqrt{\frac{2(p_m - p_0)}{\alpha}}.$$

Hence

$$v(\xi) = -\frac{k}{\mu} p'(\xi) = \frac{k}{\mu} \alpha \sqrt{\frac{2(p_m - p_0)}{\alpha}} = \sqrt{\frac{2bk(p_m - p_0)}{\mu}}.$$

In the case of circular tissue growth, neglecting curvature, we can approximate the growth rate of irs radius R by the formula

$$\frac{dR}{dt} = v.$$

Hence we obtain the formula for the tissue area $A = \pi R^2$:

$$A(t) = \pi \frac{2bk(p_m - p_0)}{\mu} t^2. \tag{10}$$

Figure 9b shows the results of numerical simulations of tissue growth and comparison with the analytical approximation. At the beginning of growth, when the pressure-dependent proliferation is not yet established, all cells divide, and the growth rate is exponential. Therefore, instead of Formula (10), we approximate it by the expression

$$A(t) = at^2 + b, \tag{11}$$

where the coefficients a and b are chosen to fit the simulations presented in Section 3.1 with two different values of maximal pressure: $p_m = 5$ and $p_m = 6$. The curves are well approximated by Formula (11) with $a = 0.0033, b = -1142$ and $a = 0.0045, b = -2227$.

In order to compare more precisely the values of a obtained in numerical simulations with the coefficient

$$a = \pi \frac{2bk(p_m - p_0)}{\mu} \tag{12}$$

in (10), we need to specify the value of pressure p_0 at the boundary. This is the pressure in the cells at the outer layer. It varies during cell growth. Its average value depends on the values of parameters.

For the basic set of parameters, $p_0 \approx 4$. Hence the right-hand side in (12) increases twice when we compare $p_m = 5$ and $p_m = 6$ while the coefficient a on the left-hand side obtained from numerical simulations in $0.0045/0.0033 \approx 1.5$ times. This difference is related to the fact that intracellular pressure in the numerical model (Section 3) is only a part of the total pressure in the analytical model. The latter also takes into account the contribution from elastic forces.

If we decrease the value of the stretching coefficient, $k_1 = 30$ (instead of $k_1 = 40$ above), then pressure in cells at the outer layer decreases. Therefore, growth accelerates and we get $a = 0.004$. This example shows how mechanical properties of cells influence the growth rate of the tissue and how they influence macroscopic phenomenological parameters.

5. Discussion

In this work, we developed a deformable cell model of growing tissue where cells are attached to each other. Two neighboring cells have the same boundary and cannot be separated. Another possible approach is to consider separated cells which can adhere due to additional forces acting between them [47,48]. The direction of cell division is chosen along the shortest diagonal which divides the cell into two cells with approximately equal areas. This algorithm appears to be very robust and allows us to simulate tissue growth with more than 10^4 cells. Pressure-dependent proliferation, which corresponds to biological observations, can result in the appearance of asymmetric tissue structures.

The spring model of cells (Section 2) can be considered as an approximation of an elastic medium. Together with viscosity in the equation for particle displacement, we obtain a viscoelastic medium. Using the porous medium equation to describe it, we simplify the model but we obtain a good approximation of the tissue growth rate.

Modelling of tissue growth with the deformable cell model can be applied to study tumor growth. In the case of pressure-dependent proliferation, it describes the linear growth rate of the tissue radius specific for tumors after a short initial stage of exponential growth [54]. The growing tumor can lose its radial symmetry, resulting in the appearance of spatial structures. This instability can be related to cell competition for nutrients, and it can be modeled with partial differential equations [60–64] or with cell-based models [32,55] (see also references in [54]). However, as is indicated in [54], in vitro experiments show a smoother shape of the growing tumor. It is suggested that another possible mechanism of pattern formation can be related to mechanical stresses: cells diffuse along the surface searching for a free space. Results presented in this work show that indeed, competition for nutrients is not the only possible mechanism of instability. Mechanical constraints lead to the emergence of spatial structures. The introduction of nutrients increases their roughness. Hence pressure-dependent proliferation, a linear growth rate (exponential rate at the beginning) and various mechanisms of pattern formation of growing tissues observed in numerical simulations are in agreement with the experiments in vitro.

Another classic example of tissue growth is wound healing. It is conventionally modelled with reaction–diffusion equations for the concentrations of cells and some substances which determine their proliferation. A wave of cell proliferation propagates in the wound region and fills it. The deformable cell model of tissue growth is an appropriate tool to study wound healing. Even without additional concentrations, pressure-dependent proliferation allows us to control wound closure. When two borders of the wound meet and cells touch each other, their proliferation stops. However, if we consider the wound cross-section perpendicular to the epidermis, the wound area is not bounded by the remaining tissue from one side. Therefore, the problem here is different: how to control the form and the size of the growing tissue in an open domain. In this case, we need to introduce the rate of cell proliferation which depends on its position. This question requires further investigation.

The model presented in this work has certain limitations. First of all, we consider a two-dimensional tissue (cell sheet) while most biological tissues are essentially three-dimensional. Numerical simulations in this case become more involved but we expect that the main properties discussed above remain the same. Cell division and death are determined by the intracellular and extracellular regulations which can be described by ordinary or partial differential equations. Such hybrid discrete-continuous models [65] are used in the case of a simplified cell representation (e.g., soft sphere model) but not for the deformable cell models. Let us also note that mechanical properties of the tissue can influence molecular transport [66] and, consequently, cell fate. Mechanical forces can influence cell division and migration [67]. These and other questions require further investigation and the development of more specific models.

Author Contributions: N.B. developed computational software and V.V. performed the simulations. N.B. and V.V. wrote the paper.

References

1. Basan, M.; Elgeti, J.; Hannezo, M.; Rappel, W.-J.; Levine, H. Alignment of cellular motility forces with tissue flow as a mechanism for efficient wound healing. *Proc. Natl. Acad. Sci. USA* **2013**, *110*, 2452–2459.

2. Chauviere, A.; Preziozi, L.; Verdier, C. (Eds.) *Cell Mechanics: From Single Cell-Based Models to Multi-Scale Modeling*; CRC Press: London, UK, 2010.

3. Friedman, A. (Ed.) *Tutorials in Mathematical Biosciences III*; Cell Cycle, Proliferation, and Cancer; Springer: Berlin, Germany, 2006.

4. Capasso, V.; Gromov, M.; Harel-Bellan, A.; Morozova, N.; Pritchard, L. (Eds.) Pattern Formation in Morphogenesis; In *Springer Proceedings in Mathematics*; Springer: Berlin, Germany, 2012; Volume 15.

5. Glade, N.; Stephanou, A. (Eds.) *Le Vivant Entre Discret et Continu*; Editions Matériologiques: Paris, France, 2013.

6. Karttunen, M.; Vattulainen, I.; Lukkarinen, A. *A Novel Methods in Soft Matter Simulations*; Springer: Berlin, Germany, 2004.

7. Bodenstein, L. A dynamic simulation model of tissue growth and cell patterning. *Cell Differ.* **1986**, *19*, 19–33.

8. Markov, M.A.; Markov, A.V. Computer simulation of the ontogeny of organisms with different types of symmetry. *Paleontol. J.* **2014**, *48*, 1–9.

9. Drasdo, D.; Loeffler, M. Individual-based models to growth and folding in one-layered tissues: Intestinal crypts and early development. *Nonlinear Anal.* **2001**, *47*, 245–256.

10. Bessonov, N.; Pujo-Menjouet, L.; Volpert, V. Cell modelling of hematopoiesis. *Math. Model. Nat. Phenom.* **2006**, *1*, 81–103.

11. Bessonov, N.; Demin, I.; Pujo-Menjouet, L.; Volpert, V. A multi-agent model describing self-renewal or differentiation effect of blood cell population. *Math. Comput. Model.* **2009**, *49*, 2116–2127.

12. Bessonov, N.; Crauste, F.; Demin, I.; Volpert, V. Dynamics of erythroid progenitors and erythroleukemia. *Math. Model. Nat. Phenom.* **2009**, *4*, 210–232.

13. Bessonov, N.; Demin, I.; Kurbatova, P.; Pujo-Menjouet, L.; Volpert, V. Multi-Agent Systems and Blood Cell Formation. In *Multi-Agent Systems—Modeling, Interactions, Simulations and Case Studies*; Alkhateeb, F., Al Maghayreh, E., Doush, I.A., Eds.; InTech: Rijeka, Croatia, 2011.

14. Ranfta, J.; Basan, M.; Elgeti, J.; Joanny, J.-F.; Prost, J.; Jülicher, F. Fluidization of tissues by cell division and apoptosis. *PNAS* **2010**, *107*, 20863–20868.

15. Meineke, F.A.; Potten, C.S.; Loeffer, M. Cell migration and organization in the intestinal crypt using a lattice-free model. *Cell Prolif.* **2001**, *34*, 253–266.

16. Van Leeuwen, I.M.; Mirams, G.R.; Walter, A.; Fletcher, A.; Murray, P.; Osborne, J.; Varma, S.; Young, S.J.; Cooper, J.; Doyle, B.; et al. An integrative computational model for intestinal tissue renewal. *Cell Prolif.* **2009**, *42*, 617–636.

17. Kansal, A.R.; Torquato, S.; Harsh, G.R.; Ciccaeb, E.A.; Deisboeck, T.S. Simulated Brain Tumor Growth Dynamics Using a Three-Dimensional Cellular Automaton. *J. Theor. Biol.* **2000**, *203*, 367–382.

18. Kansal, A.R.; Torquato, S.; Harsh, G.R.; Chiocca, E.A.; Deisboeck, T.S. Cellular automaton of idealized brain tumor growth dynamics. *BioSystems* **2000**, *55*, 119–127.

19. Ramis-Conde, I.; Drasdo, D.; Anderson, A.R.A.; Chaplain, M.A.J. Modeling the Influence of the E-Cadherin-b-Catenin Pathway in Cancer Cell Invasion: A Multiscale Approach. *Biophys. J.* **2008**, *95*, 155–165.

20. Ramis-Conde, I.; Chaplain, M.A.J.; Anderson, A.R.A.; Drasdo, D. Multi-scale modelling of cancer cell intravasation: The role of cadherins in metastasis. *Phys. Biol.* **2009**, *6*, 016008.

21. Bessonov, N.; Eymard, N.; Kurbatova, P.; Volpert, V. Mathematical modelling of erythropoiesis in vivo with multiple erythroblastic islands. *Appl. Math. Lett.* **2012**, *25*, 1217–1221.

22. Eymard, N.; Bessonov, N.; Gandrillon, O.; Koury, M.J.; Volpert, V. The role of spatial organization of cells in erythropoiesis. *J. Math. Biol.* **2015**, *70*, 71–97.

23. Fischer, S.; Kurbatova, P.; Bessonov, N.; Gandrillon, O.; Volpert, V.; Crauste, F. Modelling erythroblastic islands: Using a hybrid model to assess the function of central macrophage. *J. Theor. Biol.* **2012**, *298*, 92–106.

24. Kurbatova, P.; Eymard, N.; Volpert, V. Hybrid Model of Erythropoiesis. *Acta Biotheor.* **2013**, *61*, 305–315.

25. Tosenberger, A.; Ataullakhanov, F.; Bessonov, N.; Panteleev, M.; Tokarev, A.; Volpert, V. Modelling of thrombus growth in flow with a DPD-PDE method. *J. Theor. Biol.* **2013**, *337*, 30–41.

26. Tosenberger, A.; Bessonov, N.; Volpert, V. Influence of fibrinogen deficiency on clot formation in flow by hybrid model. *Math. Model. Nat. Phenom.* **2015**, *10*, 36–47.

27. Bessonov, N.; Kurbatova, P.; Volpert, V. Particle dynamics modelling of cell populations. *Math. Model. Nat. Phenom.* **2010**, *5*, 42–47.

28. Colombi, A.; Scianna, M.; Preziosi, L. A measure-theoretic model for collective cell migration and aggregation. *Math. Model. Nat. Phenom.* **2015**, *10*, 4–35.

29. Kurbatova, P.; Panasenko, G.; Volpert, V. Asymptotic numerical analysis of the diffusion-discrete absorption equation. *Math. Methods Appl. Sci.* **2012**, *35*, 438–444.

30. Anderson, A.R.A.; Chaplain, M.; Rejniak, K.A. *Single Cell Based Models in Biology and Medicine*; Birkhäuser: Basel, Switzerland, 2007.

31. Deutsch, A.; Dormann, S. *Cellular Automaton Modeling of Biological Pattern Formation*; Birkhäuser: Boston, MA, USA, 2005.

32. Gerlee, P.; Anderson, A.R.A. A hybrid cellular automaton model of clonal evolution in cancer: The emergence of the glycolytic phenotype. *J. Theor. Biol.* **2008**, *250*, 705–722.

33. Patel, A.A.; Gawlinskia, E.T.; Lemieuxe, S.K.; Gatenby, A.A. A Cellular Automaton Model of Early Tumor Growth and Invasion: The Effects of Native Tissue Vascularity and Increased Anaerobic Tumor Metabolism. *J. Theor. Biol.* **2001**, *213*, 315–331.

34. Simpson, M.J.; Merrifield, A.; Landman, K.A.; Hughes, B.D. Simulating invasion with cellular automata: Connecting cell-scale and population-scale properties. *Phys. Rev. E* **2007**, *76*, 021918.

35. Simpson, M.J.; Landman, K.A.; Hughes, B.D. Distinguishing between Directed and Undirected Cell Motility within an Invading Cell Population. *Bull. Math. Biol.* **2009**, *71*, 781–799.

36. Anderson, A.R.A.; Rejniak, K.A.; Gerlee, P.; Quaranta, V. Microenvironment driven invasion: A multiscale multimodel investigation. *J. Math. Biol.* **2009**, *58*, 579–624.

37. Stephanou, A.; McDougall, S.R.; Anderson, A.R.A.; Chaplain, M.A.J. Mathematical modelling of the influence of blood rheological properties upon adaptive tumour-induced angiogenesis. *Math. Comput. Model.* **2006**, *44*, 96–123.

38. Chung, C.A.; Lin, T.H.; Chen, S.D.; Huang, H.I. Hybrid cellular automaton modeling of nutrient modulated cell growth in tissue engineering constructs. *J. Theor. Biol.* **2010**, *262*, 267–278.

39. Binder, B.J.; Landman, K.A.; Simpson, M.J. Modeling proliferative tissue growth: A general approach and an avian case study. *Phys. Rev. E* **2008**, *78*, 031912.

40. Merks, R.M.H.; Glazier, J.A. A cell-centered approach to developmental biology. *Phys. A* **2005**, *352* 113–130.

41. Albert, P.J.; Schwarz, U.S. Dynamics of Cell Ensembles on Adhesive Micropatterns: Bridging the Gap between Single Cell Spreading and Collective Cell Migration. *PLoS Comput. Biol.* **2016**, doi:10.1371/journal.pcbi.1004863.

42. Scianna, M.; Preziosi, L. *Cellular Potts Models: Multiscale Extensions and Biological Applications*; Chapman and Hall: London, UK; CRC: Boca Raton, FL, USA, 2013.

43. Bessonov, N.; Babushkina, E.; Golovashchenko, S.F.; Tosenberger, A.; Ataullakhanov, F.; Panteleev, M.; Tokarev, A.; Volpert, V. Numerical modelling of cell distribution in blood flow. *Math. Model. Nat. Phenom.* **2014**, *9*, 69–84.

44. Peskin, C.S. The immersed boundary method. *Acta Numer.* **2002**, *11*, 479–517.

45. Newman, T.J. Modeling multicellular systems using subcellular elements. *Math. Biosci. Eng.* **2005**, *2*, 613–624.

46. Koumoutsakos, P.; Bayati, B.; Milde, F.; Tauriello, G. Particle simulations of morphogenesis. *Math. Models Methods Appl. Sci.* **2011**, *21*, 955–1006.

47. Rejniak, K.A.; Anderson, A.R.A. A Computational Study of the Development of Epithelial Acini: I. Sufficient Conditions for the Formation of a Hollow Structure. *Bull. Math. Biol.* **2008**, *70*, 677–712.

48. Rejniak, K.A.; Anderson, A.R.A. A Computational Study of the Development of Epithelial Acini: II. Necessary Conditions for Structure and Lumen Stability. *Bull. Math. Biol.* **2008**, *70*, 1450–1479.

49. Rejniak, K.A.; Dillon, R.H. A single cell based model of the ductal tumour microarchitecture. *Comput. Math. Methods Med.* **2007**, *8*, 51–69.

50. Tozluoglu, M.; Tournier, A.L.; Jenkins, R.P.; Hooper, S.; Bates, P.A.; Sahai, E. Matrix geometry determines optimal cancer cell migration strategy and modulates response to interventions. *Nat. Cell Biol.* **2013**, *15*, 751–762.

51. Lober, J.; Ziebert, F.; Aranson, I.S. Collisions of deformable cells lead to collective migration. *Sci. Rep.* **2015**, doi:10.1038/srep09172.

52. Bessonov, N.; Mironova, V.; Volpert, V. Deformable cell model of root growth. *Math. Model. Nat. Phenom.* **2013**, *8*, 62–79.

53. Merks, R.M.; Guravage, M.; Inze, D.; Beemster, G.T. VirtualLeaf: An open-source framework for cell-based modeling of plant tissue growth and development. *Plant Physiol.* **2011**, *155*, 656–666.

54. Brú, A.; Albertos, S.; Subiza, J.L.; García-Asenjo, J.L.; Brú, I. The Universal Dynamics of Tumor Growth. *Biophys. J.* **2003**, *85*, 2948–2961.

55. Bessonov, N.; Kurbatova, P.; Volpert, V. Pattern Formation in Hybrid Models of Cell Populations. In *Pattern Formation in Morphogenesis: Problems and Mathematical Issues Series*; Capasso, V., Gromov, M., Harel-Bellan, A., Morozova, N., Pritchard, L., Eds.; Springer: Berlin, Germany, 2012; pp. 107–119.

56. Murray, J.D. *Mathematical Biology II: Spatial Models and Biomedical Applications*, 3rd ed.; Springer: Berlin, Germany, 2003.

57. Bessonov, N.; Levin, M.; Morozova, N.; Reinberg, N.; Tosenberger, A.; Volpert, V. On a model of pattern regeneration based on cell memory. *PLoS ONE* **2015**, *10*, doi:10.1371/journal.pone.0118091.

58. Caraguel, F.; Bessonov, N.; Demongeot, J.; Dhouailly, D.; Volpert, V. Wound healing and scale modelling in Zebrafish. *Acta Biotheor.* **2016**, *64*, 343–358.

59. Tosenberger, A.; Bessonov, N.; Levin, M.; Reinberg, N.; Volpert, V.; Morozova, N. A conceptual model of morphogenesis and regeneration. *Acta Biotheor.* **2015**, *63*, 283–294.

60. Friedman, A.; Hu, B. Bifurcation from stability to instability for a free boundary problem arising in a tumor model. *Arch. Ration. Mech. Anal.* **2006**, *180*, 293–330.

61. Friedman, A.; Hu, B. Asymptotic stability for a free boundary problem arising in a tumor model. *J. Differ. Equ.* **2006**, *227*, 598–639.

62. Friedman, A.; Hu, B. Bifurcation from stability to instability for a free boundary problem modeling tumor growth by Stokes equation. *J. Math. Anal. Appl.* **2007**, *327*, 643–664.

63. Friedman, A.; Hu, B. Bifurcation for a free boundary problem modeling tumor growth by Stokes equations. *SIAM J. Math. Anal.* **2007**, *39*, 174–194.

64. Hogea, C.S.; Murray, B.T.; Sethian, J.A. Simulating complex tumor dynamics from avascular to vascular growth using a general level-set method. *J. Math. Biol.* **2006**, *53*, 86–134.

65. Stephanou, A.; Volpert, V. Hybrid Modelling in Biology: A Classification Review. *Math. Model. Nat. Phenom.* **2016**, *11*, 37–48.

66. Netti, P.A.; Berk, D.A.; Swartz, M.A.; Grodzinsky, A.J.; Jain, R.K. Role of extracellular matrix assembly in interstitial transport in solid tumors. *Cancer Res.* **2000**, *60*, 2497–2503.

67. Roca-Cusachs, P.; Conte, V.; Trepat, X. Quantifying forces in cell biology. *Nat. Cell Biol.* **2017**, *19*, 742–751.

10

Energetic Study of Clusters and Reaction Barrier Heights from Efficient Semilocal Density Functionals

Guocai Tian [1,2,*]**, Yuxiang Mo** [2] **and Jianmin Tao** [2,*]

[1] State Key Laboratory of Complex Nonferrous Metal Resources Clean Utilization, Kunming University of Science and Technology, Kunming 650093, China

[2] Department of Physics, Temple University, Philadelphia, PA 19122-1801, USA; yuxiangm@gmail.com

[*] Correspondence: tiangc@kmust.edu.cn (G.T.); jianmin.tao@temple.edu (J.T.)

Academic Editor: Karlheinz Schwarz

Abstract: The accurate first-principles prediction of the energetic properties of molecules and clusters from efficient semilocal density functionals is of broad interest. Here we study the performance of a non-empirical Tao-Mo (TM) density functional on binding energies and excitation energies of titanium dioxide and water clusters, as well as reaction barrier heights. To make a comparison, a combination of the TM exchange part with the TPSS (Tao–Perdew–Staroverov–Scuseria) correlation functional—called TMTPSS—is also included in this study. Our calculations show that the best binding energies of titanium dioxide are predicted by PBE0 (Perdew–Burke–Ernzerhof hybrid functional), TM, and TMTPSS with nearly the same accuracy, while B3LYP (Beck's three-parameter exchange part with Lee-Yang-Parr correlation), TPSS, and PBE (Perdew–Burke–Ernzerhof) yield larger mean absolute errors. For excitation energies of titanium and water clusters, PBE0 and B3LYP are the most accurate functionals, outperforming the performance of semilocal functionals due to the nonlocality problem suffered by the latter. Nevertheless, TMTPSS and TM functionals are still good accurate semilocal methods, improving upon the commonly-used TPSS and PBE functionals. We also find that the best reaction barrier heights are predicted by PBE0 and B3LYP, thanks to the nonlocality incorporated into these two hybrid functionals, but TMTPSS and TM are obviously more accurate than SCAN (Strongly Constrained and Appropriately Normed), TPSS, and PBE, suggesting the good performance of TM and TMTPSS for physically different systems and properties.

Keywords: first-principles; density functional theory; semilocal density functional; excitation energy; cluster; reaction barrier height

1. Introduction

Kohn–Sham density functional theory (DFT) [1,2] is the most popular electronic structure theory, and has achieved practical success in the first-principles prediction of the electronic structure of matter. In this theory, only the exchange-correlation energy component—which accounts for all many-body effects—remains unknown and has to be approximated as a functional of the electron density. As such, the predictive power of DFT largely depends on the density functional approximation to the exchange-correlation energy. Therefore, the development of exchange-correlation density functionals with better accuracy and wider applicability has been the central topic of the field [3–8]. More importantly, achieving high accuracy for wide-ranging properties and diverse systems will greatly enhance the computer design of new materials and devices.

The exchange-correlation energy is defined by

$$E_{xc} = \frac{1}{2} \int d^3r \int d^3r' \frac{n(\mathbf{r})\rho_{xc}(\mathbf{r},\mathbf{r}')}{|\mathbf{r}'-\mathbf{r}|}, \tag{1}$$

where $n(\mathbf{r})$ is the electron density and $\rho_{xc}(\mathbf{r},\mathbf{r}')$ is the exchange-correlation hole at $\mathbf{r}'$ around the electron at $\mathbf{r}$ (spin index has been suppressed and atomic units ($\hbar = e = m = 1$) are used). Density functionals can be developed by imposing the exact constraints on the exchange-correlation energy E_{xc}, or on the exchange-correlation hole $\rho_{xc}(\mathbf{r},\mathbf{r}')$, or on both. The constraints on the exchange-correlation energy are global, while the constraints on the exchange-correlation hole are local and thus are more difficult to impose. Most density functionals have been proposed from the energy constraints. While the functional form is rather restricted for the local spin-density approximation (LSDA) [3,4], the GGA (Generalized Gradient Approximation) [5] is more flexible and can incorporate more constraints. A meta-GGA [6–8] is even more flexible and can incorporate more local ingredients or inputs than LSDA and GGA. The simplest construction is the LSDA [3,4], in which the exchange part (i.e., Slater exchange) is calculated from the noninteracting plane wave, while the correlation part is calculated numerically with the quantum Monte Carlo (QMC) method. The LSDA is uniquely defined, although different parameterizations of the QMC data have been proposed. Since the typical valence electron density in solids is nearly uniform, the LSDA has been widely used in solid-state calculations. However, the LSDA tends to overestimate the short-range interaction arising from the orbital overlap of valence electrons in a molecule or solid and thus displays strong overbinding tendency. This tendency becomes more serious when the electron density becomes more inhomogeneous. For example, the LSDA yields moderately too-high cohesive energies of solids, but it significantly overestimates the atomization energies of molecules, in which the electron density is not slowly varying, leading to too-short bond lengths and lattice constants.

GGA [5] is designed to correct the overbinding tendency of the LSDA. It was shown that GGA can significantly reduce the error of the LSDA in molecular atomization energy by a factor of about 10. However, this correction leads GGA to produce too-long bond lengths and lattice constants, and worsens the good performance of the LSDA for molecular solids, physisorption, and layered materials, in which the long-range van der Waals (vdW) interaction is important. A fundamental reason for this is that the excess short-range interaction of the LSDA effectively compensates for the absent long-range part of the vdW interaction. GGA removes the excess short-range interaction of the LSDA, but it is unable to provide the nonlocal long-range vdW interaction, because it is semilocal after all. This leads GGA to yield too-long bond lengths and lattice constants. In other words, GGA approaches experiments from the opposite side of the LSDA. To cure the shortcoming of GGA, meta-GGA functionals have been developed by including the orbital kinetic energy densities $\tau_\sigma = \sum_i^{occ} |\phi_{i\sigma}(\mathbf{r})|^2$ as an additional input [6–8] beyond those of GGA. Using the kinetic energy density as another local ingredient makes the functional form of meta-GGA very flexible. This flexibility enables a meta-GGA to recover the correct slowly varying gradient expansion of the exchange-correlation energy up to fourth order in density gradient, and at the same time can reduce the self-interaction error of GGA. As a result, meta-GGA can extend the short-range part of the vdW interaction to a wider range. The former can improve the GGA description of usual bulk solids and molecules, while the latter can greatly improve GGA functionals for systems in which the long-range vdW interaction is important (e.g., molecular complexes and solids). There are two ways to achieve this goal. One is to include many parameters fitted to many sets of properties such as M06L (Minnesota 06 Local functional) meta-GGA [6], and the other is to incorporate many known constraints on E_{xc}, such as TPSS (Tao–Perdew–Staroverov–Scuseria) [7] and SCAN meta-GGAs [8].

A more appealing approach for developing meta-GGA functionals is to incorporate exact constraints not only via E_{xc}, but also via the hole $\rho_{xc}(\mathbf{r},\mathbf{r}')$. This will allow one to build more exact constraints into a meta-GGA than a meta-GGA constructed by only the constraints on the energy E_{xc}, and thus has a better chance of achieving high accuracy. The starting point of this method is to approximate the hole directly, rather than approximating the hole with the reverse engineering approach [9], as is done in most density functionals. From the hole, one can calculate the underlying functional via Equation (1). Then, one can establish a desirable one-to-one relationship between a density functional and the associated hole. This is a natural method. The difficulty is that the conventionally defined exchange hole is nonlocal in nature. It was shown that this difficulty can be largely reduced with a general coordinate transformation [10], because the conventional exchange hole becomes localized under the general coordinate transformation. This offers a way to approximate the exchange hole with a semilocal functional. We have recently illustrated this approach by developing a nonempirical Tao-Mo (TM) meta-GGA functional [11]. Numerical tests show that this functional can achieve remarkable accuracy for wide-ranging properties of molecules and solids [12,13].

Here we apply the TM meta-GGA to study the excitation and binding energies of titanium dioxide and water clusters, as well as reaction barrier heights. To have a better understanding of the performance of the TM functional, a combination of the TM exchange part with the original TPSS correlation (i.e., TMTPSS) is also included in this study. The selection of these systems is based on two considerations. First, these systems are formed with different bonding types (e.g., ionic bonds, covalent bonds, and hydrogen-bonds), and are thus physically different systems. Second, these clusters by themselves are of great interest, due to their remarkable properties and applications. All of these properties (i.e., excitation energies of clusters and reaction barrier heights) are closely related to electronic nonlocality. They represent a stringent test for semilocal DFT methods. Our calculations show that in all the cases, the TM and TMTPSS functionals consistently show better accuracy, improving upon commonly-used semilocal functionals. It is competitive with computationally more expensive hybrid functionals, pushing cost-effective first-principles prediction to higher accuracy.

2. Results

2.1. Binding Energies and Excitation Energy of Titanium Dioxide Cluster

Titanium dioxide (TiO_2) has attracted great attention in the past few decades [14–17], due to its low cost, environmental compatibility, and experimentally proven potential for photocatalytic and photovoltaic applications [14,15]. In particular, the use of TiO_2 as heterogeneous catalysts for photochemical splitting of water to produce renewable hydrogen and dye-sensitized solar cells has been the subject of intense research [14–17].

To understand the microscopic structure of TiO_2, the binding energies of $(TiO_2)_n$ with $n = 2$–4 clusters in the gas phase are investigated. Figure 1 shows the chemical structure of $(TiO_2)_n$, while Table 1 displays the binding energies of $(TiO_2)_n$ clusters from density functional calculations. From Table 1, we observe that the binding energies between TiO_2 molecules are in the range of a normal chemical bond. However, due to the large practicabilities of the O^{2-} ion and transition-metal ions, there exist strong vdW interactions in these ionic solid clusters. Because the long-range vdW interaction is missing in standard density functionals, this effect leads to large mean absolute errors (MAE) of all conventional DFT methods studied for this kind of cluster. Nevertheless, the TM and TMTPSS functionals give good improvement upon other semilocal DFT methods studied, such as PBE (Perdew–Burke–Ernzerhof) and TPSS. They are comparable to the more expensive hybrid PBE0 or even more accurate than B3LYP, as shown in Table 1. This performance is consistent with other recent studies [18,19].

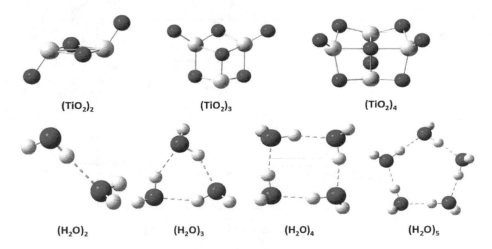

Figure 1. Equilibrium structure of $(TiO_2)_n$ and $(H_2O)_n$ clusters .

Table 1. Binding energy per molecule (kcal/mol) of $(TiO_2)_n$ (n = 2–4) clusters evaluated with different methods using the 6-311++G($3df,3pd$) basis set. B3LYP: a hybrid functional with Beck's three-parameter exchange part and Lee-Yang-Parr correlation; PBE: Perdew–Burke–Ernzerhof functional; PBE0: Perdew–Burke–Ernzerhof hybrid functional; TM: Tao-Mo density functional; TPSS: Tao–Perdew–Staroverov–Scuseria correlation functional; TMTPSS: combination of the TM exchange part with the original TPSS correlation; MP2: Møller-Plesset expansion truncated at second-order. ME: Mean Error; MAE: mean absolute error; ME = Theory-MP2.

N	PBE	TPSS	TM	TMTPSS	B3LYP	PBE0	MP2
2	55.54	56.94	59.37	59.09	57.49	59.55	73.97
3	74.16	76.18	79.79	79.45	77.09	80.11	98.75
4	84.38	87.28	91.42	91.00	87.86	91.67	113.74
ME	24.13	22.02	18.63	18.97	21.34	18.38	
MAE	24.13	22.02	18.63	18.97	21.34	18.38	

Table 1 also shows that the binding energy per molecule (TiO_2) increases with cluster size, as predicted by all DFT methods. This trend qualitatively agrees with MP2 prediction. For all methods including MP2, the increasing rate becomes smaller and should be gradually saturated to the cohesive energy of the bulk titanium dioxide when $n > 7$ [20].

Next, we study the lowest singlet excitation energies of titanium dioxide clusters with time-dependent DFT (TDDFT) within the adiabatic approximations. These excitation energies correspond to the HOMO–LUMO energy gaps of the cluster. In the large-size ($n > 7$) or bulk limit, they should converge to the band gap of bulk titanium dioxide [20,21]. Figure 2 shows the lowest excitation energies of the $(TiO_2)_n$ (n = 1–4) clusters calculated from PBE, TPSS, TM, TMTPSS, B3LYP, and PBE0 within the adiabatic TDDFT. As shown in Figure 2, for small $(TiO_2)_n$ clusters with $n = 1$–4, all these excitation energies show strong odd–even oscillation in accordance with previous DFT results [20], and the predicted values are still far above the experimental results [20,21]. All of these clusters show a large energy gap consistent with the previous calculations [20]. However, the calculations overestimated the gaps considerably, probably because relaxation effects were not included [21,22].

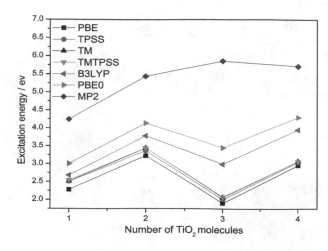

Figure 2. Lowest singlet excitation energies (eV) of $(TiO_2)_n$ ($n = 1$–4) calculated with different methods at 6-311++G($3df,3pd$) basis set.

From Figure 2 we can see that all these DFT methods exhibit a similar trend for the lowest excitation energies of the $(TiO_2)_n$ ($n = 2$–4) clusters. All DFT lines show a drop of the excitation energy from 2 to 3 TiO_2 molecules, but MP2 shows an increase. There is a noticeable excitation energy shift between semilocal and hybrid functionals, leading to the excitation energies of hybrid functionals being closer to the accurate MP2 values. This shift clearly arises from the Hatree–Fock (HF) exchange built in these two hybrid functionals. The magnitude of the shift is dependent upon the amount of the HF exchange included in a hybrid functional. For example, PBE0 contains 1/4 HF exchange, while B3LYP contains 1/5 HF exchange. The HF exchange not only provides electronic nonlocality, which is necessary for some properties discussed above, but also improves the density tail behaviour of the exchange potential and reduces self-interaction error. As a result, hybrid functionals are more accurate than semilocal DFT for excitation energies, as argued by Becke and demonstrated in the literature [23]. However, this does not mean that the more HF exchange contained in a hybrid functional, the more accuracy we can achieve, because one needs to consider the balance between the exchange and correlation parts or error cancellation.

Figure 2 also shows that the deviation of semilocal functionals from hybrid functionals becomes slightly larger as cluster size increases. Similar to hybrid functionals, the lowest singlet excitation energies of all the semilocal functionals will eventually saturate to the band gap of the bulk titanium dioxide. We observe that among the semilocal functionals, TM and TMTPSS are more accurate than others. In contrast, PBE gives the lowest excitation energies. While PBE0 does correct the exchange description relative to PBE, there is no correction whatsoever in PBE0 when it comes to dispersive interactions—a nonlocal correlation effect.

2.2. Binding Energies and Excitation Energy of Water Cluster

Water is the most abundant matter that covers about four-fifths of the Earth's surface. It has a complicated structure and anomalous properties that have not been well understood [24]. Despite considerable efforts, many of the properties of water remain puzzling [25]. Study shows that liquid water is not homogeneous at the nanoscopic level [26]. To understand the detail of the structure, a fundamental understanding of water clusters is important [27,28]. A feature of water clusters is their intermolecular interaction consisting of hydrogen bonds and a smaller part of the vdW interaction. Accurate description of these weak interactions presents a great challenge to DFT [29]. Figure 1 shows the optimized structures of various water clusters, while Table 2 shows the comparison of the binding energies of water clusters $(H_2O)_n$ ($n = 2$–5) between DFT methods and MP2. From Table 2, we can observe that TM can achieve high accuracy, substantially improving upon other DFT methods. From Table 2, one can find that PBE0 performs worst. This is because PBE0 corrects the exchange description relative to PBE, but there is no correction whatsoever in PBE0 when it comes to dispersive interactions—a nonlocal correlation effect.

Table 2. Binding energies (kcal/mol) of $(H_2O)_n$ (n = 2–5) clusters from various DFT methods at the 6-311++G(3df,3pd) basis set. MP2 values of water clusters are taken from Reference [26]. ME = Theory-MP2. D3BJ: Grimme's third generation dispersion with Becke-Johnson rational damping.

N	PBE	PBE-D3BJ	TPSS	TPSS-D3BJ	TM	TMTPSS	B3LYP	PBE0	MP2
2	−5.41	−5.83	−4.98	−5.50	−5.02	−4.83	−4.83	−5.28	−4.97
3	−17.05	−18.44	−15.72	−17.43	−16.29	−15.56	−14.97	−16.42	−15.82
4	−30.64	−32.92	−28.65	−31.43	−28.22	−26.91	−27.04	−29.35	−27.63
5	−40.41	−43.29	−37.97	−41.45	−36.77	−35.08	−35.74	−38.75	−36.31
ME	−2.19	−3.93	−0.65	−2.77	−0.39	0.59	0.54	−1.27	
MAE	2.19	3.93	0.70	2.77	0.39	0.59	0.54	1.27	

Dispersion plays a vital role in the energetics of water systems. Table 2 also shows the results of PBE-D3BJ and TPSS-D3BJ developed by Grimme [30,31] for comparison. It is shown that the addition of dispersion (DFT-D3) to a semi-local functional always increases binding energy, as expected [29,32], but is not correctly described by the semi-local functionals. The same results are obtained by others [29,32]. The addition of dispersion to a semi-local functional can bring large changes in the structure and equilibrium density of the liquid, so that errors are large [29].

To have a better understanding of water clusters, we calculate the lowest vertical excitation energies of a few small water clusters, in which the accurate ab initio values are available for comparison. The results are displayed in Figure 3. From Figure 3, we observe that the lowest vertical excitation energy of a water cluster quickly saturates to the band gaps of ice, which are smaller than experiment (8.8 ± 0.4 eV) [33–40], but with PBE0 being the closest one, followed by B3LYP and semilocal DFT methods for the same reason discussed above. We also observe that TM and TMTPSS give good match results with MP2 value among semilocal DFT methods, although the discrepancy is still too large due to the nonlocality issue. This indicates the robustness of the TM exchange. From Figure 3, we can also observe that all the calculated excitation energies tend to be red-shifted with respect to the MP2 values, as expected.

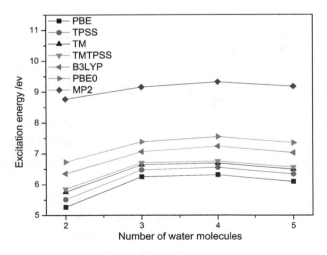

Figure 3. The lowest excitation energy (eV) of $(H_2O)_n$ (n = 2–5) calculated with different methods at 6-311++G(3df,3pd) basis set.

2.3. BH76 Barrier Heights

Prediction of reaction barrier heights presents a great challenge to semilocal DFT, due to the presence of stretched bonds in a transition state, which is closely related to electronic nonlocality.

The BH76 (76 Barrier Heights) test set consists of 38 hydrogen transfer barrier heights and 38 non-hydrogen transfer barrier heights. It is a standard test set that has been widely used to benchmark the theoretical methods [41,42]. Table 3 shows the statistical errors of the reaction barrier heights evaluated with the TM and TMTPSS functionals, compared with other density functionals.

Table 3. Summary of deviations of the calculated reaction barrier heights from best values [41] for the BH76 test set. Results are taken from Reference [42] for M06L, Reference [8] for SCAN, and Reference [41] for local spin-density approximation (LSDA), PBE, TPSS, B3LYP, and PBE0. All values are in kcal/mol. ME = theory − best values from Reference [41].

Method	LSDA	PBE	TPSS	TM	TMTPSS	B3LYP	M06L	PBE0	SCAN
ME	−14.78	−8.66	−8.14	−7.08	−6.86	−4.15	−3.9	−3.68	−7.7
MAE	14.88	8.71	8.17	7.08	6.86	4.28	4.1	3.99	7.7

From Table 3, we can see that like other semilocal functionals, the TM and TMTPSS functionals tend to underestimate reaction barrier heights. The order of MAE for the BH76 set with different methods is PBE0 < M06L < B3LYP < TMTPSS < TM < SCAN < TPSS < PBE < LSDA. Reaction barrier heights are generally predicted more accurately with nonlocal density functionals, because such functionals exhibit a small delocalization error [43] for species with stretched bonds (i.e., transition states). From Table 3, we can also see a large reduction of errors in reaction barrier heights from non-hybrid to hybrid functionals (e.g., from PBE to PBE0). Since BH76 was used to parameterize the M06L meta-GGA functional, we have not included it for comparison, but list it in Table 3 for reference.

3. Materials and Methods

All calculations of clusters were carried out using the modified Gaussian 09 [44] with 6-311++G($3df,3pd$) basis set. The ground-state geometries of molecules and clusters were performed self-consistently with respective density functionals. Based on the optimized geometries, we evaluated the lowest vertical excitation energies of clusters with TDDFT within the adiabatic approximation. The binding energies of $(TiO_2)_n$ clusters were calculated as energy difference between cluster and constituent molecules. Since our calculations involve the treatment of both the ground state (optimization of molecular geometry) and excited states, for consistency, the same basis was used in all calculations. The ultrafine grid (Grid = Ultrafine) in numerical integration and the tight self-consistent field convergence criterion (SCF = Tight) were used. To make comparison consistent, we performed the calculations with all density functionals, rather than taking the data directly from the literature for $(H_2O)_n$ and $(TiO_2)_n$ clusters. Since reaction barrier height calculations are highly sensitive to the basis set, in this work, TM and TMTPSS methods were used to perform the geometries optimization and frequency analysis of the reactants, transition states, and products with MG3 (Multi-coefficient Gaussian-3) basis set by using their QCISD(Quadratic configuration interaction single and double excitation methods)/MG3 structure [41]. Throughout the paper, ME and MAE are mean error (deviation) and absolute mean error (deviation) respectively.

4. Conclusions

We have studied the binding energies and excitation energies of clusters, as well as the BH76 barrier heights, which cover all bonding types, with recently proposed semilocal functionals. In this study, commonly-used semilocal and hybrid density functionals have also been included for comparison. Our calculations show that the TM and TMTPSS functionals can achieve good performance for these properties and systems, improving upon commonly-used semilocal DFT methods. We find that in some cases, they are competitive to the most popular hybrid functionals, but with lower computational cost.

A striking feature of the TM functional is that it incorporates many exact constraints through the underlying exchange hole, such as uniform coordinate scaling [45], negativity, correct uniform-gas limit, and spin scaling relationship [46]. The high accuracy of the TM functional may greatly benefit from its exchange enhancement factor, which has the same small oscillatory behavior as M06L [47]. Therefore, the TM functional can capture or extend the short-range part of the van der Waals interaction due to the de-enhancement (relative to the LSDA) in some regions, leading to an improvement for most properties. The TM correlation functional was developed separately from the exchange part, which respects all the exact conditions that the TPSS correlation satisfies, and improvement over TPSS in the low-density (strong-interaction) limit. Therefore, it is not surprising that the TMTPSS (TMx+TPSSc) functional can give the best results of energy calculation in many systems studied.

Acknowledgments: G.T. was supported by National Natural Science Foundation of China under Grant No. 51264021, the China Scholarship Council and by Back-up Personnel Foundation of Academic and Technology Leaders of Yunnan Province under Grant No. 2011HR013. J.T. and Y.M. acknowledge support from the NSF under Grant No. CHE-1640584. J.T. also acknowledges support from Temple start-up via John Perdew. Partial computational support was provided by Temple University.

Author Contributions: G.T. conceived and designed the experiments; G.T. performed the experiments; G.T. and J.T. analyzed the data; G.T. wrote the paper; G.T., Y.M. and J.T. contributed the discussions and revisions of the manuscript.

References

1. Kohn, W.; Sham, L.J. Self-consistent equations including exchange and correlation effects. *Phys. Rev.* **1965**, *140*, A1133–A1136.
2. Parr, R.G.; Yang, W. *Density-Functional Theory of Atoms and Molecules*; Oxford University Press: Oxford, UK, 1989.
3. Vosko, H.; Wilk, L.; Nusair, M. Accurate spin-dependent electron liquid correlation energies for local spin density calculations: A critical analysis. *Can. J. Phys.* **1980**, *58*, 1200–1201.
4. Perdew, J.P.; Wang, Y. Accurate and simple analytic representation of the electron-gas correlation energy. *Phys. Rev. B* **1992**, *45*, 13244–13249.
5. Perdew, J.P.; Burke, K.; Ernzerhof, M. Generalized gradient approximation made simple. *Phys. Rev. Lett.* **1996**, *77*, 3865–3868.
6. Zhao, Y.; Truhlar, D.G. A new local density functional for main-group thermochemistry, transition metal bonding, thermochemical kinetics, and noncovalent interactions. *J. Chem. Phys.* **2006**, *125*, 194101.
7. Tao, J.; Perdew, J.P.; Staroverov, V.N.; Scuseria, G.E. Climbing the density functional ladder: Nonempirical meta-generalized gradient approximation designed for molecules and solids. *Phys. Rev. Lett.* **2003**, *91*, 146401.
8. Sun, J.; Ruzsinszky, A.; Perdew, J.P. Strongly constrained and appropriately normed semilocal density functional. *Phys. Rev. Lett.* **2015**, *115*, 036402.
9. Constantin, L.A.; Perdew, J.P.; Tao, J. Meta-generalized gradient approximation for the exchange-correlation hole with an application to the jellium surface energy. *Phys. Rev. B* **2006**, *73*, 205104.
10. Tao, J.; Springborg, M.; Perdew, J.P. Properties of the exchange hole under an appropriate coordinate transformation. *J. Chem. Phys.* **2003**, *119*, 6457–6502.
11. Tao, J.; Mo, Y. Accurate semilocal density functional for condensed-matter physics and quantum chemistry. *Phys. Rev. Lett.* **2016**, *117*, 073001.
12. Mo, Y.; Tian, G.; Car, R.; Staroverov, V.N.; Scuseria, G.E.; Tao, J. Performance of a nonempirical density functional on molecules and hydrogen-bonded complexes. *J. Chem. Phys.* **2016**, *145*, 234306.
13. Mo, Y.; Car, R.; Staroverov, V.N.; Scuseria, G.E.; Tao, J. Assessment of a nonempirical semilocal density functional on solids and surfaces. *Phys. Rev. B.* **2017**, *95*, 035118.
14. Gratzel, M. Photoelectrochemical cells. *Nature* **2001**, *414*, 338–344.
15. Tyo, E.C.; Vajda, S. Catalysis by clusters with precise numbers of atoms. *Nature Nanotech.* **2015**, *10*, 577–588.

16. Cernuto, G.; Masciocchi, N.; Cervellino, A.; Colonna, G.M.; Guagliardi, A. Size and shape dependence of the photocatalytic activity of TiO$_2$ nanocrystals: A total scattering Debye function study. *J. Am. Chem. Soc.* **2011**, *133*, 3114–3119.

17. Cho, D.; Ko, K.C.; Lamiel-Garcia, O. Effect of size and structure on the ground-state and excited-state electronic structure of TiO$_2$ Nanoparticles. *J. Chem. Theory Comput.* **2016**, *12*, 3751–3763.

18. Mo, Y.; Tian, G.; Tao, J. Performance of a nonempirical exchange functional from the density matrix expansion: Comparative study with different correlation. *Phys. Chem.* **2017**, resubmitted.

19. Tian, G.; Mo, Y.; Tao, J. Performance of a nonempirical semilocal density-functional on noncovalent interactions. *J. Chem. Phys.* **2017**, resubmitted.

20. Qu, Z.; Kroes, G.J. Theoretical study of the electronic structure and stability of titanium dioxide clusters (TiO$_2$)$_n$ with $n = 1$–9. *J. Phys. Chem. B* **2006**, *110*, 8998–9007.

21. Wu, H.; Wang, L.S. Electronic structure of titanium oxide clusters: TiO$_y$ ($y = 1$–3) and (TiO$_2$)$_n$ ($n = 1$–4). *J. Chem. Phys.* **1997**, *107*, 8221–8228.

22. Zhai, H.J.; Wang, L.S. Probing the Electronic Structure and Band Gap Evolution of Titanium Oxide Clusters (TiO$_2$)$_n^-$ ($n = 1$–10) Using Photoelectron Spectroscopy. *J. Am. Chem. Soc.* **2007**, *129*, 3022–3026.

23. Becke, A.D. Density-functional thermochemistry. III. The role of exact exchange. *J. Chem. Phys.* **1993**, *98*, 5648–5652.

24. Armstrong, G. Supercooled water: Ice maybe. *Nat. Chem.* **2010**, *2*, 256.

25. Moore, E.B.; Molinero, V. Structural transformation in supercooled water controls the crystallization rate of ice. *Nature* **2011**, *479*, 506–508.

26. Xantheas, S.S.; Burnham, C.J.; Harrison, R.J. Development of transferable interaction models for water. II. Accurate energetics of the first few water clusters from first principles. *J. Chem. Phys.* **2002**, *116*, 1493–1499.

27. Liu, K.; Cruzan, J.D.; Saykally, R.J. Water clusters. *Science* **1996**, *271*, 929–931.

28. Pradzynski, C.C.; Forck, R.M.; Zeuch, T.; Slavíček, P.; Buck, U. A fully size-resolved perspective on the crystallization of water clusters. *Science* **2012**, *337*, 1529–1532.

29. Gillan, M.J.; Alfé, D.; Michaelides, A. Perspective: How good is DFT for water? *J. Chem. Phys.* **2016**, *144*, 130901.

30. Grimme, S. Accurate description of van der Waals complexes by density functional theory including empirical corrections. *J. Comput. Chem.* **2004**, *25*, 1463–1473.

31. Grimme, S. Semiempirical GGA-type density functional constructed with a long-range dispersion correction. *J. Comput. Chem.* **2006**, *27*, 1787–1799.

32. Santra, B.; Michaelides, A.; Fuchs, M.; Tkatchenko, A.; Filippi, C.; Scheffler, M. On the accuracy of density-functional theory exchange-correlation functionals for H bonds in small water clusters. II. The water hexamer and van der Waals interactions. *J. Chem. Phys.* **2008**, *129*, 194111.

33. Hahn, P.H.; Schmidt, W.G.; Seino, K.; Preuss, M.; Bechstedt, F.; Bernholc, J. Optical absorption of water: Coulomb effects versus hydrogen bonding. *Phys. Rev. Lett.* **2005**, *94*, 037404.

34. Fang, C.; Li, W.-F.; Koster, R.S.; Klime, J.; van Blaaderen, A.; van Huis, M.A. The accurate calculation of the band gap of liquid water by means of GW corrections applied to plane-wave density functional theory molecular dynamics simulations. *Phys. Chem. Chem. Phys.* **2015**, *17*, 365–375.

35. Warren, S.G. Optical constants of ice from the ultraviolet to the microwave. *Appl. Opt.* **1984**, *23*, 1206–1225.

36. Minton, A.P. Far-ultraviolet spectrum of ice. *J. Phys. Chem.* **1971**, *75*, 1162–1164.

37. Painter, L.R.; Birkhoff, R.D.; Arakawa, E.T. Collective oscillation in liquid water. *J. Chem. Phys.* **1969**, *51*, 243.

38. Seki, M.; Kobayashi, K.; Nakahara, J. Optical spectra of hexagonal ice. *J. Phys. Soc. Jpn.* **1981**, *50*, 2643–2648.

39. Shibaguchi, T.; Onuki, H.; Onaka, R. Electronic structures of water and ice. *J. Phys. Soc. Jpn.* **1977**, *42*, 152–154.

40. Engel, E.A.; Monserrat, B.; Needs, R.J. Vibrational renormalisation of the electronic band gap in hexagonal and cubic ice. *J. Chem. Phys.* **2015**, *143*, 244708.

41. Zhao, Y.; Gonzlez-Garca, N.; Truhlar, D.G. Benchmark Database of barrier heights for heavy atom transfer, nucleophilic substitution, association, and unimolecular reactions and its use to test theoretical methods. *J. Phys. Chem. A* **2005**, *109*, 2012–2018.

42. Sun, J.; Haunschild, R.; Xiao, B.; Bulik, I.W.; Scuseria, G.E.; Perdew, J.P. Semilocal and hybrid meta-generalized gradient approximations based on the understanding of the kinetic-energy-density dependence. *J. Chem. Phys.* **2013**, *138*, 044113.

43. Cohen, A.J.; Mori-Snchez, P.; Yang, W. Challenges for Density Functional Theory. *Chem. Rev.* **2012**, *112*, 289.

44. Frisch, M.J.; Trucks, G.W.; Schlegel, H.B.; Scuseria, G.E.; Robb, M.A.; Cheeseman, J.R.; Scalmani, G.; Barone, V.; Mennucci, B.; Petersson, G.A.; et al. *Gaussian 09, Revision A.02*; Gaussian, Inc.: Wallingford, CT, USA, 2009.

45. Levy, M.; Perdew, J.P. Hellmann-Feynman, virial, and scaling requisites for the exact universal density functionals. Shape of the correlation potential and diamagnetic susceptibility for atoms. *Phys. Rev. A* **1985**, *32*, 2010.

46. Oliver, G.L.; Perdew, J.P. Spin-density gradient expansion for the kinetic energy. *Phys. Rev. A* **1979**, *20*, 397.

47. Johnson, E.R.; Becke, A.D.; Sherrill, C.D.; DiLabio, G.A. Oscillations in meta-generalized-gradient approximation potential energy surfaces for dispersion-bound complexes. *J. Chem. Phys.* **2009**, *131*, 034111.

A Discrete Approach to Meshless Lagrangian Solid Modeling

Matthew Marko

Naval Air Warfare Center Aircraft Division, Joint-Base McGuire-Dix-Lakehurst, Lakehurst, NJ 08733, USA; matthew.marko@navy.mil

Abstract: The author demonstrates a stable Lagrangian solid modeling method, tracking the interactions of solid mass particles rather than using a meshed grid. This numerical method avoids the problem of tensile instability often seen with smooth particle applied mechanics by having the solid particles apply stresses expected with Hooke's law, as opposed to using a smoothing function for neighboring solid particles. This method has been tested successfully with a bar in tension, compression, and shear, as well as a disk compressed into a flat plate, and the numerical model consistently matched the analytical Hooke's law as well as Hertz contact theory for all examples. The solid modeling numerical method was then built into a 2-D model of a pressure vessel, which was tested with liquid water particles under pressure and simulated with smoothed particle hydrodynamics. This simulation was stable, and demonstrated the feasibility of Lagrangian specification modeling for fluid–solid interactions.

Keywords: lagrangian; continuum mechanics; solid modeling; smoothing function; SPAM; SPH

1. Introduction

Computational solid modeling is an incredibly valuable tool for todays engineers [1–6], thankfully due to the powerful computers available at low costs. Finite element analysis (FEA) is just one of many meshed solid modeling techniques used in countless industries to study mechanical stresses in numerous different components today. Computational fluid dynamics (CFD) is constantly evolving and is an important tool in engineering design [7–9]. These numerical techniques enable a detailed and robust study of complicated geometries and nonlinear behavior with far less need for costly and time-consuming experimental studies.

The vast majority of numerical methods in engineering, including finite element, are meshed, analyzing stresses and mass flows in a fixed region of space. This approach to solving continuum mechanics is considered the Eulerian specification. This has the advantage of keeping the relative distances between discrete particles and elements fairly constant. One of the main disadvantages of this method is that the entire domain needs to be modeled, and if there are large voids and empty spaces, there is a waste in computational effort as empty domains are studied repeatedly at each time step.

Another approach to avoid this wasted computational effort is to use meshless numerical methods, studying the stresses and forces in the Lagrangian specification [10–13]. The Reynolds transport theorem is most often used to convert a continuity equation from the Eularian to the Lagrangian domain,

$$\frac{D}{Dt}\int_V F \cdot dV = \int_V [\frac{\partial F}{\partial t} + \nabla \cdot (F \cdot \mathbf{v})] \cdot dV, \tag{1}$$

where $\mathbf{v}$ (m/s) is the velocity vector, V (m^3) is the volume,

F is an arbitrary function, $\partial/\partial t$ is the partial derivative, and D/Dt is the total derivative,

$$
\begin{aligned}
\frac{DF}{Dt} &= \frac{\partial F}{\partial t} + \mathbf{v}\cdot\frac{\partial F}{\partial \mathbf{x}}, \\
&= \frac{\partial F}{\partial t} + v_1\cdot\frac{\partial F}{\partial x_1} + v_2\cdot\frac{\partial F}{\partial x_2} + v_3\cdot\frac{\partial F}{\partial x_3}, \\
&= \frac{\partial F}{\partial t} + \nabla\cdot(F\cdot\mathbf{v}).
\end{aligned}
\tag{2}
$$

When characterizing continuum mechanics in the Lagrangian specification, rather than studying the mass that travels in and out of a specific discrete meshed domain, the mass itself is simulated as a set of discrete particles. Each particle has its own unique location, velocity, and stresses. At every time step, every particle is affected by all neighboring particles; because of this it is necessary to calculate the changes in relative distances between individual particles. A big challenge of meshless methods is the need to constantly determine the relative distances between all of the neighboring particles, a task that grows exponentially with increasing particle quantity. This can be mitigated with link-listing and other optimizing techniques [14,15]. Meshless methods, however, have the advantage of not requiring a grid space for empty regions of the domain. This can be advantageous for simulations such as large deformations and explosion studies, the study of planetary motion, or extremely small nanoparticles floating through a nanofluid.

While meshless methods form a minority of numerical methods in practical applications, a few have been investigated. One popular method is smoothed particle hydrodynamics (SPH) [16–20]. SPH utilizes a host of different smoothing functions in order to determine the magnitude of the force impacts from each of the neighboring particles, to discretely solve the Lagrangian Navier–Stokes equations [10–12,21],

$$
\begin{aligned}
\rho\cdot\frac{Dv_i}{Dt} &= -\frac{\partial P}{\partial x_i} + \mu\cdot\Sigma_{j=1}^{3}\left(\frac{\partial^2 v_i}{\partial x_j^2}\right) + (\rho B_i), \\
&= \rho\cdot\left(\frac{\partial v_i}{\partial t} + \Sigma_{j=1}^{3} v_j\cdot\frac{\partial v_i}{\partial x_j}\right),
\end{aligned}
\tag{3}
$$

where v_i (m/s) is the velocity in the i-direction, B_i (Newtons) is the body force (such as gravity), P (Pa) is the pressure, and μ (N·s/m^2) is the dynamic viscosity.

At every time-step, it is necessary to calculate the separation distance and smoothing function for each neighboring pair of particles, and thus the computational resources grow exponentially with particle quantity; link-listing is often used to mitigate this. SPH also only models fluids, often but not exclusively using a modified Lennard–Jones (LJ) potential force to represent a fixed solid boundary [16,17,19,22].

Attempts have previously been made to branch off SPH to apply to solid modeling; this has been referred to as smoothed particle applied mechanics (SPAM) [23–26]. SPAM has its origins as an effort to model planetary interaction in space, as well as statistical mechanics [27]. The Lagrangian-based method is quite practical when dealing with relatively small particles (such as planets and stars) in a large domain filled with empty space; it is computationally wasteful to model vast sums of empty space with no activity in it. At smaller scales, however, SPAM and SPH suffer from tensile instability [28–32], as particles under tensile stress eventually become unstable regardless of the size of time-integration steps. Efforts to use artificial viscosity approaches have only had limited success [23,26]. If these limitations could be overcome, SPH and SPAM could be used together for fluid–solid interaction (FSI) simulations [33–39], a capability that many commercial FEA and CFD software packages lack.

This effort is to investigate meshless modeling of solid mechanics, with the goals of eventually evolving into a practical SPAM-like tool for modeling solid mechanics. The eventual goal is to have a tool that can interact with SPH fluid particles, and perhaps become a useful FSI tool for fluid flows over a large domain. With an accurate model consisting of particles of liquids and solids interacting, an engineer could investigate eventual material failures and crack propagation in real time for highly dynamic fluid flow within a moving solid boundary.

2. Mechanics

In a Lagrangian solid modeling algorithm such as SPAM, each neighboring particle's relative distance would be defined by a smoothing function W (m^{-3}), such as,

$$
\begin{aligned}
W(\lambda, h) &= (10/(7\pi \times h^3)) \times (1 - 3\lambda^2/2 + 3\lambda^3/4), & \lambda < 1 \\
&= (10/(7\pi \times h^3)) \times (2 - \lambda)^3/4, & 1 < \lambda < 2 \\
&= 0, & \lambda > 2
\end{aligned} \tag{4}
$$

where λ is the dimensionless ratio of the absolute distance between two specific particles (m) and the smoothing length h (m),

$$
\lambda_{ab} = |x_a - x_b|/h. \tag{5}
$$

The density is calculated as,

$$
\rho_a = \Sigma_b m_b \cdot W(\lambda_{ab}), \tag{6}
$$

where ρ_a (kg/m^3) is the density of particle a, and m_b (kg) is the mass of neighboring particle b.

The Lennard–Jones potential [16,22,23] acceleration $\delta v_{LJ}/\delta t$ (m/s^2) is calculated as,

$$
\begin{aligned}
\delta v_{LJ}/\delta t &= D \cdot \left\{ \left(\frac{r_0}{r_{ab}}\right)^M - \left(\frac{r_0}{r_{ab}}\right)^N \right\} \cdot \left(\frac{x_{ab}}{r_{ab}}\right)^2, & r_{ab} < r_0, \\
&= 0, & r_{ab} > r_0,
\end{aligned} \tag{7}
$$

where D (m/s^2) is a constant of acceleration proportional to the particle velocity squared, r_0 (m) is the specified width of a solid particle, r_{ab} (m) is the total distance between particle a and b,

$$
r_{ab} = \sqrt{\Sigma_{i=1}^3 (x_{i,a} - x_{i,b})^2}, \tag{8}
$$

and x_{ab} (m) is the directional distance between particle a and b. The values of M and N are arbitrary coefficients; $M = 12$ and $N = 4$ often have the best results in practical applications of SPH [16,17].

The acceleration $\delta v_a/\delta t$ (m/s^2) of a particle a by a neighboring particle b is thus,

$$
\frac{\delta v_a}{\delta t} = -\Sigma_b \{ (P_a/\rho_a) + (P_b/\rho_b) \} \cdot \nabla W(\lambda_{ab}), \tag{9}
$$

where P_a (Pa) is the pressure of particle a, and can be calculated by the stress tensor σ_{ij} (Pa),

$$
P = -\Sigma_{i=1}^3 \sigma_{ii}/3, \tag{10}
$$

and ΔW_{ab} (m^{-1}) is the gradient of the *normalized* smoothing function between particles a and b.

One of the biggest challenges of Lagrangian solid modeling is overcoming the tensile instability [16,23,26]. If the fluid or solid is under pressure ($P > 0$), these Lagrangian specification methods work well. If the solid is under tension, however, where ($P < 0$) and the particles of mass are attracted to each other, there is a tendency for all of the mass particles to clump together due to the fact that the derivative of most smoothing functions grows exponentially as the particles become closer together. This is a challenge to Lagrangian modeling of solid mechanics that must be overcome.

3. Algorithm

In previous studies [23,26], the solid particles were treated similarly to liquid particles with SPH algorithms, with various techniques to avoid the tensile instability. Rather than using the traditional smoothing algorithms seen in SPAM, this model works by applying different steps for liquid–liquid, solid–solid, and liquid–solid particle interactions. All of the particles move freely (unless specified as fixed) within the domain, but accelerations and stress calculations are specific to the different classes of particles. The liquid–liquid particle interactions were all studied using the established Lagrangian CFD method of SPH [16–18].

The solid–solid particle interactions, however, used a much different approach from traditional SPH. The solid particles are given a specific cubic shape (that undergoes elastic strain), and particles of mass connected in tension are linked together in a specific contact matrix. Only particles linked together in this matrix can experience tension stress with a displacement apart from each other. Non-linked particles exert no stress on each other when they are proximate to each other unless they are close enough to be within the particle's shaped boundary; in this circumstance they are under compressive stress. While this bears similarities to a meshed approach, it is not Eulerian as the contact matrix merely relates to each mass particle which can travel freely within the domain.

This approach avoids the concerns of the tensile instability entirely. Some of the solid particles are not fused together, and thus have no attractive forces; they only experience a repulsive force when in close proximity to each other (such as during an impact). For particles pre-defined as in contact and fused together, they only experience a tensile force when pulled apart; this force reverses itself entirely when the particles are close enough that they cross each other's solid boundaries. By using this approach, the issue of tensile instability, where the attractive forces of particles in tension grow exponentially and result in solid particle clumping, is avoided entirely.

This algorithm models solid–solid forces with a numerical approach to Hooke's law [13,40]

$$\sigma = E_Y \times \epsilon, \tag{11}$$

where σ (Pa) is the tensile stress, E_Y (Pa) is Young's modulus, and ϵ is the dimensionless tensile strain,

$$\epsilon = \frac{\delta L}{L}, \tag{12}$$

where δL (m) is the material deflection of an object with a natural length of L (m). This strain can occur from particle pairs that are in both compressive and tensile contact. Each solid particle represents a cubic particle of mass, with a predetermined length, width, and height of δx (m). If the length between two particles δx_{ab} (m) is ever less then the particle length, the particle is then under a compressive acceleration repulsing the two particles apart; if particles linked in contact are ever farther apart than the particle length, then an attractive acceleration is applied to each particle.

While the particle cubic dimension δx is constant, the true particle shape is rarely a cube, as it is subjected to strain. When the stress is determined, the particle strain is calculated, and thus the particle dimension δx^u in the u direction,

$$\delta x^u = \delta x \times (1 + E_{uu}), \tag{13}$$

where E_{uu} is the component of the strain tensor,

$$E_{uu} = \frac{\sigma_{uu}}{E_Y}, \tag{14}$$

where σ_{uu} (Pa) is from the stress tensor.

The equivalent strain between two particles is thus,

$$\epsilon_{ab} \;=\; \frac{\delta x_{ab}}{\delta x \times (1 + E_{uu})}, \tag{15}$$

which can be used in Hooke's law to find the equivalent acceleration δv_{ab} (m/s^2) of particle a due to compressive or tensile forces from particle b,

$$\delta v_{ab} \;=\; \frac{E_Y \times \delta x_{ab}}{\delta x \times (1 + E_{uu}) \times m_a} \times \delta x^2 \times (1 + E_{vv}) \times (1 + E_{ww}) \times \delta t, \tag{16}$$

where m_a (kg) is the mass of the particle a, and v and w represent dimensions that are not u; the dimension of contact between the two particles being u.

When there is liquid–solid particle interaction, the particles exert a repulsive force on each other not dissimilar to Lennard Jones with some unique differences. The traditional LJ approach (Equation (7)) was originally developed to describe and model the interactions of molecules subjected to Van der Waal forces; at times using this approach for macroscopic fluid solid interactions results in liquid particles passing through a boundary of solid particles, and at other times the exponential nature of the equation results in unrealistic repulsive accelerations. Rather than use LJ, this effort approaches this problem by applying a force on the particles in contact proportional to what is needed to stop the particle from crossing the boundary and stop it from further travel. A variation of this approach was previously taken with SPH and discrete multi-hybrid physics (DMP) models to study the effects of blood and tissues in the human body [33–39]. By using the combination of these approaches, a stable Lagrangian simulation of solid mechanics and fluid–solid interactions can be achieved.

The first step in this algorithm is to establish the model; this is a list of unique mass particles with their own locations, velocities, stresses, and (in the case of solids) strains. The next approach is to refresh the link-list; particles move and therefore the link-list database needs to be updated regularly to avoid errors. The link-list, by definition, is a quasi-grid that segregates particles into neighboring regions, so computer resources are not wasted calculating the impacts of neighboring particles far too separated to have a meaningful impact. The next step is to determine how much acceleration each particle can expect as a result of the tension (from linked solid particles), impacts, repulsive forces from solid–solid interactions, liquid accelerations based on SPH forces defined in Equation (9), and liquid–solid interactions. When the accelerations are determined, the velocities are updated to reflect such an acceleration over the time step, followed by a change in location depending on the individual velocity and time step duration of each particle. The final step of a given time step is to recalculate the new tensions, stress, and strains (for solid particles) based on the new particle locations.

4. Study

4.1. Tension and Compression

A series of studies was conducted to verify this Lagrangian algorithm as a valid means of studying solid mechanics. First, a simple 3-D bar was pulled in tension, to determine if the tensile stress would match Hooke's law (Equation (11)). In addition, the simulation aimed to verify that the *necking* that occurred would properly match the *Poisson's* ratio v,

$$\delta d \;=\; -d \times \left\{ 1 - \left(1 + \frac{\delta L}{L} \right)^{-v} \right\}, \tag{17}$$

where L (m) and d (m) are dimensions of the solid under stress.

For this case study, the material parameters of steel will be used. For steel, the Young's modulus is $E_Y = 207$ GPa, and the Poisson's ratio is $v = 0.3$. The 3-D steel block was represented by a series of cubic particles, 23.4 mm in length per particle, with the particle dimensions of $5 \times 11 \times 5$ in the $x, y,$ and z direction, respectively, for a total length of 25 cm in the y direction. The steel bar was pulled

1.7132 μm in tension along the axial y direction. All of the particles were in tensile contact with their nearest neighbor. The peak tensile stress of 1.4758 MPa was observed at the center of the bar, identically matching to the analytical stress predicted with Hooke's law. In addition, the width in the X and Z direction decreased at a distance of 0.1329 μm, yielding an equivalent Poisson's ratio of 0.34125, well within the numerical error that can be expected with a 5×5 cross-section resolution.

This study was then reversed for the model, but in compression rather than tension. The $5 \times 11 \times 5$ block with a Young's modulus of 207 GPa and a Poisson's ratio of 0.3 was compressed to have 1.7132 μm of deflection, and as expected, the magnitude of the stress was identical to the tension case, with 1.4758 MPa of compression stress. In addition, the width in the X and Z direction increased the exact same distance of 0.1329 μm; the only difference was the direction. As is observable in Figure 1, the tensile pulling of the bar resulted necking in the bar in the X and Z direction, whereas compression results in a bulging in the X and Z direction.

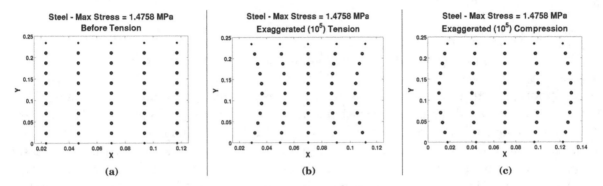

Figure 1. The steel bar (**a**) with no stress, (**b**) in tension, and in (**c**) compression, with 10^5 exaggerated deflection.

4.2. Shear

The next step in the validation of this numerical model would be to test it in shear. This model would also be in steel, with a $11 \times 3 \times 3$ block of cubic particles, 23.4 mm in length, for an overall length of 25 cm. With the Young's modulus E_Y of 207 GPa and a Poisson's ratio of 0.3, the shear modulus G_Y (Pa) can be found simply as,

$$G_Y = \frac{E_Y}{2\times(1+\nu)}, \tag{18}$$
$$= \frac{207}{2\times(1+0.3)},$$

which ultimately results in a shear modulus of $G_Y = 79.6154$ GPa. The shear modulus can be used to find the shear stress as a linear function of shear strain,

$$\tau = G_Y \times \gamma, \tag{19}$$

where τ (Pa) is the shear stress, and γ is the dimensionless shear strain,

$$\gamma = \frac{\delta L}{H}, \tag{20}$$

where δL (m) is the tangential deflection, and H is the height of the object 90° tangent to the deflection.

The model used was subjected to a shear deflection of 18.3429 μm in the X direction. The dimensionless shear strain γ is found by taking the deflection over the height (9.3619 cm) of the bar (Equation (20))

$$\gamma = \frac{18.3429 \times 10^{-6}}{9.3619 \times 10^{-2}} = 1.9593 \times 10^{-4},$$

and the shear strain can be used in Equation (19) to find the shear stress τ,

$$\tau = (79.6154 \times 10^9) \times (1.9593 \times 10^{-4}) = 15.5992 \times 10^6.$$

The numerical maximum shear stress was observed to be 15.8993 MPa, an error of less than 2%. This close match further validates this Lagrangian numerical method as a reasonable approach to solving simple solid mechanics.

4.3. Hertz Contact Simulation

After this Lagrangian solid modeling approach was demonstrated effective in tension, compression, and shear of a simple 3-D steel bar, it was then further validated by simulations of Hertz contact [41–44] between a large disk and a flat elastic plate. The 2-D model comprises a 51 by 10 flat plate of steel, with a particle dimension of 159 μm, to form a 8-mm by 1.5-mm plate. The 2-D disk is represented as a series of 53 μm particles of identical relative dimensions assembled to give a disk, three particles thick, with a radius of 12.7 mm (Figure 2). This disk will experience no elastic deflection due to having an infinite Young's modulus; the disk would be forced down up to 49 μm into the elastic plate in five discrete increments. The elastic plate particles are free to move, except for the final bottom row (opposite side of the Hertz contact); these particles are fixed. The model will be validated by comparing the deflection and stresses in this elastic plate, and comparing the numerical results to analytical Hertz predictions.

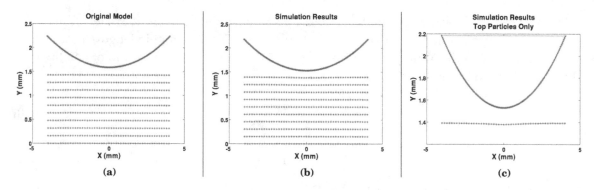

Figure 2. The disk-flat model.

The control parameter in this simulation is the actual deflection down at the center of the point of contact δ (m); this deflection can be used within the Hertz contact model to determine the maximum stress. The first step is to determine the reduced Young's modulus E_Y' (Pa) and reduced radius R'. As the disk does not deflect, it is treated as an infinitely stiff material $E_Y = \infty$, and thus,

$$\frac{1}{E_Y'} = \frac{1 - v_{flat}^2}{E_{Y,flat}} + \frac{1 - v_{disk}^2}{E_{Y,disk}}, \tag{21}$$

where E_Y (Pa) is the Young's modulus, and v is the dimensionless Poisson's ratio. The disk is infinitely stiff, $E_{Y,disk} = \infty$, and thus the reduced Young's modulus (in MPa) is,

$$E_Y' = \frac{E_{Y,flat}}{1 - v_{flat}^2} = \frac{207}{1 - 0.3^2} = 227.4725. \tag{22}$$

The reduced radius is easily found as,

$$\frac{1}{R'} = \frac{1}{R_{flat}} + \frac{1}{R_{disk}} = \frac{1}{\infty} + \frac{1}{R_{disk}} = \frac{1}{R_{disk}}, \tag{23}$$

$$R' = R_{disk}.$$

Because the disk is of infinite stiffness and does not deflect elastically, the width a (m) of the contact region can be found with simple trigonometry,

$$a = R_{disk} \times sin(cos^{-1}\{\frac{R_{disk} - \delta}{R_{disk}}\}). \tag{24}$$

where δ (m) is the deflection distance. Hertz theory would therefore predict that the maximum stress at the point of contact would be,

$$P_{max} = \frac{a \times E'}{2 \times R'}. \tag{25}$$

One significant challenge of using the Lagrangian methods to model Hertz contact is to make sure the time step is short enough so that the model is stable. The maximum time step δt_{max} (s) allowed in these simulations,

$$\delta t_{max} = \frac{\delta x}{4 \times C_s}. \tag{26}$$

where δx (m) is the minimum particle width, and C_s (m/s) is the speed of sound; this approach has been used in successful applications of SPH [16,17]. This is the longest permitted time step; to better ensure stability, a variable time step δt (s) was determined at each time step,

$$\delta t = \frac{0.1 \times \delta x}{V_{max}}, \tag{27}$$

where V_{max} (m/s) is the maximum particle velocity at a given time step. The benefit of Equation (27) is that it ensures that at no point will a particle ever move further than 10% of a particle-width in a given time-step, ensuring the model remains stable. The value of δt is found with each time step, and if it is ever greater than the value of δt_{max} found with Equation (26), then δt_{max} is used as the time step. While this approach is extremely stable, it also results in extremely short time steps; the simulation under discussion uses time steps ranging from 15 to 56 nanoseconds.

The model described was run for five simulations of forced deflections, ranging from 26 to 49 μm. In a given simulation, the disk would be forced down a given increment, and the plate particles would have time to settle; after they settled the disk would be forced down to the next displacement increment. According to Hertz contact mechanics equation, the analytical load to accomplish this would be 2.66 to 5.98 kN, with the peak stress ranging from 7.3 to 10 GPa (Equation (25)). As observed in Figure 3, the load and peak stress matched remarkably with the analytical Hertz predicted stresses and loads, and the displacement (Figure 4) and velocity (Figure 5) all settled into place after a period of time. The error percentages for the load varied from 2% to 10.4%; the error percentages for the peak stress were even lower, ranging from 0.2% to 5.4%. This close match was repeated for models of identical dimensions, with small disk radii ranging from 2 to 5 inches as well as 20 to 50 meters, and in all cases, the predicted load and maximum stress always matched the Hertz predicted values remarkably (Figure 3). This Hertz study strongly demonstrates the feasibility of this Lagrangian numerical model to predict the stresses and strains in a solid model.

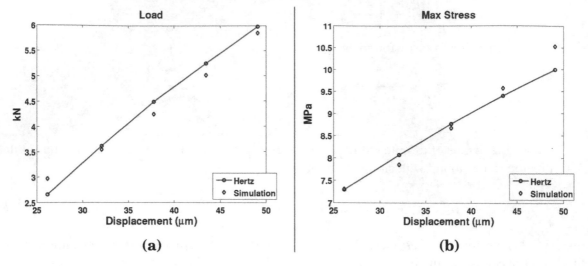

(a)   **(b)**

Figure 3. Comparison of Hertz and numerical solid modeling, for both (**a**) the numerically integrated total load, and (**b**) the maximum stress, calculated as a function for a given displacement δ.

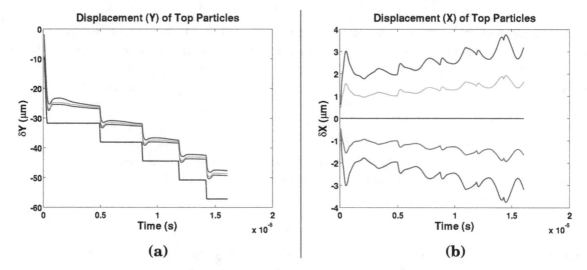

(a)   **(b)**

Figure 4. The displacement, where each line represents the displacement of a specific mass particle in the (**a**) y and (**b**) x direction, for the top five center-most particles. The black dashed line in (**a**) represents the forced displacement of the infinitely-stiff disk.

4.4. Pressure Vessel

The last step in this effort is to join the Lagrangian specification solid modeling efforts with smoothed particle hydrodynamics; this was demonstrated with a 2-D pressure vessel. A model of a 2-D circular pressure vessel was built; the solid pressure vessel was five particles thick, whereas the liquid was comprised of a 2-D circular region with a radius of twenty particles (Figure 6). Each particle, both fluid and solid, had a particle length of 23.4 mm. The solid particles were steel, with the same parameters as the earlier studies; the Young's modulus is $E_Y = 207$ GPa, the Poisson's ratio is $\nu = 0.3$, and the default density $\rho = 7800$ kg/m^3. The liquid water has a default density of $\rho = 1000$ kg/m^3, and a bulk modulus of $K_{bulk} = 2.15$ GPa. The water is initially set in the pressure vessel at a pressure of 1 atmosphere (101,135 Pa).

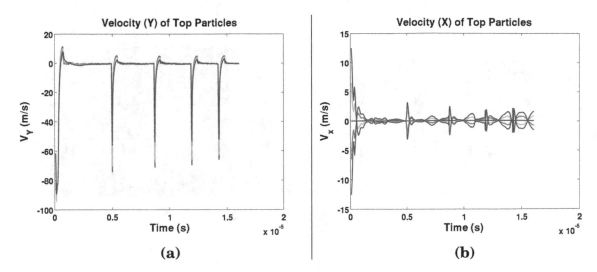

Figure 5. The velocity change, where each line represents the velocity of a specific mass particle in the (a) y and (b) x direction, for the top five center-most particles.

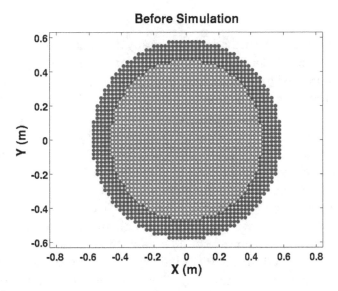

Figure 6. The pressure vessel, at the start of the simulation. Green circles represent water particles, and blue dots represent steel particles.

One fundamental distinction was the effective shape of the particles; the solid particles were cubic (as was the case in all the prior examples), whereas the liquid particles were effectively spherical. The reason for this is that the solid particles undergo shear in all three dimensions, and the cubic approach is necessary to accurately determine the tensions between fused solid particles. The liquid particles are shapeless (liquid inherently has no shape), but as SPH uses the smoothing length (Equation (4)), the impacts of neighboring particles are all proportional to the radial separation distance and the smoothing length.

The simulation was ran for 400 time steps, averaging 146.8 nanoseconds in duration. The model was stable, with few dramatic shifts in particle position; this is expected as in the pressure vessel, only elastic expansions are expected as the particles settle into place. It was observed that the steel particles are all pushed outwards (Figure 7a) as the liquid pressure stabilizes within the pressure vessel (Figure 7b). This model demonstrated the feasibility of merging the Lagrangian liquid numerical method of SPH with Lagrangian solid modeling, with applications in the study of fluid–solid interactions.

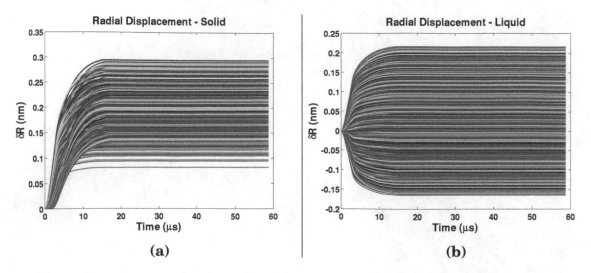

Figure 7. The pressure vessel steel particle radial movement as a function of time, both for the (**a**) solid particles and the (**b**) liquid water particles.

5. Conclusions

This effort demonstrated a stable method to numerically model solid mechanics with a Lagrangian specification. Rather than using Eulerian mechanics which utilize a meshed grid, this model used a Lagrangian approach that tracked individual particles of the mass, and how these particles interacted with each other. This approach has the advantage of not being confined to a fixed domain, as well as having reduced computational expense for models with large regions of open space, and has models with large deformations. A solid bar in compression, tension, and shear was simulated, and it matched the stresses and strains remarkably with the analytical results expected with Hooke's law. A much more detailed simulation of a rigid disk being applied to a flat plate was then studied, and the model matched the analytical loads, strains, and stresses expected with Hertz contact theory; the Hertz model matched the numerical model for a large host of loads, particle dimensions, and disk sizes. Finally, this Lagrangian solid model was implemented with the Lagrangian computational fluid dynamics method of smooth particle hydrodynamics to build a stable model of water under pressure in a 2-D pressure vessel. This demonstrated the ability of the Lagrangian solid mechanics method to study fluid–solid interactions simultaneously with the modeling of the fluid and the solid, which are often modeled separately. By using this model, a host of solid mechanics applications can be better modeled, resulting in overall better engineering design.

Acknowledgments: Sources of funding for this effort include the Navy Air Systems Command (NAVAIR)-4.0T Chief Technology Officer Organization as an Independent Laboratory In-House Research (ILIR) Basic Research Project (Smooth Particle Applied Mechanics), and the Science Mathematics And Research for Transformation (SMART) fellowship. The author thanks Elon Terrell, Jonathan Kyle, Yuanyuan Sabrina Wang, Emil Sandoz-Rosado, Tirupati Chandrupa, Aleksander Navratil, Michael Singer, and Jenny Ardelean for fruitful discussions.

Abbreviations

The following abbreviations are used in this manuscript:

FEA	finite element analysis
CFD	computational fluid mechanics
SPH	smoothed particle hydrodynamics
SPAM	smoothed particle applied mechanics
FSI	fluid–solid interactions
DMP	discrete multi-hybrid physics

References

1. Garcia, A. *Numerical Methods for Physics*, 2nd ed.; Addison-Wesley: Boston, MA, USA, 1999.
2. Arfken, G.B.; Weber, H.J. *Mathematical Methods for Physicists*, 6th ed.; Elsevier: Burlington, MA, USA, 2005.
3. Zill, D.G.; Cullen, M.R. *Advanced Engineering Mathematics*, 2nd ed.; Jones and Bartlett Publishers: Sudbury, MA, USA, 2000.
4. Strang, G. *Linear Algebra and Its Applications*, 3rd ed.; Thomas Learning Inc.: Horsham, PA, USA, 1988.
5. Birmingham, E.; Grogan, J.A.; Niebur, G.L.; McNamara, L.M.; McHugh, P.E. Computational modelling of the mechanics of trabecular bone and marrow using fluid structure interaction techniques. *Ann. Biomed. Eng.* **2013**, *41*, 814–826.
6. Kojić, N.; Milošević, M.; Petrović, D.; Isailović, V.; Sarioglu, A.F.; Haber, D.A.; Kojić, M.; Toner, M. A computational study of circulating large tumor cells traversing microvessels. *Comput. Biol. Med.* **2015**, *63*, 187–195.
7. Dalrymple, R.; Rogers, B. Numerical modeling of water waves with the SPH method. *Coast. Eng.* **2006**, *53*, 141–147.
8. Altomare, C.; Dominguez, J.M.; Crespo, A.J.C.; Suzuki, T.; Caceres, I.; Gomez-Gesteira, M. Hybridization of the wave propagation model swash and the meshfree particle method SPH for real coastal applications. *Coast. Eng. J.* **2015**, *57*, 1550024–1550034.
9. Tafuni, A.; Sahin, I.; Hyman, M. Numerical investigation of wave elevation and bottom pressure generated by a planing hull in finite-depth water. *Appl. Ocean Res.* **2016**, *58*, 281–291.
10. Currie, I.G. *Fundamental Mechanics of Fluids*, 3rd ed.; Marcel Dekker Inc.: New York, NY, USA, 2003.
11. Lai, W.; Rubin, D.; Krempl, E. *Introduction to Continuum Mechanics*, 4th ed.; Butterworth-Heinemann of Elsevier: Burlington, MA, USA, 2010.
12. Timoshenko, S.; Goodier, J. *Theory of Elasticity*, 3rd ed.; McGraw Hill: New York, NY, USA, 1970.
13. Riley, W.F.; Sturges, L.D.; Morris, D.H. *Statics and Mechanics of Solids*, 2nd ed.; John Wiley and Sons: Hoboken, NJ, USA, 2002.
14. Stroustrup, B. *The C++ Programming Language*, 3rd ed.; Addison-Wesley Professional: Boston, MA, USA, 2000.
15. Chen, S.; Gordon, D. Front-to-back display of bsp trees. *IEEE Comput. Graphic. Appl.* **1991**, *11*, 79–85.
16. Liu, G.R.; Liu, M.B. *Smoothed Particle Hydrodynamics: A Meshfree Partical Method*; World Scientific Publishing Co.: Hackensack, NJ, USA, 2003.
17. Kyle, J.P.; Terrell, E.J. Application of smoothed particle hydrodynamics to full-film lubrication. *J. Tribol.* **2013**, *135*, 041705.
18. Monaghan, J.J. Why particle methods work. *SIAM J. Sci. Stat. Comput.* **1982**, *3*, 422–433.
19. Libersky, L.D. High strain lagrangian hydrodynamics: A three-dimensional SPH code for dynamic material response. *J. Comput. Phys.* **1993**, *109*, 67–75.
20. Lucy, L. A numerical approach to the testing of the fission hypothesis. *Astron. J.* **1977**, *82*, 1013–1024.
21. White, F. *Fluid Mechanics*, 5th ed.; McGraw-Hill: Boston, MA, USA, 2003.
22. Jones, J.E. On the determination of molecular fields. *Proc. R. Soc. Lond. A* **1924**, *106*, 463–477.
23. Hoover, W.G. *Smooth Particle Applied Mechanics: The State of the Art*; World Scientific Publishing Co.: Hackensack, NJ, USA, 2006.
24. Hoover, W.G.; Pierce, T.G.; Hoover, C.G.; Shugart, J.O.; Stein, C.M.; Edwards, A.L. Molecular dynamics, smoothed-particle applied mechanics, and irreversibility. *Comput. Math. Appl.* **1994**, *28*, 155–174.
25. Batra, R.C.; Zhang, G.M. Modified Smoothed Particle Hydrodynamics (MSPH) basis functions for meshless methods, and their application to axisymmetric Taylor impact test. *J. Comput. Phys.* **2008**, *227*, 1962–1981.
26. Antoci, C.; Gallati, M.; Sibilla, S. Numerical simulation of fluid–structure interaction by SPH. *Comput. Struct.* **2007**, *85*, 879–890.
27. Pathria, R.K. *Statistical Mechanics*, 2nd ed.; Butterworth-Heinemann: Burlington, MA, USA, 1972.
28. Balsara, D.S. Von Neumann stability analysis of smoothed particle hydrodynamics-suggestions for optimal algorithms. *J. Comput. Phys.* **1995**, *121*, 357–372.
29. Dyka, C.T.; Ingel, R.P. An approach for tension instability in smoothed particle hydrodynamics (SPH). *Comput. Struct.* **1995**, *57*, 573–580.
30. Dyka, C.T.; Randles, P.W.; Ingel, R.P. Stress points for tension instability in Smoothed Particle Hydrodynamics. *Int. J. Numer. Meth. Eng.* **1997**, *40*, 2325–2341.

31. Swegle, J.W.; Attaway, S.W. On the feasibility of using smoothed particle hydrodynamics for underwater explosion calculations. *Comput. Mech.* **1995**, *17*, 151–168.

32. Swegle, J.W.; Hicks, D.L.; Attaway, S.W. Smoothed Particle Hydrodynamics stability analysis. *J. Comput. Phys.* **2002**, *116*, 123–134.

33. Wu, K.; Yang, D.; Wrightb, N. A coupled SPH-DEM model for fluid-structure interaction problems with free-surface flow and structural failure. *Comput. Struct.* **2016**, *177*, 141–161.

34. Stasch, J.; Avci, B.; Wriggers, P. Numerical simulation of fluid-structure interaction problems by a coupled SPH-FEM approach. *Proc. Appl. Math. Mech.* **2016**, *16*, 491–492.

35. Bajd, F.; Serša, I. Mathematical modeling of blood clot fragmentation during flow-mediated thrombolysis. *Biophys. J.* **2013**, *104*, 1181–1190.

36. Alexiadis, A.; Stamatopoulos, K.; Wen, W.; Batchelor, H.; Bakalis, S.; Barigou, M.; Simmons, M. Using discrete multi-physics for detailed exploration of hydrodynamics in an in vitro colon system. *Comput. Biol. Med.* **2017**, *81*, 188–198.

37. Ariane, M.; Allouche, M.H.; Bussone, M.; Giacosa, F.; Bernard, F.; Barigou, M.; Alexiadis, A. Discrete multi-physics: A mesh-free model of blood flow in flexible biological valve including solid aggregate formation. *PLoS ONE* **2017**, *12*, e0174795.

38. Alexiadis, A. The discrete multi-hybrid system for the simulation of solid-liquid flows. *PLoS ONE* **2015**, *10*, e0124678.

39. Sinnott, M.; Cleary, P.; Arkwright, J.; Dinning, P. Investigating the relationships between peristaltic contraction and fluid transport in the human colon using Smoothed Particle Hydrodynamics. *Comput. Biol. Med.* **2012**, *42*, 492–503.

40. Callister, W.D. *Materials Science and Engineering: An Introduction*, 6th ed.; John Wiley and Sons: Hoboken, NJ, USA, 2003.

41. Hiermaier, S.; Konke, D.; Stilp, A.J.; Thomas, K. Computational simulation of the hypervelocity impact of Al-sphere on thin plates of different materials. *Int. J. Impact Eng.* **1997**, *20*, 363–374.

42. Johnson, K. *Contact Mechanics*; Cambridge University Press: New York, NY, USA, 1987.

43. Gohar, R. *Elastohydrodynamics*, 2nd ed.; World Scientific Publishing Co.: Bergen, NJ, USA, 2001.

44. Stachowiak, G.; Batchelor, A. *Engineering Tribology*, 4th ed.; Butterworth-Heinemann: Oxford, UK, 2005.

Numerical Simulation of the Laminar Forced Convective Heat Transfer between Two Concentric Cylinders

Ioan Sarbu * and Anton Iosif

Department of Building Services Engineering, Polytechnic University of Timisoara, Piata Victoriei, no 2A, 300006 Timisoara, Romania; anton.iosif@upt.ro
* Correspondence: ioan.sarbu@upt.ro

Academic Editor: Demos Tsahalis

Abstract: The dual reciprocity method (DRM) is a highly efficient numerical method of transforming domain integrals arising from the non-homogeneous term of the Poisson equation into equivalent boundary integrals. In this paper, the velocity and temperature fields of laminar forced heat convection in a concentric annular tube, with constant heat flux boundary conditions, have been studied using numerical simulations. The DRM has been used to solve the governing equation, which is expressed in the form of a Poisson equation. A test problem is employed to verify the DRM solutions with different boundary element discretizations and numbers of internal points. The results of the numerical simulations are discussed and compared with exact analytical solutions. Good agreement between the numerical results and exact solutions is evident, as the maximum relative errors are less than 5% to 6%, and the R^2-values are greater than 0.999 in all cases. These results confirm the effectiveness and accuracy of the proposed numerical model, which is based on the DRM.

Keywords: concentric annular tube; laminar flow; heat convection; heat flux; boundary condition; dual reciprocity method; numerical model

---

1. Introduction

Modern computational techniques facilitate solving problems with imposed boundary conditions using different numerical methods [1–9]. The numerical analysis of heat transfer [10–14] has been independently, though not exclusively, developed in four main streams: the finite difference method (FDM) [15,16], the finite volume method (FVM) [17], the finite element method (FEM) [18–20], and the boundary element method (BEM) [21–23]. The FDM is based on using Taylor series expansion to find approximation formulas for derivative operators. The basic concept of the FVM is derived from physical conservation laws applied to control volumes. The FDM, FVM and FEM depend on the mesh that discretizes the domain via a special scheme. The FEM and BEM are based on the integral equation for heat conduction. This equation can be obtained from the differential equation using the variational calculus.

The BEM uses a fundamental solution to convert a partial differential equation to an integral equation. In the BEM, only the boundary is discretized and an internal point's position can be freely defined. This method has the immediate advantage of reducing the dimensionality of the problem by one. Additionally, the BEM naturally handles the problems caused by dynamic geometry. Unlike the FEM, which requires that the domain be meshed, the BEM only discretizes the boundary. Therefore, the amount of data necessary for solving a problem can be greatly reduced [21–24]. A complete review of the BEM's domain integrals is presented in [25].

The BEM, an effective and promising numerical analysis tool due to its semi-analytical nature and ability to reduce a problem's dimension, has been successfully applied to the homogeneous linear heat conduction problem [26]. In the context of BEM-based velocity-vorticity formulation, the work of Žagar and Škerget [27] was one of the first attempts to solve 3D viscous laminar flow by BEM. The BEM has also been used to solve direct and inverse heat conduction problems [22,28,29]. However, its extension to non-homogeneous and non-linear problems is not straightforward. Therefore, applications of the BEM to heat convection problems have not been sufficiently studied, and are still in the development stage. Because the effects of convection are of considerable importance in many heat transfer phenomena, more research should focus on these effects. However, applying the BEM to such problems has drawbacks—the required fundamental solution depends on the thermal conductivity, and it is difficult to model heat generation rates (due to heat sources), because they introduce domain integrals [30].

Several researchers have also worked on a combination of boundary element and finite element methods. A combined BEM-FEM model for the velocity-vorticity formulation of the Navier-Stokes equations was developed by Žunič et al. [31] to solve 3D laminar fluid flow. In the field of viscous fluid flow numerical simulation, an important work was done by Young et al. [32] using primitive variable formulation of Navier-Stokes equations. They computed pressure fields with BEM and momentum equation with a three-steps FEM. In the field of viscous fluid flow numerical simulation with velocity-vorticity formulation of Navier-Stokes equations, contributions were made by Young et al. [33]. In their work, BEM was used to obtain boundary velocities and normal velocity fluxes implicitly, and then explicitly the internal velocities and boundary vorticities were computed by derivation of kinematical integral equations. Simulations, as well as experiments, of turbulent flow have also been extensively investigated [34]. Hsieh and Lien [35] considered numerical modelling of buoyancy-driven turbulent flows in enclosures, using the Reynolds-average Navier-Stokes approach.

Recently, the radial integration method (RIM) has been developed by Gao [36], which did not require fundamental solutions to basis functions, and can remove various singularities appearing in domain integrals. However, although the radial integration BEM is very flexible in treating the general non-linear and non-homogeneous problems, the numerical evaluation of the radial integrals is very time-consuming compared to other methods [37–39], especially for large 3D problems.

To approximate a solution to the heat conduction equation using boundary integrals, the dual reciprocity method (DRM), introduced by Nardini and Brebbia [40], can be used. The DRM preserves the advantages of the BEM: a shorter computational time than the FEM, and a reduced number of boundary elements. Since its introduction, the DRM has been applied to engineering problems in many fields [41–43]. In the DRM, an available fundamental solution is used for the complete governing equation, and the domain integral arising from the heat source-like term is transferred to the boundary using radial interpolation functions [44–46].

In this paper, the velocity and temperature fields of laminar forced heat convection in a concentric annular tube with constant heat flux on the boundaries were studied using numerical simulations. The DRM was used to solve the governing equation, which is expressed mathematically in the form of a Poisson equation. A test problem was employed to verify the DRM solutions with different boundary element discretizations and different numbers of internal points, and the results of the numerical simulations are discussed and compared with exact analytical solutions to determine their convergence and accuracy. A concentric annular tube was chosen because of its simplicity and ability to provide an exact solution, allowing the basic nature of the proposed model for convection problems to be analysed in detail [47,48]. Therefore, present research efforts aiming at the establishment of the DRM's applicability to heat convection are confirmed, and could eventually be extended to the study of other heat transfer systems.

2. Physical Problem and Its Mathematical Formulation

Consider an incompressible Newtonian fluid of density ρ, thermal conductivity λ, and specific heat c contained between two stationary concentric cylinders (i.e., in a concentric annular tube). The inner and outer cylinders have radii of R_i and R_o, respectively. Figure 1 shows a schematic of the annular tube and co-ordinate system.

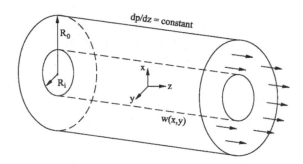

Figure 1. Schematic of the concentric annulus and co-ordinate system.

In the system to be analysed, the z co-ordinate represents the axial direction and the x–y co-ordinate plane is attached to the cross-sectional surface. To simplify the problem and its solution, the steady laminar flow is assumed to be fully developed with constant transport properties and negligible body forces. Under these conditions, the Navier-Stokes equation becomes the simple pressure-driven Poiseuille flow equation. Because the flow is fully developed, the axial flow velocity is a function of only the x and y co-ordinates, and the axial pressure gradient is constant. In the energy equation, the viscous dissipation and axial heat conduction are neglected.

2.1. Governing Equations

The governing equations of the laminar fluid flow, expressed in the form of a Poisson equation, are obtained from the momentum and energy conservation equations [49]:

$$\nabla^2 w = \frac{\partial^2 w}{\partial x^2} + \frac{\partial^2 w}{\partial y^2} = \frac{1}{\eta}\frac{dp}{dz} \tag{1}$$

$$\nabla^2 T = \frac{\partial^2 T}{\partial x^2} + \frac{\partial^2 T}{\partial y^2} = \frac{w}{a}\frac{dT}{dz} \tag{2}$$

where w is the axial velocity of the flow; η is the dynamic viscosity; p is the pressure; T is the temperature; and $a = \lambda/\rho c$ is the thermal diffusivity.

For the fully developed thermal flow with constant heat flux on the boundaries and using the mixed mean temperature T_m [48], Equation (2) becomes:

$$\nabla^2 T = \frac{\partial^2 T}{\partial x^2} + \frac{\partial^2 T}{\partial y^2} = \frac{w}{a}\frac{dT_m}{dz} \tag{3}$$

where $\partial T/\partial z = dT_m/dz$ is a constant derived from the given conditions.

2.2. Boundary Conditions

The boundary conditions associated with Equations (1) and (3) are:

$$w = 0 \text{ at } r = R_i \text{ and } r = R_o \tag{4}$$

$$T = T_i \text{ at } r = R_i; \quad T = T_o \text{ at } r = R_o \tag{5}$$

where R_i is the radius of the inner cylinder and R_o is the radius of the outer cylinder.

To solve for the temperature, the velocity is first obtained from Equation (1); then Equation (3) can be solved, because the assumption of negligible buoyancy decouples the momentum and energy equations.

3. Numerical Model

3.1. The DRM Formulation

To solve using the BEM, Equations (1) and (3) subject to Equations (4) and (5) can be generalized as the following type of Poisson equation [43]:

$$\nabla^2 u(x,y) = b(x,y), \qquad (x,y) \in \Omega \tag{6}$$

with the boundary conditions:

$$u(x,y) = \overline{u}, \qquad (x,y) \in \Gamma_1 \tag{7}$$

$$q(x,y) = \frac{\partial u(x,y)}{\partial n} = \overline{q}, \quad (x,y) \in \Gamma_2 \tag{8}$$

and the convective heat transfer problem is represented by:

$$u(x,y) = w, \quad b(x,y) = \frac{1}{\eta}\frac{dp}{dz} = \text{const.}$$
$$u(x,y) = T, \quad b(x,y) = \frac{w}{a}\frac{dT_m}{dz} \tag{9}$$

where: $\Gamma_1 + \Gamma_2 = \Gamma$ is the total boundary of the domain Ω; n is normal to the boundary; and $\overline{u}$ and $\overline{q}$ are the values specified at each boundary.

Applying the usual boundary element technique to Equation (6), an integral Equation can be derived as described in [21]:

$$c_i u_i + \int_\Gamma u q^* d\Gamma - \int_\Gamma q u^* d\Gamma = \int_\Omega b u^* d\Omega \tag{10}$$

where the constant c_i depends on the geometry at point i as follows:

$$c_i = \begin{cases} 1 & \text{for } (x_i, y_i) \in \Omega \\ \frac{\theta}{2\pi} & \text{for } (x_i, y_i) \in \Gamma \end{cases} \tag{11}$$

where θ is the internal angle at the source point.

The key part of the DRM is to calculate the domain integral term of Equation (10) on the boundary and remove the need for a complicated domain discretization. To accomplish this, the source term $b(x, y)$ is expanded, using its values at each node j and a set of interpolating functions f_j as in [41,42]:

$$b(x,y) \cong \sum_{j=1}^{N+L} \alpha_j f_j \tag{12}$$

where α_j is a set of initially unknown coefficients; and N and L are the number of boundary nodes and internal points, respectively.

Using Equation (12), the coefficients α_j can be expressed in terms of the nodal values of the function $b(x, y)$ in matrix form as:

$$\alpha = \mathbf{F}^{-1}\mathbf{b} \tag{13}$$

where $\mathbf{F}$ is a matrix with coefficients f_j and $\mathbf{b} = \{b_i\}$.

The radial basis functions f_j are linked with the particular solutions $\hat{u}_j$ to the equation:

$$\nabla^2 \hat{u}_j = f_j \tag{14}$$

Substituting Equation (14) into Equation (12) and applying integration by parts to the domain integral term of Equation (10) twice leads to:

$$c_i u_i + \int_\Gamma u q^* \mathrm{d}\Gamma - \int_\Gamma q u^* \mathrm{d}\Gamma = \sum_{j=1}^{N+L} \alpha_j \left(c_i \hat{u}_{ij} + \int_\Gamma \hat{u}_j q^* \mathrm{d}\Gamma - \int_\Gamma \hat{q}_j u^* \mathrm{d}\Gamma \right) \tag{15}$$

On a two-dimensional domain, u^*, q^* and $\hat{u}$, $\hat{q}$ can be derived as:

$$u^* = \frac{1}{2\pi} \ln(\frac{1}{r}); \quad q^* = \frac{-1}{2\pi r} \nabla r \cdot \vec{n} \tag{16}$$

$$\hat{u} = \frac{r^2}{4} + \frac{r^3}{9}; \quad \hat{q} = (\frac{r}{2} + \frac{r^2}{3}) \nabla r \cdot \vec{n} \tag{17}$$

where r is the distance from a source point i, or a DRM collocation point j to a field point (x, y). As for Equation (14), an interpolating function is chosen as a radial basis function (RBF). Two relevant expressions for RBFs are frequently used for this purpose in the engineering community: $f = 1 + r$ and $f = 1 + r + r^2$ [44,45].

In the numerical solution of the integral Equation (15), u, q, $\hat{u}$ and $\hat{q}$ are modelled using the linear interpolation functions as follows:

$$\int_{\Gamma_k} u q^* \mathrm{d}\Gamma = u_k h_{ik}^1 + u_{k+1} h_{ik}^2 \tag{18}$$

$$\int_{\Gamma_k} q u^* \mathrm{d}\Gamma = q_k g_{ik}^1 + q_{k+1} g_{ik}^2 \tag{19}$$

$$\int_{\Gamma_k} \hat{u}_j q^* \mathrm{d}\Gamma = \hat{u}_{kj} h_{ik}^1 + \hat{u}_{(k+1)j} h_{ik}^2 \tag{20}$$

$$\int_{\Gamma} \hat{q}_j u^* \mathrm{d}\Gamma = \hat{q}_{kj} g_{ik}^1 + \hat{q}_{(k+1)j} g_{ik}^2 \tag{21}$$

where:

$$h_{ik}^1 = \int_{\Gamma_k} \Phi_1 q^* \mathrm{d}\Gamma, \quad h_{ik}^2 = \int_{\Gamma_k} \Phi_2 q^* \mathrm{d}\Gamma \tag{22}$$

$$g_{ik}^1 = \int_{\Gamma_k} \Phi_1 u^* \mathrm{d}\Gamma, \quad g_{ik}^2 = \int_{\Gamma_k} \Phi_2 u^* \mathrm{d}\Gamma \tag{23}$$

The first subscript in Equations (22) and (23) refers to the specific position of the point where the flow velocity or temperature is evaluated. The second subscript refers to the boundary element over which the contour integration is performed. The superscripts 1 and 2 designate the linear interpolation functions Φ_1 and Φ_2, respectively, with which the u^* and q^* functions are weighted in the integrals in Equations (18) to (21).

When the boundary $\Gamma = \Gamma_1 \cup \Gamma_2$ is discretized into N elements, the integral terms in Equation (15) can be rewritten as:

$$\int_\Gamma u q^* \mathrm{d}\Gamma = \sum_{k=1}^N \int_{\Gamma_k} u q^* \mathrm{d}\Gamma = \sum_{k=1}^N \left[h_{i(k-1)}^2 + h_{ik}^1 \right] u_k = \sum_{k=1}^N H_{ik} u_k \text{ or } = \sum_{j=1}^{N_n} H_{ik} \hat{u}_{kj} \text{ for } \hat{u}_j \tag{24}$$

$$\int_\Gamma q u^* \mathrm{d}\Gamma = \sum_{k=1}^N \int_{\Gamma_k} q u^* \mathrm{d}\Gamma = \sum_{k=1}^N \left[g_{i(k-1)}^2 + g_{ik}^1 \right] q_k = \sum_{k=1}^N G_{ik} q_k \text{ or } = \sum_{j=1}^{N_n} G_{ik} \hat{q}_{kj} \text{ for } \hat{q}_j \tag{25}$$

where $h_{i0}^2 = h_{iN}^2$ and $g_{i0}^2 = g_{iN}^2$.

Substituting Equations (24) and (25) into Equation (15), after several manipulations, yields the dual reciprocity boundary element Equation:

$$c_i u_i + \sum_{k=1}^{N} H_{ik} u_k - \sum_{k=1}^{N} G_{ik} q_k = \sum_{j=1}^{N+L} \alpha_j \left(c_i \hat{u}_{ij} + \sum_{k=1}^{N} H_{ik} \hat{u}_{kj} - \sum_{k=1}^{N} G_{ik} \hat{q}_{kj} \right) \tag{26}$$

3.2. Numerical Solution

Equation (26) can now be written in a matrix-vector form as:

$$\mathbf{HU} - \mathbf{GQ} = (\mathbf{H\hat{U}} - \mathbf{G\hat{Q}})\boldsymbol{\alpha} \tag{27}$$

where $\mathbf{H}$ and $\mathbf{G}$ are matrices with elements H_{ik} and G_{ik}, with c_i incorporated into the principal diagonal element; and $\mathbf{U}$, $\mathbf{Q}$ and their terms $\mathbf{\hat{U}}$, $\mathbf{\hat{Q}}$ correspond to vectors with elements u_k and q_k, and matrices with $\hat{u}_{kj}$ and $\hat{q}_{kj}$ as the jth column vectors.

Substituting $\boldsymbol{\alpha}$ from Equation (13) into the above equation yields:

$$\mathbf{HU} - \mathbf{GQ} = (\mathbf{H\hat{U}} - \mathbf{G\hat{Q}})\mathbf{F}^{-1}\mathbf{b} \tag{28}$$

Introducing the boundary conditions into the nodes of the u_k and q_k vectors, and rearranging by moving known quantities to the right-hand side and unknown quantities to the left-hand side, leads to a system of linear equations of the form:

$$\mathbf{AX} = \mathbf{B} \tag{29}$$

Using the DRM matrix equation, a numerical solution to the problem of laminar convective heat transfer between two concentric cylinders can be readily obtained for the flow velocity w from the momentum equation, and the temperature T from the energy equation or for their normal derivatives.

This numerical model has been implemented as a computer program in the FORTRAN programming language for PC-compatible microsystems.

3.3. Testing the Model

The geometry illustrated in Figure 2 is used for testing purposes. To simplify the problem, the surface temperatures of the two cylinders are assumed to be equal. Thus, the solution satisfies the following boundary conditions:

$$\begin{aligned}
w(x,y)|_{R=R_i} &= w(x,y)|_{R=R_o} = 0 \\
T*(x,y)|_{R=R_i} &= T*(x,y)|_{R=R_o} = 0 \\
T* = T - T_w, \quad T_w &= T_i = T_o
\end{aligned} \tag{30}$$

For the numerical test case, the following numerical values are introduced to Equations (1) and (3) from [50], in which the spectral collocation method is used to analyse heat convection in an eccentric annulus:

$$\begin{aligned}
R_i &= 0.030\,\text{m}, \quad R_o = 0.055\,\text{m} \\
\frac{1}{\eta}\frac{dp}{dz} &= -836\,\text{m}^{-1}\text{s}^{-1} \\
a &= 1.3418 \times 10^{-9}\,\text{m}^2/\text{s} \\
\frac{dT_m}{dz} &= 0.47\,^\circ\text{C}/\text{m}
\end{aligned} \tag{31}$$

To confirm the accuracy of the DRM for the actual heat convection problem, the boundaries of the external and internal surfaces are discretized into 36, 48, 60, 72, or 84 elements. The nodes on every boundary and at the internal points of the analysis domain are located as shown in Figure 2. Therefore, the total number of internal points used in the analysis is 90, 120, 150, 180, and 210 in the 36, 48, 60, 72, and 84 boundary element cases, respectively.

Some statistical methods, such as the root mean square error (RMSE), the coefficient of variation (c_v), the coefficient of multiple determinations (R^2), and the relative error (e_r) may be used to compare simulated and analytical (exact) values of the flow's velocity and temperature to validate the model.

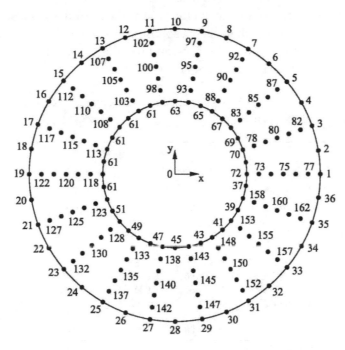

Figure 2. Boundary element nodes and internal points.

The error can be estimated using the RMSE, defined as [51]:

$$\text{RMSE} = \sqrt{\frac{\sum_{i=1}^{n}\left(y_{\text{sim},i} - y_{\text{anal},i}\right)^2}{n}} \tag{32}$$

In addition, the coefficient of variation c_v, in percent, and the coefficient of multiple determinations R^2 are defined as follows:

$$c_v = \frac{\text{RMSE}}{\left|\overline{y}_{\text{anal},i}\right|} 100\% \tag{33}$$

$$R^2 = 1 - \frac{\sum_{i=1}^{n}\left(y_{\text{sim},i} - y_{\text{anal},i}\right)^2}{\sum_{i=1}^{n} y_{\text{anal},i}^2} \tag{34}$$

where n is the number of analytical data points in the independent data set; $y_{\text{anal},i}$ is the analytical value of one data point i; $y_{\text{sim},i}$ represents the simulated value; and $\overline{y}_{\text{anal},i}$ is the mean value of all of the analytical data points.

The relative error e_r is calculated using the following formula:

$$e_r = \frac{\left|y_{\text{anal},i} - y_{\text{sim},i}\right|}{y_{\text{sim},i}} 100\% \tag{35}$$

where $y_{\text{anal},i}$ is the analytical solution; and $y_{\text{sim},i}$ is the potential value at point i obtained by the numerical method.

4. Simulation Results and Discussion

To obtain the axial flow velocity $w(x, y)$, Equation (1) is solved first. The results for the boundary and internal nodes are shown in Tables 1 and 2 for the RBFs $f = 1 + r$ and $f = 1 + r + r^2$, respectively. In these tables, the normal derivative of the velocity w at the boundary is also listed, and all of the numerical solutions are compared with the exact solutions [47], in order to determine their accuracy. In addition, statistical values such as the RMSE, c_v, and R^2, which correspond to different numbers of boundary elements in the analysed system, are given in Tables 1 and 2.

Table 1. Dual reciprocity method (DRM) results and analytical solution for the boundary and internal points in flow velocity simulation ($f = 1 + r$).

Variable	Radial Location r [m]	DRM Solution					Analytical Solution
		Number of Boundary Elements					
		36	48	60	72	84	
$\partial w/\partial n$	0.055	−9.570611	−9.614363	−9.632446	−9.646733	−9.649446	−9.667904
$\partial w/\partial n$	0.030	−11.961390	−11.931682	−11.910987	−11.902295	−11.900702	−11.883840
w	0.0342	0.040336	0.039937	0.039755	0.039656	0.039614	0.039413
w	0.0383	0.061518	0.061112	0.060926	0.060825	0.060760	0.060591
w	0.0425	0.066727	0.066320	0.066133	0.066030	0.065973	0.065803
w	0.0466	0.057611	0.057196	0.057006	0.056908	0.056853	0.056682
w	0.0508	0.035084	0.034883	0.034733	0.034638	0.034606	0.034439
RMSE		0.000741	0.000427	0.000275	0.000191	0.000149	−
$c_v\%$		2.018	1.162	0.749	0.521	0.405	−
R^2		0.999724	0.999908	0.999962	0.999981	0.999988	−

Table 2. DRM results and analytical solution for the boundary and internal points in flow velocity simulation ($f = 1 + r + r^2$).

Variable	Radial Location r [m]	DRM Solution					Analytical Solution
		Number of Boundary Elements					
		36	48	60	72	84	
$\partial w/\partial n$	0.055	−9.570477	−9.615427	−9.632632	−9.647164	−9.651780	−9.667904
$\partial w/\partial n$	0.030	−11.960900	−11.929878	−11.906732	−11.899952	−11.898130	−11.883840
w	0.0342	0.040334	0.039938	0.039754	0.039654	0.039601	0.039413
w	0.0383	0.061519	0.061112	0.060927	0.060820	0.060761	0.060591
w	0.0425	0.066725	0.066321	0.066136	0.066031	0.065974	0.065803
w	0.0466	0.057609	0.057193	0.057012	0.056906	0.056850	0.056682
w	0.0508	0.035080	0.034880	0.034726	0.034635	0.034604	0.034439
RMSE		0.000740	0.000426	0.000276	0.000189	0.000146	−
$c_v\%$		2.015	1.160	0.750	0.516	0.397	−
R^2		0.999725	0.9999087	0.999961	0.999982	0.999989	−

Figures 3 and 4 shows the convergence of the DRM's solutions for the velocity and its normal derivative, as the numbers of boundary elements and internal points increase. The DRM solutions agree well with the exact solutions, and the relative errors are within 2.3% when the number of elements is greater than 36. The values of the RMSE and c_v are between 0.00014% and 0.00074%, and 0.40% and 2.01%, respectively, for the two radial basis functions. The R^2-value for any number of boundary elements is approximately 0.9997% for both of the radial basis functions, a result that is very satisfactory. Thus, the simulation model is analytically validated.

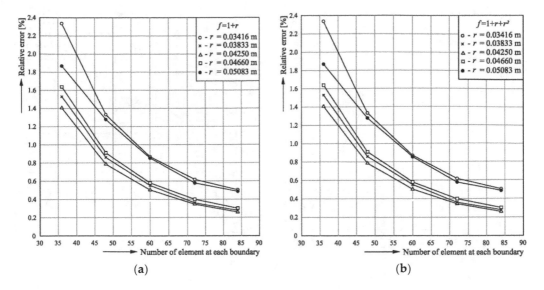

Figure 3. Accuracy of the solution for the velocity at the internal points: (**a**) Radial basis function $f = 1 + r$; (**b**) Radial basis function $f = 1 + r + r^2$.

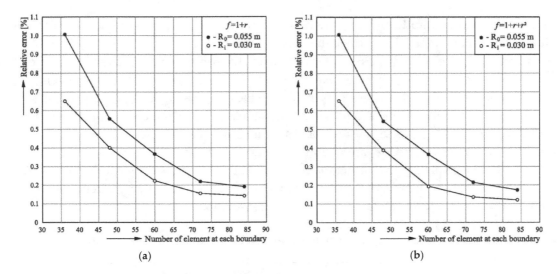

Figure 4. Magnitude of the error in the solution for the normal derivative of the velocity at the boundaries: (**a**) Radial basis function $f = 1 + r$; (**b**) Radial basis function $f = 1 + r + r^2$.

As noted in Figure 3, the velocities calculated at $r = 0.0508$ m and $r = 0.0342$ m are less accurate than the others, and the solution at $r = 0.0342$ is less accurate than it is at $r = 0.0508$. The solutions for the normal derivative of the velocity on the boundary at $r = 0.055$ m is less accurate than it is at $r = 0.030$ m, as shown in Figure 4. This is because the outer boundary elements are larger than the inner boundary elements, and the distribution of internal points becomes sparse in the outward direction, whereas a rapid change in the velocity occurs at the inner and outer boundaries, as shown in Figures 2 and 5.

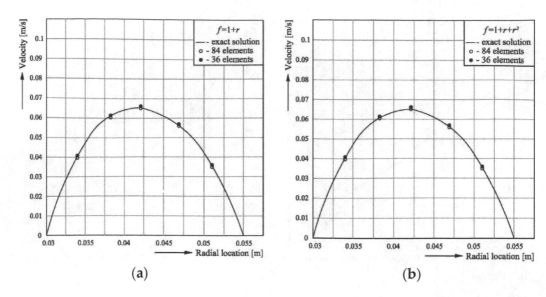

Figure 5. Comparison of velocity profile obtained using analytical solution and DRM results: (**a**) Radial basis function $f = 1 + r$; (**b**) Radial basis function $f = 1 + r + r^2$.

Therefore, the magnitude of the solution's error in the radial direction is closely related to the physical and the mathematical aspects of the problem; hence, the overall accuracy of the solution is fairly acceptable. Therefore, when 36 elements are used, the solution has a maximum error of 2.34% at radial position $r = 0.0342$ m, and the next step results in an accurate solution for the temperature. The DRM solutions for the velocity are, in turn, used in the energy equation (Equation (3)) to solve for the temperature distribution. Tables 3 and 4 show the simulation results for temperature and statistical values such as the RMSE, c_v, and R^2. The DRM solutions are in excellent agreement with the exact solutions and the relative errors e_r are within 5% when 36 elements are used (Figures 6–8). The c_v values are in the range of 0.3%–5.0%, and the R^2-value is approximately 0.999 for the two radial basis functions with any of the tested numbers of boundary elements. This is a very acceptable result, and thus, the simulation model is validated by the analytical solutions.

Table 3. DRM results and analytical solution for boundary and internal points in temperature ($f = 1 + r$).

Variable	Radial Location r [m]	DRM Solution					Analytical Solution
		Number of Boundary Elements					
		36	48	60	72	84	
$\partial T^*/\partial n$	0.055	172056.38	170824.22	171362.75	171600.75	171628.56	170484.20
$\partial T^*/\partial n$	0.030	233420.45	229217.02	230340.65	230698.70	230771.22	229506.90
T^*	0.0342	804.26	828.59	847.40	853.78	855.04	858.72
T^*	0.0383	1268.86	1298.52	1311.65	1315.86	1317.26	1320.13
T^*	0.0425	1383.48	1413.28	1426.46	1429.68	1431.26	1433.69
T^*	0.0466	1180.68	1209.26	1224.48	1230.46	1231.92	1234.96
T^*	0.0508	711.52	730.65	741.78	746.86	747.90	750.34
	RMSE	42.3739	20.1408	7.8869	3.6070	2.4750	–
	$c_v\%$	5.298	2.518	0.986	0.451	0.309	–
	R^2	0.998102	0.999571	0.99934	0.999986	0.999993	–

Table 4. DRM results and analytical solution for the boundary and internal points in temperature ($f = 1 + r + r^2$).

Variable	Radial Location r [m]	DRM Solution					Analytical Solution
		Number of Boundary Elements					
		36	48	60	72	84	
$\partial T^*/\partial n$	0.055	171989.88	170768.08	171293.14	171535.45	171598.75	170484.20
$\partial T^*/\partial n$	0.030	233300.36	229286.02	230294.05	230618.22	230708.55	229506.90
T^*	0.0342	805.85	829.69	848.14	854.14	855.78	858.72
T^*	0.0383	1271.14	1299.86	1312.24	1316.04	1317.68	1320.13
T^*	0.0425	1385.24	1414.58	1427.24	1430.02	1431.76	1433.69
T^*	0.0466	1182.72	1210.64	1225.78	1230.98	1232.04	1234.96
T^*	0.0508	713.38	731.68	742.87	747.12	748.03	750.34
RMSE		40.7741	19.1179	7.1300	3.3248	2.1458	–
$c_v\%$		5.098	2.390	0.891	0.415	0.268	–
R^2		0.998243	0.999613	0.999946	0.999988	0.999995	–

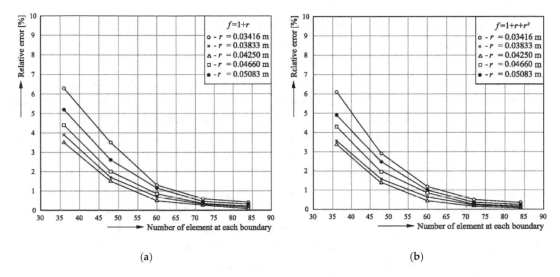

(a)   (b)

Figure 6. Accuracy of the solution for the temperature at the internal points: (**a**) Radial basis function $f = 1 + r$; (**b**) Radial basis function $f = 1 + r + r^2$.

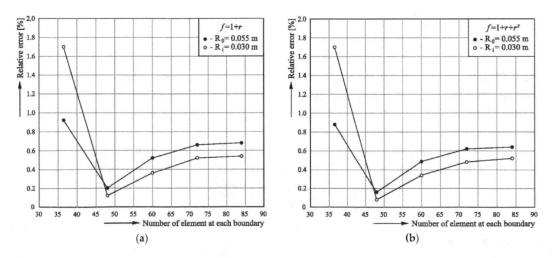

(a)   (b)

Figure 7. Accuracy of the solution for the normal derivative of the temperature at the boundaries: (**a**) Radial basis function $f = 1 + r$; (**b**) Radial basis function $f = 1 + r + r^2$.

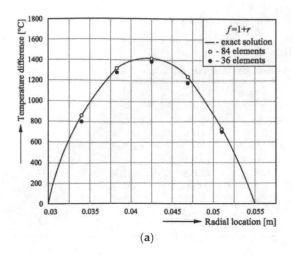

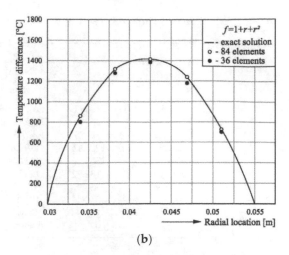

(a)   (b)

Figure 8. Comparison of temperature profile T^* obtained using analytical solution and DRM results: (a) Radial basis function $f = 1 + r$; (b) Radial basis function $f = 1 + r + r^2$.

Although the convergence trend shown in Figure 7 is not monotonic and the radial location's effect on the magnitude of the error does not exactly follow the trend shown in the previous case, the solution trends can be considered indistinguishable within 1% relative error.

These test results validate the power of the dual reciprocity boundary element method and the accuracy of its solutions. This is because the numerical solution for the velocity was used as an input in Equation (3), and the source-like function $b(x, y)$ of Equation (12) in Equation (3) was approximated using interpolating functions and the nodal values of internal points.

As a final note, all of the numbers of elements tested are adequate for solving this problem. The amount of error in the solutions for the velocity and temperature is acceptable. Using the fourth-order RBFs, the accuracy of the DRM is increased insignificantly, so that only minor differences are observed between errors (0.2%). The errors can be decreased using only a higher adequate number of boundary elements and internal points limited by computational capacity.

5. Conclusions

A numerical simulation model based on the dual reciprocity boundary element method has been developed for the solution of the laminar heat convection problem between two concentric cylinders with a constant imposed heat flux.

The DRM is different than the standard implementation, as was proposed for Poisson-type equations due the use of RBFs. The DRM matrix was formulated to perform numerical computation, and five boundary element discretizations were tested with corresponding numbers of internal points. Five radial locations were selected, at which solution for the velocity and temperature was obtained. The numerical results were shown to be in excellent agreement with exact solutions for the 36-element case, and the simulation model was analytically validated.

This numerical model was successfully used to solve the laminar convective heat transfer problem in a concentric annular tube. This study also shows that the DRM has strong potential for further applications. Although this method has been applied to 2D problems, an extension of the approach to 3D problems is straightforward.

Author Contributions: All authors conceived the research idea and the framework of this study. Iosif Anton performed the theoretical study and Ioan Sarbu analysed the data and wrote the paper. Both authors have read and approved the final manuscript.

References

1. Irons, B.M.; Ahmad, S. *Techniques of Finite Elements*; John Wiley: New York, NY, USA, 1980.
2. Rao, S. *The Finite Element Method in Engineering*; Pergamon Press: New York, NY, USA, 1981.
3. Nowak, A.J.; Brebbia, A.C. The multiple reciprocity method: A new approach for transforming BEM domain integrals to the boundary. *Eng. Anal.* **1989**, *6*, 164–167. [CrossRef]
4. Partridge, W.P.; Brebbia, A.C. Computer implementation of the BEM dual reciprocity method for the solution of general field Equations. *Commun. Appl. Numer. Methods* **1990**, *6*, 83–92. [CrossRef]
5. Chen, G.; Zhou, J. *Boundary Element Methods*; Academic Press: New York, NY, USA, 1992.
6. Reddy, J.N. *An Introduction to the Finite Element Method*; McGraw-Hill: New York, NY, USA, 1993.
7. Paris, F.; Cañas, J. *Boundary Element Method: Fundamentals and Applications*; Oxford University Press: Oxford, UK, 1997.
8. Power, H.; Mingo, R. The DRM Subdomain decomposition approach to solve the two-dimensional Navier-Stokes system of equations. *Eng. Anal. Bound. Elements* **2000**, *24*, 107–119. [CrossRef]
9. Sarbu, I. *Numerical Modelling and Optimizations in Building Services*; Polytechnic Publishing House: Timisoara, Romania, 2010. (In Romanian)
10. Lavine, A.S.; Incropera, F.P.; Dewitt, D.P. *Fundamentals of Heat and Mass Transfer*; John Wiley & Sons: New York, NY, USA, 2011.
11. Popov, V.; Bui, T.T. A meshless solution to two-dimensional convection-diffusion problems. *Eng. Anal. Bound. Elements* **2010**, *34*, 680–689. [CrossRef]
12. Bai, F.; Lu, W.Q. The selection and assemblage of approximating functions and disposal of its singularity in axisymmetric DRBEM for heat transfer problems. *Eng. Anal. Bound. Elements* **2004**, *28*, 955–965. [CrossRef]
13. Asad, A.S. Heat transfer on axis symmetric stagnation flow an infinite circular cylinder. In Proceedings of the 5th WSEAS International Conference on Heat and Mass Transfer, Acapulco, Mexico, 25–27 January 2008; pp. 74–79.
14. Nekoubin, N.; Nobari, M.R.H. Numerical analysis of forced convection in the entrance region of an eccentric curved annulus. *Numer. Heat Transf. Appl.* **2014**, *65*, 482–507. [CrossRef]
15. Wang, B.L.; Tian, Y.H. Application of finite element: Finite difference method to the determination of transient temperature field in functionally graded materials. *Finite Elements Anal. Des.* **2005**, *41*, 335–349. [CrossRef]
16. Wu, Q.; Sheng, A. A Note on finite difference method to analysis an ill-posed problem. *Appl. Math. Comput.* **2006**, *182*, 1040–1047. [CrossRef]
17. Shakerim, F.; Dehghan, M. A finite volume spectral element method for solving magnetohydrodynamic (MHD) equations. *Appl. Numer. Math.* **2011**, *61*, 1–23. [CrossRef]
18. Sammouda, H.; Belghith, A.; Surry, C. Finite element simulation of transient natural convection of low-Prandtl-number fluids in heated cavity. *Int. J. Numer. Methods Heat Fluid Flow* **1999**, *5*, 612–624. [CrossRef]
19. Sarbu, I. Numerical analysis of two-dimensional heat conductivity in steady state regime. *Period. Polytech. Mech. Eng.* **2005**, *49*, 149–162.
20. Wang, B.L.; Mai, Y.W. Transient one dimensional heat conduction problems solved by finite element. *Int. J. Mech. Sci.* **2005**, *47*, 303–317. [CrossRef]
21. Brebbia, C.A.; Telle, J.C.; Wrobel, I.C. *Boundary Element Techniques*; Springer-Verlag: New York, NY, USA, 1984.
22. Kane, J.H. *Boundary Element Analysis in Engineering Continuum Mechanics*; Prentice–Hall: New Jersey, NJ, USA, 1994.
23. Goldberg, M.A.; Chen, C.S.; Bowman, H. Some recent results and proposals for the use of radial basis functions in the BEM. *Eng. Anal. Bound. Elements* **1999**, *23*, 285–296. [CrossRef]
24. Yang, K.; Peng, H.-F.; Cui, M.; Gao, X.-W. New analytical expressions in radial integration BEM for solving heat conduction problems with variable coefficients. *Eng. Anal. Bound. Elements* **2015**, *50*, 224–230. [CrossRef]
25. Sedaghatjoo, Z.; Adibi, H. Calculation of domain integrals of two dimensional boundary element method. *Eng. Anal. Bound. Elements* **2012**, *36*, 1917–1922. [CrossRef]
26. Divo, E.A.; Kassab, A.J. *Boundary Element Methods for Heat Conduction: Applications in Non-Homogeneous Media*; WIT Press: Southampton, NY, USA, 2003.
27. Žagar, I.; Škerget, L. Boundary elements for time dependent 3-D laminar viscous fluid flow. *J. Mech. Eng.* **1989**, *35*, 160–163.

28. Choi, C.Y. Detection of cavities by inverse heat conduction boundary element method using minimal energy technique. *J. Korean Soc. Non-Destr. Test.* **1997**, *17*, 237–247.

29. Garimella, S.; Dowling, W.I.; van der Veen, M.; Killion, J. Heat transfer coefficients for simultaneously developing flow in rectangular tubes. In Proceedings of the ASME 2000 International Mechanical Engineering Congress and Exposition, Orlando, FL, USA, 5–10 November 2000; 2, pp. 3–11.

30. Skerget, L.; Rek, Z. Boundary-domain integral method using a velocity-vorticity formulation. *Eng. Anal. Bound. Elements* **1995**, *15*, 359–370. [CrossRef]

31. Žunič, Z.; Hriberšek, M.; Škerget, L.; Ravnik, J. 3-D boundary element–finite element method for velocity–vorticity formulation of the Navier-Stokes equations. *Eng. Anal. Bound. Elements* **2007**, *31*, 259–266. [CrossRef]

32. Young, D.L.; Huang, J.L.; Eldho, T.I. Simulation of laminar vortex shedding flow past cylinders using a coupled BEM and FEM model. *Comput. Methods Appl. Mech. Eng.* **2001**, *190*, 5975–5998. [CrossRef]

33. Young, D.L.; Liu, Y.H.; Eldho, T.I. A combined BEM–FEM model for the velocity-vorticity formulation of the Navier-Stokes equations in three dimensions. *Eng. Anal. Bound. Elements* **2000**, *24*, 307–316. [CrossRef]

34. Ravnik, J.; Škerget, L.; Hriberšek, M. Two-dimensional velocity-vorticity based LES for the solution of natural convection in a differentially heated enclosure by wavelet transform based BEM and FEM. *Eng. Anal. Bound. Elements* **2006**, *30*, 671–686. [CrossRef]

35. Hsieh, K.J.; Lien, F.S. Numerical modeling of buoyancy-driven turbulent flows in enclosures. *Int. J. Heat Fluid Flow* **2004**, *25*, 659–670. [CrossRef]

36. Gao, X.W. The radial integration method for evaluation of domain integrals with boundary-only discretization. *Eng. Anal. Bound. Elements* **2002**, *26*, 905–916. [CrossRef]

37. Cui, M.; Gao, X.W.; Zhang, J.B. A new approach for the estimation of temperature-dependent thermal properties by solving transient inverse heat conduction problems. *Int. J. Therm. Sci.* **2012**, *58*, 113–119. [CrossRef]

38. Gao, X.W.; Peng, H.F. A boundary-domain integral equation method for solving convective heat transfer problems. *Int. J. Heat Mass Transf.* **2013**, *63*, 183–190. [CrossRef]

39. Peng, H.F.; Yang, K.; Gao, X.W. Element nodal computation-based radial integration BEM for non-homogeneous problems. *Acta Mech. Sin.* **2013**, *29*, 429–436. [CrossRef]

40. Nardini, D.; Brebbia, C.A. A new approach for free vibration analysis using boundary elements. In *Boundary Element Methods in Engineering*; Computational Mechanics Publications: Southampton, NY, USA, 1982; pp. 312–326.

41. Wrobel, C.L.; DeFigueiredo, D.B. A dual reciprocity boundary element formulation for convection diffusion problems with variable velocity fields. *Eng. Anal. Bound. Elements* **1991**, *8*, 312–319. [CrossRef]

42. Partridge, P.W.; Brebbia, C.A.; Wrobel, L.C. *The Dual Reciprocity Boundary Element Method*; Computational Mechanics Publications: Southampton, NY, USA, 1992.

43. Tezer-Sezgin, M.; Bozkaya, C.; Türk, Ö. BEM and FEM based numerical simulations for biomagnetic fluid flow. *Eng. Anal. Bound. Elements* **2013**, *37*, 127–1135. [CrossRef]

44. Yamada, T.; Wrobel, L.C.; Power, H. On the convergence of the dual reciprocity boundary element method. *Eng. Anal. Bound. Elements* **1994**, *13*, 91–298. [CrossRef]

45. Karur, S.R.; Ramachandran, P.A. Radial basis function approximation in the dual reciprocity method. *Math. Comput. Model.* **1994**, *20*, 59–70. [CrossRef]

46. Ilati, M.; Dehghan, M. The use of radial basis function (RBFs) collocation and RBF-QR methods for solving the coupled nonlinear Sine-Gordon equations. *Eng. Anal. Bound. Elements* **2015**, *52*, 99–109. [CrossRef]

47. Kays, W.M.; Crawford, M.E. *Convective Heat and Mass Transfer*; McGraw-Hill: New York, NY, USA, 1993.

48. Kakac, S.; Yener, Y.; Pramuanjaroenkij, A. *Convective Heat Transfer*; CRC Press: New York, NY, USA, 2014.

49. Jawarneh, A.M.; Vatistas, G.H.; Ababneh, A. Analytical approximate solution for decaying laminar swirling flows within narrow annulus. *Jordan J. Mech. Ind. Eng.* **2008**, *2*, 101–109.

50. Sim, W.G.; Kim, J.M. Application of spectral collocation method to conduction and laminar forced heat convection in eccentric annuli. *KSME Int. J.* **1996**, *10*, 94–104. [CrossRef]

51. Bechthler, H.; Browne, M.W.; Bansal, P.K.; Kecman, V. New approach to dynamic modelling of vapour-compression liquid chillers: Artificial neural networks. *Appl. Therm. Eng.* **2001**, *21*, 941–953. [CrossRef]

Permissions

All chapters in this book were first published in COMPUTATION, by MDPI AG; hereby published with permission under the Creative Commons Attribution License or equivalent. Every chapter published in this book has been scrutinized by our experts. Their significance has been extensively debated. The topics covered herein carry significant findings which will fuel the growth of the discipline. They may even be implemented as practical applications or may be referred to as a beginning point for another development.

The contributors of this book come from diverse backgrounds, making this book a truly international effort. This book will bring forth new frontiers with its revolutionizing research information and detailed analysis of the nascent developments around the world.

We would like to thank all the contributing authors for lending their expertise to make the book truly unique. They have played a crucial role in the development of this book. Without their invaluable contributions this book wouldn't have been possible. They have made vital efforts to compile up to date information on the varied aspects of this subject to make this book a valuable addition to the collection of many professionals and students.

This book was conceptualized with the vision of imparting up-to-date information and advanced data in this field. To ensure the same, a matchless editorial board was set up. Every individual on the board went through rigorous rounds of assessment to prove their worth. After which they invested a large part of their time researching and compiling the most relevant data for our readers.

The editorial board has been involved in producing this book since its inception. They have spent rigorous hours researching and exploring the diverse topics which have resulted in the successful publishing of this book. They have passed on their knowledge of decades through this book. To expedite this challenging task, the publisher supported the team at every step. A small team of assistant editors was also appointed to further simplify the editing procedure and attain best results for the readers.

Apart from the editorial board, the designing team has also invested a significant amount of their time in understanding the subject and creating the most relevant covers. They scrutinized every image to scout for the most suitable representation of the subject and create an appropriate cover for the book.

The publishing team has been an ardent support to the editorial, designing and production team. Their endless efforts to recruit the best for this project, has resulted in the accomplishment of this book. They are a veteran in the field of academics and their pool of knowledge is as vast as their experience in printing. Their expertise and guidance has proved useful at every step. Their uncompromising quality standards have made this book an exceptional effort. Their encouragement from time to time has been an inspiration for everyone.

The publisher and the editorial board hope that this book will prove to be a valuable piece of knowledge for researchers, students, practitioners and scholars across the globe.

List of Contributors

Ehsan Kian Far, Martin Geier, Konstantin Kutscher and Manfred Krafczyk
Institute for Computational Modeling in Civil Engineering, TU Braunschweig, 38106 Braunschweig, Germany

Seshaditya A. and Luigi Delle Site
Institute for Mathematics, Freie Universität Berlin, D-14195 Berlin, Germany

Luca M. Ghiringhelli
Fritz-Haber Institute, Faradayweg 4-6, D-14195 Berlin, Germany

Aris Lanaridis, Giorgos Siolas and Andreas Stafylopatis
Intelligent Systems Laboratory, National Technical University of Athens, Athens 15780, Greece

Seyyed Mahdi Najmabadi, Moritz Hamann, Guhathakurta Jajnabalkya and Sven Simon
Institute for Parallel and Distributed Systems, University of Stuttgart, Universitätsstraße 38, 70569 Stuttgart, Germany

Colin W. Glass and Philipp Offenhäuser
The High Performance Computing Center Stuttgart (HLRS), Nobelstraße 19, 70569 Stuttgart, Germany

Fabian Hempert
Robert Bosch GmbH, Robert-Bosch-Allee 1, 74232 Abstatt, Germany

Mirjam S. Glessmer
Physics Education, Leibniz Institute for Science and Mathematics Education, Olshausenstraße 62, 24118 Kiel, Germany

Christian F. Janßen
Institute for Fluid Dynamics and Ship Theory, Hamburg University of Technology Am Schwarzenberg-Campus 4, 21073 Hamburg, Germany

Le Wang, Qiang Pan and Shunsheng Yang
School of Civil Engineering, Southwest Jiaotong University, Chengdu 610031, China

Jie Chen
School of Energy and Power Engineering, Xi'an Jiaotong University, Xi'an 710049, China

Mohamed Hamada
Software Engineering Lab, Graduate School of Computer Science and Engineering, University of Aizu, Aizuwakamatsu 965-8580, Japan

Mohammed Hassan
Software Engineering Lab, Graduate School of Computer Science and Engineering, University of Aizu, Aizuwakamatsu 965-8580, Japan
Department of Software Engineering, Bayero University Kano, Kano 700231, Nigera

Animesh Agarwal
Institute for Mathematics, Freie Universität Berlin, Berlin 14195, Germany

Brooks D. Rabideau
Department of Chemical and Biomolecular Engineering, University of South Alabama, Mobile, AL 36688, USA

Ahmed E. Ismail
Department of Chemical and Biomedical Engineering, West Virginia University, Morgantown, WV 26506, USA

Nikolai Bessonov
Institute of Problems of Mechanical Engineering, Russian Academy of Sciences, 199178 Saint Petersburg, Russia

Vitaly Volpert
Institut Camille Jordan, UMR 5208 CNRS, University Lyon 1, 69622 Villeurbanne, France

Guocai Tian
State Key Laboratory of Complex Nonferrous Metal Resources Clean Utilization, Kunming University of Science and Technology, Kunming 650093, China
Department of Physics, Temple University, Philadelphia, PA 19122-1801, USA

Yuxiang Mo and Jianmin Tao
Department of Physics, Temple University, Philadelphia, PA 19122-1801, USA

Matthew Marko
Naval Air Warfare Center Aircraft Division, Joint-Base McGuire-Dix-Lakehurst, Lakehurst, NJ 08733, USA

Ioan Sarbu and Anton Iosif
Department of Building Services Engineering, Polytechnic University of Timisoara, Piata Victoriei, no 2A, 300006 Timisoara, Romania

Index

A

Adaline, 118, 121-122, 128-132, 135

Adaptive, 52-53, 55-56, 58, 60, 62-63, 66, 68, 74, 76, 117, 121-123, 134-135, 154

Aeroacoustic Simulation, 55-56, 64

Affinity Maturation, 31-32, 34

Analytical Approximation, 156, 167, 169

Ansatz, 23, 87

Antibodies, 31-32, 34-35, 41, 43-44, 51

B

Bem, 197-198, 200, 209-210

Boltzmann Equation, 2, 19

Boundary Condition, 89, 93, 105-106, 167, 169, 197

C

Cfd Simulations, 2, 7, 56, 64, 93, 97-98, 117

Classifier Systems, 31-33, 39, 45, 51-53

Cluster, 53, 74, 174, 176-180

Coarse Graining, 154

Coefficient, 1, 4, 7, 19, 101-103, 117, 127, 150, 162-163, 167, 169-170, 180

Collision Operator, 89

Compression, 55-58, 60, 62-76, 162, 184, 188-190, 194, 210

Computational, 1-2, 18, 20-22, 26, 28-29, 34, 52-53, 55-56, 64, 75, 81-83, 86, 96-98, 100, 119-120, 133, 136-138, 152, 163-164, 171-173, 180-181, 185, 194-198, 207-208, 210

Computational Techniques, 21, 197

Concentric Annular Tube, 197-198, 208

Continuum Mechanics, 184-185, 195, 209

Coulomb Interaction, 23

Cylindrical Orifice, 4

D

Deformable Cells, 156, 173

Density, 7, 21-29, 55-56, 64, 70, 73, 83, 98, 102, 106-107, 137, 145-146, 148-153, 174-183, 186, 192, 199

Dimensionality, 21, 25, 32, 197

Discharge, 1, 7, 19

Discharge Coefficient, 1, 7, 19

Disk, 55, 184, 190-192, 194

Drm, 197-198, 200-202, 204-209

Dual Reciprocity Method, 197-198, 204-205, 209-210

E

Eddy Simulation, 1, 18-19, 93, 98

Elastic Plate, 190

Electrons, 21-23, 25, 27-29, 175

Ellipsoidal Surface, 31, 51

Engineering Education, 78, 97

Evolutionary Algorithms, 31, 33, 54

Excitation Energy, 174, 176, 178-179

F

First Principles, 29, 182

Fluid Dynamics, 1, 20, 55, 75, 77-78, 81-83, 94, 97, 100, 105-106, 117, 184, 194

Fluid Mechanics, 4, 20, 55, 78-81, 86-89, 95-96, 195

Functionals, 21-22, 25, 28-29, 174-176, 178-180, 182-183

G

Genetic Algorithm, 33, 56, 118, 122, 124, 135

H

Heat Convection, 197-198, 202, 207, 210

Heat Flux, 197-198, 207-208

I

Immune Networks, 31, 51

Immune Systems, 31, 52-53

Implicit Large, 1, 18, 93

Innate, 31-32

Input Pressures, 1-2

Interaction, 23, 25, 30, 62, 79, 82-83, 88, 93-94, 97-98, 137, 140-143, 147, 150, 155, 157, 175-176, 178, 180-182, 185, 188, 195-196

Interactive Simulation, 78, 80

K

Kinetic Energy, 14, 21-23, 25, 29-30, 175, 183

L

Lagrangian, 10, 20, 57, 115, 184-188, 190-195

Laminar Flow, 1, 197-198

Lattice Boltzmann Method, 1-2, 4, 7, 18-19, 78, 93, 95, 97-98

Learning, 31-33, 35, 38-39, 45, 51-54, 76, 78-79, 81, 85-90, 92, 95-97, 118-119, 121, 125, 127-128, 132-134, 195

Levenberg, 118, 122, 134

Loss Coefficients, 4

Lossy Data, 55-56, 71, 75

M

Magnitude, 5, 8-11, 14, 17, 47, 50, 71-72, 80, 83-84, 102, 107-108, 137, 142, 178, 185, 189, 205-208

Marquardt, 118-119, 122, 134

Minimization, 29, 122

Monte Carlo, 21-25, 28-30, 123, 134, 136-138, 140-141, 143-144, 148, 152-155, 175

Multiscale Simulations, 136

N

Neural Network, 54, 118, 121, 124, 129, 132-135

Numerical Model, 90, 170, 184, 189, 192, 194, 197, 200, 202, 208

O

Orifice, 1-2, 4-10, 14, 17-20, 73

P

Pattern Classification, 31-32, 35

Pattern Formation, 156, 170-173

Polymer Chains, 136-138, 140-141, 146-148, 150-152, 154-155

Predictive Coding, 55, 58

R

Reaction Barrier, 174, 176, 179-180

Recommender Systems, 118-120, 126, 132-135

Rmse, 70-71, 75, 204-207

S

Sampling, 21, 23, 28-29, 123, 139-140

Semilocal Density, 174, 181-182

Simulated Annealing, 118-119, 123-124, 127, 134-135

Simulation, 1-2, 4-5, 7, 17-20, 22, 55-60, 63-64, 68, 72-78, 80-83, 97-101, 104-108, 115-117, 124, 133, 142, 144-148, 150, 152-155, 171, 184, 188, 190-191, 196-198, 204-210

Smoothing Function, 184-186

Solid Modeling, 184-186, 190, 192-194

Spam, 184-187, 195

Sph, 184-188, 191, 193, 195-196

T

Tissue Growth, 156-157, 160, 164-165, 168-173

Turbulent Stresses, 1-2, 11, 17-18

V

Velocity, 1-2, 4-5, 7-11, 17, 64, 80, 83-84, 89, 100-101, 103, 105-112, 114-116, 156, 167, 184-186, 188, 191, 193, 197-202, 204-208, 210

Vena Contracta, 1, 4-5, 7

Visualization, 55, 58, 71-72, 75, 80-83, 88, 92-93, 97-98, 106-107

W

Wavelet Transform, 57, 75-76, 136-139, 146, 152, 154, 210

CPSIA information can be obtained
at www.ICGtesting.com
Printed in the USA
BVHW011418240519
549249BV00004B/350/P

9 781682 856437